DREAM MAKER

DREAM MAKER

THE RISE AND FALL OF JOHN Z. DeLOREAN

IVAN FALLON & JAMES SRODES

G. P. Putnam's Sons / A Boston Book
New York

The authors gratefully acknowledge permission from the following
sources to quote from material in their control:
Crain Automotive Group, Inc., for material published in *Automotive
News*. Copyright © 1972, 1973, 1979 by Crain Automotive Group, Inc.
All rights reserved.
Dow Jones & Company, Inc., for excerpts from "Taking on Detroit,
John DeLorean Says He'll Show Industry How to Build Cars!" by John
R. Emshwiller, published in *The Wall Street Journal*. Copyright © Dow
Jones & Company, Inc. 1979. All rights reserved.
Lawrence Institute of Technology for material published in the *Tech
News*. Copyright © 1943, 1947, 1948, 1980 by Lawrence Institute of
Technology.
Multimedia Product Development, Inc., for excerpts from *On a Clear
Day You Can See General Motors* by J. Patrick Wright. Copyright © by
Wright Enterprises, 1979.

Designed by Richard Oriolo

Library of Congress Cataloging in Publication Data

Fallon, Ivan.
Dream maker: the rise and fall of John Z. DeLorean.

1. DeLorean Motor Company.   2. DeLorean, John Z.
3. Businessmen—United States—Biography.   I. Srodes,
James.   II. Title.
HD9710.N594D43 1983   338.7′6292222′0924 [B]   83-9497
ISBN 0-399-12821-2

Printed in the United States of America

ACKNOWLEDGMENTS

This book is the result of an enormous research program that never could have been accomplished by two men working alone on opposite sides of the Atlantic. We were blessed with a team of colleagues who were unstinting reporters and editors and encouraging friends as well.

A special note of thanks goes to Stella Shamoon of the *Sunday Telegraph*, whose early discoveries about John DeLorean sparked our own efforts. Dr. Philip Beresford, also of the *Sunday Telegraph*, contributed a unique insight into the tangled tragedy of Northern Ireland; indeed all of the staff members of the *Sunday Telegraph* from Editor J. W. M. Thompson to Deputy City Editor Ian Watson and the City staff gave generously of their support.

Once under way, Sue Fallon and Christine Tierney proved to be adept and unstoppable interviewers and researchers. Maritsa Blackman in London and Maryse Rhein in Washington kept us both on time and on target. Irene Saunders Goldstein checked and queried and edited the avalanche of manuscript and notes we generated. And Christine Jennings typed it all, at least once, and always on deadline. Thanks too, to John Cushman, our agent, whose good counsel was as invaluable as his faith, and to Richard Sykes, our peerless legal adviser. Authors should always be grateful to publishers such as Phyllis Grann of G. P. Putnam's Sons in New York and Penny Hoare of Hamish Hamilton in London, who put their support behind us early when it really counted. Nor would we be authors at all if it were not for Putnam's superb editor Christine Schillig, who combined enthusiasm and professionalism to make it all happen.

Finally, there is a debt owed to the scores of men and women who were interviewed or who provided us with documentation or expert advice during the nearly two years of our investigation. These ex-

DMC employees, relatives of our subject, friends, enemies, attorneys, bankers, and automobile executives as well as the officials of the governments of the U.S., U.K., Northern Ireland, the Republic of Ireland, and the Commonwealth of Puerto Rico brought invaluable perspectives to our research. Many had to relive painful personal episodes; others risked jobs and even prosecution to help. Some are named in the chapters that follow, many are not. However, we know who they are and hope that our efforts repay them for their contributions.

IVAN FALLON
London

JAMES SRODES
*Washington,
D.C.*

TO

Sue, Tania, Lara &
Robert Fallon
&
Louise and Cecile Srodes

CONTENTS

AUTHORS' NOTE

The authors conducted numerous interviews in the preparation of this book. Quotations cited throughout the text and descriptions of scenes witnessed by them are based on personal communications from the following persons:

Barrie Askew
Humphrey Atkins
Walter Avrea
Robin Bailie
John Banham
Charles Bennington
Alan Blair
C. R. Brown
Kenneth Bunker
Frederick Bushell
Adam Butler
George Clarke
William Collins
Alan Curtis
Kenneth Dahlinger
David E. Davis
Charles DeLorean
George DeLorean
John DeLorean
Robert Dewey
Harry DeWitt
Manuel Dubon

Jeanne Farnan
John Freeman
Nathan Gantcher
Marian Gibson
William Haddad
Shaun Harte
Michael Hayes
Clark Higley
Robert Holberg
Tony Hopkins
Clarence Jones
Arvid Jouppi
Peter Kalikow
Michael Kimberley
Semon Knudsen
Kurt Kuennecke
William Kuntz
Gary Laughlin
Michael Loasby
Brendan Macken
Bruce McWilliams
Rupert Murdoch

Tony O'Reilly
Colin Pinn
Jim Prior
Sir Lindsay Ring
John Simpson
Colin Spooner
Walter Strycker
John Thomas

Alejandro Vallecillo
James Wangers
Alan Watson
Barrie Wills
Nicholas Winterton
Jacques Wittmer
J. Patrick Wright

The authors have also talked to a number of politicians, officials, former executives, lawyers, and advisers who have greatly contributed to the information in this book but for a variety of reasons preferred to remain anonymous. We have also made extensive use of letters, memos, company files, board minutes, and other documents.

Information in Chapters 1 and 2 concerning John DeLorean's early life and years at General Motors was taken from *On a Clear Day You Can See General Motors* by J. Patrick Wright (Wright Publishing, Chicago, 1979). Material on the history and organization of the automotive industry included in Chapters 1 and 2 was provided by *American Automobile Manufacturers* by John B. Rae (Chilton Company, Radnor, Pa., 1959).

Much of the information contained in Chapters 6 through 19 regarding events in Northern Ireland and the United Kingdom came from confidential interviews, public staff-level documents, and other records pertaining to the Northern Ireland Development Authority and Her Majesty's Government's Department of Commerce.

DREAM MAKER

PROLOGUE

In the cold, blue-gray flicker of the video monitor screen, the nagging question would not be silenced. What was that guy doing there? Every rookie cop and street dope pusher knows the rule by heart: never make the buy yourself. Hand the cash over—but have someone else, somewhere else, take the delivery. But there was John DeLorean, media celebrity, international automobile tycoon, standing in a Los Angeles airport hotel room that was so wired for sound it could generate a magnetic field.

What could he be thinking of? He says something that is lost in the noise of other men moving around and opening suitcases. Somebody laughs. Why not? It's a law-enforcement convention and DeLorean is the guest of honor.

Doesn't he sense the danger? There is tension in the room, but DeLorean appears to be in good humor. He moves to a suitcase and picks up one of the kilo bags of cocaine. He hefts it with both hands the way a farmer would a sack of flour.

"It's as good as gold, and just in the nick of time," he says. This time everyone in the room chuckles. *

The truth was that John DeLorean had no one else to make that buy for him. For all his legendary charisma, for all the money he had lavished on an army of hangers-on, he ended up alone that day. He had been called a maverick many times, and indeed he was—isolated from any satisfaction in his engineering talent or business accomplishments, a fantastic, appealing personality who could draw beautiful women and loyal aides, but who ultimately drove most of them away.

---

* Affidavit of special agent Jerry G. West before U.S. District Court for Central District of California, October 20, 1982.

This sad, wretched, lonely man ended up in a hotel room drug trap because he could not bear to be found out, to confront his own failure.

This is the story of how John DeLorean began a public career that promised great hope and benefit to the world and how that promise was broken. It is the story of a man who once preached the social duties of the business executive, but who ended up cheating thousands of the poorest and hundreds of the richest people in the world—from Hollywood's exclusive Bel Air to the grimy slums of Belfast—and how he dared not be unmasked.

But this also is a story about the ideals of our society, and how far we are willing to go to have our dreams fulfilled. It is about the limitations of the institutions that we have established to protect our dreams from those who would pervert them. The DeLorean story tells how one man could amass a fortune—at one time his company had as much as $500 million in economic clout behind it—and how today nothing is left except a few hundred luxury sports cars of questionable value and millions of dollars in debts.

This story is not really about the U.S. government drug charges against John Z. DeLorean or the other defendants who still face their day in court. Nor is it merely a breathless listing of the sex-drug-celebrity innuendos that have fascinated the popular magazines and broadcast media.

Rather, the story began as a search for answers to a swarm of questions that surrounded the DeLorean Motor Company project in Northern Ireland. In late 1981 the future of the "Dream Car," as the DMC-12 was called, still shone brightly enough. Full production had not yet been reached, but prospective buyers were offering as much as $35,000, a full $10,000 over its list price, to win an early place in the delivery line.

Yet there were troubles. There were reports of embezzled funds and of production problems that could be traced back to poor design and bad management decisions. As the company's prospects daily became more convoluted and doubtful, the search for answers generated serious questions about John DeLorean himself and the men who followed him from Detroit's top executive suites to the green fields outside Belfast, where the most modern automobile plant in the world would soon become an empty, rusting reminder of how greed and fraud can sour the dreams of thousands.

Other men must share the blame for the wreck of the DeLorean dream machine, but so do many of the institutions we rely on to protect us from just this kind of disaster. Because this is also a story about the failure of government watchdog agencies, the probity of our financial centers, and the dubious accuracy and credulity of our news-gathering organizations.

Finally, the DeLorean story is about a world standard of morality that places the highest value on immediate reward and pays less attention to the true worth or actual success of an enterprise. It is about world-celebrity status granted on the basis of lifestyle and conspicuous consumption, and ignoring the real character and substance of the individual.

The DeLorean story warns us to be more cautious and reluctant to entrust our dreams to others.

1

HAPPY CHILDHOOD
-UNHAPPY HOME

It was election day in Northern Ireland—October 20, 1982. Voters were being asked to turn out for candidates for the British Parliament in London that served as Britain's proof of self-government for the six Irish counties under its control. It was a brisk, sunny day that made the green, low rolling hills of the Irish countryside appear at their best.

In Belfast the improbable good weather brought the shoppers out to wend their way through the iron turnstiles and checkpoints designed to keep the terrorists out of the main department-store district. Still, bomb blasts rocked the surrounding city in unusual number as the Irish Republican Army tried to discourage voters from giving respectability to the Parliament at Westminster.

The sunny day did nothing to penetrate the gloom inside the seventy-two-acre DeLorean Motor Company plant in the nearby suburb of Dunmurry; this was the last day the DMC-12 gull-wing sports car would be coming off the factory's assembly lines. Most of the 2,400-man work force had already been sent home weeks before, but that day there was a finality to it all. Once a plant closes, it rarely opens its doors again—especially in Northern Ireland.

Inside the brightly lit main assembly building, the entire production process stood frozen in time. Small groups of men puttered around the various work areas, sweeping up, gathering tools, talking quietly among the piles of fiberglass bales and mattings that formed the basic outlines of the DMC-12. All along the line were large wire hampers filled with the parts that were added at various production stages, and farther down were the huge mold presses that produced the top and bottom halves of the car's body shell. At the end was a line of cars, each with one gull-wing door extended into the air like an injured bird.

But for the men who were spending their last day on the job—perhaps their last job ever—there was something else to talk about. The overnight wire service reports from California had filled the morning radio programs with little else. John Z. DeLorean had been arrested near a Los Angeles airport hotel and charged by United States government investigators with taking part in a plot to smuggle in 100 kilos of cocaine that could have been resold on American streets for $50 million. Justice Department officials said they believed DeLorean was making a frantic effort to raise the money he needed to save his bankrupt car company in Northern Ireland.

They could not know just how frantic he was. Nor could they know that ironically he was close to lining up a far bigger legitimate rescue deal, that even as he flew from New York to Los Angeles, his more reputable lenders were frantically telephoning to get him to sign the loan agreements that would have given him a potential new lease on life. All that the federal agents knew about John Z. DeLorean was what almost everyone else knew—what they were told by the admiring journalists who built the DeLorean myth. According to that myth, DeLorean was the iconoclastic big businessman who had "fired General Motors" and gone on to found a flashy, high-flying sports car company.

He was still a glamorous figure, as likely to turn up as the subject of a glowing profile in some high-fashion magazine as on the business pages of *The Wall Street Journal.* The general news media knew him as a swinger who dated movie stars and who was now married to one of the world's top fashion models; a gifted engineer who had switched with style and grace into the world of high finance; a classy guy on the fast track of life—that was John DeLorean.

Little wonder that he impressed even the agents of the combined strike force that was trying to slow the flood of cocaine, heroin, and marijuana entering the United States. Most of their arrestees were members of a sleazier segment of society. Few of the agents on the case from the Internal Revenue Service, the Drug Enforcement Administration, and the Federal Bureau of Investigation had ever met such a celebrity. So they were impressed, if not exactly surprised. After all, drug smuggling and illegal sales had become so pervasive in American life that more than one businessman had tried to bail himself out of trouble with the quick riches to be had from one small cocaine deal.

Nowhere was DeLorean's reputation better than in Northern Ireland, where the 2,400 jobs provided by the car plant had injected an enormous economic boost into that desolate, strife-torn region. The men who were collecting their final paychecks that afternoon had seen John DeLorean only on rare occasions as he regally toured the kingdom of his factory in West Belfast. But his fall was their fall, too. Outside, a cluster of workers stood in the bright sunshine having a last cigarette before going home. They watched silently as two large trucks pulled through the plant gate, each carrying six of the shining steel sports cars to the storage yard at the port of Belfast. The trucks seemed like hearses carrying loved ones away.

Had the men heard about Mr. DeLorean's arrest? A sad thing, said one as the others nodded. He did his best for this area. It was a shame what had happened to the company, to their jobs, and now to him.

"Some of the lads never had jobs before; now they stand a chance of never having another. This summer I was able to take my kids to the seaside for the first proper holiday they've ever had. Now there'll be no Christmas," one man said, turning toward home.

A journalist walked after him; where could he be found later on? "Oh, you'll be able to find me all right. I'll be down on the Falls Road dole from now on."

In London there was shocked bewilderment. But there was also some undisguised glee. By the time of his arrest, DeLorean had made powerful enemies in British government circles. For months ministers had been arguing that the government should not deal with him at all because he was a "crook." But they never had any real proof, only hunches. Now they felt they had good evidence. It was a day full of "I told you so." It seemed a fitting end to one of the biggest disasters in British corporate history.

The bewilderment was centered mostly in the office of Sir Kenneth Cork. Sir Kenneth was the British government-appointed bankruptcy receiver charged with either restructuring DeLorean Motor Cars Limited of Northern Ireland or with selling it off and settling as many of its huge debts as he could. He was a tough professional with an impeccable reputation. One London newspaper called him the "familiar provider of a better class of financial funeral service." For eight months he had been running DeLorean's factory and was in almost daily touch with DeLorean himself.

Cork had been on the phone most of the day before, making one last try to save the factory. For months DeLorean had been telling him he had "the head of a Middle Eastern state" or a "friend from the West Coast" or a "wealthy industrialist" who was going to invest $30 to $50 million. Every one of them had fallen through—except one. And that last one was coming through with the money. Even the skeptical Cork was persuaded of it.

The night before, Cork had received a call from Virginia, from the woman representing the bank that would transfer the money. It was all ready, she told him. All it needed was a signature from DeLorean, but she was not able to get hold of him—he had apparently left New York to fly to Los Angeles without signing the document. That morning a shocked Cork heard about the arrest on the seven o'clock news. A few hours later he arrived at his office to find a Telex from the bank confirming the money was there. It was waiting for a simple "John Z. DeLorean" signature. But John Z. DeLorean was not available that morning. The final hope for the Belfast factory had gone.

There was a feeling of relief, too. In one of the Northern Ireland ministry offices in Whitehall complex, across from London's St. James's Park, a junior minister gazed out the window at the misty greenness. A colleague sat at his desk regarding the bold headlines of the *London Evening Standard*, which was full of John DeLorean's arrest.

"Well, look at it this way. What if he *had* come up with the money, bailed out the factory with his drug money—and *then* been arrested. How would we look then?"

The minister turned abruptly from the window. "Good Lord—I hadn't considered that! *That* would have been the end of a couple of bright, promising careers."

The British official was not the only one to be astonished by the implications of the arrest. News reports and radio and television talk shows devoted to it all produced disquieting public reaction to the scandal. Such was the apparent level of cynicism in America about government and institutions that people thought of John DeLorean as a fast-track version of Robin Hood. A veteran investigative journalist who had tracked DeLorean's long history of business vandalism emerged shaken from one national radio show on which listeners were asked to telephone their reactions to the arrest.

"You wouldn't have believed it," he recounted later. "The calls ran seven or eight to one in sympathy for John. There was one poor guy called all the way from Buffalo. He'd lost his job when the factory he'd worked at for twenty years went bust and he said, 'I just wish my boss had sold some cocaine or anything just to keep that plant open.' That still bothers me. How can people still support him after all the harm he's done? How can they ignore what he has done to other people and then consider *him* some kind of victim?"

To be sure, there were people who did not consider John DeLorean a victim at all. To them, he had been and remained a firsthand threat to their lives; they were victims of previous encounters well before DeLorean and Northern Ireland had ever heard of each other.

In Phoenix the news of the arrest brought telephone calls from friends and relatives to the home of Pete and Shirley Avrea, who had suffered through the lengthy lawsuits and threats that came so close to breaking Shirley's health. In 1974 Pete had relied on DeLorean to help market an invention—a device that keeps automobile radiators from boiling over and that is now on almost every car in North America. During one trial, the judge estimated that Pete Avrea had been cheated out of royalties worth $70 million. In the end, Avrea had to give up his efforts to recover his losses because of his wife's deteriorating health. He took no joy in the calls about the arrest; he wished he had never heard of John DeLorean.

Across the country, in the resort town of Cape Coral, Florida, Kenneth Dahlinger reacted to a radio report of DeLorean's arrest by changing the route he took to work that morning. Dahlinger was now the owner of a prosperous business in the growing resort town, but he had once owned an even more prosperous Cadillac dealership in Wichita. DeLorean and a henchman left Dahlinger bankrupt, and the continuing threats against his life forced him to move, to keep changing his unlisted telephone number, to keep looking over his shoulder and changing his daily routine—even with John DeLorean 3,000 miles away, locked up in the Terminal Island federal jail awaiting his bond hearing.

Elsewhere across America, still others would suddenly realize just how wrong they had been to trust DeLorean.

Houston's sprawling glass and concrete airport has an exclusive section of hangars and support buildings set aside for the private planes that wealthy Texans use to cover the frequent huge distances between home and work. Out in the parking lot, Gary Laughlin sat staring at his waiting plane, momentarily paralyzed by the news he had just heard on the radio. Laughlin had wrenched his fortune out of the ground in the Texas oil patch as a wildcat driller and investor. He had trusted John DeLorean's outspoken individualism and his seeming integrity. Laughlin also had invested $500,000 of his own money and convinced friends and relatives to invest still more in the car venture.

Show business superstar Sammy Davis Jr. was even harder hit. Although Davis had earned several fortunes during his fifty-year career on stage and in the movies, he had been ill-served by early managers and was frequently in trouble over taxes and alimony. The $150,000 Davis had given John DeLorean had been earned by the sweat of his brow and was the entertainer's hope for winning some financial independence. "Sammy can't come to the phone," an aide told a sympathetic caller. "He's really in mourning over that man DeLorean."

To be sure, DeLorean had plenty of friends in high places—James Aubrey, the ex-CBS boss, Dave Mahoney, president of Avis Car Rental, and Herb Siegel, chairman of Chris-Craft Industries, who even then was trying to arrange DeLorean's $2-million bail demanded by the federal court.

And he had his inner circle of faithful supporters. The horde of journalists and television cameramen that jammed Los Angeles airport a day later to cover the arrival of DeLorean's cover-girl wife, Cristina Ferrare, paid no attention to the tough, heavyset man in a windbreaker who met her at the arrival gate and whisked her to a waiting car. It was Roy Nesseth, DeLorean's long-time comrade in many shady business deals. It was Nesseth who struck terror into the heart of any business associate or DeLorean employee who interfered with his desires. "Roy enjoys ruining people," DeLorean would boast. Threats from Nesseth caused Pete Avrea to drop his suits to regain control over his invention and forced Kenneth Dahlinger to move into hiding in another part of the country.

Another associate sat in stunned disbelief in his New York hotel room as the World Series baseball game between Milwaukee and St. Louis was interrupted when the announcement of DeLorean's arrest flashed across the bottom of his screen. Thomas W. Kimmerly, sixty-two, took to his bed with a 100-degree temperature. Kimmerly had given up a thriving Detroit law practice as a tax and securities specialist to follow John DeLorean on his odyssey from the executive suite at General Motors to the ill-fated and now bankrupt car company across the Atlantic. Kimmerly was totally devoted to John DeLorean, and even tolerated snide teasing from other company officials that he might be in love with his boss. It was Kimmerly who worked out the details of DeLorean's many business ventures, who plotted the securities offerings and the tax strategies that shifted funds from one enterprise to another and ultimately to DeLorean himself.

After the company crashed, former officials fell into the habit of referring to DeLorean, Nesseth, and Kimmerly as one entity—an overpowering combination of drive, muscle, and shrewdness. Indeed, at the end, there were those who argued that DeLorean himself had become dominated by the other two, that he was powerless to resist Kimmerly's plots and Nesseth's predations.

But DeLorean was very alone in that Los Angeles airport hotel room. Kimmerly and Nesseth were never considered suspects by the federal strike force agents.

Who is John Z. DeLorean?

The task of separating the real nature of any man or woman from his or her public mask is difficult, and the temptation to perform an armchair psychoanalysis is greatest when the details are the sketchiest. But a great deal is known about the early, formative years of John DeLorean's life. Later he would exaggerate the poverty and the violent instability of his childhood.

These exaggerations—and sometimes lies—served to make the distance he had come in later life all the more remarkable. This fact, too, remained a central thread in his character. There is no doubt that he hated the shame and insecurity that pressed in on him during his youth. Nor is there any doubt that it left him dissatisfied with many of the innumerable genuine successes that followed. There always had to be something more—something bigger and grander.

John Zachary DeLorean was born on January 6, 1925, in Detroit, the eldest of four sons of Zachary and Kathryn DeLorean. Pervasive hard times were soon to become a fact of life for the millions of Americans who were lucky enough to find industrial jobs. DeLorean's father was an immigrant French-Alsatian whose irregular jobs at the Ford Motor Company foundry left him drinking and raging at the frustrations of his life. A gifted millwright, Zachary DeLorean was nevertheless kept to relatively menial, insecure jobs at the foundry because of his poor command of English. Furious at the snubs he endured at work, the six-foot-one, 220-pound DeLorean vented his anger in barroom fights that only added to the family's hardship.

Kathryn DeLorean was also an immigrant, a refugee from the wreckage of the Austro-Hungarian Empire. Necessity forced her, too, onto the factory floor, and throughout most of young John's life his mother worked as a tool assembler for the Carboloy Products Division of General Electric.

How poor were John DeLorean's family and childhood?

"You don't know what poor is until you know how poor we were. We were really poor," he said in a recent interview. "When I was twelve I got one of those Sears and Roebuck suits that cost about twelve bucks in those days, and I wore that suit until I got out of college to go into the service. It was the only one I had; it was bought so you could let the pants out as I grew taller and I didn't weigh anything then anyway. No, no, we were really poor."

Even if it were true, the DeLorean family was hardly an example of the grinding poverty that millions of Americans endured in the middle 1930s. Many American boys had no suit at all or they got hand-me-downs from older brothers—an embarrassment young John did not have to endure as he grew toward his eventual six-foot-four-inch height.

No, the less dramatic truth was that through much of his childhood, John DeLorean lived in a pleasant, if small, frame house near Six Mile Road and Dequindre on Detroit's Near East Side. He would describe it as a tough, lower-middle-class neighborhood, but it was considerably better than that. There were three bedrooms, and thus the four brothers had the relative privacy of sleeping two to a room. There was enough food and love. And there was enough money for school and even for music lessons for John, who used his talent in playing the clarinet to win scholarships to the better Detroit schools.

It is also clear that the DeLorean family suffered considerably from Zachary DeLorean's emotional flareups. Three times during his early years, John's parents separated and the boys were taken by Kathryn to the sanctuary of her relatives in Los Angeles. Each reconciliation lasted a year or so, through John's early teenage years. Finally, in 1942, when John was seventeen, Kathryn and Zachary took the unusual step in those days of divorcing. After that, the boys saw little of their father. He died at the age of sixty-one of throat cancer.

It is hard to say how much of an imprint was made on John De-

Lorean by his father's frightening explosions and subsequent neglect, but it is easy to sympathize with a new arrival in a hard land at a hard time. Perhaps Zachary DeLorean could have done better for his family, yet he took care of them for as long as he could and prophetically instilled in his sons a familiarity with and love for the automobile. Like every other mechanic in Detroit, the elder DeLorean tinkered with cars at home when he wasn't building them at work. One of John's earliest memories, he later recalled, was helping to put cylinder heads on Ford Model As in his father's backyard workshop.

If there are two central themes that characterize John DeLorean's childhood, they are his disappointment in and lack of respect for his father's perceived weakness, and the boy's own embarrassment at coming from a factory-class background. DeLorean acknowledges that as a child he was fairly content and was adequately sheltered from the hunger and homelessness that millions of other Americans endured during the 1929–1941 Depression. In his own words:

> Kids are inherently happy if you give them half a chance, and I thought we had a pretty happy childhood. Part of the reason is that while we had the humble surroundings that come with lower-middle-class existence, we didn't know we were being deprived of some of the great fruits of American life because we didn't have the means of instant communication then as we do today. So while we didn't have a lot, we also weren't aware of what other people had. That comfortable picture was shattered one day when I was about 13, and two classmates, a brother and sister, at Nolan Intermediate School asked me to their house for dinner. They lived in a very plush area known as Palmer Woods, at Woodward and Seven Mile Road. And while their house wasn't the biggest in the area, it was the largest I'd ever been in. I remember feeling awkward at dinner, not sure of how to act or eat. The conversation covered some things I'd never heard of, like going to summer camp and traveling on vacations. Vacations, for the most part, when I was young, meant getting out of school and playing around the house for three months. The experience opened a new vista for me. I began to realize what things were possible and available in America. *

---

* J. Patrick Wright, *On a Clear Day You Can See General Motors* (Wright Publishing Company, 1979).

Palmer Woods, where Detroit's Municipal Golf Course is located, is a very pleasant neighborhood, to be sure. But on Detroit's grid system of streets and neighborhoods, the Six Mile Road (now called McNichols) and Dequindre neighborhood where the DeLoreans lived was less than a mile away from his schoolmates, and that was scarcely the impenetrable class barrier he would later portray it to be. If school holidays did not mean summer camps for young John DeLorean, neither did they mean summer jobs to help the family make ends meet.

The point is that John DeLorean plainly felt ashamed of his family and background. This is a common enough story in the families of new immigrants. Some families stick together in tight units and work their way to a better life for all. In others, individual members abhor the embarrassment of the old ties to old ways. They seek their success through education and advancement.

Young John DeLorean was to take full advantage of the open American public school system as it existed in those days. After the family's last return from Los Angeles to reconciliation, John went to Cass Tech, Detroit's High School for honor students. There he qualified for a music scholarship to the Lawrence Institute of Technology, the top-flight training school that turned out the army of draftsmen and designers for the region's manufacturing complex.

At Lawrence, DeLorean specialized in industrial engineering studies and was good enough to be elected to the school's Honor Society. He also played in the school dance band and wrote for the school newspaper, the *Tech News.* John also ran for the presidency of Lawrence's Student Council organization in 1947, but lost.

Photographs from the various newspapers, school yearbooks, and other publications of the period at Lawrence show John DeLorean as he was—a tall, slender American teenager: a soft and dreamy-eyed boy who would probably grow up to be a handsome man. If he pushed hard at his studies, that was why the boys were at Lawrence Tech: to get ahead. If he was brash and slightly self-promoting, his classmates and teachers also remember him as being willing to help less gifted students with tough engineering problems. He also showed a barbed sense of humor in his newspaper writings and often sank a shaft or two into himself.

In his final newspaper column before going off to the Army in 1943, he wrote: "In my spare time I've written a book on how to stay out of the Army. Those who wish to secure a copy of this infallible booklet should send 25 cents to Pvt. J. Sachelpants DeLorean at Camp Custard. But, seriously, the best way to stay out of the Army is to join the Navy. . . . s'long JD ERC."

World War II interrupted DeLorean's studies at Lawrence Tech, as it did for millions of other Americans. He returned to Detroit after his three-year hitch and got a job with the city's Lighting Commission until he had enough money to re-enroll at Lawrence. During his final two years there, he worked part-time in a Chrysler plant (a job arranged by an uncle) and at a neighborhood body and fender shop.

When DeLorean resumed his column in the *Tech News* in early 1947, the following appeared in the letters column:

> Dear Editor,
> I would like to compliment you on securing the services of that distinguished and polished journalist, Mr. DeLorean. Seldom, if ever, does a college of this size boast an author of such proportions. In issue after issue his subtle witticisms, fluent prose and lofty philosophy have brought warmth and joy to the hearts of his avid readers. Truly such literary grace and charm must come from a pen driven by a noble mind. I know most of the student body joins me in this sincere tribute to high endeavor and the matchless style which Mr. DeLorean exemplifies. Sincerely, Naeroled Nhoj.

He also was still young and self-confident enough to risk writing the following discourse for *Tech News* on the topic "Know You What It Is to Be an Engineer?"

> It is to have a dream without being conscious you are dreaming lest the dream break, it is to be trapped in a terrible tower of pure science.
> It is to live in a mean, bare prison cell and regard yourself the sovereign of limitless space; it is to turn failure into success, mice into men, rags into riches, stone into buildings, steel into bridges, for each engineer has a magician in his soul. . . .
> It is to give imagination full play, to accept the inventions of nature, to tell stories born of silence that fill the world with wonder. . . .
> It is to be a conquerer and a coward, a king and a captive, a savior and a slave, it is to be good unto seeming Godlike while

contrasting evil incarnate; it is to suffer a throne alone in your terrible temple of science while companions roam the city streets making carefree carnival. . . .

It is loving and winning only to lose and love again and again, for engineering is a fanciful goddess, clad in fickle fantasy, form fitting fortune and flaming fool's gold who recognizes neither disaster nor despair.

Without putting too much emphasis on the anecdote, it is also worth noting that when DeLorean graduated from Lawrence in 1948, his colleagues on the *Tech News* published the following tongue-in-cheek farewell.

We mourn the passing of our dear departed *Tech News* columnist John "B.S. ME" DeLorean, whose aim it was to remain a ward of the Veteran's Administration throughout his declining years, as he has finished the prescribed obstacle course of four undergraduate years and passed beyond to the ranks of the unemployed. It is with a wistful tear in our eyes that we realize that we shall no longer see his neat soldierly form bent over the tasks of plant layout and electrical experiments long into the night. But though he has departed to seek his eternal reward, those of us who knew him will draw inspiration from his example. We shall miss his sober countenance and the lofty idealism of his "5 with D" column. But as he stumbles through the future, we wish him the best of luck and may all his opponents' kings be infessable [sic]. We shall always remember his sage remark, "Eternal vigilance is the price of dishonesty."

But DeLorean would desert his "fanciful goddess" of engineering almost at once. He claimed later that his part-time work as an industrial draftsman had disillusioned him about the prospects for the field. His first jobs after Lawrence were as an insurance salesman and as a salesman for the Factory Equipment Company, a concern that made machine tools. By all accounts he was quite successful, and won a trip to Bermuda for selling the rather considerable sum, for the late 1940s, of $850,000 in insurance policy coverage.

But his restlessness and unwillingness to focus were becoming evident even at that early time. A relative helped him get a job at the

Chrysler Institute, a postgraduate facility run by the car company to train higher-level engineers. In 1952 he graduated with a masters degree in automotive engineering and went to work at Chrysler while pushing on to earn the credits necessary for a masters in business administration from the University of Michigan.

It was during that time that two other patterns emerged in John DeLorean's persona. One was his recognizable skill as an automotive engineer. He would be comfortable with that skill, secure in his ability for the rest of his life. He also developed the patterns of diligent, hard work that brought him advancement and promotion throughout his career.

Chrysler soon bored DeLorean and he shifted over to a job with the legendary Forest McFarland, the head of Research and Development for the Packard Motor Company. DeLorean was assigned to work on the new central hydraulic systems and the innovative "ultramatic" transmission system. These were important formative years for his professional life, for they imbued him with the spirit of Detroit's classic auto engineer and set him firmly on his career path.

Up to this point there was very little that would set John Z. De-Lorean apart from any other young man trying to get a foothold in life in the years immediately after World War II. He was middle class, had a decent education, had served his country honorably during the war. Afterward, he worked hard to finish his training and moved from job to job trying to better himself. He was not above using the help of relatives to find jobs, and he was ambitious enough to move on if the opportunities looked better elsewhere. Like millions of others, DeLorean also married. His wife was the former Elizabeth Higgins, a secretary. He continued to play his clarinet as a pickup addition to the jazz bands that played in Detroit's interracial black-and-tan clubs, but even that was more for enjoyment than for the money it brought in.

The discontented aimlessness that re-emerged later in DeLorean's life disappeared at least temporarily when he joined McFarland's design shop at Packard. Here was something that absorbed his interest, something he could respect and even aspire to.

It is no exaggeration to say that the automobile industry is one of the key expressions of that personal yearning that has turned into cliché as the American dream. Central to the American experience from the time the first settlers arrived in the New World are the themes of personal mobility and individual independence and enterprise. If times are hard, move on. Go west. Go somewhere.

In the early twentieth century, the automobile ceased being just a convenience for the rich and emerged as a source of social change. The car itself became an object of fantasy and speculation. Exploration of the innards of the internal combustion engine became a rite of passage for most American boys—John DeLorean and his brothers were no exceptions—so much so that few American adult males have ever really outgrown this fascination and romance.

And why should they? A man could grow rich by building a better automobile. Indeed, the entire nation profited by the unprecedented development of the automobile. General Motors Chairman Charles E. "Engine Charlie" Wilson never said, "What's good for General Motors is good for America." What he did say that fateful day in 1952 at a U.S. Senate hearing was, "I have always believed that what was good for America was good for General Motors and vice versa." And the statement has proven to be an accurate observation rather than an expression of incredible arrogance as it was considered to be by some at the time.

Since World War II, car production has been far and away the largest manufacturing enterprise in America. That explosive growth has fueled thousands of other business enterprises, provided employment for millions, and valuable mobility and convenience to others.

If one pauses to consider, the present-day automobile is essentially the same product it was in the early 1920s. Steam and electricity had been discarded as sources of power because of technological weaknesses or because they failed to catch the public's fancy. So, too, had manufacturers dropped a variety of notions about the number of wheels, the random location of the driver, and buggylike body designs. From that point on, all technological changes from the Ford Model T to the DMC-12 were refinements and improvements rather than drastic innovation.

Moreover, by the 1920s, the supply of automobiles in America had caught up with the demand for them. The industry could produce more cars than there were buyers. The increased competition led the U.S. car industry steadily away from its entrepreneurial founding days and inexorably onward to the consolidations and increasingly complex corporate organizations that were forged to survive.

By the 1920s the old myth of the genius mechanic in his modest workshop, which had always been more fiction than fact, was being replaced. Henry Ford, Ransom Olds, David Dunbar Buick, Louis Chevrolet, and even the five Studebaker brothers were shirtsleeves inventors, to be sure. And it is a little-known fact that these men—even the stiff, reclusive Henry Ford—raced their cars against each other. That was how they proved an auto's worth: They built it, then hauled it out to some county fair dirt track and raced it until someone won or the engine blew up.

But these same men, to the varying degrees that they were successes, were also pioneer industrialists. They invented the manufacturing techniques that would make their particular cars sell profitably, and the parts and innovative elements of the cars were frequently a second consideration to the enterprise. Ford, for example, continued to buy his engines from the Dodge Brothers up through the Model N Ford, the immediate precursor of the legendary Model T.

To some extent, that decentralization survives today in the network of independent suppliers currently maintained by each of the Big Four American producers (General Motors, Ford, Chrysler, and American). The real revolution of the 1920s was the consolidation of management controls and decision-making for a wide range of activities into one group of senior executives, often under the leadership of a single man.

At the base of this change was a truly revolutionary idea for its time —the offering of a variety of products to suit broader market tastes. Henry Ford had become rich making a car that the average American could buy for $500. Other men had varying successes selling luxury cars to the very rich. But by the middle of the First World War, William C. Durant was busily putting together the structure of General Motors from the disparate parts of Buick, Oldsmobile, Cadillac, and Oakland. Into his conglomerate he folded other autos whose names read like a museum of old cars—the Carter, the Elmore, Ewing, Marquette, Rapid, Reliance, and Welsh. The new General Motors also included the Northway Motor Manufacturing Company, which made engines, and the Champion Ignition Company of Flint, Michigan, which produced the porcelain spark plug designed by Albert Champion.

Durant's strategy was sharply rejected by Henry Ford at the time. Durant reasoned that if a company offered a model to fit every definable market category, then that very variety was insurance against the entire company failing because one product line had hit a slump. Ford, on the other hand, argued for most of his life that one should do only what one does well; that the complexities of making so many kinds of cars would ultimately drag such a conglomeration down. Durant lost control of General Motors in 1911 but regained it again in 1916 with the help of Pierre S. DuPont, John Jacob Raskob, and the profits generated by Chevrolet, which Durant had acquired in the meantime.

In the end, Billy Durant died a penniless failure. But the trends he set in motion became part of the folkways of the industry. Where Durant stumbled, other men pushed ahead, many of them set on their way by the old conglomerator himself.

Alfred Sloan, W. S. "Bill" Knudsen, and other General Motors chief executives would take Durant's philosophy and refine it over the next thirty years. Sloan set up the lines of organization and decision-making that last to this day. Knudsen contributed his own emphasis on product development and improvement. He guided Chevrolet to its rivalry with Ford by the simple principle of trying to offer the buyer a visibly better product than Ford, even if the price was just noticeably higher.

It is important to remember that these now-mythic figures of the American automobile industry were still alive and functioning when young John DeLorean was beginning his career. Knudsen had abandoned his presidency of GM in 1941 to take charge of the war industrialization effort. Sloan would be a father figure to the industry until his death in 1966. Their theories and achievements would be among the lessons DeLorean absorbed along with his technical training. The myth and reality of Detroit and its car-making industry are an important element in examining his character and why he would later do what he did, become what he was.

For now John DeLorean was learning valuable technical skills at the Packard design shop. Packard was one of the independent luxury-car holdovers from before World War II. It was justifiably proud of its precisely engineered heavyweight engines and was now trying to design its way back to profitability with innovations in its power train and transmission.

Because Packard lagged behind in meeting the public's quick-changing tastes for style in the middle 1950s, the company's fortunes never recovered. But while he was there, DeLorean benefited from access to both the assembly shops and the production facilities where Packard designers worked side by side with the toolmakers.

Packard also had an institutional pride that attracted DeLorean: it was a bit old-fashioned and stuffy. In fact, it was the pride of the individual craftsmen, with the inherent disdain that such men hold for any mass-produced products.

In 1956, four years after joining Packard, DeLorean succeeded Forest McFarland, who moved to Buick as assistant research engineer. DeLorean was now in charge of a small research and development operation at a fatally troubled firm. But his reputation was good enough to win a call from the newly appointed chief of General Motors' troubled Pontiac Car Division.

Semon E. "Bunkie" Knudsen was a true prince of Motor City. He was the son of GM's former president and was himself an MIT-trained automotive engineer who had nevertheless retained his father's predilection for getting his hands dirty building cars that others would buy. Knudsen needed new engineering talent to revive Pontiac. He hired Elliott "Pete" Estes as chief engineer and DeLorean as his assistant for advanced design work.

As DeLorean would recall, the impending merger of Packard with Studebaker Corporation in 1956 left him with several unsatisfactory prospects. He could move to South Bend, Indiana, where Studebaker's headquarters was located. But he reasoned that the merger would not make one stronger company out of two ailing ones. His other option was a job offer from a small Cleveland firm, Thompson Products, an auto parts supplier. Bunkie Knudsen's call to join him at Pontiac was a welcome alternative.

2

THE GENERAL MOTORS YEARS

"There were two of them. This other fellow and John, and the other guy right away started asking me about benefits and raises and things like that. John just wanted to know about the job. The other fellow was gone in a week.

"In those days John was a bit on the heavy side, about 190 pounds. And like everyone else back then, he didn't dress with much style, and he had the short hair. But he worked hard enough."

These days, Semon Emil Knudsen is not the retired elder statesman that he is entitled to be. Knudsen is now seventy-one but looks as if he's in his mid-fifties. His immaculate suits and reserved manner mask the fact that he feels equally at home in the executive suites of Detroit and in the pits at a racetrack. These days, Knudsen is in active partnership with American racing's supermechanic, Smokey Yunik, in the development of a high-compression, low-pollution, fuel-efficient engine that produces the same horsepower with two cylinders that most engines do with four. Until April 1982, Yunik and Knudsen were being actively courted by John DeLorean, who wanted the design for his 1985 model DMC-12 car.

William S. "Big Bill" Knudsen emigrated from Denmark to Buffalo, where he married and where young Semon was born in 1912. The boy was an only son with three younger sisters, but Bunkie—from the old Army slang for bunkmate or buddy—would hardly be the spoiled crown prince of Detroit he could have been. Not even when the senior Knudsen took his skills as a toolmaker and engineer to Dearborn, Michigan, to work for Henry Ford. By 1926 the elder Knudsen had become vice president of the Chevrolet division at General Motors; and that year, he gave his fourteen-year-old son a new Chevy, completely unassembled. Bunkie was told that the car would be his if he could put together the 1,000 or more parts unaided. It took him just two months to complete the task.

In 1937, the year after Bunkie graduated from M.I.T. as a fledgling automotive engineer, Bill Knudsen was elected president of General Motors and stayed in that post until 1940, when Roosevelt named him to head the war mobilization production effort for World War II. Instead of taking a plush GM job as might have been expected, Bunkie got a job at a machine shop and then went to work in a roller bearing plant that turned out 100,000 units a day so he could have the experience with mass production.

When he finally did join GM, it was to tour the outposts of the giant corporation, working in the plants that produced engines for aircraft and for the diesels. By 1956, at age forty-four, Bunkie Knudsen would be the youngest man ever to head one of GM's five automobile divisions. He was made general manager of Pontiac. The age distinction is important—it will be repeated.

A common belief around Detroit is that Bunkie Knudsen was the father John DeLorean never had. Up to a point, that is probably so. In an uncharacteristic acknowledgment, DeLorean will recall later in his book that he was "a naive, rough-edged engineer . . . [when] I came under the tutelage and into the friendship . . . of Bunkie Knudsen. He showed me another side of life I never knew existed."

Knudsen, for his part, has the kind of sober regret one has for an old comrade in arms who has fallen on hard times. John DeLorean may well have been a surrogate son to Bunkie Knudsen, but the older man was never blind to John's flaws.

The regret is real enough; you rarely wish ill of someone who was there at the beginning. John DeLorean came along just as Knudsen was setting off on his campaign to match his own father's legend—to become president of General Motors—so he still has a regretful fondness for one of the men who began the march with him.

In that summer of 1956, when Knudsen entered the lists with John DeLorean among his squires, Detroit was just becoming the engineering backwater it is today among other U.S. industries. The real name of the car game by then was less one of manufacturing transportation and more like the fashion industry.

Perhaps World War II and the Korean War were to blame. Other industry groups (aerospace, chemicals, and communications, for example) all received enormous technological boosts during wartime that were immediately translated into improved commercial products in peacetime, just as our high-technology industries of today are still feeding off the advances of the space program. What the wars and the space program had in common was that they forced companies to solve problems and improve products well in advance of market demand—indeed, they created the demand for products that were unknown to the consumer until then.

Detroit, however, went the other way. The last commercial automobile rolled off a Detroit assembly line in 1942. From that time until late in 1946, when the first Chevrolets, Plymouths, and Fords went on sale again, Detroit had effectively been on a sabbatical. There would be some improvement in the new cars—higher-compression engines, better transmissions, and the first experimental electric power-assisted luxury items—but for the most part the automobile emerged from the war years in almost indistinguishable form from its prewar predecessors. It was still a box on four wheels powered by an internal combustion engine.

Ironically, not even the advances in engine development were all that useful because they emphasized speed rather than efficiency. Tooling and manufacturing costs placed limits on just how fast a mass-produced car could go, and besides, even speed-happy Americans have little use for a car that can exceed 200 mph, then or now. So Detroit settled for making its cars prettier or more novel in appearance. Since public tastes in America have been in an almost constant state of revolution since that time, the industry has drifted along, changing the image of its product without substantially altering the product itself. Today, of course, Detroit is paying a high price for its failure to innovate in the postwar era.

But just as with the other, luckier industry groups, Detroit was under enormous pressure to get back into the business of producing for the consumer market as quickly as it could when World War II ended. For a while it was a seller's market as pent-up demand outstripped the ability to put new cars into dealer lots fast enough. By 1956, however, the industry was being steadily nudged to pay more attention to how popular taste could be motivated and manipulated.

This is where men like Bunkie Knudsen and John DeLorean represented a break with Detroit's tradition of shirtsleeve engineers and managers. They both were engineers, but they also had an eye for fashion and public taste. There would be differences between the two men as they evolved over the years. Knudsen never ended his love affair with the automobile. Recently, he told with pride of how he failed to get the dealer who had sold him a new Ventura to fix a complicated ignition problem. Finally, Knudsen took the afternoon off, grabbed his toolbox, and solved the problem himself. DeLorean, on the other hand, lost that enthusiasm as his increasing cynicism overwhelmed even the one talent that everyone agreed he possessed —his engineering skill. But at the beginning, he and Bunkie Knudsen had more in common. They were both good engineers and the future in Detroit beckoned to them both.

We are encumbered with myths about the way things are done in America. One of the more pervasive is about the way top management is chosen for the biggest American corporations. Cartoonists have relied for years on the image of callow Junior being inserted into a top vice presidency of Dad's firm over the heads of senior, more qualified people. Another myth is the conspiracy theory that envisions a web stretching from the Ivy League business schools to Wall Street and out across the land to the executive suites of the 2,000 major corporations.

Despite the current popularity of the MBA degree, the truth is that the business school graduate has only recently become a major component of the management pool for big U.S. firms. The tradition of most heavy industries has been to select chief executives and senior officers from the ranks, and to put a premium on men who have the greatest experience on the manufacturing side of the enterprise, sometimes to the exclusion of colleagues who come from backgrounds in research, marketing, or even administration. The prejudice of management to replace itself with persons "who know how to make what we sell" over those known as "bean counters" is still remarkably strong, even in the 1980s.

There was sound reason for this tradition at the start. It allowed senior managers to watch men come up through the manufacturing ranks, with each candidate performing at increasingly difficult levels of responsibility. It is a painfully slow process, with each successive promotion narrowing the field of possible contenders for the ultimate top job. It becomes important to be accepted at every step along the way, and John DeLorean, in later years, would be especially scornful of this tradition. To him, it smacked of stagnating conformity; it put a premium on those who could mask their lack of ability by wearing the same clothing styles and by adopting the same public attitudes as their mentors and judges.

He believed that the later generation of General Motors executives —his bosses—were poor inheritors of the industry's traditions; that they had become dependent on the perquisites of office and on an old-boy network of power, instead of improvements and innovation and organization.

As I grew in General Motors it became apparent that objective criteria were not always used to evaluate an executive's performance. Many times the work record of a man who was promoted was far inferior to the records of others around him who were not promoted. It was quite obvious that something different than job performance was being used to rate these men.

That something different was a very subjective criterion which encompassed style, appearance, personality and, most importantly, personal loyalty to the man (or men) who was the promoter, and to the system which brought this all about. These were rules of this fraternity of management at GM. Those pledges (initiates) willing to obey the rules were promoted. In the vernacular they were the company's "team players." Those who didn't fit into the mold of a manager, who didn't adhere to the rules because they thought they were silly, generally weren't promoted. "He's not a team player," was the frequent, and many times only, objection to an executive in line for promotion. It didn't mean he was doing a poor job. It meant he didn't fit neatly into a stereotype of style, appearance and manner. He didn't display blind loyalty to the system of management, to the man or men doing the promoting. He rocked the boat. He took unpopular stands on products or policy which contradicted the prevailing attitude of top management.

At General Motors, good appearance meant conservative dress. In my very first meeting as a GM employee in 1956 at Pontiac, half the session was taken up in discussion about some vice president downtown at headquarters who was sent home that morning for wearing a brown suit. Only blue or black suits were tolerated then. I remember thinking that was silly. But in those days I followed the rules closely.

What DeLorean did not say about the men who ran Motor City when he was beginning his career was that they were men who had spent those careers adjusting to a depression and a global war that forced tremendous dislocations and accommodations on them and their industry. They were conservative, to be sure; too much had happened to them already to countenance flamboyance or even much reliance on intuition.

But however conformist GM was in its dress code, the path to the executive suite on the 14th floor of the West Grand Avenue head-quarters was not an automatic treadmill where loyalty to one's sponsor was the key for those who served and waited their turn. General Motors was then and is now a place of sharp-elbowed, aggressive personalities. Like many of its sister industrial centers, Detroit has always been a tough town, and the scramble to survive reaches from its streets and factory floors to the paneled offices of senior manage-ment.

It is possible that DeLorean never quite realized how tough these older men could be—and when he found that out it was too late.

To the extent that he was correct, he also exaggerated the confor-mity charge. No senior management group or individual chief execu-tive is ever so secure that he can fill a line of succession with clones of himself. This was doubly so at General Motors where the average tour of duty as president or chairman of the board was less than five years.

Rather, it is more accurate to say that the pressure on young exec-utives in those days was that they "make their numbers"—that is, achieve the goals or quotas set out for them by the demands of profit-ability and productivity set by senior managers. Personal style had very little to do with it. DeLorean was right to complain about that part of the life on the 14th floor: dullness was endemic.

What he apparently never accepted or appreciated fully was that one's reward or demotion depended upon success with immediate goals, not on attractive promise or even in being right over the long haul in spite of being wrong today. You made today's numbers today and collected today's reward. To get tomorrow's reward, you kept on succeeding. It could be done. Bunkie Knudsen had seen it done!

Without a doubt, in 1956 Bunkie Knudsen was the hottest young engineer-manager in Detroit. But he had learned several good lessons from his father's career, one of them being that you are only as good as the team working for you. If they don't make their numbers, you don't make yours.

So you need a good team, good enough to meet the immediate challenges and good enough to grow with you, to advance when you advance and to share, to have a vested interest in your success. For Knudsen, that team was John DeLorean and Pete Estes.

Estes was the man Bunkie Knudsen needed most. He was forty-one and the engine wizard at GM. Unlike Knudsen, his background was more akin to DeLorean's. Like other boys of his day, he had begun fooling around with cars at an early age and was skilled enough to make repairs on his father's Flying Cloud. At fourteen he had attached a one-cylinder engine to his coaster wagon to make it self-propelled.

So Pete Estes was the man Knudsen needed, a real up-from-the-ranks engineer. He had worked his way through the General Motors Institute, that company's farm system for draftsmen. Later he had come under the tutelage of Charles F. Kettering, head of GM research labs, where he worked on diesel injectors and radial aircraft engines during the war. At the same time, he continued his studies at the institute, washing dishes at night to help pay his living expenses (something John DeLorean somehow escaped). In 1946 Estes moved over to GM's Oldsmobile division. It was the time of the postwar buying frenzy—Americans were rushing to buy any car at all, just to replace their old, deteriorated models. But a new sales environment was already visible on the horizon.

Old brand-loyalties counted for nothing with the millions of young men who were returning from war. They were making money in their new civilian jobs; they were getting married; a new car was more important than a new home in those days. It offered mobility, privacy, excitement; but more than anything, having a new car symbolized to the world that the interruption caused by the global war was over. Life had begun again!

Styling counted for much in this new market—styling and speed. Estes' design for the Olds Rocket 88, the world's first high-compression V-8, captured the fancy of that coming-home generation. By 1949 the medium-priced Olds outsold every other car in America except the cheaper Ford and Chevy models. By 1954 Estes was chief engineer at Oldsmobile; and by 1956 he was looking for other challenges. In joining Knudsen at Pontiac, Estes lined up with a man who complemented his own engineering bent, and gained the opportunity to learn the management skills he would need to rise up the ladder.

In the meantime there was work enough for all. Pontiac had turned into "an old lady's car" in the public mind. A heavy metal, stolid model, Pontiacs were still being turned out according to the die-hard Detroit vision of an America in which both the men and women who drove their cars wore hats and so needed large, boxlike car bodies to accommodate their headgear in comfort.

So, too, the Pontiac had clung to its old hood ornament with a fierceness that took one back to the 1930s, when every car had its own readily identifiable hood ornament signature, recognized by every schoolboy and prospective customer. In Pontiac's case, it was the profile of the Indian chief Pontiac. In the last years, the old warrior was sometimes even made of plastic and lit from within so that at night his grim visage stared into the dark road ahead.

Knudsen and Estes were under direct orders to turn Pontiac around fast, to completely change the car's image. To do that, Knudsen reasoned, his team would have to make Pontiac the first-choice car of the growing generation of post-Korean War new-car buyers. He and Estes set to work rounding up a support team and trying to make the maximum impact in the minimum amount of time. As *Motor Trend* magazine said in February 1965, "Estes . . . bought, borrowed and stole some of the best engineering brains in Detroit."

It is important to realize how little time there was to make major changes. DeLorean joined the team in September 1956, even as the 1957 models were going into production. Automobile designs are not made overnight, but the Knudsen-Estes team moved with speed. As a symbolic gesture more than anything else, Knudsen chopped off the Chief Pontiac hood ornament and removed the chrome side strips that had been the model's concession to modernity.

DeLorean's task was to begin advance planning both for the styling and power train changes that would push the model into top sales contention. The next five years were perhaps the happiest and certainly the most productive period in DeLorean's engineering career. It was the start of more than 200 innovations, from power trains to recessed windshield wipers, that would be patented in his name. Joining the team put him on the track that would ultimately lead out of engineering and into management.

Crucial to Knudsen's broader campaign was a strategy that was novel then, but which is considered standard practice today. He took the Bill Durant notion of using various product lines as disaster insurance and applied it to the Pontiac division. Pontiac, by tradition, had been a single-identity car, a metal behemoth that conveyed assurance and stability to the driver.

But America was growing younger as it grew more affluent. Increasing numbers of teenagers and college-age customers were entering the new-car market. Tastes were varied. Small imported sports cars were a popular novelty. Bigger, more powerful cars with flashy designs also offered new sales opportunities. Knudsen decided that Pontiac would compete at both ends of the market.

Pervasive to the DeLorean image is the myth that he alone was responsible for the revival of Pontiac's fortunes. That it was his own flair for styling, his own keen sense of what young Americans wanted, that led him to "create" the G.T.O. muscle car of the 1960s, which captivated a generation. The irony is that very little is remembered about the car for which he genuinely contributed basic design improvements, the Pontiac Tempest.

The Knudsen-Estes-DeLorean team knew where to look in creating the new Pontiac models. Dirt-track racing had long been Detroit's real design proving ground. And Knudsen had made himself a fair reputation as a driver when the sport was revived in the early 1950s, both as an entertainment medium and as a magnet for the growing number of independent car customizers and stylists. These independents—often no more than garage mechanics working in their spare time—took Detroit's boringly standard models and turned them into sleek, growling, power mills.

It was an exciting time in racing. It was the early days of the Don Garlitz dragster shop and the early Daytona stock car races in Florida, of Fireball Roberts and Junior Johnson in the Carolinas; and it was a time when the body and engine customizers of California were chopping and channeling chunky Fords and Chevys into pink-candy-striped muscle cars for the long boulevard racecourses of suburban Los Angeles.

The first thing the new Pontiac team did when they began to work in earnest in early 1958 was to sponsor field racing teams at the major stock car races around the country. Pontiac sponsored Joe Weatherby and Fireball Roberts to punch around the dirt-track circuits the models that would later be refined into designs for the LeMans and the Catalina. Much of the important testing of new ideas and designs was done by the three men themselves.

"Let the car tell you," was an Estes motto.

Under Knudsen's leadership, engineers and design executives were encouraged to put innovative designs or bits of test equipment on standard models and drive them home each night. Woodward Avenue, which slashes north to the wooded Bloomfield Hills area, where top Detroit executives live, became a unique part of the street drag racing scene. Detroit's grid system of streets created one-mile stretches of three-lane highway between intersections and stop lights going north on Woodward Avenue from the city's center—an ideal length for drag racing. So Detroit's teenagers became used to having their homemade hot rods challenged by older men (in their forties), pulling up to stop lights in dull-looking standard sedans. It was a laugh, really. These old guys, goosing the accelerators of these old locomotives, the universal signal of challenge to these cherried, chopped, decked, and channeled street rods. There they would be, the kids with their tailpipes grumbling from backyard tinkering, goosing and backing off, goosing and backing off as the stop light went from red to green.

As the months went by, word began to spread among Detroit's hotrodders. These old dudes in their square cars could fool you every once in a while. There was this little car they were driving. It didn't look like anything recognizable, and there was no brand name on it. But it could move! It was fast and light, and from stop light to stop light it was hard to beat.

The key to the new Tempest's success was an innovative 225-horsepower engine created by Estes that features an overhead cam designed by DeLorean. In fact, the entire drive train for the Tempest was put together by DeLorean's advance planning staff.

When the Tempest was introduced in 1959, it became the most popular of America's compact cars. By 1961 it was voted Car of the Year by *Motor Trend*'s poll; and it helped boost the sales of the Pontiac division from sixth place to third behind Chevrolet and Ford. The 1960-model year was Knudsen's year of triumph at Pontiac. Not only did the Tempest catch on among the new generation of economy-minded buyers, but the Estes-DeLorean engineers also unveiled the Grand Prix sports car as well as the luxury-market LeMans, an important addition to the Pontiac arsenal.

But if 1960 and 1961 were hot years for Pontiac, they were down years for Detroit in general. Chevrolet, in particular, was giving GM problems. Its basic design had not been changed since the classic 1956 model, which had become stale and boring.

In 1961 GM's top management predictably moved Knudsen to the post of general manager of the Chevrolet division and, at his suggestion, made Estes his successor as general manager of Pontiac. DeLorean, who had been promoted to assistant chief engineer in 1959, was named chief engineer to succeed Estes on November 7, 1961.

What kind of man was DeLorean at that time?

"He was very secure as an engineer, and so he was fairly easy to get along with. You could test out an idea of his and go to him and say, 'John, this just doesn't work.' He would say, 'Well, you're the one who tested it so you know best. Let's try something else,' " recalls one of his original design team:

> He could be tough to work for though; everyone worked hard in those days and you didn't expect to go home at 5 o'clock and get ahead, not with Knudsen and Estes around either. But while Pete Estes was a pleasant man with a good sense of humor, John wasn't much with the jokes and the friendly approach. People liked and respected Pete. They respected John, and worked for him, even when they didn't like him a lot. I can't think of any single thing that stands out, except that John never really cultivated close ties to anyone. He didn't have friends among the younger engineers, and he didn't really cultivate his bosses either.

As chief engineer of the division, DeLorean's life changed dramatically. Before, he could bury himself in his work and leave the administrative duties to Estes, while Knudsen did the politicking within GM for the extra resources the team needed. Now he had to take on an increasing share of both the administrative and corporate political maneuvering. He did not do well at it; not surprisingly, he did not like it.

Another GM engineer who followed DeLorean's career from a few steps behind noted:

> He was a great engineer. The word genius is overused, but he was certainly at the top of his profession in those years. He had

a sense of what the public wanted, even if it didn't know what it wanted already. He could create style, and that is a precious commodity. But he was a godawful administrator.

So when he took Estes' job, he formed a small cadre of people he trusted implicitly and shut everybody out. If you were in with John, you were in; and anything you said was okay with him. If you were out, he would walk all over you; he would shut you out.

The worst thing was for a man to be imposed or inserted into John's shop by upstairs management. Then John walked all over the poor bastard; he never had a chance. John began to develop a very hard attitude to people, but at the time, you could excuse it as being the price you pay to get ahead.

And times were competitive, both within the car industry and within GM itself. The sixties' boom was under way. It was the time of new fashions, of the Kennedys and their informal but elegant style. America was repudiating the fifties dullness and looking for exciting things.

But coming out of the recession of 1959–1960, Detroit was still feeling cash poor; budget-cutting for research and development was the order of the day. For Estes and Pontiac that meant no more new-model experiments. No new chassis or engine designs. Work with what you have. In mid-1963, the company pulled Pontiac's racing team off the stock car circuit as a cost-cutting measure, but in so doing, it robbed Estes of an immediate way of testing engine and body designs. His response was to look for a new body style and image that could be built around the wide-track LeMans. The result was the Pontiac G.T.O., named after the Ferrari coupe, Gran Turisimo Omologato. It was a car that would symbolize a generation, and it was the basic root of the John DeLorean myth.

In later years the myth that would be repeated in every newspaper in the United States and much of the rest of the world was that John DeLorean single-handedly came up with a design for the G.T.O. which was so radically successful that it rescued a troubled division of General Motors and set the American automobile scene on its ear for years.

The truth was something else.

"In the sense that John worked on the Tempest, he can take credit for the G.T.O., because the Tempest was just a small G.T.O. But by that same sense, you should give credit to Ronnie and the Daytonas," said David E. Davis, current editor of *Car & Driver* magazine, who was part of the public relations and advertising team that helped boom the G.T.O. into America's consciousness.

Burly and now bearded, Davis had a unique vantage point from which to watch DeLorean's GM career. A former race car driver, he became one of DeLorean's inner circle—to his discomfort—at the Campbell and Ewald agency, which for fifty years had held the $100 million annual advertising budget for Chevrolet. As a veteran writer for *Car & Driver*, before he joined Campbell and Ewald, he has since returned and made that trade publication into the world's most outspoken and independent magazine for car enthusiasts. Davis explains:

> To go back to the beginning, Knudsen started the original four-cylinder Tempest, and as did all of those compact cars of that period, it grew and got a V-8 engine. Then it became the LeMans. Then, later, when GM cracked down, all they had to do was drop in a great big engine, put on different wheels and tires and they had a G.T.O. They were able to take off the LeMans name and just make it a G.T.O., and it was easy to do within the corporate structure because it wasn't a new car by any stretch of the imagination. It was just a model spun off an existing line of cars.
>
> But to be absolutely scrupulously honest, if you want to name the man who came up with the *concept* of the G.T.O., you have to name Jim Wangers. It was Wangers who was the wild-eyed drag-racing enthusiast—he was very much tuned to the street-racing crowd of the sixties—and he had a lot of latitude when Knudsen was running Pontiac.

At that time, Jim Wangers was the product sales promotion specialist for the Pontiac division's outside advertising agency. He urged Estes to have Pontiac give the hot-rodder a mass-produced version of what he was building at home—a high-gloss, heavy-engine, close-to-the-ground street racer—something with class but with real brute muscle.

The G.T.O., which actually came out in 1962, had been doing well enough around the country, but in early 1964 sales of the car went from good to spectacular. Again, industry insiders credit Wangers with coming up with the sales pitch that caught on.

"There was this singing group, Ronnie and the Daytonas; and they came to GM with a song about the G.T.O. They were pretty damn good. They had a California surfin' sound, much like the Beach Boys. It got recorded and we bought thousands of copies to send to our dealers. The record went on to sell a million copies and reached third place in the top-40 charts. It was nothing but a two-and-a-half-minute commercial for the Pontiac G.T.O.," Wangers said.

But in 1964, sales of the G.T.O. were boosting Pontiac's lead over Oldsmobile as the third-best seller, by 173,000 cars a year. Pontiac was the hot car-division in Detroit, and the motor industry press began looking for celebrities to help explain the division's phenomenal success. John DeLorean knew very well indeed how that game worked.

The version of the G.T.O. story put about by John was that he had come up with the concept of the car because of his close contact with the world of the teenage dragster.

"These rock stations, the things they say, what they discuss, that's what counts. It's the cheapest education you can get," he told *Newsweek* in September 1968.

In another version published by *Current Biography* in 1976: "When the management of General Motors prohibited its divisions from racing their new models in 1963, DeLorean introduced the sporty G.T.O. . . . to attract and hold racing enthusiasts. To promote the new car, he backed a massive publicity campaign that included T-shirts, emblems and the hit recording, 'Little G.T.O.,' as well as more traditional advertising techniques. By the end of the model year, the entire run of 31,000 G.T.O.'s had been exhausted. Within two years, G.T.O. sales nearly tripled."

DeLorean had good reason to push himself forward. Knudsen was making his play for a berth on the 14th floor top executive suite at GM, and Estes was rumored to be his successor at Chevrolet. By rights, DeLorean could move into the management track behind Estes if he played it right. He was making his numbers, and so he pushed for his reward.

Moreover, the ever-energetic DeLorean had burnished his credentials for promotion. What time he hadn't spent working for Estes and the design team over the last eighteen months, he'd spent working on a masters degree in business administration from the University of Michigan in nearby Ann Arbor. There was even time for a course on business law at the Detroit College of Law. DeLorean was also an active joiner of all the professional engineering and automotive societies and industry associations.

While he may have been something of a joiner, he was not much of a success in the social circuit to which he had been elevated. He and his wife, Liz, now lived in Bloomfield Hills. Appearances at the Bloomfield Golf and Country Club were now a weekend ritual. So was dinner out at the Kingsley Inn Hotel dining room on Woodward Avenue, the restaurant of choice of the motor industry social set.

"Liz loved it. She was beautiful and blond—really a dish—and very lively. John hated it. Even then, he didn't drink to speak of. He had no small talk. But at the same time he sometimes couldn't keep his mouth shut. He would name-drop or tell really bad jokes. Some of his stuff was really teenage dirty joke humor. But people excused it. They liked Liz because she was so enthusiastic, and I guess they figured John would grow out of it in time," remembers a long-time social friend.

"It was really strange. At a big party John would just stand there with one drink, shifting from one foot to another while Liz danced and had fun. At a small dinner party, he would try to dominate, telling those awful, coarse jokes and name-dropping, name-dropping all the time. So-and-so had said his design of something was the best he'd ever seen. That sort of thing," another recalled.

But social clumsiness had never been a bar to promotion at General Motors. Far from it. Detroit's upper management was an almost total reflection of the American tastes of the upper middle class. Pete Estes complained that his elevation to the managership of Pontiac forced him to travel overseas; he hated the unfamiliar food, the uncomfortable strangeness of foreign language barriers, and chilly hotel rooms. A thick charcoaled steak at the Kingsley Inn and a few bourbons at the country club—with the obligatory turn around the dance floor to keep the wife happy—that was how these men relaxed on Saturday night. Real fun was a round of golf on Saturday afternoons (after a morning in the office) and a few beers in the locker room. John DeLorean took up golf, too.

On July 1, 1965, it all paid off. Knudsen had been elevated to head of GM's North American car and truck vice presidency and moved to the 14th floor sanctum sanctorum. Estes was named general manager of the all-important Chevrolet division, which was the conglomerate's largest sales unit and Ford's direct competitor. And John Zachary DeLorean was named general manager of the Pontiac motor division.

One long-time journalist who had covered Detroit for more than twenty years recalled:

> I'll never forget John DeLorean's first press conference as general manager of Pontiac. Most of us had only seen him once or twice as an engineer, so we really didn't know what to expect. So here is the automobile industry press corps all ready to meet this guy and he starts off the conference with a joke. I've never forgotten the joke, either.
>
> It seems there were two guys who were in a big city on some convention and they went to a whorehouse. And one of the conventioneers says to the madam, "Look, lady. We've been here three days already so we're a little jaded. Can you fix me up with something special?" "Sure," says the madam, "I have a girl you'll like. She's half-French, half-Chinese." So the guy goes upstairs and comes down a little bit later. His friend asked him, "What was it like?" And the conventioneer says, "Really strange. She ate my laundry."
>
> None of us knew what to do, we were so embarrassed for him. It was such a dumb, juvenile joke and it was also clear that he thought it was enormously funny. Some gave him a break and wrote it off to being nervous and young, and nobody wrote about it. But I've always remembered it.

As with the press releases that had announced the promotions of Knudsen and Estes to head Pontiac, DeLorean's announcement noted that "at 40, he is the youngest man to ever become general manager of one of General Motors' ten main divisions."

Although the promotion moved John DeLorean onto the fast track to General Motors' management, it took him further away from hands-on engineering, which he liked, and involved him more in the tedious but nonetheless crucial tasks of management and planning. There were committee meetings to attend if one wanted something. DeLorean had learned to his vexation that you just did not ask for something and get it; you had to campaign and convince and even fight for a larger share of corporate resources if your division was to prosper with the GM family.

"It's relatively easy when you are an engineer. If you want to do something, you ask your boss and if he says yes, you do it. But wanting something, even when you are right to want it, is not enough in the corporate structure. John didn't like to politic for things. And he began to get frustrated with the way things are done at GM much too early in the game," Knudsen later would recall.

There were other distractions, too, now. His marriage was becoming increasingly troubled. Liz was an office secretary for a small Detroit firm when she met John. She was distressed that they never had any children, so she devoted herself to the life of a Bloomfield Hills housewife, to the Lily Pulitzer shop and the long lunches.

Like other bored wives of other managers, she concentrated on decorating their home and on planning what their life would be as John worked his way further up the GM ladder and eventually into retirement, either in Palm Beach, Florida, or Palm Springs, California, or some other fashionable haven for the burned-out executives of America.

But John had other ideas. Turning forty reminded him forcefully that he had a great deal of distance to travel before he could fulfill his still vague ambitions. One good thing about being Pontiac general manager was that it got him away from Detroit. Unlike Estes and other GM management, who felt faintly uncomfortable away from home, John reveled in his newly won celebrity and the power that came with it.

From Knudsen and Estes he had learned the importance of the division's network of car dealers and how critical it was to pay attention to the advertising campaign that supported the cars he was trying to sell. Both tasks required going on the road for extended periods of time. Liz never enjoyed the noisy dealer conventions and was a comparatively drab companion when her husband made his initial forays to California's glitter and glamour world. He began to resent her demands on his time at home. Who wanted Bloomfield Hills after seeing Beverly Hills for the first time?

It was not an uncommon problem among Detroit management families. The generally prescribed remedy of the sympathetic wives of Bloomfield Hills was patience. Wait until he's had his fling and then he'll come home. Sometimes it worked, sometimes it didn't.

November 1967 was the turning point in Bunkie Knudsen's GM career. Detroit had been in turmoil for much of the two previous years as changing public tastes led to growing public and government criticism of the safety of some of the hot-off-the-drawingboard designs that the major producers were turning out.

It was also a period of changing management styles. Conglomerates were the buzz word of the day, and the intuitive Wall Street gunfighter, the investment strategist who melded corporations by looking at balance sheets and not product lines, was the glamour figure of the time.

The middle-1960s saw even staid corporations become unsettled by the advent of "the professional manager," the man who was at home running a conglomerate or any one of its diverse constituent parts. The art of management, with its supposedly arcane superiority in accounting and controls, was deemed more important than knowledge of production techniques or abilities on the factory floor. The engineer-executive might deride these newcomers to the corporate suite as "bean counters," but he made way for them nevertheless.

James Roche had been a bean counter all his life. What set him apart from the typical nonproduction executive was that he was a superb bean counter and had worked for General Motors all his life, starting as a sales statistician and climbing the administrative and labor relations ladder with increasing plaudits. A decade before, he might have ended his career as an executive vice president for management. In 1965 the 14th floor was shocked to find Roche becoming president of GM and also taking over the roles of chief operating officer and head of the GM administration committee. But that was also the year of the Corvair controversy, and the publication of Ralph Nader's *Unsafe at Any Speed,* an attack on the design dangers of a number of major automobile brands put out by Detroit. The industry was also just struggling back onto its feet from a disastrous strike in which Roche played an active role as negotiator.

The situation at GM did not improve at all during 1966. First-half sales were bumped down by nearly 7 percent to 2.1 million units. There were persisting troubles with the Chevrolet division and its unhappy dealer network. The Nader controversy spread like a brushfire as the book became a best-seller—the Bible of the newly formed American consumer movement.

In March 1966 Nader charged before a Senate hearing that he was the target of a concentrated campaign to intimidate him. Private detectives hired by GM were harassing him and his friends, and a smear campaign could be traced back to the 14th floor. It was Roche who went to Washington to apologize.

Aside from the blow to GM's public image, the Nader affair had a serious impact on GM sales. Worse, the scandal and sales slump produced chaos within 14th floor management circles, and the other executives waited with increasing impatience for Roche to take a hand and turn things around. What alarmed the executives most of all was growing data that quality control was an endemic problem throughout the company—that Nader had been right.

Then GM internal estimates projected that the 1966 profits slump would sag even further in 1967. Roche had to go. GM's experiment with a bean counter had been judged a failure.

So it had to be a production man who would succeed him. But who? Bunkie Knudsen would clearly be taking a chance if he tried to step over the two or three men ahead of him in seniority from the engineering ranks. The man just ahead of him in line, Edward N. Cole, was perhaps a more adroit politician than Knudsen. Cole was an engineer who had gone from Cadillac to tanks during the Korean War to resurrect Chevrolet during the early 1950s just as Knudsen was rescuing Pontiac. Cole raced his Chevies, put V-8 engines in them, and ultimately invented the Corvette sports car.

But Ed Cole was also the father of the Corvair, the rear-engine compact that he believed was his division's response to the same growing market that Knudsen pegged for the Tempest. When the Corvair hit the market to applause in 1960, Cole used the success to lever himself onto GM's board and in 1965 into the executive vice presidency in charge of research, engineering, manufacturing, and marketing plus public relations. Knudsen, by contrast, had home appliances and heavy engines. And when the Corvairs of 1961 and 1963 developed appalling suspension problems, Cole was far away from the chain of responsibility.

More to the point, in that spring of 1967 Cole campaigned hard for the presidency. He had a platform. General Motors must get away from the concept of decentralized divisions, the independent fiefdoms which Alfred Sloan had devised. GM management must be centralized, the 14th floor must take a more active role in the separate strategies of its product lines. That way, labor relations would not unravel; that way the Naders would have nothing to carp about.

Cole's philosophy was an important break with Detroit's longstanding tradition of separate product lines and management teams that made independent decisions. At its best, the old way had allowed men to fully explore technological frontiers and to come up with innovative designs. It was a system that put the maximum responsibility load on the individual shoulders of the production line managers.

But now it was obvious that the damage that could be caused by the failure of one man or a small design team could have dangerous impact on the whole corporation. Look at the uproar caused by the Corvair. There were too many men out there in the GM product management divisions who were off on their own schemes and dreams. Bunkie Knudsen's attitude was to let them go, as long as they made their numbers. Ed Cole argued more persuasively that the senior management should have more control over the basic decisions and planning. Projects should be conceived for the entire company, not one division competing against another.

With good reason John DeLorean could consider Ed Cole's campaign a direct attack on his own personal management style; not a few of his worries came from his close identification as a Knudsen protégé. But even if DeLorean and Cole had been on close personal terms, what Cole advocated—however inevitable it all seems now—ran contrary to everything the younger man had been taught to know about the automobile industry. Committees don't build cars; geniuses conceive them.

In November 1967, by a tiny margin, Ed Cole made it into the president's chair and Roche was kicked upstairs to the chairmanship.

On January 31, 1968, Bunkie Knudsen resigned his $182,000-a-year job, noting that the management changes were in place for at least four years and that he was ready for another assignment. Less than a week later, he was president of Ford Motor, just forty-five years after his father had quit Ford to go to GM.

To offset his losses on leaving GM management, Henry Ford II paid Knudsen stock bonuses valued at $750,000 and guaranteed him a base annual salary of $200,000 for five years. Knudsen stayed with the mercurial Ford until he in turn was replaced by another ambitious hard charger named Lee Iacocca. During the late 1970s, Knudsen added to his reputation by taking control of and rescuing the faltering White Motor Corporation, which specializes in tractors and heavy equipment. On his retirement from corporate life, he had built a personal fortune of more than $30 million.

But even in those hectic mid-1960s, Bunkie Knudsen had not lost track of John DeLorean:

I had made a point, and so had Pete Estes, of getting John out on the road to the dealer's meetings. You have to listen to them because they are our front line troops. They hear what the buyer says, and they are quick to pick up on why a buyer buys one kind of car in preference to another. By the time John became manager at Pontiac, though, I was well away from that division so I have no idea how he arranged his management of the division, except that he appeared to travel a lot, which I thought was a good thing at the time.

The trouble with being a manager of a major automobile division is the sudden celebrity that goes with the job. I remember that when I took over Chevrolet, I got a call my first day on the job from Dinah Shore and she wanted me to come out to Hollywood that weekend for a party that she was going to give for me. Gregory Peck and a lot of other stars were going to be there.

Now you have to remember that the Dinah Shore Show was the biggest show on television in those days. Campbell and Ewald, our advertising agency for Chevrolet, had a $100 million budget that was one of the biggest in advertising; so the general manager of Chevrolet was very much a show business celebrity whether he wanted to be or not. That "See the U.S.A. in your Chevrolet" song she sang was important. But I had very strong feelings about that sort of thing and I said, "Miss Shore, I enjoy your program very much, and I thank you for your kindness. But it might be in the best interest of Chevrolet for me to fire you some day, and I wouldn't want our social friendship to get in the way of such a decision. So I'll do my job, and you keep doing yours."

But John DeLorean did not see it that way.

"No, John was on the first plane to Hollywood he could get," Knudsen recalled. "He got in with that crowd and went through all sorts of changes."

If the rest of General Motors was in turmoil just after DeLorean's appointment as general manager at Pontiac, his division at least continued to build sales, not only on the firm popularity of the G.T.O., but with the other spin-off lines—the Bonneville, Firebird, and Catalina.

Racetrack testing may have been a thing of the past, but DeLorean continued to press his design team for new stylings and features. Vertically stacked headlights, split grilles, and passenger compartments that resembled airplane cockpits were all part of the DeLorean search for the next generation of popularity.

But the search for a new design change that would fuel Pontiac's popularity was slowed by DeLorean's increasingly chaotic administrative practices and his penchant for centralizing the responsibility for all key decisions within a tight circle of trusted aides—without regard to whether they had been assigned to those tasks by General Motors senior management. David E. Davis recalls:

> He was probably one of the worst administrators that ever lived. Not because he didn't have the skills, but because he had such contempt for the administrative arts. He believed that was all bullshit and that you handled the staff work by bypassing the people officially in charge and finding some bright young guy who would be knocked out by your charisma. Then he would go straight to that guy and get answers from him, leaving the superior off in limbo, wondering what had happened to them.
>
> That was what was so strange. He was a curiously complex guy. He was extraordinarily talented, a really good engineer. There was absolutely no question in the mind of anybody who worked closely with him that he was a good engineer. But his organization was just nightmarish because John would take a dislike to a guy and cut him out of the decision-making process whether he really knew anything or not.
>
> In fact, that's how I got to work with John later on. I joined Campbell and Ewald because he announced that everyone there was an old fart and he would only talk to me. He had known me when I worked on the magazine back when he was doing research at Pontiac.
>
> So there was John, the head of Pontiac, building his little coterie, freaking out the people he didn't like. There is really nothing so very wrong about that except that the people who surrounded John tended to echo his own tastes. And that was where John started to leave the rails. When Knudsen and Estes and Wangers—all real racing enthusiasts—were there, Pontiac was well in tune with the market that was developing. But left to his own devices, John's intuition was to build a Pontiac lim-

ousine! He got that under way at Pontiac and took it with him to Chevrolet, but Jim Roche found out about it and there was a wild panic among John's henchpersons to destroy all evidence of how that money had been spent building a limousine version of a car whose image was that of a street dragster.

By DeLorean's own account, the limousine idea came while he was at Chevrolet. The object was to compete with Ford, which in 1968 had garnered some welcome publicity by presenting President Johnson with a new, specially constructed limo for White House ceremonial purposes.

Davis continues:

> Don't you believe it. It was a Pontiac and then later a Chevrolet; and there was a hell of a lot of money wasted on both versions. But it was also a serious indictment—John didn't quite know what the hell the image and product business was all about. By the midterm of his period at Pontiac, he had bought the entire California package of the youth culture—being intuitive, letting your feelings hang out, that sort of thing.
>
> So, in 1968, he directed a promotional film that is still famous in the advertising group, and it was what everyone was supposed to look at to learn "where John is coming from" so it would guide us in dealing with him. It was a nicely photographed job showing beautiful cars smoking down the road with gorgeous young people at the wheel. The background music was the theme, or something like it, from the French film A Man and a Woman. Everything was soft and oh, so California. John had seen A Man and a Woman and went nuts over the picture.
>
> So there was a constant fight at Pontiac about any effort to put content into advertising. It embarrassed John to think that an institution like Pontiac had to reach out and really provide potential customers with hard information about how to go and buy the car, or to convince them that they should want to buy it. And remember, in the late sixties, coming out of that sales jolt GM had just had, people needed to be convinced about the product all over again.
>
> Instead, John said the best you could hope to do is leave a nice impression. You did that with nice music, beautiful pictures of

Ivan Fallon & James Srodes

the most beautiful young people with a nice warm feeling, and they would go for it. But don't try to tell them how big it is or what it weighs or about gas mileage. "Who cares about that?" he would ask. "Nobody wants to know that bullshit," he said. "That's Detroit talking."

John was wrong about the advertising. Certainly, the traditional Detroit advertising of the day wasn't very good; but John wanted to eliminate any useful information from the traditional message so that it became, if anything, worse. Somebody once described John's vision as being like peeing in your pants—all you get is a nice warm feeling.

But DeLorean was doing more than breaking up traditional chains of command within Pontiac and experimenting with advertising images. In California he was meeting a new kind of businessman. What an enormous contrast it must have been to match up the blue-suited, plainspoken, pens-in-shirt-pockets engineers of Detroit against the laid-back, California wheeler-dealers who did their business by poolside or in a restaurant and not on the top floor of some boxlike office complex.

The man who clearly caught John's imagination was James T. Aubrey, the whiz kid of broadcasting and movie production of the late 1960s and early seventies. Seven years older than DeLorean, Aubrey was already a megacelebrity, dubbed "the Silver Fox" for his ruthless management techniques. He was also recognized as a genius whose intuitive grasp of public tastes radically changed both television entertainment and motion picture production and made them what they are today.

Aubrey was the man who had the instinct for "instant pop," that indefinable quality about a performer or program that would catch the public's fancy in a big way. At ABC he had churned out such popular (if not critically acclaimed) smash hit series as "The Real McCoys," "Maverick," "The Donna Reed Show," "77 Sunset Strip," and "The Rifleman."

After boosting ABC into a contender for the third network, Aubrey joined the Columbia Broadcasting System as vice president for creative services and put his instant pop vision to work with a mixture of low comedy and adventure sit-coms including "Mr. Ed," "Gomer Pyle," "Route 66," and "The Munsters."

But in 1965, the year John DeLorean took over at Pontiac, Jim Aubrey's luck appeared to have run out. Several of his production efforts bombed. Viewer ratings fell and advertising revenues fell with them. In his heyday, Aubrey's imperious manner, his image as the original swinging jet-setter, and his abrasive business ethics had been overlooked. But after the failures began to accumulate, Aubrey's enemies came out of the woodwork in droves. Finally, without specifying why, CBS President Frank Stanton sacked him.

Down but not out, Aubrey walked away from the sacking with millions of dollars' worth of CBS stock options, which he exercised. He plunged immediately into the red-hot Los Angeles real estate market and into the equally hot Wall Street stock market. He set up an import-export firm that specialized in pearls and, with his production company, sold series ideas to Screen Gems, which in turn had contracts with half the studios in Hollywood.

Tall and lean, a health and exercise fanatic, Aubrey continued his high-profile, jet-set escapades; always impeccably dressed in informal but studied fashions of the West Coast, always putting in heroic working hours, always sniffing ahead to the trends and shifts in taste that would put his career back on track.

John DeLorean was fascinated by Aubrey when they met in 1965, and the older man enjoyed the unabashed admiration of his protégé. He helped introduce the new Pontiac boss to other media chiefs, to advertising "creative" specialists, to wealthy men whose money came from vague sources.

"Aubrey was probably the closest thing to a friend John had out in California. Neither of them drank much, and Aubrey nagged John into losing weight and shaping up his clothes," a former Pontiac offical who had been based in Los Angeles at the time would recall.

The Aubrey career bloomed again in 1969 when Las Vegas financier Kirk Kerkorian seized control of the moribund Metro-Goldwyn-Mayer Studios and installed Aubrey as president. The deal was done over a handshake, and Aubrey set out with an enormous, sharp knife to pare back production costs and to personally censor MGM movies so they could qualify for the GP rating, which brings in larger audiences.

Aubrey was riding high that year of 1969. He was back on top of the heap at MGM, and was rumored to be Jacqueline Susann's model for her sex-obsessed antihero in *The Love Machine*.

And he took John DeLorean along for the ride, introducing him to still more important people. DeLorean met Kerkorian himself, and Herb Siegel, who later became the chairman of Chris-Craft. Dave Mahoney, the chairman of Avis, became a friend, as did a host of show business stars including Sammy Davis Jr., Engelbert Humperdinck, and, perhaps most important, Johnny Carson, who was in the process of moving his wildly popular late-night talk show from New York City to Hollywood.

And there were the girls. Aubrey collected willing females without effort, and there were more than enough to go around for a friend.

Although DeLorean's marriage to Liz was over, for a time, at least, he was simply too busy to get a divorce. Too busy grappling for control over Pontiac, too busy exploring a new lifestyle, a new business style in California. Everybody loved John DeLorean's classy cars in California.

After he left Pontiac, scores of cars were discovered to be missing from the California inventory.

A recently retired GM corporate counsel, who refused to be identified, explains: "From the time John DeLorean took over at Pontiac until the time he left, we had to deal with a whole string of shabby business practices that he got involved in. I never trusted him from the beginning; and the more I saw of him, well, nothing I saw ever changed my mind."

But why didn't GM management come down hard on DeLorean at that early date? Or if early warnings failed, why wasn't he fired? The former Pontiac executive continues:

> Remember the time. We'd had all the scandals we needed in those days. Pontiac was doing well enough, and the rest of the company had plenty of problems. Also, DeLorean was getting tremendous publicity and quite a few people in top management in those days saw John as a comer—a bit rough around the edges, but too valuable a property to lose just over a few cars he had given away. Things were not as centralized as they became when Ed Cole took over, so a division general manager had far more autonomy than he does today. They could give cars away if they wanted to; they could even have special custom jobs fitted out for themselves and a few friends. But the standard was a few, not dozens; so the perception was that John had just stepped over the line into greediness, not criminality.

The retired lawyer also noted, "Make sure you understand that no one ever accused John of stealing those cars. It was never brought to us on that basis. It was never brought to us formally at all. In any event, we had other things that John was doing that worried me more." Indeed, General Motors executives had plenty of things to worry about. The consumer movement sparked by Ralph Nader showed no signs of going away, the company's union problems were worsening, and the profitability of several key product lines was slipping alarmingly. The October 1967 realignment of GM top management placed Ed Cole in the presidency instead of Bunkie Knudsen and cost John DeLorean a friend and mentor.

But Cole's victory had strengthen the prestige of the engineers over the bean counters within the corporate hierarchy, and DeLorean benefited plenty from that. Then, too, Pontiac had its best year in 1968. The division sold 877,000 cars, almost 200,000 more than in 1964.

The selection of Cole over the more strait-laced Knudsen was also a signal of another kind within the GM management circle, for Ed Cole also was something of a swinger. On taking over Chevrolet in 1952, he had, as Knudsen described it, "gone Hollywood." An active, hearty sort, he became involved with Hollywood movie starlet Monique Van Vooren in the early 1960s. There was a minor scandal when, just after the Detroit Business District Association voted him "Father of the Year" in early 1963, he divorced his wife of thirty years.

But while most of Detroit concluded that Cole had thereby ruined any chances for a shot at the GM presidency, he had sense enough to scramble back across the undrawn line between propriety and excess. In 1964 he married the vivacious Dollie McVey, a divorcée who owned and operated her own line of women's designer clothes. Dollie Cole quickly installed herself as a major figure among the Bloomfield Hills wives and helped push her husband's career forward again.

So at first Cole had reason to look at John DeLorean as a promising young executive well worth cultivating. Both were engineers; both shared in that secret fraternity of disdain for hypocritical moral standards. They also shared two other affinities—a fascination with rear-mounted engines and an instinct for the consolidation of power. After all, that was what had tipped the scales for Cole in the race with Knudsen. DeLorean, too, had taken over most of the decision-making at Pontiac. Besides, in 1968 his division was making its numbers, and very good numbers at that.

So there was a somewhat tolerant mood on the 14th floor when DeLorean spent increasing amounts of time in California. He and Liz finally agreed to divorce in January 1969. There was someone else—Kelly Harmon, a twenty-year-old, honey blond, blue-eyed beauty who was a prototype of the California look that Bo Derek made world-famous a decade later. The marriage of Kelly and John DeLorean was later portrayed as having rocked Detroit's staid society to the core. It was considerably less of an event than that. Detroit was understandably fascinated, but hardly shocked—it had grown tired of being shocked by anything John DeLorean could come up with, and the town was full of equally eccentric people.

At first the executives and their wives had watched with amusement as DeLorean embarked on a crash program of weight loss in late 1967. There were persistent rumors that John had gone "Grecian"—that is, that he had begun touching up the graying sideburns of his black hair with a well-known hair preparation, Grecian Formula 16.

Then there was the "minor car accident" in California in early 1968 that kept DeLorean out of the Detroit offices for several weeks. When he returned, Bunkie Knudsen bluntly asked DeLorean what was wrong with his face; it had changed somehow.

"John mumbled something about getting some cuts in the accident; but it was a face-lift, all right," Knudsen recalled.

Shortly afterward, DeLorean was playing golf at the posh Bel Air Country Club in California in a foursome with Tom Harmon, the CBS sports broadcaster and former University of Michigan all-American halfback. Harmon invited DeLorean home for dinner.

It was love at first sight for John and Kelly. Kelly was immediately attracted to the six-foot-four DeLorean's carefully maintained good looks; but she was even more impressed by the fact that DeLorean took her seriously, listened to her opinions, and treated her as an adult. "It was his sincerity. I could recognize it right away. John's a very deep-thinking man. He's real. And a very strong man," she told the *Detroit Free Press* shortly after their wedding.

What Kelly offered DeLorean was the youth, beauty, and style—indeed, the respectability—he felt were lacking in his life. The Harmons, after all, were more than national celebrities. Tom Harmon's exploits on the gridiron with the 1939 and 1940 University of Michigan football teams made him a permanent idol for practically every teenage boy growing up in Detroit. He went on to fashion a life that dreams are made of. When World War II broke out, he became an Army Air Corps pilot and was shot down over China in the early days of the war. He returned safely to the United States and married movie star Elyse Knox in a ceremony at the University of Michigan chapel that made the front pages of every newspaper in the country. The bride's dress was given special attention—it was made from the parachute Harmon used to escape from his damaged plane.

Since the Harmons were a much-loved family in Detroit, the prospect of the forty-four-year-old DeLorean being married to a daughter of Tommy Harmon was greeted with curiosity and a little snickering, but hardly stony-faced shock. If anything, DeLorean came in for good-natured ribbing. Typical of the hometown reaction was a blind item in a *Detroit Free Press* gossip column in May 1970. The item twitted DeLorean for being forty-five and trying to "look like the Pepsi Generation." The columnist archly noted that DeLorean had recently imported a beautiful new wife from Hollywood as part of his youth quest. And the column stated flatly that in 1968 DeLorean had "a foamlike material" inserted to extend his jawline as part of a broad cosmetic surgery treatment to create a more craggy profile.

The article would be about as critical as the Detroit news media ever would be about John DeLorean during most of his career. DeLorean was a swinger, a bit sexy, perhaps a bit too wild. But nothing more. That wouldn't do for hometown consumption. Gossip was just fine for Detroit's news consumers; but never really hard news scandal, not about hometown people at least. So the media dutifully reprinted the press reports from Los Angeles as DeLorean was first divorced from Liz in January, then ordered to pay her $370,000 in alimony over fifteen years. Then there was the news that John had bought Kelly a six-carat diamond ring for her visit to Detroit on a modeling job.

On February 4 Ed Cole reshuffled his second layer of management and moved Pete Estes to Car and Truck and DeLorean to Chevrolet as general manager. DeLorean's orders were specific. He was to oversee the launching of the new Chevy Vega, which would be the division's entry into the compact car sweepstakes. And he was also to supervise the remodeling of the Camaro and Corvette for the 1970 model year.

Cole also exacted a promise from DeLorean as a condition of the move. It was a simple enough request. DeLorean was spending an increasing amount of his time overseeing his private investments—

large minority stakes in the San Diego Chargers football team and the New York Yankees baseball club—while on Pontiac trips. Doing private business on company time had to stop, Cole said.

"Ed was no saint. He told John he didn't care where he was playing around or who he was screwing. But Chevy was having troubles, and he wanted those new lines turned out fast. John promised he would buckle down, and he had lots of quick ideas about doing this and that. He agreed to the condition," a GM official recalls.

On May 31 DeLorean and Kelly were married in a civil ceremony at the Bel Air Country Club in Brentwood Hills overlooking Los Angeles. The Mitchell Boys Choir, dressed in white robes, provided the music, and Kelly was described in rapturous terms by the newspaper reporters. Her matron of honor was her sister Kris, who was married to rock star Ricky Nelson. The guests were an uneasy mixture of Harmon's broadcasting industry friends, some General Motors officials, and John's new California friends. Bunkie Knudsen flew in to be best man.

But even as the champagne flowed and the flash bulbs popped, the festivities were clearly chilled by the Harmon family's distress at their daughter's choice of a husband.

A long-time DeLorean aide remembers, "It wasn't much of an affair, laugh-wise; but then Tom Harmon put the stopper in it. John was standing there talking to Bunkie Knudsen and Tom Adams, the head of the Campbell Ewald Agency, when Tom walked up to him in the middle of the celebration and said, 'If you ever hurt her, you'll have to answer to me.' No quiet chat in the library—just the open threat. John didn't know what to do, so he just smiled."

DeLorean had little enough to smile about when he returned to Detroit with Kelly. The new compact Vega was just six months away from showroom delivery. The tools and major engine components, molds, and presses were already at work, but the car was plagued in its first year by rough engine performance and tire vibration at the higher speeds. As spring turned into summer, the production problems at Chevrolet spread to the Camaro and Corvette. By early summer it was clear that a number of design changes DeLorean had ordered for both cars could not be accomplished in time for the traditional September introduction date for the 1970 model year.

This put DeLorean in the embarrassing position of having to publicly cancel the 1970 models of both cars and announce that his division "would continue to meet the backlog of demand for the 1969 cars until we can push ahead into production of all new designs for both which we had planned for 1971."

The trouble was that there were no such new designs on the drafting tables, and the motor industry press knew it. DeLorean's credibility—and GM's—took a whacking. Unabashed, he pushed ahead that summer, trying to make a name for himself as the iconoclastic superexecutive. If he couldn't talk GM management into a scheme, he went public with it to the Detroit press corps, which was always eager for stories to feed to the national wire services.

For example, DeLorean announced the construction of a new superdivisional office complex for Chevrolet that would be in suburban Detroit, away from West Grand Boulevard. The announcement was flatly repudiated by GM public relations staff in hurried telephone calls to key reporters that afternoon. People were beginning to wonder whether John DeLorean wasn't more of a flake than he appeared to be.

"You had to wonder whether John didn't have a suicide wish or something. He went so far out of his way to insult people who didn't fawn over him or approve of everything he did," a long-time aide said. The case most frequently cited by Detroit observers of the DeLorean career was his legendary falling-out with Dollie Cole, the wife of the man who had elevated him. At a number of private dinner parties and club dances, DeLorean repeatedly teased Dollie about having married her husband on the rebound from his Hollywood fling.

The former aide recalls:

Maybe it was John's way of saying that they weren't any better than he was, having married Kelly. Anyway, Dollie didn't like it and finally told him never to mention Monique Van Vooren again. Well, Dollie loved to give costume parties for Ed's birthday, and it was his sixtieth birthday or some special occasion and everybody was to dress up in costume for a real bash. John and Kelly arrived late, and John had a huge wrapped-up present for Ed. He said in a loud voice that Ed should open the present later and not do it in front of everyone; so needless to say, Dollie got all curious and made Ed open the present. It was a painting of Monique Von Vooren in the nude. John stood there laughing and laughing and laughing. And that was it! Dollie never forgave him, and it just confirmed in Ed Cole's mind that he had made a mistake in pulling John up the ladder.

Davis also remembers DeLorean's apparent compulsion to alienate GM people who did not meet his approval:

> Once, while Cole's reorganization was still going on and Dick Terrell and Tom Murphy had both been elevated to the 14th floor [Murphy would later become GM president and board chairman] I had to see John about something one evening. I walked into his office, and he was really pleased with himself over something that had just happened.
>
> He said there had been a meeting with Terrell and Murphy and a dozen or more senior management. "I just told Murphy and Terrell that if the shareholders knew what dumb cocksuckers were running this corporation, they would sack the place. I told those two guys they don't know any more about the goddamned car business than Kelly DeLorean knows." I checked his story out, and he had done it, all right, even to calling them both dumb cocksuckers.

It was at that point in early 1970 that DeLorean resumed his forays out to California again, frequently leaving Kelly to visit her family in Bel Air or back in Detroit. Later in the year they bought the Pine Creek Ranch, near the Snake River in Idaho, as his response to her increasing involvement with impoverished youth groups. The ranch was to be a summer holiday camp for inner city kids, and for a while John was very taken with the notion of being the father figure, providing holidays for the new generation of ghetto children, with which he identified. He also had his own ranch and groves in Pauma Valley, near San Diego, which he had bought at the same time he was investing in the football team. Here he would take frequent refuge from the turmoil at Chevrolet and the troubling realization that he had made a mistake marrying someone as young as Kelly. He began to increase his weekend visits to the ranch of a neighbor, Fletcher Jones, the millionaire founder of Computer Sciences Corporation. Jones went into forced retirement from CSC for tax reasons, but he was still an active dabbler in real estate, car dealerships, and various investment schemes that interested DeLorean as well. By this time, the

$200,000 salary plus $400,000 or so in annual bonuses were causing DeLorean to seek out increasingly venturesome tax shelters. Besides that, Jones shared DeLorean's taste for young, beautiful girls, especially Hollywood starlets.

Weekends at the Jones ranch became a byword in L.A.'s fast set. Jones would hire pilot William Morgan Hetrick to fly a planeload of girls and other friends to San Diego for the weekend. A regular visitor was Jones' special girlfriend, a starlet named Cristina Ferrare, whose distinction among the other girls was that she had actually starred in a movie, *The Impossible Years*, with David Niven. There were rumors that Cristina would marry Jones. Also present at the parties was another neighbor, John Timothy Hoffman. Hoffman's name will surface again in the course of DeLorean's story.

As was true elsewhere among the swinging sets of Southern California, drugs of all varieties were plentiful, although there is no evidence that either Jones or DeLorean joined in with the heavy users. There was business to talk about, that's what they really got high on. For DeLorean it was a chance to try out his constant flow of enrichment schemes on an older and wiser mind. There were the girls to chat up and the chance to relax from a Detroit world that was becoming increasingly hostile.

At the time, it seemed obvious to DeLorean that he had to build up his financial independence so that if the worst should happen at General Motors he could still walk away with financial security for the rest of his life. An easy way to do that was to use his position as the head of one of the largest corporations in the world—for Chevrolet by itself certainly was that—to do business with men who could be of help to him later on, if and when he and General Motors parted ways.

The GM lawyer recalls:

> The schemes that he came up with were a constant bother to us. The one that caused us the most trouble was his proposal that Chevrolet franchise service centers to various gas stations with a separate franchise organization that he would head. The dealers went stark raving mad when they heard about that. Here they had gone to the expense of setting up shops to make our cars ready for delivery and we were going to give the repair business to any gas station owner who could put up the money to John.

That caused a lot of damage within the company. His other stunts were just as off the wall. He decided that Chevy salesmen were too ignorant to give the complicated sales pitch about the variety of models the division was selling, so he forced through a plan for dealers to buy these little theaters and prospective buyers would first be shown a movie about the new line of cars with all the advertising promo built in. Of course he owned a piece of that action, but he got that one by us.

David Davis confirms:

Yes, I remember the minitheaters. It started as a fairly reason-able argument that a dealership should have an audiovisual cen-ter and a salesman could take the prospect in, sit him down, plug in the cartridge and film on, say, the Impala, and show how it related to other cars and its advantages.

The obvious thing to do was to go to videotape, but John came out of left field with an incredibly stupid super-eight-millimeter projector arrangement that was at the very end of the line of super-eight technology. And there was a lot of uproar in favor of waiting until video could be used—it would be cheaper and more flexible—but John rammed his plan through. Only later did we find out that a Hollywood television producer friend of his owned the company.

Also involved in the minitheater company was a new friend of DeLorean's—California car dealer Roy W. Nesseth. In a state where car dealers are the acknowledged zero-sum standard of dishonesty, Nesseth was something of a rarity even in that profession. He had been convicted in the early 1950s on fraud charges involving forged car sale documents.[*]

When DeLorean met Nesseth, the older man was the manager of the largest Chevrolet dealership in California (in Norwalk); and the GM executive was once again attracted by Nesseth's hard attitude and tough business talk.

Throughout 1970 and 1971, DeLorean used Chevrolet's promotion budget as his own privy purse. To save money for more grandiose projects, he canceled Chevrolet's historic commitment of funds to

---

[*] People v. Nesseth 127 C.A. 2d 712, 1954.

the National Soapbox Derby in Akron, a nationally televised event that brought boys and girls from all over North America to compete in a series of downhill races in their homemade, unpowered car models.

But DeLorean needed the money for other things: for lavish television productions from Las Vegas—shows sold to Chevrolet and Campbell and Ewald by Aubrey and other producers such as Milt Scott, Bert Sugarman, and Pierre Cousette. The trouble was that the shows never achieved the kind of audience that made the expense appear worthwhile. Rumors began to circulate that John was demanding kickbacks from advertisers. Editor Davis remembers:

> There was an investigation—a full-dress internal investigation into the kickbacks thing. I remember at the time Pete Estes specifically asked me if I thought DeLorean was getting kickbacks from the people who were producing the various television shows that Chevrolet was using.
>
> And I said, "I don't think so. I think he has such contempt for all of us here in Detroit and such low regard for our ability to guess what America wants to see, that he has gone to friends of his and turned the responsibility over to them and allowed them to come up with things that they think will be good."
>
> I also told Estes that I think John is wrong and the programs are junk, but he's not on the take. He's buying those programs because he trusts these people and he doesn't trust us.
>
> And Pete said, "Gerstenberg [the GM chairman] doesn't agree with you. He's afraid there is going to be a shareholder suit over John on this."

GM officials began to worry about leaving DeLorean in charge of their single most important division, as his erratic behavior worsened. There was considerable division of opinion even at that point, as executives who prized DeLorean's undeniable engineering skills opposed those who worried about the increasingly public controversy he was stirring up.

The Vega had finally shaped up and boosted Chevrolet sales: 1971 was the first year that a General Motors division ever achieved sales of 3 million cars and trucks. Furthermore, DeLorean was successful in slashing scores of production duplications from within the division's lines. In one instance he cut the possible dashboard option combinations in the Camaro line from 2,700 to 96. Within a year of his taking over, Chevrolet was running just 200,000 cars behind Ford's total U.S. output.

But for every success there was more than one failure. DeLorean campaigned hard to build a compact version of each of the Chevy division's midrange lines: the Nova, Camaro, and Ventura. He also enraged union officials by demanding that styling and tooling changes be done at night or on weekends in order to cut lost production time. Both efforts were countermanded by senior management.

His attempts to use GM for his own personal gain offended others among the management group. And his clear attempts to make internal company matters public, through Detroit's always credulous press corps, also helped turn the tide against him.

Starting in late 1972, GM officials became worried about another problem as well. A number of highly secret internal discussions were finding their way into print in the Detroit newspapers and automotive industry periodicals. The information being leaked was too detailed not to be coming from someone privy to the innermost workings of GM management. At the time, no one connected the beginning of the leaks with the decision to replace DeLorean as head of Chevrolet with Jim McDonald.

DeLorean was moved up to the 14th floor and became vice president of car and truck production. It was a promotion, to be sure; but it was also a test. Ed Cole was loath to admit having made a mistake in the first place.

DeLorean's marriage to Kelly was widely rumored to be on the rocks, despite their decision to adopt a baby son, to be named Zachary. The kick upstairs was his last chance to survive at GM, provided that he stay out of trouble for a while.

But DeLorean stepped up his public criticism of the company. By now his public image was complete. He was six-foot-four John Z. DeLorean—the hip, socially conscious business wizard. He was a fashion plate with a heart. He was at home with Hollywood swingers, ghetto kids, and big businessmen. He was saving General Motors from itself. He was going to succeed Ed Cole as president.

Arvid Jouppi, Wall Street's leading auto industry analyst, remembers the time: "John DeLorean was the most exciting thing going in Detroit. Folks thought he was the greatest thing since Billy Durant, and he was the new generation of engineer-executive the industry needed. After all, he was projecting this image of being pro-civil rights, pro-consumer, pro-safety and fuel efficiency; and yet, he was making his numbers. The stuff with the clothes and sideburns and the dyed hair didn't count against him with those people. If you want to know how John got away with it, ask the people at GM who knew better but kept promoting him."

DeLorean by now had an international press following for his public speeches and writings on various social issues. In late 1969, he met William F. Haddad, a former John F. Kennedy speechwriter and liberal activist journalist. Haddad was compiling a book on the black economic struggle in the United States that would feature chapters on topics written by major business executives.

DeLorean had an introductory chapter whipped up for the book by GM's publicity shop, in which he urged the white business establishment to make a greater commitment to the promotion of black business enterprise.* Much of what he had to say needed saying in those days, yet those closest to him felt his beliefs were as carefully tailored as the new European fashions he wore.

Much, much later, a disillusioned Haddad (who served as the public relations director for the ill-fated DeLorean Motor Car effort in Northern Ireland) would discover, "John was a racist. He really was afraid of black people; and the sad irony was that he positively hated the Irish, the very people he was supposed to be trying to save."

Another crisis came in September 1972. The three-year marriage to Kelly came to an end. Kelly left and filed for legal separation in Los Angeles. She moved in with her parents, taking the adopted son, Zachary.

"We're trying to do it like a lady and a gentleman, the best we can. I'm trying to keep Zachary with me, but I guess it's up to the adoption agency and the court," Kelly told a *Detroit Free Press* reporter at the time.

But she had not figured on DeLorean's capacity for anger over what he felt was a desire to embarrass him in public. Through his attorney, John Noonan, he mounted a campaign in the courts to take Zachary away from Kelly. Private detectives were called in to investigate Kelly's life before and during the marriage. It threatened to be a long, public, and bloody affair.

Finally, family attorneys stepped in and negotiated an out-of-court

---

* William F. Haddad and J. W. Pugh, *Black Economic Development* (Prentice-Hall, 1969).

settlement and kept it out of the newspapers. Kelly Harmon gave back Zachary and disappeared from DeLorean's life. She did not know it, but she was one of the lucky ones.

The divorce proceedings were still in the wrangling stage when DeLorean began appearing around Detroit in early 1973 with a new date: Fletcher Jones' girlfriend Cristina Ferrare. Jones had been killed late in 1972 in a plane crash on his own property.

DeLorean was being carefully discreet about the affair since he was intent on not losing the war with Kelly's lawyers by default. By that time Cristina was a fast-rising fashion model. Her trips to Detroit were covered by stories about a forthcoming General Motors advertising campaign.

Davis was frequently used as a stooge for the happy couple:

> I remember one time, the idea was we were supposed to be discussing a film that we were going to do for Chevrolet. That way John could be seen publicly with Cristina. So my wife and I and all these people from California were dragged along while John sat with his nose stuck in her ear all night. My wife said right then that was the last time she would be a beard for John DeLorean.
>
> John was in his image heyday at that time. His hair was jet black and he wore smart, very dark blue suits. They were three-piece suits, but he always wore the vest unbuttoned, and he had those shirts with the long collar points—really good linen, really good neckties. But it was always enforced casualness. "I'm wearing a $600 suit, but I can't be bothered to button the vest." That sort of thing. So he would swoop into a room. He was tall, and his clothes would swirl around him because of all the flapping; but after five minutes, you had to get him out of the meeting because he would initially impress people for about that long and then he would begin to turn them off.
>
> Because enough was never enough for John. If we were successfully pushing a product line or cooling down the dealers, John would turn everyone off again by bringing up something else, by bragging about something, by name-dropping. He never really bothered to learn how to deal with people.

By now it was probably past the time when John DeLorean could have talked his way out of his internal problems at GM. The leaks of corporate secrets to the press were increasing. There was an especially damaging report about the disaffection among Chevrolet dealers with their new general manager, Jim McDonald. It was March 1973, and the clock was running out for DeLorean at General Motors.

Every three years the top levels of General Motors management journeyed to the Greenbriar Hotel in White Sulphur Springs, West Virginia. There, over a long weekend, the 300 or 30 top executives played golf, drank whiskey, and relaxed. More important, they plotted long-term strategy for the mammoth corporation. The meeting was held in the strictest secrecy, and no minutes of the morning and afternoon discussion sessions were kept.

Many American corporations have similar rituals of executive think tanks. At the root of the struggle to climb the corporate ladder in the United States is the universally held belief that the ladder is worth climbing, not just in terms of personal gain, but because the company is worth fighting for, that its products are useful and beneficial. One is a member of a corporate team not just for the procedural convenience, but because it is a good team to be on.

These periodic secret conferences in which board chairmen play golf with division managers and young analysts speak freely to senior vice presidents are all part of the bonding process that gives American management its sense of continuity and purpose.

The Greenbriar meetings had been held without interruption since the 1930s. The 1973 meeting was especially important because Ed Cole and Dick Gerstenberg, the chairman, were convinced that GM had to make some fundamental changes in its production and marketing strategies if it were to prosper in the 1970s. The OPEC oil embargo would come later in the year and turn Detroit upside down; but even in that early spring, GM's chiefs were seeking new directions.

John DeLorean was asked to submit a future-planning paper. The topic was product quality and a critique on whether American car buyers were getting what they wanted. Cole told DeLorean to make the criticism as forceful as possible in order to spark the maximum discussion at the conference. It would be one of the key presentations. It might even be the first step on the long road back to rehabilitation for DeLorean, who had been effectively isolated from any real work on the 14th floor for nearly a year now.

On Thursday, March 17, the day before the executives were scheduled to embark on their weekend at the resort, Robert Irvin, senior automobile writer for *Automotive News*, the authoritative trade daily, carried a detailed advance story on DeLorean's speech, including quotes of some of the more controversial charges—ranging from the assertion that Detroit was deliberately selling substandard transportation designs to the consumer to charges that General Motors' design capability was mediocre. What intrigued the GM management was that the speech copy Irvin had obtained was clearly a copy of an earlier draft that DeLorean had circulated among the most senior management for comment prior to the conference.

Cole ordered that a private investigator be hired to check the leak, since he could not even trust the company's own in-house security personnel to do the job. Within a month, the report was back. In tracing the bootlegged copy of DeLorean's Greenbriar speech, the trail led to two places—a woman public relations officer in GM's own publicity department and DeLorean himself. Moreover, the report delved into areas that Cole and Gerstenberg really did not want to be confronted with.

Not only was DeLorean a likely source of other leaks of confidential GM information to the press, but there was substantial evidence of irregularities in his personal life that could be overlooked only at GM's peril. Specific allegations about DeLorean's sexual preferences were pinpointed to gossip stemming from Dollie Cole and Liz DeLorean, the report said; and while there was no specific proof, General Motors should be forewarned.

That was enough. Cole ordered the report suppressed and destroyed. In early April DeLorean was sent for and told he would have to resign. At first he resisted, threatening to release still more damaging documents on GM product safety standards, on its poor minority hiring record, and other scandals. A deal was finally struck.

He would be allowed to resign, that went without saying, but he would be given a Cadillac franchise in Florida that was worth at least $1 million. Better still, Gerstenberg, who was that year's chairman of the National Alliance of Businessmen, would see to it that DeLorean was named president of a group that sought employment for impoverished young people. And DeLorean's salary of $200,000 was to be continued that year.

On April 18 DeLorean flew to Gerstenberg's New York office and agreed to the final details in a meeting presided over by Cole. It was a low-key affair—no shouting or recriminations. Cole later recalled that DeLorean even appeared disinterested and somewhat distracted.

The resignation was announced to the press, to become effective May 31. "I want to do things in the social area. I have to do them; and unfortunately, the nature of our business just didn't permit me to do as much as I wanted," DeLorean told newsmen. A week later, his appointment to the business-jobs coalition was announced with a flattering comment from Gerstenberg.

Before his time was officially up at GM, DeLorean had two opportunities to make official Detroit sit up and notice him. On May 8, 1973, he and Cristina were married in a civil ceremony in Detroit.

A few weeks later General Motors top management and wives turned out in force for the retirement dinner that he had insisted be part of his separation package. Pete Estes had derided these affairs as "pickle-plate dinners" for the false sentimentality that pervaded. "You work your life off for the company and all they give you is a dinner and some damned pickle plate or other geegaw," he quipped, and the name stuck.

"You wouldn't have believed John's pickle-plate dinner," an eyewitness recalled. "The place was packed because all the wives wanted a good look at Cristina—the men too for that matter. But we all knew that John had been pushed out so it was awkward at the beginning. But not for old John; he got up and gave us all hell for half an hour. He had been the one who had warned us about this and that, he had tried to do this and that and the management wouldn't let him. He named names and raised specific complaints. We would all be sorry after he was gone. And what was amazing was that everyone sat there and took it. It was the damndest thing I've ever seen, before or since."

So, no matter that he had been pushed out of his Detroit life, John DeLorean had made sure it was he who slammed the door as he left. There would be no going back.

3

DREAM CAR

The October 1973 OPEC-led oil embargo did more than just rattle the oil industry or unsettle Wall Street; it changed forever the assumptions by which millions of Americans had lived their lives. The all-day lines at the gas pumps, the economic shock and inflation that followed, are now dimming memories to most. The diminished hopes and limited realities that spread through both the industrialized and the developing nations are the legacy of that autumn upheaval a decade ago. Whatever else the embargo did, it also provided John DeLorean's image with the instant "issue focus" the news media need to keep someone's public identity clearly defined and fresh.

So John DeLorean became the ex-General Motors executive who had warned his employers to do something about fuel economy before it was too late. His persona of the hip and socially sympathetic big businessman took on a new aura. DeLorean was *right*. He was a prophet with honor and had a fresh new lease on the public attention-span.

Not that he had been languishing since leaving the 14th floor. GM chairman Dick Gerstenberg followed through with his promise to secure the presidency of the National Alliance of Businessmen for 1973 to 1974. After his ouster from GM that April, DeLorean was visible and busy, for summer was the busy season for the NAB. Since the 1968 summer riots that had raged through frustrated black neighborhoods from Watts to Washington, D.C., the NAB had waged a campaign, for the most part in the news media, to convince the public that big business was sympathetic to the problems of the growing army of hard-to-train, impoverished urban black and Hispanic youth. DeLorean's job was to tour major industrial cities with high unemployment rates and express the desire of the big corporations to help

local businesses do more to hire these young people during the summer, with the explicit threat of more riots to come if they did not.
His speeches were DeLorean at his best, uplifting messages followed
by entertainingly caustic press conferences in which he needled
Detroit for its shabby products and constipated management techniques.

The general-readership newspapers and magazines around the
United States took their cue about DeLorean from the automotive-
industry press corps. There was a tacit acknowledgment that perhaps DeLorean *had* been fired from his GM job, but the consensus
was that GM's management had been more intolerant of his flashy
clothes and jet-set lifestyle and not a little jealous of his engineering
skills.

Automotive News set the tone of the time about DeLorean's career
at GM. It compared DeLorean's ouster with the resignation of a talented Ford executive vice president, William Innes, who had retired
at the early age of fifty-one a few weeks previously. On April 23,
1973, *AN*'s editors wondered aloud whether or not a trend against
innovative young executives was endemic to the car industry.

> The auto industry has thrived on the accomplishments of in-
> dividuals. Men like Henry Ford, Walter Chrysler and the Fisher
> brothers are only a few whose style and manner set them apart
> from the crowd in terms of accomplishments and goals. . . .
> Today more than ever before it is important for corporations to
> continue to nurture the climate for executives who do not always
> fit into the corporate mold. In a society that is fast becoming
> more and more impersonal, it seems so important that individ-
> uals be encouraged to speak up, even if their voices do not always
> echo the corporate line.
>
> John Z. DeLorean has quit General Motors. He left for a
> number of reasons, but one thing is sure: the industry will miss
> him. Now, more than ever before, the industry needs the color
> and style of a DeLorean. His most important attribute is, simply,
> credibility. People believe him—his co-workers, his dealers and
> his suppliers . . . perhaps even government and the consumer,
> too. . . . If his style set a pattern for the future, the auto business
> will be better off. If he is one of a kind, the auto industry has lost
> more than it realizes.

Moreover DeLorean was cleaning up his act, toning down the swinger-jet-set image, stressing the solid business executive image. His marriage to Cristina was an instant success from all standpoints. Even though she was twenty-three, just a year older than Kelly Harmon, Cristina Ferrare had a sharp-edged sense of reality. Born in Los Angeles, the daughter of a supermarket butcher, Cristina managed to survive the dead-end of the movie starlet system and make the jump to high-fashion modeling. She started out as a child model and endured the exploitation of the movie studio system of the 1960s, even to the point of turning her luxuriant black hair blond to land jobs.

But now her modeling career was on an upswing, and covers for *Harper's Bazaar, Vogue,* and a host of women's magazines came thick and fast. Unlike Kelly, who lived in a protected dream world where she was the benevolent, laid-back helper of poor children, Cristina knew exactly what she was and what she was getting in the forty-eight-year-old John DeLorean.

The marriage would work, she decided. It would work because they could help each other get the kind of life they both hungered for. She assured her family that the much older, twice-divorced DeLorean would make a good husband.

What kind of woman is Cristina DeLorean? Friends who remember her from the early days of the marriage use unreservedly glowing words to describe her; words such as moral, truthful, loyal, warm and feminine. Life in the DeLorean household in Bloomfield Hills was far away from the sun-and-palmtree glamour of the Hollywood of their previous lives, further still from the hard-chrome glitter of the Park Avenue life to come.

John and Cristina stayed at home during these days; their social circle was a small and tightly woven group of Detroit entrepreneurs such as promoter and developer Sonny Van Arnem. The men would talk sports and business; the women would gather in the kitchen where Cristina made them laugh with her tales of the modeling world as she prepared yet another superb Italian meal.

The sudden changeover to the stay-at-home husband from the Hollywood swinger was not as difficult as it might have been. DeLorean had never been an enthusiastic partygoer, he had no taste for alcohol, and he was indifferent to gourmet cooking because of his fixation on diets and health.

While he had been publicly linked in the show business press with many of the most beautiful women in the film colony at one time or another, many of the "dates" were public relations affairs arranged by studios or industry friends to provide both the woman and DeLorean with sufficiently prominent companions for some public function or other. His fetish for health and weight control won the interest for a while of Candice Bergen, herself a food faddist. And he was also photographed with Nancy Sinatra and Ursula Andress. In most of the cases there would be a date or two to a dinner party or film premiere, but after that no real romance.

"The fact is that John at a dinner party is pretty dull company. He has no small talk whatsoever. He picks at his food and he doesn't really enjoy drinking. Usually he would try to find some excuse to get on his host's telephone and talk business with somebody somewhere else," a social friend from Los Angeles recalls.

Others recalled that DeLorean was especially uncomfortable around women he viewed as aggressive or opinionated. His response was to become equally aggressive and to retaliate with coarse derisive humor. For more intimate relaxation during his sprees with his Hollywood friends, he preferred the more pliant, submissive girls that were procured for him.

A long-time Detroit friend and business associate comments:

John felt bad when Kelly left him, he felt betrayed somehow. And he really did miss the boy until he got him back. But he went out to California one weekend and came back all elated. He told me a wild tale about how his Hollywood friends had hired three prostitutes who looked a lot like Kelly—that same California girl face and body. So they get these girls all made up with their hair and makeup just like Kelly's so they really looked like her, all three of them. And then they put the girls in a house at Malibu and packed it full of booze and threw John in the middle of it for the weekend. His friends were saying to him, "Don't worry, there are more like her anytime you want." John thought it was great. He said it was the *classiest* thing anyone had ever done for him—that was his phrase, classy. And he said it could only have happened out there in California, that no one in Detroit would have enough class to pull off something like that. I guess he was right about that.

But all that was over now. He was getting the esteem he needed from the public and the love he wanted from Cristina. And she was proving to be a definite business plus, providing real assistance with the job he held with the NAB. The Alliance was based in Washington, D.C., and the couple threw themselves into the social whirl of a city just settling down to the second Nixon term in the White House; it was a Washington still unruffled by the gathering Watergate storm-clouds.

The DeLoreans were a success in the capital. There were many gushing comparisons between the dashing Detroit business executive with the Hollywood past and Henry Kissinger, the swinging secretary of state. Were they comparing notes on their various mutual friends? The gossip columnists drooled. Cristina drew approving reviews for her New York-chic clothes and her ability to prop John up at the interminable receptions with her gift for party small talk. He too won admirers among senior government officials for his willingness to speak against the car industry. His jeers and criticisms fitted in with the mood in official Washington that the industry must be more closely regulated in the wake of the energy crisis that had panicked them all. DeLorean went further and began speaking out in favor of a heavy tax on gasoline to force energy conservation and to help finance an expanded drive to find alternative energy sources.

But he could not afford to stand around making ego-soothing chit-chat with Washington power brokers. His year with the NAB would soon be over, and with it the $200,000 annual stipend continued by General Motors. There would be more payments from GM over the next few years, but most of them were payoffs from bonuses and stock options that he had not exercised for tax reasons while he was an active executive. At his peak earning period over the five previous years, DeLorean had been piling up bonuses of roughly $400,000 a year, but those were meant to be taken after retirement, when the tax bite would be less. DeLorean was well-heeled enough, but not so wealthy as to support the life he and Cristina were determined to maintain.

To live that kind of life, one had to control a mammoth corporation, something the size of Chevrolet, or a major conglomerate or movie studio. John was no longer atop that high a corporate pyramid, and it appeared that most of the private investments he had made over the previous few years were turning into big money losers. Being strapped for cash was unendurable to John DeLorean. It was something he could not even discuss with Cristina, whose own six-figure income from modeling was scrupulously segregated in her own accounts.

The hard truth that DeLorean had to face in early 1974 was that he needed to get back to work in a big way. His stakes in the New York Yankees and the San Diego Chargers were not turning out the profits his higher-flying friends had promised. He pulled out what he could from the two teams, and then there were rumors that he and Sonny Van Arnem would make a bid for the Detroit Wheels, a lackluster franchise of the soon-to-go-bankrupt World Football League.

The football franchise deal never came off. Another upset was the growing squabble between DeLorean and brother Chuck over a venture they had started with other partners several years previously—Grand Prix of America, Inc. The firm tried to franchise reduced-to-scale replicas of famous Grand Prix racing circuit tracks. The idea was a variation on the concept of the miniature golf course. Customers could rent reduced models of famous Formula One race cars and test their skills at the banks and turns of the minitracks.

Grand Prix was one of the business interests that DeLorean promised Ed Cole he would soft-pedal during one of the final confrontations at Chevrolet. At the time, what jolted GM management about the scheme was DeLorean's publicized decision to power the minicars with the Wankel rotary engine, which was also used in the Mazda, the newly arrived Japanese entry in the U.S. automobile sweepstakes. It just didn't look right, Cole insisted. It didn't really matter though. The franchises did not sell well and DeLorean lost interest in the scheme after a few months.

David Davis recalls one DeLorean attempt to recruit capital and technical aid for Grand Prix:

> We had a client at the advertising agency who had been an international go-kart champion and he had a little company in Ohio where he built karts and snowmobiles and the little engines to power them. John heard about him and called me and said he would like to see this guy. I thought, well, that's nice. Here is an opportunity to do a nice thing for two clients.
>
> So sometime later I usher the guy into John's office at Chevy and John's idea of a proposal was that the guy would put up all

the capital and build the cars, with John's license on the Wankel of course, and then they would ship the cars out to the franchise track operators. Well, I could see right away that this guy does not want any part of the deal when John interrupts himself and says, "Do you understand anything I'm saying?" And the guy says, "I'm listening to you." And John says, "No you're not. I can see your goddamned eyes glazing over." And out of the office we go.

In 1974 Grand Prix of America filed for bankruptcy, with one brother, Jack DeLorean, suing to recover his lost funds, and another brother, Chuck, threatening to join the litigation unless his losses were covered as well. In his suit, Jack alleged that he had been replaced as president of Grand Prix by Roy Nesseth and that John DeLorean and Nesseth had shifted needed capital into other De-Lorean ventures—capital that belonged to the partners.

The suit was later settled out of court, although Chuck DeLorean remained a bankruptcy creditor claiming $20,000 in unpaid losses. Although he disputes it, he was among the first victims of a Nesseth-DeLorean corporate looting pattern that ranged across the country for the next eight years.

"John repaid me. It took awhile but he finally did. Look, we've always been close brothers, John has always been a good businessman, a hard fighter," says Chuck DeLorean, a prosperous Cadillac dealer in Cleveland today. And Roy Nesseth?

"Well, that's a sensitive area. Roy Nesseth is a hard-driving, very shrewd negotiating businessman. I would say this: If I were dealing with some of the people that John was dealing with under the circumstances, I would have been very pleased to have a man of Mr. Nesseth's capabilities representing my interests. There are instances where John has really been taken to the cleaners by people who later claimed that he was unfair to them. In one case, a real estate deal, John turned it around with Nesseth's aid and got the guy back instead," Chuck DeLorean argues.

But John DeLorean needed something bigger than a failing go-kart franchise or a couple of football teams to put him back on top. All during the past year there were reports every few weeks or so that one major corporation or another was considering him for a top post, but somehow firm offers never came. DeLorean began to complain that

GM was on an "SOS" campaign. That decoded into "put shit on his shoes," and it meant that without charging him with any specific crime, GM was effectively getting the word out to prospective employers that there was something not quite right about him and that the aroma of misconduct followed him wherever he sought a new post.

In the meantime DeLorean kept up his own barrage of rumors, and the Detroit press corps recorded each one with open-mouthed credulity. Mary Wells, a top advertising executive, was going to use DeLorean to help launch Toyota's first major marketing offensive in the United States, according to one report. In another, DeLorean had plans to license the Isuzu truck from Japan, and then it was for Lada cars from the Soviet Union. There were talks with the Rumanian government about his building a car production plant in that country. But nothing seemed to gel in those early months of 1974.

The seeds for the dream car had been sown while DeLorean was still running Pontiac. He watched the foreign sports car craze buildup during the mid-1960s with a keen professional interest.

From England came the Triumph Spitfire and Austin-Healey Sprite —tiny two-seaters with few luxuries, but tough, zippy, and economical little cars. The Fiat 124 and the Datsun 240Z soon joined the ranks.

Why not build something to beat them? DeLorean mused.

Back at Pontiac he had his team put together a small, low-priced two-seater with the Pontiac overhead cam, a six-cylinder engine (the foreign cars had four), and a fiberglass body.

The project excited DeLorean. He presented it enthusiastically to General Motors' engineering policy group, but they turned it down. The GM executives wanted to keep the Chevrolet Corvette as their only product in the low-price sports car market; they wanted no competition, not even from Pontiac.

When DeLorean left GM in 1973, he had no reason to speak publicly about any plans he might have to build his own car. But at the back of his mind that Pontiac sports car idea lay simmering.

"The easiest car to build is a sports car," Bunkie Knudsen was fond of saying, "because you can do exciting things with the design."

DeLorean's own oft-quoted quip about his final days at GM was, "We quit designing cars and started designing committees." It was a stale old cliché, reminiscent of the corporate definition of a camel: a horse designed by a committee. But all the same it brought an appreciative chuckle from the various audiences around the country on his NAB speaking tour.

In April 1974 DeLorean addressed a meeting of the Texas Christian University management alumni association in Dallas. He had just completed his year at the NAB, and the next stage of his career—whatever it was to be—was about to unfold. What would he do?

In 1973 he had told his audience that he had designed a couple of little cars—one, similar to the Pontiac, a two-seater sports job. The other was a minicommuter car with a foreign engine.

At that point it was the commuter car that really sparked De-Lorean's enthusiasm. "Initially it will run on gasoline," he told the excited alumni group, "but down the line it will be a multifuel vehicle." Hydrogen was a possible fuel, he said. It could be in production within eighteen months to two years.

DeLorean was deliberately enigmatic. Uncertain of his welcome in the industry and in need of reassurance, he was putting his toe in the water to gauge the temperature. In March DeLorean had received nationwide publicity with a speech to the Motor and Equipment Manufacturers Association in Chicago in which he forecast that Detroit would have to abandon the "grotesque monsters of the 1960s and 1970s." Consumers, he predicted, were going to demand smaller cars with less weight, better fuel economy, and adequate room for a family.

"By 1980, less than 1,500 working days away, the largest car sold in any quantity in America will be little bigger than today's Chevy Nova."

The public response had been warmly positive. Now he was going on to the next stage in Dallas, hinting that he himself might build such a car: perhaps 350,000 cars a year, a truck line to be added later with its own production run of 200,000. What would the auto industry think of that? he wondered.

Automotive News soon told him. "We think it would be a stroke of luck for the industry and consumer alike if DeLorean would return to the auto business and build the sort of car he says will be king of the road by 1980. We're ready, John. C'mon home."

On that April day in Dallas, DeLorean talked about his deeper ambitions. "The ideal thing I would like to do with my life right now would be to build the American equivalent of the Mercedes-Benz. A car with high quality, where you wouldn't have to worry about the price, just build the best car you could."

But it would take enormous sums of money if he were to move his dream car from the talking stage to something more tangible. The importance of scoring a big bankroll become more urgent as the car project steadily crystallized in his mind after the Dallas speech. He needed money.

Earlier that April, DeLorean had been telephoned by Walter "Pete" Avrea, a Phoenix inventor who was beset by serious business problems in marketing two extremely valuable automotive patents. DeLorean reacted quickly; he flew at once to Phoenix to meet Avrea and his brother Bill, who had helped form the small stockholders company Saf-Guard Products, which sold licenses to manufacture and market the inventions.

Pete Avrea is a self-taught mechanic turned inventor. He freely admits that his goal was to be left alone in his workshop with his projects. He wanted other people to navigate the frighteningly complex world of patent development and sales. His two major inventions were big winners; both helped prevent car and truck engines from boiling away their radiator coolant and guarded against the risk of burned-out engines. One device helped recover vaporized coolant; the other was a radiator cap that prevented blowouts.

But it is just not enough to be able to prove that one has invented a product or some unique device. Even after the patent is granted, the owner must vigilantly pursue pirates who run into the marketplace with quickly copied versions. The only way to survive as an independent inventor is to aggressively use lawyers and the court system to recover royalty monies collected by pirates and to block them from future exploitation.

In theory, Pete Avrea's two inventions were worth hundreds of millions of dollars in potential sales and scores of millions in potential royalty payments to him and to whoever helped him enforce his rights. As he recalls now, "After we had been sent back from the U.S. Supreme Court to the District Court here, the judge ruled that we had valid patents and that they had been infringed on by all the major car manufacturers in the world." At that point in 1980, the judge ruled that for every one of the Avrea units made by those companies without valid licenses, the major manufacturers owed Avrea $11.30.

Avrea never came close to collecting that. The original Saf-Guard Products firm spent hundreds of thousands of dollars in suits against the big auto parts manufacturers, but the court cases dragged on and on, first in the trial courts to establish the patents, then to determine that the patents were being stolen, and finally to establish the amount of money due Saf-Guard in pirated royalties. The inevitable appeals and delays finally put Saf-Guard into bankruptcy in 1974, and that is when the appeal went out to DeLorean. Would he provide his name, his heavy Detroit reputation, and some expertise to recapture some of the lost royalties? Could he market the kits to new companies and work out profitable licensing deals with other auto parts manufacturers?

"Norm Bernier, who was president of Saf-Guard Products, called John DeLorean on a Tuesday or Wednesday. On Friday, John arrived here and after a brief talk he said he wanted to take over our company and that he could do for us what we wanted done. Norm and I just stood around in awe. He was just like they said he was in the magazines. He was such a success it was fantastic," Avrea recalls.

What Avrea and his family could not know was that John DeLorean was already familiar with the coolant recovery device. It had been put on the production run of the Vega while he was at Chevrolet. Avrea later believed that DeLorean had learned General Motors was planning to order 167,000 more units shortly after he entered into contracts with Avrea to set up a new company—Saf-Guard Systems, Inc. The new GM order would have been worth $1.8 million.

Saf-Guard Systems was the corporate vehicle under which DeLorean was supposed to be conducting Pete Avrea's business, but it was only a corporate shell throughout his relationship with the inventor. All the business—that is, all the purchasing, borrowing, licensing, and shifting of capital—was done through the corpse of Saf-Guard Products, a legally bankrupt firm with no direct ties to John DeLorean.

"He never had the phone changed, nor the building lease changed. He took no responsibility under the name of Saf-Guard Systems until the day the door closed. All the purchase orders and all the checks still continued to be in the name of Saf-Guard Products. He didn't even tell Ford or General Motors, who were using the kits under license, that there was a company name change because he would have had to pass their quality-control standards all over again," Avrea recounts.

In the meantime, Avrea was visited by Roy Nesseth, who introduced himself as DeLorean's nominee to run Saf-Guard.

"Our first meeting was so unpleasant that I went to the phone with my attorney on the line and called DeLorean and told him that if this was the man he was putting in here, we had no deal. And he said, 'Okay, I'll get him out of town. Put him on the phone and I'll tell him to get out of town and I will send another man in,' " Avrea says.

"And Nesseth did go away and another man came in as president of Saf-Guard, but Roy would come through town periodically and make a point to see me and tell me about the big wheelings and dealings he was handling for DeLorean."

While the inventor fretted over Nesseth's boorishness, DeLorean moved quickly to extract as much money as possible from Saf-Guard. Royalties that were coming into the company regularly dried up. Firms that were suspected of using Avrea coolant kits without licenses were sold licenses at cut-rate royalties without notification to Avrea, he would later charge. The Celanese Corporation lent DeLorean $200,000 for the development of the radiator cap, but the loan was shifted over as a debt of Saf-Guard Products while the capital vanished. For the moment, however, Pete Avrea went back to his workshop, unaware of what was going on. John DeLorean was now in Detroit, thinking hard about his new sports car and what it would look like.

DeLorean had been speaking publicly all summer about the development of first his commuter car, then the sports car. The idea of a superluxury American competitor for Mercedes also intrigued him. But whatever he decided upon, it would have to be a knockout, something totally distinctive and unique. Something worthy of the DeLorean name and image. But what?

The small, sporty car and the Mercedes competitor were at opposite poles of the automobile spectrum. Neither bore the slightest resemblance to the car that DeLorean was to build later. His dream car was just evolving. But that summer DeLorean discovered gull-wing doors and forgot about his commuter car—he did not mention it again.

Gull-wing doors, hinged in the roof, were by no means new. The famous Mercedes 300SL, the glamour car of the 1950s, featured them. So did the ill-fated Bricklin, the private car venture that was about to go belly-up.

DeLorean wanted his car to be different. He loved Mercedes cars—at that time he drove a Mercedes 300SEL, and Cristina had a 450.

He also owned a Cadillac, a Monte Carlo, and a Corvette, plus six trucks on his California ranch. He had always been adroit at taking the ideas of others and translating them—often brilliantly—into his production cars at Pontiac and Chevrolet. Now he decided to adopt the Mercedes gull-wing doors. Taking the words of Bunkie Knudsen to heart, he also decided that the easiest route was to build a sports car. It would fit with his image of the dashing former GM executive. The car could be produced in smaller numbers and sold at a higher price than a standard sedan. It would not require the huge fortune needed to compete in the mass markets.

"We can't play in the same concert halls as GM," he quipped to newsmen. "They play on the keys and we have to play on the cracks."

There was another attraction too. DeLorean commissioned surveys at GM that showed that sports cars were a "growth area." But most important of all, he realized they offered him the best chance of winning government subsidies. "To qualify for government financing, you need a statement from the U.S. Department of Labor confirming that your project would not displace Americans in similar employment. Well, the sports car market was mostly imported cars," he would recall later. At that time he began thinking about building his car in Pennsylvania or Texas, or so he told the press.

So a gull-wing sports car it would be. Now he needed someone to put it together for him. DeLorean was an undeniably fine engineer and knew that side of the business very well. But if he were going to launch his own company, he needed someone to take care of the mass of detailed design work that would lead to the prototype stage and on to production. He began to look around.

William T. Collins was a lanky, quietly intense project manager at General Motors. He wore a large handlebar mustache that flourished or disappeared whenever whim dictated. Collins created a great air of professional calm and proficiency around him; he was a man who knew what he was doing and liked doing it well. He was a good man to have on any team. He served six years as assistant chief engineer at Pontiac, and in the corporation was dubbed the "godfather of the Grand Am."

In 1974 Collins was project manager of the 1977 Model B Car for GM. This was to be the first down-sized car the company made. The B Car was also the first car produced at a GM "project center," where a chief engineer was in charge, put there by a vote of other car division chief engineers. The idea of the project center has been used on most new models since that time. It meant that a new model would start its life in styling, after which different divisions would take responsibility for designing and producing specific part or systems for the car. Buick might have the brakes and Pontiac the rear suspension. These divisions were spread geographically throughout the state of Michigan, but the parts would be monitored at the design center, where the project would be pulled together. Collins' B Car project was a success and he found himself sought by GM's rivals.

By coincidence, he had worked on DeLorean's two-passenger sports car experiment at Pontiac and was still irked by the way the idea had been killed off. He had stayed in touch with DeLorean since. When Grand Prix of America was getting started, DeLorean asked Collins to run it.

"John, you know I don't know anything about running tracks," he protested. "And I don't want to move out to California [where the corporate headquarters was being located] so let's pass on this one."

But now in the summer of 1974, Collins was being head-hunted. American Motors wanted him and offered him more money and a promotion. He leaned toward making the break. One of the references he gave was John DeLorean. Within days of the job interview with American, Collins received a phone call from the Miami Airport. (DeLorean could not resist making phone calls from airports.)

"Hey, Bill, you don't want to go to American. I'm just about to get my car company off the ground," DeLorean said. He had finally decided to make a two-seater sports car, he told Collins. It would have gull-wing doors and lots of new safety innovations—safety would be the theme. DeLorean ticked off the features he planned. New plastic process, very strong, very light. Everything rustproof—use plastics and stainless steel. Get one of those flashy Italian designers to come up with a body line that was really ritzy. Get government money to build it in the United States. And get the dealers to put up the money in advance.

"Bill, I want you to be in charge of the whole thing," DeLorean promised.

Collins did not resist long. "Hell," he would say later, "I guess the concept of any engineer who loves cars is to be able to do your own car." He had done it with that sports car at Pontiac. When he compared his dull task of coordinating the 1977 B Car with a chance to build a sports car for which he would be totally in control, he really had no choice. And there was the money too. DeLorean was promising good salaries to start and the lure of a large fortune for everyone once the car was off the ground.

"John, it's very, very appealing," he told DeLorean.

He knew what he was giving up at General Motors—bonuses were paid out over five years, and if he left he could forfeit them. He decided to go ahead and "throw off the golden handcuffs." Having made up his mind, Collins had to tell GM. Pete Estes had just taken over from Ed Cole a few weeks before, and it was to him that Collins offered his resignation. In the president's office on the 14th floor, Collins explained to Estes what he was doing and why.

"Geez, I wish you'd stay," Estes responded after a pause. Men like Collins did not grow on trees, even at GM, and Estes was first of all astonished that anyone would want to leave as great an organization as GM. But to leave for—of all people—John DeLorean . . . well, Estes was thunderstruck.

"John is flaky, you know," he warned Collins. "He has just plain flipped out."

Collins would have reason to remember Estes' warning. He himself observed some years later, "I am not sure if any of us understand what we all go through in our lives, but some people do have something that happens to them in their early forties."

This is a theme that will recur whenever people who knew John DeLorean from the early days pondered his subsequent fate. It might be Bunkie Knudsen's euphemistic "gone Hollywood," or David Davis' quip, "DeLorean and John Glenn both have been out into outer space. John DeLorean's problem is that he lost a few tiles on re-entry."

But all of this still lay ahead for Bill Collins. At the time of his exit interview with Estes he was inclined to dismiss the warning; like everyone he knew that bad blood had grown up between the new GM president and his former protégé. Collins concluded it was best to get to work on the sports car project as soon as he could.

So in September 1974 Bill Collins joined DeLorean in the offices of the John Z. DeLorean Corporation in Bloomfield Hills, Michigan. The concept had begun to take firmer shape in DeLorean's mind. The Corvette was selling nearly 50,000 cars a year, priced around $12,000. It was no longer exclusive. DeLorean figured he could sell 20,000 of a more exciting car at a price pitched $1,500 more than the Corvette.

That was the market he would shoot for. Why, even Porsche was selling nearly 20,000 cars a year.

That autumn, DeLorean and Collins flew to Italy for the Turin Motor Show in search of a designer. They looked at the Maseratis and the Farina designs. They spent some time talking to a man named Giorgetto Giugiaro.

Giugiaro had earned a reputation as one of the most adventurous automotive stylists of the Turin school. He had worked as Bertone's chief stylist on the Lamborghini, one of the world's most dramatic sports cars. Then he founded his own Ital Design, and performed some of the work on the new generation of highly successful Volkswagen cars that succeeded the Beetle. He had also worked on Lancias, Audis, and Alfa-Romeos. Most intriguing of all, he did the styling work for a small British sports car maker that would play a major role in the development of DeLorean's dream car—Lotus.

DeLorean and Collins decided Giugiaro was the man for them. DeLorean explained to the designer what he wanted; they spent more time discussing the materials to be used in the car, notably the stainless-steel shell and the gull-wings. DeLorean wanted the engine behind the driver. "It's more sporty—that's where it is on the Indianapolis and Grand Prix cars." That configuration demanded a wedge-shaped body design, which Giugiaro also liked. The two Americans flew home, pleased with the way the project was shaping up.

By February 1975, Giugiaro had his design ready and Collins had produced the seating and chassis design. Collins and DeLorean went to Italy again and fitted the two together. It all looked glamorous enough, even for John DeLorean. Giugiaro had come up with a sleek, low-slung, silver beauty.

The Italian presented his proposal, and by March 1975 DeLorean and Giugiaro had signed a deal. Over the next five years, Giugiaro would tweak the design here and there, but basically the silhouette produced that spring was the same one that DeLorean would send into production. And while it was later to be criticized for many other reasons, its looks were undeniably eye-catching.

By the end of July, before Giugiaro's workers went off on the traditional month-long August break, the design was essentially complete. DeLorean's dream now had a shape. His own contribution to the actual shape of that dream was something less than crucial. He was only peripherally involved in the design work, leaving that to Collins, who recalls:

> He would occasionally make sketches. Not to scale though, so we never had anything workable. He had a favorite concept he came up with that I called "Zachary's Greenhouse." He kept showing this little guy—like his son—sitting behind the front seat, and if you bulged out the rear window, supposedly little Zachary could sit back there. And I kept showing John that to scale you can't do it. It wouldn't work. And finally the idea went away. Occasionally he made sketches of areas he was interested in, but the basic engineering and all the basic design was work that I did. All the suspension parameters, the ground clearance, the seating dimensions were all put together by me.

Others verify that this is so, and Bill Collins is not by nature a boastful man.

On through the summer of 1975, Collins had been giving the Detroit press corps gentle hints about what was going on. There was no word yet on the engine—DeLorean had not decided—but leaks began to circulate about the underbody and radical design. The philosophy continued to emphasize safety as well as style.

The first Giugiaro-designed drawings and models featured the initials DSV on the front panel—they stood for DeLorean Safety Vehicle. That was never intended to be the car's name, but it produced the image DeLorean sought. The safety, and the car's special lightness and strength, were to be provided by a new plastic wonder material called Elastic Reservoir Molding, or ERM. It was not a widely known process in the United States, although it had been in use for a short time in European cars. As John DeLorean originally conceived it, ERM was the secret key to his dream—the ingredient to make his car something special. In the end it was used only for a few nonessential parts.

The ERM method was a fiberglass process originally developed by Royal Dutch Shell. DeLorean set up a company called Composite Technology Corporation (CTC), separate from his personal investment company, John Z. DeLorean Corporation, and through CTC bought an option on the license to the product for the motor industry.

CTC rented a 25,000-square-foot factory near Troy, Michigan, and DeLorean hired Peter H. Hofer as CTC's director of research and development.

Collins was enthusiastic about the process. "Based on what I know so far," he reported in July 1975, "the weight of a car body would be almost as light as if it were made entirely out of aluminum."

But it also was expected to have another important characteristic. Collins estimated that it could be used to design one of the safest cars ever built. "You could vary the [composition]," he told *Automotive News* in July, "to achieve energy management during a high-speed crash." He hoped he might even be able to achieve "barrier survivability," at forty to fifty miles per hour, which meant that a passenger would crawl out unhurt from head-on crashes at those speeds.

This safety concept was built into the legend of the car, and actively encouraged by DeLorean himself. While it was still untested, people who should have known better were claiming that one could survive an eighty-mph crash. As it turned out, the ERM process supplied just three minor parts for the final version of the DMC-12: all unimportant bits on the bumpers—the front bumper reinforcement, the rear panel, and the license plate bezel.

Collins' design work on the car, however, included the ERM. The idea he and DeLorean worked out was based on a one-piece body molded from ERM. Over this shell would be placed a skin of stainless steel, thus avoiding the need for paint. The engine would either be in the middle of the car or in the rear," so the entire front end can be devoted to energy management in a crash." The light weight of the plastic also meant the car would meet DeLorean's ambitious goals for fuel economy, which were now defined as thirty miles per gallon on the highway and twenty mpg at city street speeds. It also meant lower tooling costs—"fewer holes," said Collins happily, "a lot less nuts and bolts."

On August 18 *Automotive News* presented to the world the first glimpse of the dream car. It was just a frontal flash, with a large "DSV" on the front. The gull-wings were not in evidence—they were still on the "secret" list. But in the same issue, DeLorean's broader strategy was revealed. Although he was not quoted directly in the article, he had written down his thoughts for Collins to ascribe to him in the interview. In view of later events, it makes for ironic reading.

One word to me describes our car's concept, and that is "responsible"—no gimmicks and no compromises. It must demonstrate a responsibility for conservation of energy, human life and human resources. Responsibility also implies recognizing the customer's desires and needs, not only in the product but also in service after the sale.

Quality in all aspects, combined with durability and serviceability are paramount. I do not feel any of these needs compromise a vehicle and force it to be either unattractive or undesirable, but quite the contrary. . . .

Today's technology will allow, even encourage, all of these if you decide on your goal. Further, we feel in a position to provide an enlightened response to the needs of society without being encumbered by numerous constraints.

So there it was, spelled out for the first time. John DeLorean's dream car was to be the great ethical machine that General Motors had refused to allow him to build. It was to be safe, beautiful, economical, and what the customer wanted. What more could you ask? John DeLorean probably believed it at the time. Collins certainly did, and was doing his engineering best to make it so.

The steady erosion of this ideal into a more commonplace and unspectacular car—what Collins called the "stainless-steel Lotus"—lay years ahead. It will be June 1981 before the first DMC-12s are delivered to customers and before the car industry and the buyers realize just what a second-rate car John DeLorean ended up producing.

In these summer months of 1975 though, DeLorean was hoping to be in production by the 1978 model year—September 1977—and even with his ingrained optimism he realized that it would be a tight race. Money would help him meet his time goals; money *was* time, money was breathing room.

He had gotten one injection of help a year previously; another such windfall was unlikely. Late in 1974, to his surprise, Allstate Insurance Corporation, the insurance subsidiary of the giant Sears Roebuck merchandising chain, commissioned the John Z. DeLorean Corporation to prepare a study on car safety standards for the future.

Like other insurance companies, Allstate was alarmed that the post-oil-embargo rush toward fuel economy might have the unhappy side effect of reducing automobile safety standards. DeLorean's early

findings confirmed Allstate's fears; if Washington's goal of a 40 percent gain in fuel efficiency were to be reached by the 1980 target year,
there was a real danger that highway deaths and injuries could rise by
that same figure. There were things that could be done, DeLorean
argued, to prevent this. Cars could be designed for more fuel efficiency
in ways that did not sacrifice safety in the race to reduce vehicle
weight. Airbags could be installed in the front seats of all new cars.
He went further: his research showed that a delay of just three years
in making airbags standard equipment in U.S. cars would cost $18.8
billion in "societal loss" due to injuries and fatalities.

But with airbags and other safety-oriented design features, it was
within the technological reach of the U.S. motor industry to produce
a car that not only was fuel efficient and affordable, but could also be
run into a brick wall at 40 mph with no serious harm to its occupants.
Here it was then, another case of DeLorean billing the possible as an
almost certainty.

But the 40 mph crash survival assertion would be repeated later by
Allstate's chairman, Archie R. Boe, as he and DeLorean testified in
Washington at a Senate hearing on car safety and the energy crisis.
Allstate was so pleased with the early DeLorean work and the press
coverage of his safety remarks that they commissioned him to do the
design work on the very elements that might be included in such a
safety vehicle.

"It was a cooperative program," an Allstate spokesman said after a
recent search through the records. "Between us and the DeLorean
Corporation, in the construction of an advanced concept two-passenger safety car. The objective of the program was to demonstrate that
a truly advanced automotive design can provide the consumer with
the unique combination of product attributes that include advanced
safety features coupled with outstanding styling, excellent performance and superior fuel economy—and that it could be produced at
a reasonable price."

In Allstate's now dusty and forgotten files, the joint project targeted
a car "for a 2,200 pound weight class with fuel economy in the range
of thirty miles per gallon. It would have increased protection in those
side, rear and low-speed front end accident situations. The fuel tank
would be centrally located. A rear-mounted engine is planned. They
fulfilled the contract with a design that met our agreed-upon goals and
the design was used as our proof that such a safe car could be produced
right then in 1975."

The cost to Allstate was a reasonable $50,000; in return, it got several batches of creative designs for seating and structural design alternatives. Allstate would not own the designs by any means; rather, they would be able to show them off and claim credit for helping fund the concept so that some future manufacturer—Ford, Chrysler, yes even General Motors itself—might agree to take any or all of the innovations. But John DeLorean now had those innovations; Allstate had paid the overhead on his design work. In November 1975 DeLorean leaked more of the details of the new safety car he was going to put into production under his own name:

- The car would weigh around 2,200 pounds;
- Fuel economy would be thirty mpg on the highway and twenty mpg in the city;
- It would have an integral body construction based on a new, advanced ERM plastic technique;
- The car would have solid barrier protection for crashes at speeds exceeding minimum federal government standards;
- There would be airbags for driver and front-seat passenger;
- Front-end structure would be solely devoted to "energy management" of head-on collisions which, according to the statement, represent about 30 percent of serious road crashes;
- The foam-filled rear structure would offer similar crash protection;
- The centrally located fuel tank would be a design feature;
- The windshield would be located well in front of the occupants.

Allstate's Archie Boe apparently was even more delighted. Later that November, Bill Collins announced that Allstate had provided another $500,000 grant for the building of three "safety car" prototypes: metal, glass, and plastic full-sized machines to be tested against the realities of the wind tunnel, the test track, and public taste. But even with Allstate inadvertently footing the bills for the initial design work, DeLorean knew he was still short of money. He needed more, much more. Grand Prix of America had gone bankrupt and several of his Detroit friends (not to mention his brother) had been burned in the deal. No, Detroit was not the place to look for new funds.

As he had in the past and would again in the future, DeLorean turned to his hulking friend Roy Nesseth.

Men like Roy W. Nesseth pockmark the business landscape of all countries; they skirt along the edge of the law, preferring the fruitful shallows of the gray areas of legality. But they sometimes dart over into outright lawlessness provided they can get back quickly to the other side. Respectability is a joke to the Nesseths of the world; the posturing and public relations sensitivities of John DeLorean were just so much con job. Not that Roy Nesseth didn't enjoy a good con. He also was equally good at the veiled or not-so-veiled threat if someone stood up to him.

By the late summer of 1975, DeLorean had worked out a business and personal relationship with Nesseth that was a variation of the classic Tom-and-Jerry, good-guy/bad-guy routine used by all skilled manipulators, be they teams of detectives or swindlers. As Pete Avrea had experienced, a heated complaint about Nesseth often resulted in DeLorean unceremoniously yanking his colleague out of a situation; but never completely out.

Nesseth's criminal past goes back to 1954 when he was convicted of forgery and fraud in car sales to two elderly couples from the California dealership where he had been a salesman. An affable six-footer, Nesseth had just the mix of charm and chutzpah, when he wanted to show it, that DeLorean lacked. Roy could establish rapport. By the time the two were introduced through the General Motors dealers' network, Nesseth had become the manager of the largest Chevrolet dealership in America, the Williams Chevrolet firm of Norwalk, California. *

In one of the many suits filed against him, Nesseth was described as "the best auto salesman and closer in the field"; the last a tribute to his ability to get reluctant or undecided prospects to close the deal and buy.

In 1968, a year before Nesseth and DeLorean met, he convinced a wealthy widow, Hazel Upton Dean, to put him in charge of her extensive properties, which included a redwood sawmill; a ranch; a thoroughbred horse farm; a large art collection; a home in Palm Springs, California; and an apartment in Beverly Hills. Mrs. Dean had had a heart attack and she wanted to rest at her Palm Springs home undisturbed.

But Hazel Dean soon suspected something was wrong, that Nesseth

---

* People v. Nesseth 127 C.A. 2d 712, 1954.

was selling off her properties without her knowledge and pocketing the proceeds. He had taken over her Beverly Hills apartment and was using it as a party place; among the guests who had stayed at the apartment, she learned later, was John DeLorean. She sued, charging that Nesseth had defrauded her of property worth several million dollars; at one point she stole back one of her horses that had been spirited away to another farm. She still maintains that the grand piano from her apartment is in Nesseth's Huntington Beach, California, home. Since 1980, that same home has been listed as the property of John Z. DeLorean.

John Thomas, of La Jolla, California, an attorney who has made something of a career of representing Mrs. Dean and other people defrauded by Nesseth, says, "He has no assets listed, titled or recorded in his name. This makes him virtually litigation proof, or rather he is recovery proof, penalty proof. Yet, he enjoys a high standard of living and I allege upon information and belief that he earns very large amounts of money and has significant assets, all of which are deeply hidden from his creditors."

While DeLorean is owner of record of Nesseth's California house, it is not the first swap the two have made to confuse potential litigants. In early summer of 1975, DeLorean transferred control of the Delaware corporation that owned the Pine Creek Ranch near Salmon, Idaho, to Roy Nesseth. The ranch was the thousand-acre property he had bought for Kelly Harmon to turn into a holiday camp for ghetto kids. Although he often bragged about how he ran *two* summer camps for poor children, the truth is that DeLorean rarely visited the ranch while they were married and he stopped going there altogether after Kelly left him.

Nesseth scouted the region until he found a likely prospect to buy the ranch. Clark Higley and his wife were plainspoken farm folks who had turned a small homestead claim into a 500-acre potato farm. With their profits they bought a $125,000 house on the Snake River and two boutiques run by his wife.

As Higley tells it, "We wanted to consolidate and find someplace big enough so that my two boys and their families could come and work it with me and make a living for us all. I was getting on in years and wanted something that did not take every waking minute to take care of. DeLorean and Nesseth, they mesmerize you. They told me everything I wanted to hear. When we first started talking, they would take us to dinner and treat us super-good."

What Higley did not know was that Nesseth already had sold off some of the cattle and that DeLorean had secured a $1 million mortgage on the ranch from the Metropolitan Life Insurance Company. As an aside, the local Metropolitan representatives recommended that the property be valued for purposes of the loan for only $800,000, still half a million dollars more than DeLorean had paid for it five years before. But DeLorean was skilled at using his old ties to GM when he could; Metropolitan was a major health and life insurer at the car company, so a quick call to the head office helped boost the value of the loan on the Pine Creek Ranch.

With Nesseth rapidly quoting figures from past deals as confirmation, DeLorean suggested a way that Higley and he could construct a deal so as to minimize the tax consequences of the sale. Perhaps more importantly, although Higley would only realize this later, the DeLorean deal also did away with the necessity to do the normal title search that would have revealed the Metropolitan mortgage.

The deal worked like this: Higley was to rent the ranch with an option to buy. DeLorean was to take possession of Higley's potato farm (which he sold in 1981 for $800,000) plus he received a $300,000 cash payment from Higley for 1,100 head of cattle and various ranch equipment. Higley paid $375,000 in rent for two years, during which time the light slowly dawned that he was being taken for a very long ride by DeLorean and Nesseth.

First of all, the cattle and farm equipment—like the ranch itself—were already security against DeLorean borrowings. In the case of the cows and machinery, DeLorean had borrowed $300,000 from the First National Bank of Idaho. Instead of using the $300,000 in cash which Higley had paid him to pay off the loan, DeLorean gave the money to Nesseth so that he and a brother could open a Chevrolet dealership in Lewiston, Idaho. The dealership had its franchise yanked two years later by General Motors "for no longer serving the sales and service needs of customers."

Ultimately Higley, during one of his many court actions (most still pending), did get back most of the $300,000 he had paid after the bank collected it from DeLorean. But he was not so lucky with Metropolitan, which foreclosed because DeLorean never made a payment on the outstanding mortgage loan. Higley and his wife were finally forced off the Pine Creek Ranch in 1980; later that year, DeLorean repurchased it for $1.7 million from Metropolitan, thereby settling the mortgage against him. And a few months after that he sold the ranch again for $2.1 million.

The immediate yield of $1 million from Metropolitan's loan, plus the $300,000 cash that went to Nesseth, plus the regular monthly payments Higley made, all served to ease DeLorean's ravenous appetite for cash. For the moment.

The Higleys and DeLorean and Nesseth are still tied up in Idaho courts, but there is little hope that the Idaho farmer will ever recover his losses.

"It just ruined us. He and Roy changed lawyers on us all the time and that kept the court from pushing the trial ahead. They wouldn't pay their lawyers and the next thing you knew here was a new set of them asking for delays," Higley says.

"I will say Mrs. DeLorean was nice. When she was out, she and I would talk many times. I don't think she knew what all was going on with him. She told one of our friends that if I didn't get that Pine Creek Ranch, DeLorean would never go to heaven. Well, I never got that ranch."

By the beginning of 1976, DeLorean was talking about production being "less than two years away." Over the winter the first prototype was built. The body was tested at the Turin Polytechnic and Caltech wind tunnels. Collins used a computer to do a body-stiffness analysis, tire and suspension analysis, and simulations of what would happen to passengers during a head-on crash of up to 40 miles per hour. He also used a computer program to work out the four-wheel independent suspension.

This prototype was powered by a transversely mounted Citroën Powerplant engine. It also featured a high doorsill, which was said to provide extra side protection, but in fact was largely a structural necessity. The car had no main chassis, but rather, it had two subchasses —front and rear. DeLorean was relying heavily on the strength of his new plastic material to keep the car rigid on the road.

The prototype also featured an on-board computer with a digital readout. Few of these features were to survive development into the production car, but the basic size and shape changed only marginally. The prototype was 165.1 inches long and 72.7 inches wide—the production car was 166 inches long and exactly six feet wide. The final version ended up just one inch lower than the original 46 inches. And 2.2 inches were chopped off the wheelbase to leave it at 95 inches.

As for the all-important weight of the car, the prototype was designed to weigh a light 2,200 pounds, compared with the 3,541-pound Corvette. The production car was to weigh in at 2,844 pounds as ERM faded from the scene and the engineers installed an all-steel backbone chassis plus other unplanned additions.

True, all cars change between the prototype and production models. It would be unreasonable to expect that DeLorean's hastily put together designs would not be amended considerably—why else build prototypes? The significance of the changes to the DeLorean car, however, is that he was openly boasting about its "uniqueness," with every individual feature specifically designed for safety and durability.

John DeLorean accused General Motors and the whole auto industry of pulling a great con job on the American public by selling it the same car for twenty years with nothing more than a minor face-lift each year. His car was going to be revolutionary: safe, rustproof, economical, maintenance-free. It was going to be radically different, an ethical car.

Over the next four years there was a steady series of compromises on feature after feature. Each so-called "unique" element dropped away. Nothing new replaced them. Everything that was used had been tried and tested and had been done before. What hit the American market in June 1981 was a car that was not at all bad; it looked good, behaved relatively well, and had some useful safety features.

But it was a very different machine underneath its stainless-steel skin from the car John DeLorean promised the American public. It was just an ordinary car. It was the "stainless-steel Lotus" that not even the Lotus people were very excited about.

All through 1976, however, DeLorean was making bigger—not smaller—claims for the car. When it was equipped with an airbag, he boasted, occupants could walk away from an 80 mph head-on collision, and he was hoping to raise that to 100 mph. Later prospectuses were to quote "occupant survival" in a fixed-barrier crash at a speed of approximately 40 mph.

In March he told *Fortune* that the first model would be a two-seater, midengined sports car priced about $1,000 more than the Corvette, which then sold for $9,000. He also forecast he would be in production "sometime in 1978." His plans for adding a sedan version were first mentioned in this story too. In the article, DeLorean came back to his Mercedes theme. "My dream is to build a very small version of

Mercedes. I look at GM as the Sears, the mass merchandiser of this business, and Ford as the J. C. Penney. We want to be the Tiffany."

In June 1976 DeLorean rented Detroit's Cobo Hall and lined up an unmarked, nonrunning DMC-12 prototype with three of its potential competitors: a Corvette, still the only American-made sports car, a Datsun 280-Z, and a Porsche 911. He hired Research One of South-field, Michigan, to prepare a questionnaire and mail it out to 6,000 sports car owners in the Detroit metropolitan area. About 25 percent of them replied.

DeLorean's new marketing director, David R. T. Wood, pared the replies down to 350 people he thought would have a lively and knowl-edgeable interest in the car. He invited them to Cobo Hall to evaluate the DeLorean DMC-12. This was the first time anyone from the general public was allowed to look at the car. Ostensibly the idea was to incorporate the results from a "blind" research clinic into the car. But it appears to have been much more a part of DeLorean's steady promotion strategy, designed to create more and more excitement and interest, getting people to talk about his "revolutionary" car.

The gull-wing door was the central point of comment, not all of it favorable.

"Just like the Bricklin, huh?" remarked one furious sports car buff to Wood. (Wood resigned three months later to join Renault as vice president of marketing.)

DeLorean still talked about starting production in 1978, although there was still no definite plan for a factory site. It had not yet been decided what power unit to use on the car and virtually no work had been done on testing. It was the type of unrealistic optimism that was to haunt the project right through to its end—and even beyond.

4

THE
DeLOREAN MOTOR COMPANY

During the autumn and winter of 1975–1976, DeLorean was racing from one crisis to another, demonstrating his enormous capacity for hard work and his willingness to push ahead in the face of odds that would daunt frailer men. He was on the verge of the next step up the money-raising ladder and nothing must block his path. The kind of money he needed for the car could not be just swindled away from some gullible mark; it would have to be raised out in the open. He needed help.

Thomas W. Kimmerly was a sixty-two-year-old partner in the three-man law firm of Kimmerly, Gans & Shaler; their offices were in the same four-story glass and steel office building as those of John DeLorean, on Long Lake Road in Bloomfield Hills.

Kimmerly was the son of a well-known Detroit business executive with the Burroughs Corporation. A quiet, diffident man, he was swept off his feet by the glamour and purpose in DeLorean's manner. There was also another element to Kimmerly's personality—he was a car enthusiast and had worked as a legal adviser on both of the major new-car ventures mounted after World War II—the Kaiser, which never really got off the ground, and the Bricklin, which had gone belly-up in Canada earlier in 1975.

Kimmerly also had done a few minor bits of legal work for De-Lorean, and when DeLorean was looking for an office for his fledgling company he had suggested space where his own offices were located in a building on Long Lake Road in Bloomfield Hills. Soon DeLorean used him more and more to discuss deals and car ideas. But it was one day, as they were both standing at the office men's room urinals that (as Kimmerly later recalled) DeLorean suddenly said to him, "Let's start a car company."

In later years, those inside the DeLorean corporate structure would say that John DeLorean trusted Thomas Kimmerly more than his wife, Cristina. In any event, it was undeniably true that DeLorean turned over to Kimmerly the complex task of raising the money needed to keep the car venture going and to provide him with the cash flow he needed to live like a man at the top.

Kimmerly's first act was to create the DeLorean Motor Company (DMC). In January 1974 DeLorean founded his own personal corporation, the John Z. DeLorean Corporation, which was known by the acronym JZDC. In April 1975 JZDC had formed Composite Technology Corporation to take a license for the ERM process, but the rights to that license, while held by CTC, were also held by JZDC.

In one of the few traceable instances where John DeLorean can be said to have invested any of his own money, JZDC was capitalized at $20,000, and he had lent the company another $350,000 from his own resources.

In October 1975 Kimmerly incorporated DMC and transferred to its capital stock from JZDC all the design work done by Collins and his staff (and paid for by Allstate) and the rights to the ERM licenses —all assigned a value of $3.5 million.

At the end of the month, Kimmerly moved to set up yet another corporate structure for the purposes of raising money. The shift of assets out of JZDC and into DMC had accomplished one important purpose: DeLorean still retained total control over the assets, but now there was an intervening corporate layer between those assets and the public, not to mention the law.

By forming the DeLorean Sports Car Partnership (DSCP) in December 1975, Kimmerly created a vehicle into which outside investors could contribute large sums of money to help with testing and research on the project. Once it was set up, DeLorean again transferred the ERM method and car design work, with their established worth of $3.5 million, to DSCP, where it would be matched by cash investments worth just a shade more than $3.5 million. DeLorean retained a 49.9 percent interest in DSCP, which gave him unchallenged control.

The attraction to investors, who were being asked to put up minimum amounts of $100,000, was that as a research and development project, every dollar of investment reduced one's taxable income that year by one dollar. For an investor caught in the 70 percent tax bracket that prevailed in those days, the opportunity meant he could use only 30 cents of his own cash and 70 cents of money that would have been taxed away by Washington, to buy something with a nominal worth of one dollar, multiplied of course by $100,000. Plus the fact that there was an option to buy shares in future stages of the venture at preferred prices, and there was the romance of an exciting car development project. The money came in easily: some Merrill Lynch Pierce Fenner and Smith traders formed a special group and invested $450,000 in one chunk.

So now DeLorean had $3.5 million at his command, but even that was just the first installment if there were to be a serious effort to design, produce, and market a car. Indeed, the project was acquiring a breathless momentum of its own. People whom John DeLorean had never heard of volunteered enthusiastic support; others wanted to give him money, almost on a no-questions-asked basis. His preaching and criticism about business ethics and on the need for an ethical car had struck nerves all over America, where people who were worried about the economic future and who lamented Detroit's hard times were just waiting for a savior to support.

But if a car were going to be built, as much as $70 to $90 million would have to be raised. The project would have to go public, to offer stock on the open market and to attract a large number of cash-rich investors. For all his corporate skills, Kimmerly could not handle the flotation of a national public stock offering alone. He needed plenty of legal and financial help. Detroit attorney Malcolm Gushee was brought in to do the legal legwork involved in clearing such a major stock offering through the Securities and Exchange Commission and through the various regulatory agencies of the fifty states.

DMC also needed an expert financial planner and strategist. Robert W. Dewey had been in financial management with General Motors, and during 1974 and 1975 DeLorean had frequently turned to him for advice. Dewey recalls:

"John would call me up every once in a while and say, 'Are you having fun, Bob?' and I would say, 'Well, I'm working here.' And he'd say, 'Why don't you swing by some Saturday morning or on the way home from work and see what I'm doing.' And it was right on my way home, so I'd drop in from time to time and he'd bring me up to speed on how the project was coming. He said he was looking for a chief financial officer and at the appropriate time he'd like me to consider it."

When he finally came aboard, Dewey immediately buckled down

to the backbreaking task of getting ready to launch DMC's fund-raising effort for the kind of seed money that would make the company a serious manufacturing contender. For Dewey, the lure of being chief financial officer of an exciting new company overcame any personal misgivings he may have had about DeLorean.

"No, I didn't like him personally. Not many people did. But it was a chance to do something, to do it the way it should be done—at least I thought it could be at the time—and I couldn't pass it up," Dewey said.

Another part of the explanation is money. If John DeLorean paid himself extremely well ($125,000), he also paid his top executives very well, with the promise of more; he had to lure them away from the "golden handcuffs" of stock bonuses and various options that could make a senior GM executive a very wealthy man when he retired. Dewey got $70,000 a year, plus stock options, as secretary-treasurer of DMC.

But the key to DeLorean's ability to recruit top men was their own overwhelming wish, as Dewey phrased it, "to do something the way it should be done." The frustrations of corporate life are many, but none can be so galling as the pervasive feeling among the average senior management personnel that they are prevented from doing the best job they can within their capabilities.

The next man DeLorean recruited to the team was C. R. "Dick" Brown, a solid, quiet man who had been the U.S. chief executive of the Mazda Motor Company of Japan when it located an assembly plant in California in the early 1970s and entered the U.S. market as a sales competitor. He was hired as vice president for operations at $100,000 a year. He not only played an important role lining up potential investors, but he would also be in charge of planning the early phases of manufacturing and marketing through a dealer's net-work. Brown recalls:

> This is a very self-serving remark, but I didn't join because I thought John DeLorean could do it. I felt *I* could do it. Then why do it with him? Because he had a stronger, more interna-tional name—a General Motors name if you will. And it was his concept. I didn't really care that much for him, he was a braggart and a loudmouth and as time went on I never saw a shred of evidence of this engineering genius he was supposed to have. He

may have had it, but he never spent any of it, or any time, on the car project's design—that was Bill Collins. Dewey was the financial man. What I could provide for him was the know-how of putting the mechanics of a car company together and to establish the dealer organization.

So, in early 1976, the core of the DeLorean car executive team was in place: Kimmerly, Brown, Collins, and Dewey. There were fifteen employees now in the Long Lake Road offices, and the tempo was picking up with design and testing, money-raising, and plans for making and selling the DMC-12 moving ahead at a rapid pace.

In the meantime Roy Nesseth had been busy elsewhere. Kenneth Dahlinger was a Wichita, Kansas, businessman who was an early investor in the Pizza Hut fast-food chain. He pulled out a $450,000 profit and in 1974 reinvested it in a Pontiac dealership in this town. Later, he added a Cadillac franchise to the dealership and for a few months was doing all right.

But the 1974–1975 recession really bit into car sales, and by early 1976, Dahlinger had run up a dangerous level of debt at the Kansas State Bank and Trust. In May 1976 bank officials presented him with an unusual restructuring plan to keep his company in business and their loans secure. John DeLorean, the well-known ex-GM executive, was interested in taking over the dealership, investing new capital. He would put in his own man, a Roy Nesseth, as president, but Dahlinger's name would remain on the franchise and he could stay on as vice president.

Dahlinger was initially surprised by the deal, even though he accepted DeLorean's demand for anonymity on the grounds that he was still "a controversial figure at GM." The bank accepted Nesseth as the front man, too.

J. V. Lentell, the president of Kansas State Bank, says, "DeLorean didn't want his name on the franchise because the GM people were not too friendly. Nesseth and DeLorean were both very impressive."

Dahlinger agrees, and he still calls Nesseth "Mr. Personality" in a rueful way. "He was the best charmer I've ever seen."

The terms of the deal were that Dahlinger was to collect $80,000 for his interest in $4,000 monthly installments. He was also to look after the dealership in Nesseth's absence. At once, the deal turned sour. Nesseth ordered up an American Express card in the dealership's name. He ran up thousands of dollars' worth of champagne and hotel bills in Wichita, all of which was duly paid for by Dahlinger Pontiac-Cadillac.

Worse still was the rush of checks in and out of the dealership's accounts. More than $1 million in checks was written to Saf-Guard Systems (not Saf-Guard Products, where the actual work was going on), and checks from Saf-Guard Systems were coming back. When the final litigation ended years later, the Kansas Bank was to recover $300,000 from the Saf-Guard check-kiting scheme alone. In the final accounting, there were even checks to Clark Higley in Idaho as Nesseth and DeLorean kept draining funds out of the dealership with the high volume of incoming and outgoing checks.

Cash was not the only thing that Dahlinger lost. In plusher times, Dahlinger had restored a classic 1956 Mercedes 300SL, a design unique for its use of gull-wing doors. To cut considerable insurance on the car, it was registered to the dealership, and when DeLorean borrowed it, ostensibly to help promote the DMC-12, Dahlinger never saw the car again. After six months of trying to persuade incredulous bank officials that something terrible was going on, Dahlinger literally walked away from his dealership and moved away from Wichita. Later he sued Nesseth and collected $80,000.

But for the next three years, at least, the Dahlinger dealership remained a plentiful cash cow that DeLorean and his henchmen milked with great regularity.

In the meantime the finishing touches had been put on the DeLorean Sports Car Partnership fund-raising effort. Brown, who had valuable connections with car dealers and potential investors all over the country, had rounded up most of them. There were several early-warning signals that Brown now recognizes he should have heeded.

"I gave one presentation to a group in Palm Springs and a dealer there, I knew the guy real well, came up to me later and said he had been involved with DeLorean in something called Grand Prix of America three years before. The guy said, 'I went through all this with that guy and I wouldn't touch him with a ten-foot pole again.' "

Another signal, symptomatic of DeLorean's attitude toward money —other people's money—came when the full $3.5 million had been raised for the DSCP; he took a $200,000 consulting fee off the top.

If Brown thought about DeLorean's open greed at the time, he obviously did not spend much time worrying about it. There were more important things to do as spring turned to summer in 1976. For the project to succeed, DeLorean had to get four elements in place.

There was the design for the car, and under Bill Collins that was now coming along well. Then there was the money for it—a bigger problem but not insurmountable. At least there was breathing room, financially, for the present. And DeLorean was convinced that the investors' enthusiastic response when the DMC-12 was no more than an idea would really mushroom now that there was something tangible to show them. The third element was the dealership networks, and Dick Brown was working full time on them now that the DSCP had been fully funded.

The fourth factor in the equation was a location where he could build his car. He needed a factory—a large, new one built specially for him. Initially he left this problem on the back burner and tackled the other elements. But the day was fast coming when he would have to give the problem his full attention if he were going to have a car at all.

As the months passed during 1976 and into early 1977, the new DeLorean team members worked on crash schedules to get their individual special functions organized. Periodically, Brown flew in from the Los Angeles suburb of Anaheim, where the DMC West Coast offices were located, to meet with Dewey and Kimmerly in Detroit. There were other meetings there with Collins and the rest to plot the final strategy to finance and finish the design work on the prototypes. DeLorean himself was making increasingly frequent commuting trips to New York City. The idea was that he would meet prospective clients and keep up his media contacts. His friend Herb Siegel let DeLorean and a small staff set up housekeeping at the Chris-Craft headquarters there.

By this time DeLorean was stepping up his lifestyle and spending. Without any formal discussion with the others, he decided to locate his major headquarters in New York, and he and Cristina were often busy searching for an apartment. They finally settled on a duplex about to be sold by Johnny Carson. The superstar had moved his program to Hollywood, and his marriage to second wife Joanne Carson had broken up. Carson and DeLorean had met previously at various show business social functions in Los Angeles; the negotiations over the apartment caused Carson and the DeLoreans to become fast friends. It was to be an expensive friendship for the entertainer.

At the same time an interesting pattern was developing in the relationship between DeLorean and the team of Brown, Dewey, and Collins as the weeks wore on. Increasingly, each of the three sought to isolate DeLorean from contact or interference in his own task; each felt strongly that DeLorean had little to contribute and in some cases was a dangerous liability when he suddenly took an interest in the task at hand.

Collins had the least trouble because DeLorean was most secure around engineers and had confidence in his designer. But Collins also came to feel that DeLorean really was not very interested in the crucial drudgery of the design sequence. Indeed, the suspicion grew that DeLorean was indifferent about the details of his own car now that its basic shape and configuration had been determined.

Bob Dewey, however, took special pains to keep DeLorean away from the delicate negotiations he was conducting during that time with the Securities and Exchange Commission in Washington and with the various securities regulation agencies of the states. In December 1975 and January 1976 the DeLorean Sports Car Partnership (DSCP) had attracted $3.5 million from various investor friends of Dick Brown—dealers who were interested in getting in on the ground floor of the company and the Merrill Lynch brokers' group. But that amount would soon be spent and another, and this time public, stock offering would have to be made.

In order to make a stock offering, one must first register it with the SEC. While the agency takes no stand on the potential profits or losses of an investment opportunity, it will not register a stock offering for sale to the American public unless it meets certain standards of fair dealings on the part of the offering company. An SEC attorney who followed the DeLorean case file explained later:

> The registration statement is exhaustive. A stock issuer has to list everything from the pay of the president to the kind of widgets they are going to manufacture. Those statements are usually handled by examiners and our [legal] office rarely sees them unless there is a problem.
>
> Now, our office became involved in DeLorean before the first registration statement was filed because there were a number of

previous private financings and the [DSCP] partnership. There was a technical question in our minds as to whether we should consider the previous private financings as part of this upcoming public offering, to integrate them.

So, before submitting the registration statement for the upcoming offering, DeLorean's lawyer came to us and asked whether we would integrate. They were very good about that, it was the smart thing to do, rather than let us find out about the private offering later. So we said give us the details of both financings. We wanted to look at that private offering because sometimes a company can use a private offering to enrich its officers and majority shareholders at the expense of the smaller participants. In addition there is a technical requirement that purchasers in private offerings have to hang onto their securities for a specific time limit—you can't have them selling their private acquired shares in the middle of the public offering.

Also, just before their appearance, sometime in 1974, the SEC had finally gotten around to setting out the specific guidelines or checklist it wanted to use when reviewing private financings prior to public offerings. But in talking with DeLorean's lawyers, we got the impression that they were still operating on our old procedures, without the new changes.

But even after the initial slow start and confusion, Kimmerly and attorney Malcolm Gushee were able to submit a proper registration statement for filing in the spring of 1976. What happens next, in SEC parlance, is known as the quiet period. This is the interval between the time the company submits its stock sale plan for registration and when the agency clears the plan so the company can actually get out there and sell the stock to the waiting public. During this quiet time the company may not do anything that can be seen as a promotion of its upcoming share offering.

It was during this critical period that DeLorean got a break. The National Automobile Dealers Association was slated to hold its annual convention and car show in New Orleans that June. DeLorean had not only booked an exhibitor's booth at the show, but he also planned to have one of the DMC-12 prototypes on display and to use a special minitheater to show a promotional film to potential dealer-investors who might later become part of the nationwide DeLorean network that would be so vital to the car's marketing success. But wouldn't all this violate the SEC regulations?

The SEC attorney noted:

> We let them go to the convention and perhaps we can be criticized for being too liberal in hindsight. But after all, the SEC is not here to *prevent* stock offerings. Our mandate from Congress is to *help* companies issue shares to the public that meet standards of adequate disclosure. So we looked at the DeLorean movie and it appeared to be a fairly bare-bones engineering film. We also permitted them to have the prototype on display and to hand out a pamphlet on the car as long as it did not refer to the pending stock offering.
>
> Our reasoning was that enough time would elapse after the convention to cool off any hyping of the market. Also, to deny them attendance at the dealers' convention would probably have done them real harm and that we should not do. Also you should keep in mind that we had no knowledge and no way to know about Mr. DeLorean's legal problems, nor did we examine the reorganization of the company prior to the registration statement. Perhaps we should have. Perhaps we *would* have, but again no one came forward to tell us about these potential problems and we have no investigative facilities to go out and search every potential stock seller in America.

The attorney was referring to an occurrence that might have clouded investor enthusiasm—not to mention the agency's cooperative attitude—had it been widely known at the time. In February 1976 Pete Avrea had had enough and filed suit against DeLorean and Nesseth, alleging fraudulent behavior and demanding the return of ownership of his patents.

Throughout the winter of 1975–1976, his complaints about the falloff in royalty revenue and disturbing rumors of cheap license sales by DeLorean had come to a head. Nesseth returned to Phoenix with the news that he had purchased control of Saf-Guard Systems from DeLorean for $1. "From now on you're not dealing with Mr. DeLorean anymore, you're dealing with me."

Had Avrea known what he was in for, he might have walked away from Saf-Guard right then. It would take him four years of tedious on-again, off-again court struggles and $250,000 in legal fees and deposition costs to reach a dead end. In the meantime there were the threats and harassment.

"I can't prove who it was, but my wife believes it was Roy Nesseth who would call the house and tell her to tell me to drop the suits. If I were sure it was he, if I had heard the calls myself I would know what to do about it," Avrea says today. "But it hurt her health; she became afraid to go out and start the car in case it was a bomb meant for me. I had to do something."

And in the end, Pete Avrea gave up. He paid $400,000 to De-Lorean for the return of his patents and thereby released another $250,000 in royalties that had been impounded by the courts—royalties that were immediately turned over to the John Z. DeLorean Corporation, not to the official owner of record, Roy Nesseth. In the meantime, during most of 1976 and 1977, the rush of kited checks reached a flood tide between Saf-Guard and Dahlinger Pontiac-Cadillac. As much as $1 million in meaningless checks may have been generated among the various DeLorean enterprises, with as much as $250,000 from just the car dealership and Saf-Guard disappearing in the process. It may have been "quiet time" insofar as the SEC was concerned, but it was business as usual for Nesseth and De-Lorean.

On the twenty-ninth of June 1977, the SEC finally permitted registration of the DeLorean Motor Company Share offering. The offering sought to attract 400 investors who also wanted to be DMC-12 dealers, to contribute $10 million in capital to the project. The minimum $25,000 investment not only bought 5,000 shares of DeLorean Motor Company stock but it also secured a franchise as a dealer. The investor was presumed to be an existing operating car dealer—this was important since it provided the showroom and service facilities so necessary to successful automobile marketing, as well as the kind of local name-identification for the DMC-12 that is equally important to sales. The dealer-investor was also committed to sell between 100 and 150 (depending on the size of his dealership volume) of the DMC-12s during the first two years of the company's production run. Although this part of the investment agreement could not be enforced, it served its purpose in supporting DeLorean's claim that two years' production run had been sold out before the factory was built. In the year that followed, the stock offering would be only moderately successful; 206 dealers instead of the needed 400 came forward, and the $5.16 million in capital inflow from them, however welcome, was not enough to put the project over the top.

Part of the problem lay in the ambitious nature of the sales and investment plan cooked up by Brown, Dewey, and Kimmerly. The DMC-12 could be the instant success it had to be only if it could plug into an already existing network of dealers, more importantly the best dealers who sold only the most prestigious models in every major city and town across the United States and Canada. What that meant was that the DeLorean Motor Company had to sell shares on a nationwide basis and it had to attract dealers the same way. Normally, attempts to raise money through public stock offerings concentrate on those regions of the United States where heavy investment capital is found in the greatest abundance, or in the home state where the company will do business. The SEC registration statement clears the way for the stock issuers to seek the permission of the various state regulatory agencies where the shares will actually be sold.

Financial officer Dewey recalls: "It was a unique offering in that we went to all fifty states. Very, very few stocks are sold in every state in the union, but we had to because we wanted a dealer network in every state. Normally you don't do it that way, because each state has its standards. In some, once you are effective with the SEC in Washington, you are effective in that state. In others, like Georgia, you send them a check for $250 and you are effective and can sell shares in Georgia. In Nevada you can sell anything."

But some states have what are known as blue-sky laws, which impose a stricter standard of fairness than the federal standard. Under blue-sky laws it is not enough just to disclose the facts in an adequate and candid manner. While you may be able to sell shares as you want in Nevada and Georgia, you come up against a very tough standard indeed in states such as Texas, Wisconsin, and California.

William Kuntz, executive director of the Texas Securities Commission, handled the negotiations that followed when Dewey and Kimmerly arrived in Austin in January 1978 to file their offering there. Texas was an important state for the DeLorean offering—there were plenty of high-rollers there, and the rich market of Dallas, Houston, and Fort Worth was going to be a central point of the car's sales campaign.

Kuntz explains:

There was a Kansas judge who said there should be protection under the law against people who would sell us nothing but the blue sky. The SEC in Washington does have a standard of disclosure, but you can give them a prospectus where you disclose that Mr. XYZ is a convicted felon and intends to take the money and leave the country. Under federal law, in this admittedly extreme case, you have met the SEC requirements of disclosure and are registered.

Under blue sky laws such as we have here, we can say no, this business is not fair, you cannot do this to the investors in this state. Because we feel that even if you have adequate disclosure, the complex language of securities law is such that the layman can get lost in the underbrush and the investor is not protected.

But as it was with the scrutiny applied by the SEC in Washington, Mr. Kuntz could do only so much. They raised plenty of objections in Texas, and the record of those objections and similar complaints raised in Wisconsin, California, and the other tough blue-sky states should have been ample public warning for future investors and backers—had they cared to look. The objections raised in Texas alone should have been enough by themselves.

Kuntz continues:

First off we had problems with the cheap stock. Mr. DeLorean had trouble showing that he had paid sufficient value for the shares he owned in DeLorean Motor Company, compared to the value of the stock that was to be sold to the public. He owned some 10 million shares that were considered too cheap by our standards—California's too, apparently—and we required that Mr. DeLorean put those shares in escrow against future improvement in the worth of the other shares.

What we were saying was that we will acknowledge that as an entrepreneur you have created value for this company and that your shares do have value, but there is no way to set a value on them at this time—much less the millions you ascribe to them. So the next thing for you to do is put those shares in a bank escrow account and when your company has achieved certain earning levels for all the shares, you can reclaim ownership of those shares and enjoy the income or sell them or whatever.

Now, the next objection gets us a little ahead of ourselves in time, but in his application to us in 1977 he said he was going to have his plant located in Puerto Rico under a deal that required him to raise a certain sum of money before the Puerto Rican government and the U.S. government were to kick in their monies. So again we said this is an unfair risk to our Texas investors and we will hold all that money you raise in this state in escrow here until all the capital is in place.

It turns out that that very provision of our law worked to the advantage of our people here. As I recall it, Mr. DeLorean's deal with Puerto Rico never came off and they went to Northern Ireland. Well, under our laws our investors had the option of pulling out of the deal and getting their money back; and I believe that at least two of them did.

But what we really fought over was the dilution of the stock he was trying to sell down here. He had his own shares that he had paid nothing for, and the officers of the company had options on other shares—about 650,000—at about 10 cents apiece, and here he was charging $5 for a share to our people.

"Dilution" is one of those rare legal-financial descriptions that can be taken literally; an investor who pays money for a share of stock has that investment's value "diluted" by every share that is issued for free or at less than he paid for his shares. The percentage of dilution—or loss of equity and value—can be precisely measured by the number of shares issued and their respective prices.

When you work it out, as we did, a Texas investor or any investor was paying $5 a share that was immediately worth only 30 cents as soon as he bought it. The remaining $4.70 of value accrued to Mr. DeLorean personally—or to his officers in the future—by virtue of their cheap stock. That's a dilution of value that runs somewhere between 80 and 90 percent by my unofficial calculations at the moment. Under our laws we get worried when a share offering here gets diluted by 20 percent or thereabouts; so we were *really* worried by the DeLorean offering.

What we ended up doing was letting them have their registration here, but on a limited basis. We ruled that because the class of investor they wanted to reach was sophisticated in the area of the automobile business—they were dealers and they were involved in a franchise agreement as well—we would allow it on the basis that the shares could not be sold to the general public. We let them sell shares only to people who wanted to go into the dealership. That, finally, was the best we could do.

The objections in Texas and the other states kept Dewey, Kimmerly, and the others flitting between Detroit, Austin, Sacramento and various state capitals for most of that summer and autumn of 1977. Money came in from other states, and in August of 1977, Johnny Carson bought 250,000 shares at $2 a share, in a placement that was treated separately by most of the state securities regulators. In October the Canadian brokerage house of Wood Gundy Company, Ltd., came in with another $500,000, prompted by a young senior partner, Edward King, who was impressed by DeLorean and his venture.

For their large single investments, two seats on the DMC board were also included. King represented Wood Gundy, while Johnny Carson's attorney, Henry Bushkin, became a director. Carson had a special interest in the car project by now. One of the objectives of his major commitment to the DMC-12 was the promise that he would become the advertising symbol, the official spokesman for the car when it was up and running. While these separate placements caused some worries about dilution among the state regulators, it did not slow the flow of money into the DMC coffers.

"Restricting us to dealers-only offerings as they did in Texas really was to our advantage; it added a little zip to our deal. This wasn't something for just anybody," Dewey, the financial officer, says now. "And it was a good proposition for a dealer. His entrance fee was $25,000 and for this he got not only 5,000 shares but the opportunity to sell the cars. On the price markup for the car, which was going to run $4,000 or so, all a dealer had to do was sell the first six or eight cars and he had recovered the cost of his investment plus he had the ownership of the shares and the franchise. So it was a pretty attractive deal in its own right."

But the deal did not stand still. Sometime earlier in 1975, John DeLorean had created DeLorean Manufacturing Company and transferred into it the assets of JZDC. In October 1977 Kimmerly restructured the entire corporate alignment to strengthen John's personal control over the growing assets. First off, DeLorean Motor Company paid 300,000 of its shares—which were valued at $5 each, or $1.5 million total—to DeLorean Manufacturing Company, for ownership of Composite Technology Corporation (CTC) and for the nonautomotive development rights to the ERM plastic resin process. Over the years to come, DeLorean Motor Company paid another $1.5 million in billings to CTC, its own wholly owned subsidiary, for various engineering and design jobs, money that somehow vanished from that company's coffers. In 1982, when CTC went into bankruptcy liquidation, the bankruptcy trustees were able to win bids of only $250,000 for its assets and net worth.

But the reshuffling was even more ambitious than a selloff of questionable subsidiaries from one company to another. In another part of the restructuring, DMC *reacquired* the rights to the development of the DMC-12 car and the automotive use of the ERM method from the DSCP partnership by issuing each of the three dozen partners part of a total issue of 99,995 new shares of DMC's $8 cumulative dividend convertible preferred stock.

Dewey notes:

> This was a very attractive thing on paper for the partners. They were coming into DeLorean Motor Company with preferred stock with a conversion right downstream if they wanted to, into common stock. And their dividends were accumulating, a preferred $8 a share dividend that was piling up at a rate of about $1.6 million a year. So in theory if the company had gotten off and running, they would have had quite a windfall of dividends and they were not being diluted since there was no other preferred stock in the company. Plus of course their original partnership investment of $100,000 had had its tax writeoff consequences.

Of course, all of this was in theory. The immediate effect was that DeLorean regained control of the assets he had put into DSCP—the car development work and the ERM process. He had spent the $3.5 million the partners had invested and he had rolled them into DeLorean Motor Car company as preferred shareholders at no dollar cost to himself. The DSCP partners also had the option to become DeLorean car dealers without putting up the $25,000 entrance fee required of the later dealer-investors.

The box score at this point looked like this: John DeLorean had sold Johnny Carson half a million dollars' worth of DMC stock, 125,000 shares of which had come out of his own holdings. Thus he had picked up $250,000 in cash that had been meant for the company. Then DMC gave him 300,000 new shares for ownership of CTC. This left DeLorean owning a 64% interest in DeLorean Motor, since the DSCP partnership was now dissolved and the remaining partners had been rolled into DMC through the preferred-stock gambit. He now had firm control of the $6.1 million in new capital that the early dealers, Carson, and Wood Gundy had pumped in and it had cost him nothing. Not even the personal effort to sell the shares.

By this time, as Dick Brown would note, "We felt we could build a car company in spite of John DeLorean. I was seeing quite a bit of him during this period. He was pompous and loud. He would get on an airplane and start talking business in a loud voice, or if we were in a restaurant he would talk loud enough to make sure everyone heard him and recognized him. But he really didn't do anything and he wasn't responsible for either conceiving of or recruiting the dealer-investor network."

Brown and a former Mazda associate, Robert Holberg, had recruited many of the dealers for the DSCP partnership, and it was they who had to come up with the bulk of the 400 dealer-investors that would make the sales network credible.

Holberg recalls:

> We wanted the dealers to invest because we wanted to retain their interest and the only way to do that was to give them equity participation. And we had a solid no-nonsense presentation worked out that would appeal to the kind of sophisticated investor we wanted. After the first two presentations in Dallas and Houston, we agreed that we had to keep John out of it, otherwise he would blow the whole deal then and there.
>
> The original idea was that we would make the presentation and then John would come into the room for the closing remarks. He exaggerated so much that people lost confidence in our presentation and you could see the prospects falling off right away. He didn't just talk about the car, he bragged about how he was already moving on to bigger and better things. He confused them with claims that he was going to build this and invest in that when he hadn't really won their support yet for the car project.

And all the while, as the money flowed in from 1977 through early 1978, DeLorean's level of spending rose to meet it.

Brown remembers:

> I really hadn't anticipated that he would be so reckless and self-serving with other people's money. I was stunned by it. I criticized John for it to his face and his response was to tell me that I didn't understand, that I really wasn't participating in the management of the company there in New York. He was right about that, I was way far away in California. So he put me off.
>
> The thing about John was that in many ways he was like a child who had never had any discipline. He tried to see how far he could go with a thing and if you yelled about it, often he retreated. He'd say, "Well you're right about that, we won't do that anymore." He sent Nesseth around and Nesseth tried to take over one of the promotional meetings—one in Las Vegas, I think—and I called John and said get this guy out of here or I leave. And John said, "No don't do that," and he yanked Roy right away.
>
> But John never stopped trying things. I guess I thought that as the organization took shape, the corporate organization itself would provide the discipline on John DeLorean. We had a public offering with the dealers and we were registered with the SEC; I figured the SEC regulations alone would provide some kind of limits on him. After that I hoped the British government was not going to give him all that money without the necessary controls. But I was wrong.

However, there were people who evaded DeLorean's snares or, once ensnared, fought back and won.

On March 16, 1978, DeLorean and Robert J. Buckley, president and chief executive officer of what was then Allegheny Ludlum Industries, Inc., of Pittsburgh, agreed to yet another infusion of capital for DMC and on a much more important production relationship.

Buckley, who remains chairman of what is now Allegheny International, Inc., agreed to purchase 50,000 DMC common shares at the market price of $5 and took an option to purchase another $500,000 worth once the full financing package for the company was in place. The letter of intent signed between the two men is interesting reading for other reasons. The agreement acknowledges that both Wood Gundy and Johnny Carson have made similar purchases at less than half the price and, in Carson's case, "half of which came from John DeLorean. Mr. Carson will be a spokesman for DeLorean at an agreed upon fee."

Moreover, the agreement called on DeLorean and Allegheny to negotiate a ten-year contract during which the steel company would provide the stainless steel for the DMC-12 outer shell and that Allegheny Ludlum would be closely identified with the DMC-12 for promotional purposes.

Dick Brown remembers the deal. "Allegheny Ludlum had always been a big promoter of stainless steel. Back in the 1930s they took a couple dozen Ford sedans and made them with stainless-steel bodies and occasionally you will see one of them at an auto show; they still look great. They were all hot to help John get started, but as always happens when someone agrees to do something, John turned around and demanded still more."

Spokesmen for Allegheny's chairman Buckley will not comment on the record about the deal or why it ultimately came to nothing.

But one company official recalled:

> There we were, committed to invest $1 million and to provide steel for the car for ten years and DeLorean suddenly started demanding more money and help in locating a plant site. During that time he had looked at two sites in Pennsylvania but had been unable to get the local government clearances. He wanted us to not only increase our capital input way beyond what we felt was justifiable, but also to use our influence with the state government to get more generous training grants and assistance, well above what they could afford to do, too. So we just walked away from it.

In May Pete Avrea was joined in the litigation siege being laid to DeLorean, Nesseth, and company by the Kansas State Bank, which filed suit against DeLorean and ultimately against Nesseth. The previous September the bank had demanded and obtained a meeting with Kimmerly to discuss its loans. General Motors informed the bank that it was pulling both the Pontiac and Cadillac franchises out unless Nesseth were replaced by another buyer. When the buyer was located,

Kimmerly talked the bank into negotiating a debt consolidation. Poor Dahlinger was out of it; he had left town anyway. So the bank took all the previous financings and put them together into one $1.3-million loan to DeLorean, who used the proceeds to buy the land under the dealership. The idea was that the new dealer would pay enough rent to pay off the majority of the debt. The remainder of the debt was to come from a selloff of the used-car branch of Dahlinger Motors. DeLorean signed a personal guarantee for that part of the loan since the rest was secured by the mortgage on the land.

From September 1977 through May 1978, Nesseth used all his powers as a salesman to unload the used Cadillacs and Pontiacs from the Dahlinger lot. The proceeds of the sale disappeared, however, and in some cases the buyers of the cars had their property seized by the county government because the money that was supposed to go for taxes and license plates had been appropriated by Nesseth. Although the litigation took three years and involved appeals to the courts of both California and Kansas, Nesseth ended up having to return $130,000 from this scam and DeLorean himself had to put back nearly $300,000 more. *

Although he never announced it, DeLorean was also negotiating with Brown Ferris Industries for a deal in Texas, but that came to nothing. The state of Maine appeared briefly as a possible source of funds and a plant—some $40 million was mentioned—but a serious bid had been made by Pennsylvania.

DeLorean looked over three potential sites and even took an option on one, an eighty-acre bit of land at Fogelsville, near Allentown. If the planners objected to that, he would take one of the other townships. He was genuinely interested in Pennsylvania, but not in the financial package the state offered. There were not enough dollars to enable him to build his factory. Bob Dewey and his financial team had been working out how much was needed, and they estimated that approximately $75 million for a factory, machinery, tooling, and working capital would see the vehicle through to pilot production.

With Allegheny Ludlum dropped out of the picture, DeLorean gave up on Pennsylvania, but not on getting that money. Who in 1978 had the most money in the world? The Saudi Arabians, of course. DeLorean found himself a Saudi and turned on his charm. He could

* Binyan v. Nesseth, 231 Kans. 381

offer an almost irresistible package. At the time, the Saudis were being blamed for wrecking the world economy, and the auto industry in particular, by increasing the oil price six-fold during the previous two years. The world financing system also had a new problem: how to recycle the $60 billion surplus that OPEC had piled up? Arab money at the time had assumed a special quality: if you had an Arab backer, your financial status was assured—and of the Arabs, by far the richest were the Saudis. Having a Saudi backer meant that no one would seriously question the extent of your financial support. Everyone knew that Saudi wealth was limitless.

And what better venture was there for a rich Saudi to invest in during the mid-1970s than a new car-project, particularly the first post-oil-crisis one—a new, ethical, economical car, creating jobs and prosperity? DeLorean's dealings with the Saudi were handled by the First Boston Corporation, which was keen on both John and his dealings with their friendly Saudi. The Saudi was also keen on having the project go to a third world country—the Arabs were very hot on the north-south dialogue at the time. But like most Arabs, this particular Saudi wanted anonymity.

His name was Ojjeh Akram.

5

PUERTO RICO AND IRELAND

At various times since 1974, when he had told *Auto Week* in an interview that the car would probably be assembled by Canada, DeLorean had disclosed promises of financial assistance and government support from Maine, Ohio, Rhode Island, and "two Canadian provinces." He had also hinted that Spanish industrial sources had offered to provide capital and facilities. It is clear that as time went on, he discovered there was quite a lot of government aid about if the cards were played right—and not just in the United States, either. Officials overseas were as naive as they were anywhere: underpaid, inexperienced men and women, very impressed with the motor giant from Detroit.

In 1977, while press attention centered on Pennsylvania, DeLorean was discovering Puerto Rico. It was First Boston that brought the Caribbean island into the picture. The bank had a subsidiary there and was alerted by their man on the scene that the Puerto Rico Economic Development Administration, or Fomento as it preferred to be known, was offering large, generous aid packages to potential investors, particularly for foreign firms that would provide both jobs and prestige. A DeLorean car plant would offer both.

Early in 1977 DeLorean flew to San Juan and drove the eighty miles to the northwest corner of the island. At Borinquén there was the old, abandoned Ramey U.S. Air Force Base that Fomento planned to turn into an industrial zone. Nearby was the town of Aguadilla, one of Puerto Rico's larger cities, where the necessary labor could come from. There were few trained people, but labor was cheap and the Puerto Ricans were very enthusiastic. So was DeLorean.

Through February and into March they negotiated. By March 23 there was a written offer. A week later, Fomento set out the agreed-upon deal in a memorandum of understanding. John had had his first experience at serious negotiation with a government and had acquitted himself well. However, he made one major mistake, for which he was later to kick himself: he agreed to put $25 million up front. He was still a novice at these negotiations; by the time it came to Northern Ireland he would be a master.

The DeLorean team consisted of Collins, Dewey, Brown, and Terry Werrell, an able enough production man hired from GM. They made some calculations and estimated that they needed a 500,000-square-foot factory, plus 50,000 feet of administrative space. They would also need a test track and storage space for the finished cars. Puerto Rico was a long way from the component makers, which were mostly grouped around the big three in Detroit. But there were 185 acres of space at Ramey, an airstrip they could use, reasonable shipping facilities and, above all, money.

The memorandum of understanding, dated April 4, 1977, was the basis of an agreement that was to be argued over for the next year. Besides the initial equity of John DeLorean ($3.5 million based on his rights to the DMC-12) and the partnership (their matching $3.5 million), DMC was expected to raise "not less than $25 million additional equity capital." It was reiterated that the whole package hinged on this. DeLorean had convinced Fomento he would have the money within weeks, that his Saudi—Ojjeh Akram—was very excited about the project. He had still not signed a single dealer and would not be able to until he had updated the prospectus to take account of the plant site in Puerto Rico, but the expectation was that he could raise a minimum of $3,750,000 from 150 dealers and as much as $10 million from 400 dealers.

The memorandum went on: "DMC expects to raise the balance of the equity from private investors which shall be evidenced by commitments acceptable to Fomento by April 15, 1977"—only eleven days away. John clearly expected the Saudi to sign as soon as that, particularly if he could show him that the Puerto Ricans were in.

Alejandro Vallecillo, then the administrator of the Puerto Rico Economic Development Administration, signed the memorandum with a flourish and sent it off to DeLorean for his signature. However, DeLorean hesitated; suddenly that Arab money was not so assured. A few days later, First Boston told him the bad news, Ojjeh had pulled out. DeLorean was to claim afterward that he did so because U.S.

securities laws would have required that his identity be publicly revealed and he feared that members of his family might be kidnapped and held for ransom. The true story of Ojjeh's defection at this crucial time was more mundane and vastly more significant.

The Saudis may have had more money than anyone else at that time, but as anyone who tried to do business with them discovered, they also were about the most difficult people in the world to part from it. By that time all the rich Saudis had secured the best investment advice possible, and Ojjeh Akram was no exception, even though he was a most unusual Saudi Arabian.

Ojjeh Akram was born in Syria and became a nationalized Saudi only in 1950. Since then he had built one of that country's leading industrial companies, Technique d'Avant Garde Finance, which specialized in high-quality prefabricated building construction projects. The car project had initially appealed to him for several reasons. His son Mansour was a student at UCLA and a fan of DeLorean's, and Ojjeh himself was attracted to the concept of an "ethical car" that also would be constructed in a third world economy—as Puerto Rico certainly was.

But Ojjeh was not just going to take the word of John DeLorean, nor the recommendations of First Boston, without doing some checking on his own. He asked his principal American bank, a leading institution outside New York, to do a top-secret, for-his-eyes-only investigation of the project. The bank hired experts, including the leading automobile-engineering specialist in Detroit, Zora Duntov, to analyze all aspects of the deal from the financing of the car to a marketing analysis of its prospects.

Since Ojjeh was openly enthusiastic about the deal, the bank could have satisfied its important customer by whipping up a report that endorsed his wishes. Instead the report turns out to be the best analysis of the DeLorean project ever done. Scrupulous to the point of keeping its investigators anonymous—Duntov was referred to throughout as "Mr. X"—it put forth an astonishing array of arguments and proof against Ojjeh's participation in the project.

No one reading the analysis would put a penny into John DeLorean's dream car project. In the light of the rest of the project's history, one cannot help but speculate what would have happened if the Northern Ireland and British officials had done the same kind of exercise a year or two later.

The bank's analysts told Ojjeh that DeLorean's car might have been viable before the OPEC oil crisis, but it no longer was. The market had changed and John DeLorean had not caught up with it. He was still back in his GM days, an entirely different era. The U.S. sports car market was no longer a growth area, and a so-called "ethical car" could not be easily reconciled with building a sports car that would be bought only by the idle rich in the first place. Glamour was out; utilitarianism was in. The report went on to state that the only group that would still buy a high-performance sports car would have to be earning more than $75,000 a year; and they would prefer a Mercedes, Porsche, or Jaguar.

In addition to "Mr. X's" scathing comments about the car's design and capabilities (he had driven the prototype DMC-12s on a regular basis), the analysis also noted that the overall market for sports cars was in sharp decline in America; it had once been a 30,000-car-a-year sales environment, but it no longer was. And it was certainly not the 200,000-car market that John DeLorean had told Ojjeh it would be.

Competition in the sports car market was going to get ferocious. A new-model Corvette was to be introduced in 1979, and GM had a completely new version, freshly engineered, already on the shelf ready for launch in 1981. If DeLorean's car began to see even 10,000 units of sales, and that seemed unlikely, GM would bring out its new version even sooner. There was a new model series from Ford, and Honda was said to have a new sports car ready for the spring of 1979. These all would be priced at under $10,000. The DMC-12 was now priced at a probable $11,000-plus, which made it too expensive.

Then there was the color, which the analysis saw as a major flaw. For instance, only one-third of the Corvettes sold were silver-gray because many Corvette owners liked to have their own distinctive color. No DMC-12 owner could have that. "The more cars DeLorean sells, the more common the product will become, and thus the less attractive it will be to the prospective buyer." Since the 55 mph speed limit had been imposed, sports car owners tended to compensate by cruising with the top off. This would be impossible in the gull-wing DeLorean.

Therefore, said the analysis, the product was wrong: too high priced and not exceptional enough for the new market conditions. It might have been right for the market of four or five years earlier, when the typical sports car buff, a male between twenty-five and forty, wanted performance, styling, and exclusivity. Now they wanted safety, quality, and value for their money. Producing the DMC-12 in Puerto Rico would "definitely have a negative impact on its quality image." It was no use trying to make a unique feature out of the airbag: either it would be compulsory and all cars would have it or it would not be allowed.

This tough-minded analysis also provided some interesting insights into the DeLorean team. The bank analysis devoted much space to the comments of "Mr. X," who originally had been a supporter of the car but had reversed his position as the market changed. He felt that John had developed his market feel "in an era vastly different from what we face today and will face when the DMC is ready for production some 1½ to 2 years in the future. One of DeLorean's major achievements at GM was engineering and building 'wide-track' cars that emphasized performance. But we believe the market has evolved considerably since those days in 1965–72, as have product characteristics necessary to sell a car."

However, the report went on to say, DeLorean was "considered an outstanding automotive engineer and his successes at GM are attributable to his certain charisma." Even the hard-headed bankers noticed that.

The report continued: Bill Collins was "top-notch and one of the stronger members of the team." Bob Dewey "may not have the stature necessary to fill such a demanding job, given John DeLorean's drive for a quality product almost regardless of cost." Dick Brown, it noted a bit lukewarmly, had "performed well for a time" at Mazda. And the final member of the team, Terry Werrell, was cited as an experienced production man who "most recently worked at one of GM's most advanced production facilities."

There was more, much more, but the basic conclusion was brisk enough: "We can envision a situation where production is delayed for one year, first year sales volume is in the area of 5–7,000 units, unit costs exceeding forecast, price increases ruled out by competitive pressures, and warranty costs running $500 a car. Under this set of circumstances, shareholders equity would show a deficit of the order of $20–25 million calling into question the company's continued economic viability and/or the requirement of substantial additional capital."

That was remarkably prescient, except that the delay was two years rather than one and the deficit correspondingly larger. The Saudi was advised against making the investment of $20 million. "Our best estimate is that the car, presuming it can be built to present specifications at the forecast costs, would sell in the 5,000 to 7,000 units per annum range." At that level it could not make a profit. Rather, its operational losses would be $20 million in the first year; each month's delay, on DeLorean's own (or rather Dewey's) figures, would cost another $1 million. Ojjeh was warned he might well find he was the only source of new capital. And because the company would be public, the Saudi would face the same responsibilities—and exposure —as any other director. (The bank felt obligated to enclose a special appendix setting out the responsibilities of a director.) Finally, and this was perhaps a crucial point, Ojjeh would be a second-class shareholder, in the same way the dealers were, with his investment made at a much higher cost than DeLorean himself or the other early investors, including Johnny Carson. At the end of April, Ojjeh said "No, thanks" and walked away.

Ojjeh Akram easily found another place to invest his money. Later in 1977 he became a world celebrity when he bought the luxury ocean liner *France* for roughly $20 million. A week later he was back in the headlines when he paid another $20 million for a 202-piece collection of French antique furniture from the unique Wildenstein Collection. The furniture would grace the soon-to-be refurbished liner, Akram told the press, as part of his plan to turn it into "a little traveling French city."

But while Ojjeh Akram could blithely walk away from his near-folly, his departure left John DeLorean in a very deep hole. He had to have that money to get his Puerto Rico deal off the ground. He had counted on it. The Puerto Ricans were adamant on that $25 million of new equity before they would budge.

For the next year, DeLorean tried everything he knew to raise that money. He could not sign up a single dealer until the SEC gave its approval for the prospectus, and that approval would not be given until it was amended to allow for the proposed location in Puerto Rico. But there was no Puerto Rico deal until he had his $25 million. It was a vicious circle that left him bitter against Ojjeh in particular and later, all Arabs in general. "You just have lots of cups of tea with them. You sit, you talk and nothing happens," he once remarked. "Back in the sixties," he told the *Detroit Free Press*, "any moron with an idea could raise capital. Now it's impossible. If you want to know what raising venture capital is like; well, most people say it's impossible. If it's accomplished, it will be the most incredible accomplishment of the last 100 years!"

DeLorean was forced to extend his agreement with Puerto Rico until October 31, by which stage he had to have his minimum 150 dealers. He made that one, but he was still a long way from the requirement of 400. By the end of the year he had signed up 177 dealers, but he had wasted a full year; his whole program was now getting even further behind his original target. Then, as 1978 opened, things livened up again. He was visibly cooling on Puerto Rico, although still hunting for his money, and a new location was emerging right under his Bloomfield Hills nose: Detroit, itself—his own hometown!

On December 15 a story broke in the *Detroit Free Press:* "Detroit officials are quietly trying to assemble a financial package sweet enough to lure General Motors executive John Z. DeLorean into locating his planned $90 million sports car company in the city."

DeLorean was learning the art of bargaining for development aid money. He could toss Spain into a conversation with the Puerto Ricans, saying he had an offer to go there, and watch them sweat. Now he would do the same with Detroit. He was also at pains to point out that Detroit was pursuing him, not the other way around. Negotiations had been going on for several months and he had already been shown several pieces of land along the Detroit River near the Edison plant on the city's east side. John had met Detroit's Mayor Coleman Young a number of times, impressing him with the possibility of a plant employing 2,000 people, with an annual payroll of over $35 million and the extra jobs that would be created among the component makers. According to Anthony Devito, Detroit's planning director, "We're pursuing him. . . . We have to convince him." The Detroit officials planned to tap some of the $300 million assigned under the federal government's new Urban Development Action Grant Program, which would come into effect on January 1, 1978. This program was specifically earmarked for distressed cities with high unemployment and a need for development.

DeLorean delayed the filing of his prospectus with the SEC while waiting to see if Detroit could come up with an attractive package. He had already been trying for nearly a year and had not been able to raise the money the Puerto Ricans required. They again extended the deadline until January 31, but were showing obvious signs of impatience and annoyance that he was talking to Detroit as well.

On January 22 the Detroit City Council unanimously approved a financing plan, stepping up the pressure still further. The city held two weeks of open discussion on the project, including a public hearing at a school near the proposed site just south of Jefferson to the west of the Conner Creek Power Plant. There was, reported the *Free Press*, "only modest opposition."

Egged on by the Puerto Rican proposals, the City Council was coming up with an astonishingly attractive package for a city that was already heavily industrialized. Even Kenneth V. Cockrel, the one reluctant councilman, supported DeLorean in the vote. "There was no real alternative if the city wanted jobs," he said. "That's really the bottom line."

But DeLorean still had to find that extra $25 million. Now, however, there was new hope. Oppenheimer and Company, the Wall Street firm, was working on it for him, putting together the biggest limited partnership scheme ever attempted on the Street. The De-Lorean Sports Car Partnership was the same sort of thing, but for only $3.5 million, and that had been hard enough to raise. Now they were going for $25 million in a poor market. In Oppenheimer's favor, though, there were two factors: the investment was attractive to high-rate taxpayers because they got the advantage of the project's tax losses; and there were still plenty of people around who were auto buffs and loved an entrepreneur.

So DeLorean had two offers and could play one off against the other. It was Detroit versus Puerto Rico, and the local media in Detroit were full of the project. The city, DeLorean told the *Free Press* at the end of January, would be foolish not to back his project. "I think it's going to be successful. There's nobody who's got a better track record in the goddamned automobile business than I have."

Then, one day early in 1978, a young man called Liam Keilthy happened to be driving through Michigan. Keilthy was the Irish Industrial Development Authority's (IDA) man in Chicago; his job was to attract American companies to go to Ireland and build factories, create jobs and exports and wealth for a nation which, until ten years before, was essentially a poor farming nation.

Keilthy listened idly to the car radio tuned to the local Detroit station. Then he suddenly stiffened. The Detroit City Council, said a news announcer, had confirmed reports that it had approved a financing plan to lure former General Motors vice president John DeLorean to build an auto plant there. A similar offer from Puerto Rico expired on January 31, just a few days off. Keilthy was driving from Chicago to Detroit. Now he stopped long enough to make a phone call, check a Bloomfield Hills address, and headed north past the huge Ford plants at Dearborn. By early afternoon he was in Bob Dewey's office.

At first Dewey and Collins did not take him too seriously. Mentally, they were focused on Puerto Rico; that was where they wanted to go, they thought that was the best deal they would get, and at long last there seemed a good chance that the Oppenheimer operation would raise the necessary $20 million they were still short. But they sat down with the Irishman and spent two hours going over the project with him. In turn, Keilthy told them about the industrial prospects for Ireland: it now had the highest economic growth rate in the whole of Europe and was even ahead of Japan; it was rapidly emerging into the industrial world; there was plenty of labor, much of it trained; thousands of Irishmen had gone to the English midlands to get jobs in the car plants there and many had drifted back again. Would DeLorean Motor Company consider an approach from the Industrial Development Authority of Ireland?

"By then," said Bob Dewey, "we had people coming through the door all the time who wanted to tell us about their state or country and all their attributes. The only ones that really had any substance were Texas and Pennsylvania—I spent many days trying to put deals together there. And I spent many days in Puerto Rico. But there was also Kansas, Georgia, Detroit. And we had to go through it with each one because we never knew who the real one would be." Dewey became almost anguished as he recalled the amount of work he put in on potential sites for the factory. "I had Louisiana, I had Maine, Spain —I couldn't name them all. Spain was always John's great fallback, but I had a notion they wanted a large piece of John. There was this Spanish priest that used to come over and explain it and John would say, 'Do you understand it?' and I'd say, 'No, John, I don't understand it. I hope you do.' It was gobbledygook to me."

Keilthy, however, was convincing, even to Dewey, who was keen to put the project in Puerto Rico, where he had been the man most heavily involved. The young Irishman gave an eloquent account of the package he would like to try to put together, and it sounded good. "Go ahead," said Dewey, still not believing it would get serious. He hoped that the site for the factory was soon to be resolved.

At the end of February, however, Puerto Rico finally seemed to have won the battle to build John DeLorean's dream car. It had more money to spend than Detroit, and although Detroit still hoped to win DeLorean over, most officials privately accepted the fact that the plant would be built in the Caribbean. On February 16, with tempers fraying and irritation openly showing, the Puerto Rican Council in Washington had finally gotten DeLorean to sign a new agreement prohibiting him from negotiating with anyone else for alternative plant sites. "The agreement," said Fomento's Alejandro Vallecillo, "unequivocally states that the decision has been made to locate the plant in Puerto Rico. The agreement reaffirms the DeLorean Motor Company's commitment to locate its plant in Aguadilla and states that no other sites are being nor will be considered."

The new agreement expired at the end of May. The Puerto Ricans were ecstatic. They had won: Detroit was out! They did not know that Ireland was now in. Nor did Oppenheimer's Mike Hayes, who was busily raising money with a prospectus that carefully assessed the abilities and working habits of the Puerto Ricans.

In Dublin the IDA decided it was time to speed things up. De-Lorean was obviously skeptical about going to Ireland—why should he be anything else? The IDA used a tactic that it had employed before on Americans who were ignorant of the modern Ireland—it drafted one of the Irish "Mafia" of American businessmen who could invite DeLorean to dinner or lunch in a familiar American environment and persuade him that Ireland was to be taken seriously.

The man chosen for the task was Ireland's greatest star in the business world—in fact, in several other worlds, too. In his home country he was almost a legend. At age forty-two, Anthony O'Reilly had already been the president and chief operating officer of the huge H. J. Heinz Company of Pittsburgh for six years. (He is now president and chief executive officer.) To Irishmen, however, his greatest feats had been on the rugby field, where he was arguably the greatest player the country had produced since the war. A tall, dashing figure with flaming red hair, he had run the Heinz operation in Britain and then moved to Pittsburgh, where by the time he was thirty-six he was that worldwide company's head. He still had substantial interests in Ireland and was already a wealthy man. Not even DeLorean, with his notorious contempt for almost everyone else, could look down on O'Reilly—physically or in any other way.

In Pittsburgh O'Reilly had a call from the New York director of the IDA, who explained the situation and said, "Look, would you mind meeting with Mr. DeLorean?" O'Reilly instantly agreed—he was quite looking forward to it. So the IDA set up a dinner at the Plaza Hotel in Pittsburgh and O'Reilly and DeLorean met with several of the IDA men.

O'Reilly talked to DeLorean about the problems, perils, and potential of Ireland. There was an added advantage, from the IDA point of view, in having O'Reilly do the talking because he knew Puerto Rico well. Heinz has a large tuna and pet food plant in Mayagüez and is probably one of the three biggest employers on the island. He knew the grant structure, the problems, the advantages of Puerto Rico far better than DeLorean did. It gave his support for his native Ireland that extra degree of credibility.

At the end of the meal, one of the IDA people tried to arrange a further meeting. "Well, look, we know the minister for economic planning and development, Dr. Martin O'Donoghue, will be in America in the next three weeks or so. Could we meet with him and discuss it further?" O'Reilly offered to host a dinner party at his Pittsburgh home, get together a group of Irish-American businessmen, and have DeLorean along to meet O'Donoghue.

A few weeks later, the dinner party took place. O'Reilly had organized it well—he had some leading business dignitaries including Krome George, chairman and chief executive of Alcoa, which is also based in Pittsburgh.

DeLorean arrived after the others and started straight away on a monologue. "It was very clear," said O'Reilly, "that John DeLorean had an extremely high opinion of the notion of the DeLorean car company and in the benefits that it could bring to either Puerto Rico or Ireland or wherever, and I would have said, as someone who has been negotiating grants and talking to governments in various parts of the world for years, that perhaps he made assumptions that were a little high-handed and comported himself in that way at that dinner." He was barely civil.

O'Reilly was not offended, nor were the others. O'Reilly commented:

At the end of the meal DeLorean sort of stood up and started to phone his wife and friends, without any reference to the host. Now, Irish dinner parties often have a character of their own, so I wasn't alarmed at it, but I was a little dismayed because I didn't think he was winning friends and influencing people like that. Martin O'Donoghue had come a long way and he is an extremely intelligent, well-versed economist. There was a lot he could have told DeLorean about the Irish economy. And it is not that I felt like he was not being treated with proper reverence, but I just felt that as an evening, although it was very pleasant socially, it seemed to proceed on the assumption that whoever got the DeLorean car company would be extremely fortunate. By removing himself from the dinner almost before it had finished, there was some surprise. I think of that marvelous line "delusions of grandeur is the curse of the Celt." I think he was suffering from the curse of the Celt that night.

In March DeLorean sent Bill Collins off to Ireland to assess the working habits of the Irish and to inspect what the Irish had in mind for the DeLorean factory—a new plant in Limerick built by the IDA for the Dutch firm Akzo. Then, in April, it was DeLorean's turn to go. "It takes a lot for John to go away for four or five days," says Dewey. "You don't get him to spend that amount of time anywhere unless there is a pretty good chance he's going to get a good deal." The deal was beginning to take shape, and it looked highly promising. DeLorean was stalling Puerto Rico, keeping Ireland secret for the moment. In Dublin, the Irish industry minister, Desmond O'Malley, hosted a dinner for him. Despite himself, DeLorean responded to the place, and he was impressed with the businesslike way the IDA went about its affairs. This wasn't, as he first thought, a two-bit operation that could not be taken seriously. It was a real possibility, better than Puerto Rico, although not so much money. He was really interested; he turned his full charm and persuasive power on O'Malley.

For the minister it was riveting stuff. DeLorean's reputation preceded him. Every Irish schoolboy knows that General Motors is the biggest company in the world. Here was the man who had nearly gotten to the top of it. The Irish, too, have an almost mythical respect for Americans, particularly tall, well-groomed, tanned, and obviously wealthy Americans. The men around the table that evening were all widely traveled, probably more so than DeLorean himself, but they still inherited a feeling of inferiority in the presence of a man they saw as a sophisticated, rich Yank. O'Malley himself, a shrewd and able politician at that stage, maneuvering for the top job of Taoiseach (prime minister) in Irish politics, was far from immune.

DeLorean outlined his thesis on the decline and fall of the American automobile industry and General Motors in particular, and how it could be saved if people stopped designing committees and started designing cars again.

In Ireland, DeLorean said, he wanted to build a car to the same standards as Porsche or Mercedes. He had plans for a sedan after the sports car, new revolutionary cars that would be built with materials that would last. There would not just be 2,000 jobs, but 5,000— maybe ten. He had an idea for a bus—America didn't build buses. Everyone wanted his factory: Puerto Rico, Detroit, Spain. He had rich backers behind him, Middle Eastern money, that would come in.

O'Malley was impressed. "He's what we want here," he told a colleague. DeLorean sensed it, and he had discovered something else that day, the implications of which intrigued him. The proposed factory was in O'Malley's own constituency. It was a strange coincidence, DeLorean reasoned, that the factory he should be offered by an agency that was ostensibly part of the Ministry of Industry should be in that minister's constituency. Even if it were pure coincidence (and he doubted it), that would still make the minister all the more eager to announce that he was filling the factory with workers again. There had to be a lever here that no one had thought of yet, and he, John DeLorean, was going to use it. When he did, he found he had misjudged his men.

At Oppenheimer, the team led by Nate Gantcher and Mike Hayes had completed their analysis of Puerto Rico. They were getting ready to close. By April 22 they would have $22 million ready to go into the DeLorean project. They had sold $150,000 unit shares in a limited partnership to be called, simply, the DeLorean Research Limited Partnership. The partners would put up 20 percent of the new company's capital and in return could write off 99 percent of the company's losses against their own income. It meant that effectively they were investing "30-cent dollars"—they were all in the 70 percent tax bracket, and through Oppenheimer's clever scheme they would get tax relief on their investment. Or so they thought at the time. If the project succeeded, they would be able to take either royalties or stock. At last, at long last, John DeLorean was about to get his money. However, there was one little problem. DeLorean hadn't yet told Oppenheimer that he was thinking of going to Ireland, and they hadn't told their clients. As far as everyone was concerned, it was Puerto Rico. After all, John had signed an exclusive agreement with them, had he not?

Mike Hayes had done most of the donkey work, often taking DeLorean with him to meet the potential investors, traveling widely with him around the country. The two had become good friends, and Hayes had decided to invest his own money in the project. But he had been working flat-out on it for six months and needed a vacation. With everything now complete, he took his family to Virginia Beach, a small resort near Norfolk, Virginia.

Hayes, for no reason he could fathom, suddenly felt a stir of unease. He had learned that John DeLorean was secretive, difficult to get information from. Hayes trusted what DeLorean did give him, but felt he had to drag it out. DeLorean never volunteered anything. There was only one phone Hayes could use in Virginia Beach, and he called the lawyers, Javits and Javits, in New York. How was the closing going? Everything being signed okay? No, it was not! "DeLorean's delaying it," the lawyer told him. "There's something wrong."

The phone was in an Italian delicatessen, and Hayes spent the next seven hours on it, with the proprietor ready to kill him. He soon discovered what was wrong. The governor of Puerto Rico had made a statement. DeLorean was breaking his agreement and negotiating with the Irish.

Oppenheimer had a number of men still down in Puerto Rico working on the details. They had spent weeks on the island. Now, the anger of the Puerto Ricans could almost be felt in New York. The team had to call all their investors, saying, "It's not Puerto Rico anymore. It's the Republic of Ireland." They did not even know what the wage rates were there, had not assessed the transportation situation, the package itself. The long, detailed analysis they had done on Puerto Rico was now a waste of time.

Oppenheimer would earn a $2-million fee for putting the partnership together and for running it; but if there was no deal—and that was the way it looked—then there was no fee.

It was a gloomy Hayes who drove back to New York to start work on a new fact sheet and analysis of building the car in Limerick. He had one interested investor in Des Moines whom he called to advise that the vehicle was going to be built in Ireland. "Then I'm out of the deal," said his client. "I'm not putting a cent in. You can't manufacture anything there. I had a little company there and couldn't make any money. There were labor problems and all kinds of other problems. I'm out." Enough investors stayed in, however, to make it still workable. Instead of $22 million, Oppenheimer now had about $20 million.

By late April the Irish package was basically in place. The IDA would put up $13 million equity, which would consist of the factory. Then there would be $22 million in grants, which would have to be repaid if the company failed within ten years. There would be no taxes, no royalties to pay. Worked out over the period of the project, it was roughly in line with the Puerto Rican deal, although with less cash. With the Oppenheimer money, it was enough.

But DeLorean now asked for more, believing he had O'Malley hooked. He said he wanted more Irish government money by way of training or employment grants. He wanted to put in less himself. Control would be from DMC in New York, which would become a large conglomerate, the Irish factory a small part of the whole. Dr. Michael Killeen, the head of the IDA, was getting suspicious. It was Killeen who had turned the IDA into the success it was and he had laid down strict vetting procedures for every venture that not even DeLorean was going to short-cut. As a result of other investigations, the Irish were doing some rethinking.

Killeen had met DeLorean only once, briefly, at a cocktail party in New York when someone had thought they should be introduced. Martin O'Donoghue had not reported favorably, and O'Donoghue carried a good deal of weight. But Killeen did not allow himself to get too close, leaving the direct dealings to other negotiators. In May they were getting close to signing. The lawyers were drawing up the papers, supervised by Dewey and Walter Strycker, a San Francisco financial consultant who had recently joined the team. Strycker, then fifty, had been raising venture capital on his own for about three years after having served as vice president and treasurer of Wheelabrator Frye in Pittsburgh.

The change in the Irish stance began to come through during those final days of negotiation. "We felt somewhere during the course of that week," says Dewey, "that they were starting to play games with us and that there was something else going on. We weren't getting a true reading about whether the Republic was really going to fulfill all the promises, or whether there were people up the hierarchy who were throwing cold water on it. We didn't quite understand what was going on. It became a mystery when you didn't get to sit down and talk with the top people."

Then, what had already been going sour turned even more so. At a meeting between the two teams, DeLorean suddenly opened up about his huge dreams. "It was a sort of Global Motors—he was envisioning this huge conglomerate as only he can do. All you have to do is encourage John a little bit and he will start puffing and puffing and puffing and going into his dreams," says Dewey. "And these people were sitting there, visualizing this man going on and acquiring General Motors and someday making a tender offer. And they got really blown out of proportion and everybody became very alarmed. I felt that the Irish became very alarmed about whether they weren't just a stepping-stone in a huge pyramid. And the whole deal just started crumbling."

Afterward, Walter Strycker described the reactions of the IDA people and the Irish officials: "Their jaws just kind of dropped and their eyes got big, and then they recessed for a special meeting. And then they came back and said they wanted absolute control over the management of the company for seven years." DeLorean, of course, would not accept that.

Dewey comments:

They had already started changing the deal on us. They started backing down on the promises we'd heard in our offices in Bloomfield Hills. I felt there was some backpedaling and they started upping the ante for the factory, placing a value on it and things like that. If anything, they were tightening the screws on us relative to the offering and they weren't really coming forward with what they had led us to believe was going to be offered. And there was some reneging.

And then I think the thing was really lost when we started discussing constraints on John, and he was playing hardball and it was all unnecessary. It really became an unnecessary discussion. It was all over.

Of course DeLorean could not accept that. He still believed he had O'Malley on his side and that would swing the deal his way. Instead, Killeen called his team together for his own meeting at the IDA. They reviewed the project. There were technical doubts—the car had no clearance on emissions, or safety or, indeed, on anything else. One member of the team, John Kerrigan, believed the DMC-12 was too expensive at over $11,000—too close to the Porsche and too far above the Corvette. The surveys showed the market was very price-sensitive. He didn't believe the costing figures either; and there was no provision in the financing plan for new models. But above all it was DeLorean's character and behavior they were all worried about. Like the Saudi, the Irish could see themselves as the only source of funds if things went bad. "It could be a huge gobbler of money," someone remarked. They were also disturbed by DeLorean's unshakable and unreal optimism. He simply would not admit that there were any circumstances, no matter how bad, under which the project could fail. "The minister's keen on it," one of the IDA men said. They all knew that by now and had come to resent very much the way DeLorean was trading on O'Malley's enthusiasm, but they also knew something DeLorean had not bothered to find out: the minister did not make the decisions at IDA. Its success was in large measure due to its recruitment of professional practicing businessmen to its board, and its autonomy. IDA may have been dependent on the Department of Industry for its funds, but it made its own decisions. Now Killeen decided to reject John DeLorean. He picked up the phone and asked for Desmond O'Malley. The minister accepted Killeen's decision without argument.

Back in New York, Mike Hayes and his team began calling their clients again. "That DeLorean project—well, it's not Ireland after all. We're back in Puerto Rico."

"Okay," said the investor in Des Moines. "I'll go back in. I'll reinvest."

In fact, however, they were not back in Puerto Rico. The Republic of Ireland might have gone, but there was another part of Ireland: richer, less critical, and desperate for jobs. John DeLorean was going to Belfast!

6

NORTHERN IRELAND

"Why don't you try the North?" said a Dublin lawyer to Walter Strycker, as DeLorean's deal with the Southern Irish was breaking down. "They'll invest in almost anything."

For centuries Northern Ireland had been the only part of Ireland that could boast any real industry. For a hundred years it led the world in fine linen and was a major shipbuilder and producer of complex and sturdy textile machinery. Its Harland and Wolff shipyard had built the "unsinkable" *Titanic,* not perhaps its proudest achievement, but it was no fault of the craftsmen who lived in the rows of houses huddled around the huge shipyard that she hit an iceberg on her maiden voyage.

In the sixty years since Ireland was divided between the twenty-six counties of the South and the six "Loyalist" counties in the North, Ulster had modernized much more rapidly than its neighbor, producing manmade fibers, motor industry components, and aircraft. The Short Brothers plant in East Belfast turned out small, box-shaped, commuter aircraft and guided missiles.

But for all that, it remained the poorest, most neglected part of the United Kingdom. And for a brief spell, its neighbor, the Irish Republic, was enjoying the fastest growth rate in Western Europe. Killeen's organization was attracting foreign investment to Ireland that the Belfast officials felt should have gone there; and in 1978 competition between the two was considerable. But Killeen, in Dublin, had to be sparing and careful with his money. Because of the violent reputation of the North, the policy was to take greater risk, offer more money.

In 1976 Dr. George Quigley, a senior civil servant who was soon to play a major role in the DeLorean story, prepared a report on the Province's economic and industrial strategy. His conclusions were not encouraging. "The Northern Ireland economy is in serious difficulty, and if no measures are taken, the outlook is grim," he wrote. "The wide gap between average income per head of population here and in Great Britain must, at best, endure and, at worst, enlarge." This report was especially concerned with the growing division in the population, not just between Catholic and Protestant, although there was that too, but between the haves and the have-nots. The haves, essentially, were those with jobs: the have-nots, the growing population of the unemployed.

For the recession had hit Ulster hard, harder than any other part of Europe. Its shipyard could still boast the largest crane in Europe, dominating the Belfast skyline, but each of its 7,000 workers cost the State a subsidy of about $8,000 a year. In 1950 the shipyard employed 20,000 people; now it was a third of that. Belfast's textile industry had declined by two-thirds in twenty-five years. Manmade fibers were in heavy world oversupply. The automobile industry in mainland Britain was apparently in terminal trouble, causing cutbacks in Ulster's engineering firms.

So the Dublin lawyer had a point that day. Male unemployment of 50 percent in towns such as Strabane, Newry, Fermanagh, and West Belfast meant they were breeding grounds for the men of violence. It was there that the IRA could recruit at will, feeding on the festering hatred of the Catholic population which for generations past had seen themselves as an oppressed people, still fighting the ancient enemy across the Irish Sea.

In his report, Dr. Quigley recommended a reorganization and beefing up of the inducements to encourage blue chip overseas companies (particularly American) to come and invest in Northern Ireland. Against the reputation of the place for bombings and outrage, it was an uphill task. But by the time DeLorean came along, Quigley's plan was winning, although the IDA in Dublin still had the edge. "We conclude that existing arrangements need to be revised in order to restore Northern Ireland's competitiveness and, more particularly, its ability to compete with the Irish Republic," he wrote. "Competition with the Republic is likely to be especially severe in respect to overseas investment."

That had happened. Northern Ireland now offered 40 to 50 percent capital grants, plus employment grants, interest-relief grants, grants toward houses for key foreign employees, and even rent grants. The

Department of Commerce had soft loans, loan guarantees, and hard loans. There were experts and factories and factory sites—anything and everything the prospective investor could desire if he would just come to Northern Ireland and create jobs. For jobs and prosperity were the one answer the politicians could agree on as a possible solution to the violence. "Jobs, homes and hope—that's the way to beat the IRA," said Roy Mason, secretary of state for Northern Ireland.

John DeLorean was now about to become part of the battle against the IRA. Specifically, he was to be the best weapon of the security forces against the terrorist crèche in West Belfast, where the Northern Ireland Development Agency (NIDA) had put its first great new project under the reorganized scheme. Strathern Audio had started with high hopes, but had gone bust within two years.

Roy Mason, the Labour government's minister in charge of Northern Ireland, was squat, thickset, and beetle-browed—a rough, tough-looking man, pale from too many late sittings in the House of Commons and the grueling schedule that all ministers have to put up with. Beside him, John DeLorean appeared extra tall and thinner than ever, his mass of gray hair and white shirt setting off his California tan. Mason looked the coal miner he once was, while DeLorean seemed to be straight off a Hollywood set.

They sat in front of the microphones and the gathered Belfast press to give the world the glad tidings. Forty-five days after starting their negotiations, Northern Ireland and DeLorean had signed a deal. John DeLorean would not be going to Aguadilla or to the East Bank of the Detroit River. A 550,000-square-foot factory would be constructed on a seventy-two-acre site on the Twinbrook industrial development at Dunmurry, six miles to the southwest of the city. It was, said Mason, a tremendous breakthrough for the government. An initial 800 jobs would be created immediately just to build the factory; 600 permanent jobs after 1979; 1,500 more after that as the company hit its full stride of 30,000 cars a year.

DeLorean was enjoying himself. No more Puerto Rican officials tying him down, no more kowtowing to Arabs, no more petty questions from the Southern Irish. Now he would have money, real money, for the first time! He would be able to do the things he had been planning for years. Of all the places in the world, John DeLorean had struck it rich in Belfast.

"We aim to move from cow pasture to production within eighteen months," he told the press conference. His audience laughed appreciatively. Mason had already made the point that the site was now nothing more than a couple of boggy fields where cattle grazed.

"But isn't it a rather high-risk venture?" asked a reporter.

"We have orders as of now for 30,000 cars," said DeLorean smoothly. "That is $300 million worth of business. Of course there are going to be difficulties, a lot of hard work, and many taxing problems. There always are. But I cannot agree with the description of this as a high-risk venture."

Although he did not say it, the risk was now mostly taken by the British government. DeLorean had talked Mason into giving him $106 million in grants, equity, and loans. More important, DeLorean himself did not have to put in a penny. He could afford to be magnanimous. One of the reasons he had settled on Northern Ireland, he said, was that of all the places that were chasing him, it had the most highly motivated, stable, and dedicated work force. The financial incentives, he added offhandedly, were attractive but not compelling. They were in fact approximately three times as attractive as the Dublin offer and twice those in the Puerto Rican deal. That was a lot of compulsion.

As the news from Belfast flashed around the world, however, there were some who did not find it compelling at all—Governor Carlos Romero-Barceló of Puerto Rico, for example. The governor had put up with a great deal from DeLorean and pulled out all the stops to get that plant at Aguadilla. Eighteen months of torturous negotiations had finally ended. He had even gone to New York to sign a deal with DeLorean. Now there was no deal. He had some choice words to say about DeLorean in private, and in public he accused him of "an open violation of good faith," "duplicity," and of going "behind our back." He would be suing, he added venomously.

In the Wall Street office of Oppenheimer and Company, there was some discomfort, too. The DeLorean team had to telephone its whole list of prospective investors yet again with the third change of location. Mike Hayes got on to his man in Des Moines. "Surprise, surprise! Remember we were going to Southern Ireland? Well, as you know, it's not Southern Ireland, but it's not Puerto Rico, either. It's —wait for it—Northern Ireland!"

The phone exploded in his ear. "Are you guys crazy? Do you know what you're doing? I'm going to get in my car, drive to New York, come up to your office, and beat the shit out of you. You're torturing me. Go anywhere in the world! Go to hell! It beats calling me up and telling me you're going to Southern or Northern Ireland." The phone slammed down. The man in Des Moines did not invest. Hayes walked warily for the next few days, glancing nervously over his shoulder.

John DeLorean had played cat-and-mouse with the Puerto Ricans for eighteen months. The IDA in Dublin took five months to vet his project and turn him down. In Northern Ireland, from first approach to the final signing on August 3, 1978, it took only forty-five days. Mason was to say later that the project had been subjected to a very thorough evaluation. Yet not one of the details in this book, which surely would have caused them to run from the project, were ever uncovered or even suspected. The Northern Ireland ministers saw and heard only what John DeLorean wanted them to.

It was late evening on Sunday, June 18, when the DeLorean team flew into Belfast for the first time. With Walt Strycker were Alan Cohen from the New York law firm of Paul Weiss Rifkind Wharton & Garrison, and John Plaxton from Wood Gundy, the Toronto stock-brokers. DeLorean himself was due in the next morning. Plaxton, the contact man with NIDA, had joined them from London. Wood Gundy was to get a handsome finder's fee for the introduction. The three men booked into the battle-scarred Europa Hotel in the center of Belfast, not the most lively place on a Sunday evening. But outside the hotel, the city was experiencing business as usual.

The day before, a police patrol had been ambushed by the Provisional IRA (the Provos) near Bessbrook in South Armagh. One policeman was killed and his partner abducted. In retaliation that morning, the extremist Protestant group, the Ulster Freedom Fighters, kidnapped a Catholic priest. As DeLorean and his colleagues were settling in to their evening meal, the Protestant extremists released him. The Provos announced their victim had been executed. The policeman's body did not turn up for three weeks, and then a postmortem established that he had died in the ambush. The abduction was simply a tactic of the IRA to tie down the security forces.

None of the DeLorean team had very high hopes for Belfast, but Plaxton assured them there was money there, and DeLorean was convinced enough to make the trip. The next morning they drove east out of the city's center, past the towering cranes of Harland and

Wolff, and on to the sweeping six-lane highway that runs past the Short Brothers plant and landing strip, along the coast to Holywood, an exclusive suburb of Belfast where the wealthy businessmen, civil servants, and executives live well away from the violence. Here it was another world: fine houses looking out over the sparkling bay, the countryside lushly green in midsummer, the Army patrols and armored cars they had seen on the way and in the city center now invisible.

Out here, loosely grouped around the bulk of Stormont Castle, a massive classical building that had been the gift of the British government to the people of Northern Ireland in 1932 and which had housed the Province's Parliament when it still had one, was a series of government offices. Among them, at 100 Belfast Road, was the modern building that housed NIDA.

The next two days were to be the most fruitful in John DeLorean's career. At the end of them, he would have a rough agreement for a deal and a plant in Northern Ireland. He himself stayed only an hour at NIDA. He introduced his team, made his opening remarks, then got back into his car, went to the airport, and flew back to London. It was Walter Strycker who made the deal.

Back in Detroit, the others were only too happy it worked out that way. "We've got to keep John out of it," said Brown. "He'll blow the deal for sure." And Strycker had seen the same thing in Dublin. Here, it was up to him, at least for the next few crucial days.

By now Strycker had the figures and presentation at his fingertips. The tall, slim Californian was low-key, sincere, persuasive. He had an attractive, educated voice. At that stage, he believed the DeLorean dream was going to work, and the officials were visibly impressed that DeLorean was represented by such a man.

He showed them a business plan prepared for Puerto Rico by Booz Allen & Hamilton. He had a summary of it ready, projecting sales of 20,960 cars in 1980, meaning revenues of $195 million and a profit of $6.8 million. By 1984 the projections showed sales of $280 million and profits of $45 million. There were some even healthier balance sheet projects: the company would have cash of $152 million in the bank within five years. The manufacturing project they were planning to build would cost around $85 million, and although the company hoped to raise approximately $40 million from dealers and other sources, that would be needed for development work on the car and for the distribution network. Unfortunately there was a possibility that because the plan had now switched from the Irish Republic to the North, the Oppenheimer Limited Partnership would not go ahead. Would NIDA be prepared to fill that gap if necessary?

Strycker was able to inject a certain amount of urgency into the talks because Puerto Rico still had an offer on the table. By the end of the first day, there was already a rough deal. On Tuesday morning NIDA had a special board meeting to review the creation—it normally met the last Wednesday in every month at ten in the morning. The operation looked very promising. The Department of Commerce seemed happy to come in for $55 million—$20 million to pay for the factory itself and another $35 million in grant assistance. That left NIDA to find $30 million, and it seemed possible. The board nodded approval. Then Dennis Faulkner, NIDA chairman, Belfast businessman, colonel in the part-time Ulster Defence Regiment, and brother of Northern Ireland's former prime minister, went into a huddle with the Commerce officials. He took with him Londonderry businessman Sean O'Dwyer, the nominal Catholic on the NIDA board, and the deputy chief executive, Tony Hopkins, and went to see Dr. Quigley, Permanent Secretary of the Department of Commerce.

Both the agency and the Commerce Department were in agreement. It was well worth pursuing, particularly if they could agree on a site in West Belfast, the constituency of member of Parliament Gerry Fitt, for many years Northern Ireland's leading Catholic politician.

The assumption (one of the more naive ones, as things turned out) was that a Wall Street investment house would be no bad judge of the risk involved. Oppenheimer's senior partner, Jack Nash, was investing his own $150,000, and another Oppenheimer associate, Sisyphus, was investing $300,000. If a Wall Street firm was willing to stake its own money and reputation, and if Northern Ireland could get in on the same basis, surely it couldn't be bad. The officials nodded agreement. It seemed a reasonable argument.

By Tuesday evening, after numerous meetings among the NIDA officials and with Strycker, there was an initial agreement: NIDA would invest $17.5 million not in the parent DMC, but in a new Northern Ireland company identified for the moment as DeLorean Motor Company Northern Ireland.

On top of this, there would be another $11.5 million over ten years, with no repayments for three years. The exchange rate being used was $1.825, although the pound was starting to rise rapidly against the dollar. NIDA's shares should be linked to the value of the DMC parent, and NIDA would have an option to be bought out on the basis of the value of the parent's share price. In return, for four years DMC could buy out NIDA at cost plus 15 percent annual interest. So, even at this stage, the deal was already shaping up on the basis that if all went well, NIDA did no better than get its money back; if it went badly, then NIDA would lose the lot.

The officials were dealing with DeLorean as they were used to dealing with the big multinationals such as Du Pont or GM itself, which had all invested in Northern Ireland. Their thinking and negotiating stance were thus based on the premise that here was a substantial company setting up a manufacturing subsidiary in Northern Ireland. They would tie up that subsidiary good and proper, with guarantees from the parent, because it was unthinkable that the parent would default. It never seemed to occur to anyone that there *was* no parent—only a cashless shell that would be dependent on their money.

The result was that even at those early stages the fatal pattern was set. NIDA's money would be in the subsidiary, for which it would put up 94.5 percent of the capital but get 5.5 percent of the votes. Including the Commerce Department's $55 million, the Northern Ireland authorities were already at this early stage agreeing to invest $83 million, or £54 million, while DeLorean's contribution was to be exactly $1 million, or £546,000. DMC would have an exclusive license to sell the cars made in Belfast, weakening control by the Belfast authorities.

On Wednesday the officials drew up the agreement. The preamble read: "Based on the tripartite discussions held on 19 and 20 June 1978, the following assistance will, subject to the approval of the Secretary of State for Northern Ireland, be offered by the Department of Commerce and the Northern Ireland Development Agency respectively to the company to be formed in Northern Ireland by the DeLorean Motor Company."

On three pages it then laid out the terms: the grants and loans from the Commerce Department and the lease of the factory at Twinbrook at £1,000 a year for three years plus another 50,000-square-foot factory free for five years. It went on to NIDA's contribution, including the right to appoint one director to the board of DMC and to the new Northern Ireland company. Then there were a few general conditions: DeLorean would use its "best endeavours" to employ 600 people when production started, 1,000 after a year, and 2,000 after five years. A fourth condition related to the Oppenheimer money and would soon cause a major reworking of the arrangement. It stated that DMC would "complete a satisfactory agreement in respect to the formation and financing" of the new limited partnership on the basis of the prospectus dated March 14, 1978. Although Strycker had hinted there might be problems, everyone assumed the Oppenheimer money was on the way.

The agreement was dated June 21, 1978, and was signed first by Walter P. Strycker with a flowing elegant hand. Next, Brian Lyttle signed for the Department of Commerce; finally, it was signed by Ronnie Henderson, NIDA's chief executive. Less than three days after opening negotiations in Belfast, the DeLorean team had a deal, signed and on the table. It was far from a final deal, of course. It was subject to checks, searches, and investigations, but the broad terms had been set—Strycker's job was done. He rang John DeLorean in New York.

"John, it's all done. You've got a deal, subject only to ratification by Parliament and the board." Strycker assumed there would be no problems with the first. He knew full well that there would be no problems with the second—John DeLorean *was* the board. Strycker flew home.

In the Oppenheimer office at One New York Plaza, a stone's throw from Wall Street, there was no great joy, however. Howard Phillips, Nathan Gantcher, and Mike Hayes, the men essentially putting the limited partnership together, had been concentrating again on Puerto Rico since the Dublin deal looked as if it were going to collapse. Now, all of a sudden, it was Northern Ireland.

"That was when we found out what John was like," said an Oppenheimer man later. "He would just go off in his own way, and you couldn't find out what the hell he was doing. He wasn't reachable or whatever. But then Mike would corral him in his office and sit down for four or five hours with him and get the whole story laid out. Of course, our problem was that our investors wanted to know what the hell was going on and we couldn't provide them with the information because we didn't know. At this point we were shell-shocked."

Oppenheimer was so annoyed that it decided it would not invest in Northern Ireland. It would forfeit its huge fee, but in the heat of the moment that seemed a small price to pay. The limited partnership it was attempting was already extremely delicate and difficult. They had tapped their own friends, DeLorean's friends, clients, anyone they thought was a high-rate taxpayer interested in either cars or John DeLorean, and who had $150,000 to spare. Sammy Davis Jr. had agreed to invest that amount. So had the country singer Roy Clark; Amon G. Carter, the publisher from Fort Worth; author Ira Levin; the Craig Corporation, which made the stereo equipment for the DMC-12; and DeLorean's old friends Herb Siegel of Chris-Craft Industries (from whose office on Madison Avenue DeLorean was still working) and Gary B. Laughlin from Fort Worth. Laughlin's former wife, Vivienne Wilson, was also in for another $150,000.

The $20-million issue had been oversubscribed for Puerto Rico and had come down a bit for the Irish Republic, but Oppenheimer still had nearly $20 million on the table. Now the company decided it would not use it—not for Northern Ireland!

On Monday, June 26, the DeLorean negotiating team was back at NIDA. By now it consisted only of John Plaxton of Wood Gundy, who had flown in from his base in London. Plaxton announced himself as the negotiating link between the agency and DeLorean. DeLorean was handling the negotiations personally—but wasn't there. He was in New York, available by phone.

Faulkner was away, so the NIDA team was led by its deputy chairman, John Freeman—a shrewd, bright, trade union leader, skilled in negotiating deals for his members but without DeLorean's experience in international negotiations. That day's negotiations, however, would have perplexed Henry Kissinger. There was to be no Oppenheimer money now, so would NIDA fill the gap? What was the gap? Oppenheimer had promised to raise $20 million, really only $18 million after its fat fee was deducted. So DeLorean needed another $18 million. How about $18 million from NIDA, made up of $12 million on the same terms as Oppenheimer investors in the parent company and another $6-million secured loan? Plaxton rang DeLorean in New York to confirm that this would do the job.

"Nothing doing," DeLorean shot back. He could sense the enthusiasm at the other end and he had the bit between his teeth now. "Tell them this is what we want . . ." When Plaxton related it, the

NIDA officials could only gasp: $47 million in equity, with DMC paying the Irish company a royalty of $600 per car up to a maximum of $80 million, at which stage DMC would have the right to buy out the original equity for a nominal $5 million. Now it was "nothing doing" at the Belfast end.

DeLorean's next proposal was just as cavalier and audacious: $23.5-million equity to be repaid on a royalty basis with a return of 15 percent, plus an $11.5-million loan, plus that $12 million on the limited partnership basis to be repaid at $267 a car. DeLorean sat in an office on Madison Avenue, doodling on his pad, tracing out artistic shapes and figures, all the time playing with the numbers coming over the phone. If NIDA wanted equity in his business, then it was going to have to pay highly for it. He didn't think they would press too hard.

Now NIDA came back to the original starting point of $12 million on the same basis as the Oppenheimer investors, plus a $6 million guaranteed loan. DeLorean contemptuously dismissed it. The deal seemed to be falling apart. The perplexed NIDA officials decided they had better consult higher authority. They went all the way to the top: the secretary of state, Roy Mason.

Mason was at Hillsborough House, ten miles southwest of Belfast, the home of the Northern Ireland Secretary. Freeman and the officials arrived there about 7:30 P.M. to find Mason giving a dinner for his Labour Cabinet colleague Roy Hattersley. He emerged, however, to hear the state of the negotiations and listened attentively. "That's quite good, John," he said. "But for Christ's sake sign it. It'll be a great psychological boost for Ulster." He went back to his dinner party.

The NIDA people were visibly upset by their first taste of John DeLorean's cavalier approach to taxpayers' money. If he was going to be like this now, what would he be like later? But Mason wanted that deal made. DeLorean had told the NIDA team that the governor of Puerto Rico was on his way to New York to sign the agreement. The documents were ready. They now passed that on to Mason. "Try to complete the deal," he told them. "Give way a bit—not more money."

Back again to the negotiations. Now NIDA changed the mix of its $18-million offer: $15 million in equity in a third class of share in the Northern Ireland company and another $3 million in loans. In return, the Northern Ireland Company would pay NIDA $333 per car sold on the first 90,000 and $80 after that.

DeLorean did some more bargaining. The extra equity would go into the Northern Ireland company, with NIDA's voting shares still less than control. Now DeLorean would have 73.5 percent of the votes. He had just gotten himself another £10 million of British money without surrendering anything.

Freeman and Ronnie Henderson from NIDA now met with Quigley and Brian Lyttle from the Department of Commerce to review the scene so far. Quigley was disturbed about the Oppenheimer situation. Why were they not investing? Freeman and Henderson were not too sure. Was Oppenheimer pulling out because it knew something about John DeLorean that they did not? Or were they saying they would not invest in Northern Ireland at all? To Quigley, concerned as he was with persuading far bigger fish than DeLorean to come to the Province, that was a serious point. Further inquiry was clearly necessary.

Gordon Booth, the British consul general in New York, was asked by Quigley to find out from Oppenheimer what the true situation was. Booth asked Howard Phillips to explain. The Oppenheimer man was anxious to avoid saying that Oppenheimer would not invest in Northern Ireland under any circumstances, which was what NIDA was worried about. Carefully, he explained that Oppenheimer, "being a bank of very high repute," could not seek investors for a project or a country without doing its full vetting procedure first. It had studied Puerto Rico in depth. It had studied the Irish Republic. It simply had had no time to study Northern Ireland. Oppenheimer would, he added, if asked by John DeLorean, seek investors for a project there, but only after a proper study.

Booth cabled the message back to Belfast, with the further information that "the limited partnership was a device by which high-income earners in the United States could use a tax-haven country such as Puerto Rico or the Republic of Ireland to invest with large benefits to their own personal tax position." Northern Ireland did not offer those advantages. This struck the Belfast officials as nothing more than an excuse, as indeed it was.

Two days later the NIDA board met again at Holywood, this time for the regular board meeting. If they were going to take it further (and they all decided they would), then it was time for the process of "due diligence." Someone would have to go to the United States, see that the company had title to the things it said it did, that there was a car at all, look at the offices, talk to the complete management team, check with the auditors, lawyers, consultants, and so forth. Whom to send?

Tony Hopkins, the obvious candidate, was on vacation. But there was a new man who had joined the staff two weeks before: Shaun Harte, a loquacious, dark-haired, Irish accountant. He was given the job and so was Gil Wilson, another NIDA official. The Department of Commerce was to send Frank McCann and Robin Bailie, a local Belfast lawyer who had done a lot of work for the agency recently, was to go also. Bailie was something of a Belfast whiz kid. He had already been minister of commerce in the Brian Faulkner government in the early 1970s and now had a thriving practice in Belfast. Later Bailie would represent the DeLorean Company in Belfast. With everyone's approval, it was agreed that on this trip Bailie would act for NIDA and would go to Detroit.

On Thursday, June 29, the team of Harte, Wilson, McCann, and Bailie flew to London and then caught a plane to Detroit. In Bloomfield Hills, however, they were not overpoweringly welcome, at least as far as the chief financial officer, Bob Dewey, was concerned. Dewey thought they should not even be there. "I thought Puerto Rico looked good, and I didn't want to be all the way over in Northern Ireland."

It seemed to him another of John's aberrations, another way-out plan that would come to nothing but would waste everyone's time— except John's. He was not even going to be there that weekend—it was the Fourth of July holiday.

"You know, this is a national holiday here, and we've got a long weekend we take off," he told the Belfast team before they started.

"We're coming anyway," was the reply. "You've got to make yourselves available."

Dewey afterward recalled he was "not very cordial." The visitors never noticed. Collins was his usual bluff, enthusiastic self. Strycker was there. So was Brown. They made a good team: experienced, capable, friendly but businesslike.

At that time the DeLorean empire consisted of only fourteen professional men. In addition to Collins, Brown, Dewey, and Strycker, who was a consultant, there was A. Lawrence Cobb, who enjoyed the title of general manager although there was little to manage. He had come from Rockwell International in February. Harry DeWitt was an old hand, although he was only twenty-eight. He had been there since the end of 1976, helping Dewey in general accounting. Collins had a couple of people to help him: Alan Cross, who had worked on the ill-fated Bricklin (the only man to work on both the Bricklin and the DeLorean), was doing development work on the chassis; Robert Manion, from Chrysler, was in charge of electrical. Then there was the team of Terry Werrell and Marshall Zaun, who had been involved in the new Chevrolet Vega plant at Lordstown, Ohio—a two-million-square-foot plant built in fifteen months, employing 5,000 people and turning out sixty cars an hour. They were standing by to build the DeLorean factory.

Dick Brown had brought his own team from Mazda: James Fearer, Louis O. Glasgow, and William A. Morgan. Tom Kimmerly did not officially join until later, although his law firm had a well-established relationship with the company. His vanguard was Jeffrey B. Levine, who became a full-time employee in April 1978, hired from Kimmerly's law firm.

And that was all! The British government was considering an investment of more than $100 million in it.

Bob Dewey had another reason for not welcoming the Irishmen that July Fourth weekend. He had made a momentous decision: he would leave John DeLorean just as soon as he possibly could—the first member of the team to go. He nearly quit in May, but he knew that would have put up too many red flags, and there would be no project. And he did not want to kill it, merely get away from it. He was increasingly concerned by the way money was going out the window faster than it was raised.

Since he had joined, more than $8 million had been spent (most, in his view, senselessly and wastefully), with little to show for it. Much of it seemed to be going for John's private projects and for his lifestyle. The original sports car limited partnership had put in $3.5 million and that was gone. Wood Gundy had invested $500,000 and that was gone. Johnny Carson's $500,000 was gone. The dealers to date had invested over $5 million and that was gone. DeLorean was flying around the world with teams of people, spending money like water on consultants and legal fees without any visible objective or plan, taking up projects and dropping them again. But it was DeLorean's company—he owned 84 percent of the common stock and

Dewey could not argue. But there were minority shareholders. Dewey knew what his fiduciary responsibility as chief financial officer was, and he was worried by it.

Through 1978, he said, he spent more and more time minding the till. By summer it was so bad that "I was guarding that till twenty-four hours a day, seven days a week."

"John, we have entirely different attitudes about how you go through money," he finally told him.

DeLorean sent him a letter, pointing out the alternatives: "You can do it my way or you can leave."

In an odd way, Dewey admired that. As he remarked to a friend, "You know, that's very straightforward. His name is on the door, and I'm not necessarily going to do everything his way, so my alternative is to leave."

Now he was spending his July Fourth weekend showing the Irish team the books, resenting them and resenting DeLorean even more. That weekend they split up the team. Brown, Collins, and Dewey each took a day with them in the office, and Strycker was there too. DeLorean was "available by telephone," but no one bothered him. They met the DeLorean auditor, Dick Measelle, from the accounting firm of Arthur Andersen in Detroit. Measelle supported their already favorable impressions and also laid out in more detail why the Oppenheimer limited partnership was no longer available.

Then Gil Wilson went to California, taking Shaun Harte's camera to photograph the prototype, as someone remarked "to prove there really is a car after all this." The others went to New York, where Ronnie Henderson joined them from Germany.

In New York they tried to see the Oppenheimer people, who were still annoyed and refused. But on Monday they finally saw DeLorean at his office in the Chris-Craft building. It was still the holiday weekend, and there was no one about. They had seen the investors' prospectus and were impressed by that. If it was good enough for the SEC to pass on and to get through the blue-sky regulations of various states, then that was another major plus. Not a bad first trip, they decided, as they flew back across the Atlantic.

But something more detailed, more professional, was needed, and there was now a great hurry. The British Cabinet would have its last full meeting at the end of July, at which stage Parliament would go into recess and even the prime minister would go on holiday. If they missed that (and the project was going to require full cabinet approval), then it would have to wait until September.

The end of July was also the final, final, final signing date given by the Puerto Ricans. The head of Fomento in San Juan, Manuel Dubon, who had recently replaced Vallecillo and who opposed the project, had been pressing to get out of the agreement, and Governor Romero agreed with him. Now they indicated that unless the deal was signed by August 2 at the latest, the offer would be finally and irrevocably withdrawn.

On Friday, July 7, the Department of Commerce asked the consulting firm of McKinsey to investigate. In Britain, McKinsey is something of an institution in financial consultancy. It had organized such institutions as the Bank of England and the island of Hong Kong. Now it was the turn of McKinsey's John Banham to go to Detroit and New York and be back with a report exactly a week later.

It was not favorable. In that first unwritten report, Banham did not advise against investment in the DeLorean project, but within a week he had spotted most of the weak points and laid them out for the Commerce civil servants in Belfast.

"The project is very risky, and it is not difficult to see why Mr. DeLorean has found it hard to raise private risk capital. High-risk projects require higher returns."

Quigley asked Banham to do some more detailed research and let them have a written report—when could he do that? Banham gulped and promised it for the following Tuesday. His feet had not touched the ground and would not touch it again for another week.

On July 18 Banham turned up with his final McKinsey report. It was even more critical than his oral one but still did not definitely come down against the investment. He had seen the DeLorean corporate plan only two days before. Banham could point to lots of reasons for not going ahead with the project, but the Northern Ireland politicians palpably wanted it, so he started by looking on the bright side, stating why it might be attractive "if the formidable odds against its success can be overcome." He underlined the "if."

There were all those jobs, and in West Belfast, too. The project would be a morale booster for the Province and help keep up the impetus generated by the announcements that both General Motors and Michelin were to invest in Ulster. "The DMC investments would further strengthen the local automotive industry, particularly since the luxury and sports car segments of that industry are less sensitive to business cycles as a whole," he went on.

In his efforts to find good points at the beginning, Banham then went over the top:

> The project itself would be an attractive advertisment for the province in terms of its quality and the technical innovation involved. (Porsche is also researching the possibilities of a 20-year car.) Many of the likely purchasers could be in a position at some stage in their careers to influence U.S. investment overseas. The Ulster operation would not be marginal to DMC success and, thus, vulnerable to closure in a recession. On the contrary, the plant would be essential to the whole venture; so the province would be acquiring high quality managerial talent. Finally, Mr. DeLorean himself would be a very effective ambassador to the U.S. industry for the province. As the press clippings demonstrate, DeLorean is well known and highly regarded in industrial circles in the United States and had an impressive record during his career at General Motors. Moreover, he is likely to be familiar with the Washington scene, which could be important if anti-dumping actions are brought against the DeLorean Motor Company in Northern Ireland.

Perhaps it is unfair to subject that paragraph to the test of hindsight, but it does illustrate as clearly as anything the way the minds of politicians and officials were working at the time.

Instead of an "attractive advertisement" for Ulster, the DeLorean project turned into the worst possible publicity. There was no technical innovation worth speaking of in the car, and to compare it with Porsche's idea of a twenty-year car was nonsense.

The "likely purchasers" did not become DeLorean and Ulster fans. The car had so many problems in the United States that the opposite was true. The Ulster operation was never intended to be central to John DeLorean's corporate schemes. On the contrary, it was only part of his plan for a General Motors-type conglomerate, which so scared the Dublin officials and greatly worried his fellow directors. In fact, a month or so after the deal was signed, DeLorean shook up some of his colleagues by suddenly saying, "I don't think we'll ever build the car in Northern Ireland; the IRA will blow it up."

Then there was that final point of Banham's: that DeLorean would be a good ambassador for the Province and that he knew Washington well. None of his executives recall DeLorean saying anything favorable about Northern Ireland. Brown's father was a Northern Ireland Protestant and he still had family there. He became very upset with DeLorean, who characterized the Northern Irish as "dummies," "morons," "incompetents," and worse. Nor did DeLorean know much of the politics of Washington and he remained extraordinarily naive about them.

Banham, however, was on surer ground in assessing the risks in the project and he now listed them in detail. For a start, he did not believe the sales targets. DeLorean was projecting sales of 20,000 cars a year immediately, rising to 30,000. Yet the sales of the Porsche 924, priced below the DeLorean, were only 13,657 in 1977. The Porsche 911 had sold only 5,709 and the Lancia Beta Scorpion, which McKinsey figured was also a competitor, a mere 1,375. The entire Lotus line managed fewer than 1,000 cars worldwide in 1977, Banham added, little knowing at the time that Lotus was to play such a key part in the DeLorean story. Part of that Lotus line was designed by Giorgetto Giugiaro, just like the DMC-12, and Banham had clippings from *Road and Track* that indicated Giugiaro saw the DeLorean designs as little more than one of the family of cars he designed for manufacturers all over the world.

Banham also worried about the color problem. Chevrolet, he pointed out, had so many potential colors that each of its 42,000 Corvette owners could have been unique—and liked to imagine themselves so. With DeLorean, you only got stainless steel. There was no allowance for competition. If his car really sold well, the others would react fast enough, and DeLorean was planning to capture 15 percent of the market.

The report was dubious about the ERM plastic process, pointing out that if it could not be used, the plant and equipment budget would have to be increased by $29 million, the extra money presumably to be taken from the British taxpayer. Then there was the time involved. DeLorean was promising to do it all in eighteen months. Yet the standard time for developing a new car with an established company and experienced management was three years. Porsche took seven or eight.

In general, there were too many optimistic assumptions and no margin for error. All estimates and projections were worked out on the basis that nothing could go wrong, that the whole setup from day one would click into top gear, be as efficient as General Motors or Porsche or BMW, which had generations of accumulated experience. DeLorean was blithely assuming that with untried management, a new distribution network, new suppliers, new work force, new location, and a new car using new and untested technology, he would not just match "but be able to exceed the best industry practice." This section summed up forebodingly: "On the face of it, these projections seem hazardous."

There was some gentle irony in the report. Banham, clearly, was a man of subtle wit. He wrote: "Labour productivity is assumed at North American rates—that is, the Northern Ireland unit labour cost is based on standard hours per unit developed for a possible site in Pennsylvania and adjusted for Belfast labour rates. If this can be achieved, it will be a remarkable performance, and one that has eluded the management of Ford, Chrysler and GM in the United Kingdom—not to mention British Leyland."

Then there was a section headed "Undue Dependence on One Man." The man, of course, was John DeLorean and this was by no means all negative. "One of the (few) reassuring aspects of this project is that Mr. DeLorean's personal reputation depends on its personal success, and that he also stands to gain substantially if the odds can be overcome. Under the latest proposals he would retain a 34-percent interest in DMC and its subsidiaries—and his equity stake could be worth $60 million."

On the other hand, the project would be threatened if anything happened to him, and that was possible "given the nature of the project and the location of the plant." Banham suggested that an insurance policy could be taken out, although the premiums "will almost certainly be quite significant."

He then got to the crux of the matter: "In summary, the Department is being asked to fund an extraordinarily risky venture. The combination of DOC grants and NIDA equity investment will mean that a large proportion of the financial risk ($116 million out of a total funds requirement to April 1, 1980, of $118.1 million) will be carried by the U.K. taxpayer in return for a 22 percent stake (after conversion) in the company if it can succeed in overcoming the odds. Moreover, by the nature of the investment, most of the funds have to be committed at the front end: working capital amounts to less than £9 million [about $16.2 million] of the total Northern Ireland investment of £61 million [about $109 million]."

Banham didn't know it, but of course Puerto Rico had insisted that not a penny of government money go in until DeLorean had spent $25 million.

Banham's final paragraph was not exactly reassuring to Dr. Quigley at the Department of Commerce. The analysis, Banham said, suggested that the chances of the project succeeding as planned were "remote." But analysis was not everything, he then admitted: "The odds can be beaten, even though this may seem unlikely. Mr. DeLorean has a formidable record behind him, and he has committed his personal reputation, not to mention $3.5 million of his personal funds, to the project. He has persuaded some competent people to join him, and they also appear to believe in the project's viability."

To justify investing in the high-risk DeLorean venture, said Banham, "the political and image benefits . . . will have to be very substantial and the opportunity costs to NIDA . . . will have to be low." Except for that one naive and uninformed paragraph at the beginning, it was a remarkably prescient and penetrating report for eleven days' work.

It was Tuesday, July 18, when Quigley received it. In the Department of Commerce building in Chichester Street, in the heart of Belfast, the McKinsey report went down like a lead balloon. It did not raise much cheer in the NIDA office either when the officials heard about it.

In the Commerce Department, McCann was apparently enthusiastic about the project. Quigley wanted it, too, but not at any price, and he was worried. At NIDA, Chief Executive Henderson was enthusiastic; so was Harte. Hopkins, who had been on vacation with his family in Donegal in the early stages, had now taken over from Harte and was deeply involved with the figures. He was in favor, too, but was already worried by it.

McKinsey had raised some serious questions. What were the answers? More frantic Telexes flew to and from Belfast and Detroit, but it seemed only reasonable that the DeLorean team in Detroit should have the report in its entirety.

Banham's office was in St. James's Street in London. The next day Buck Penrose, a new DeLorean executive who had joined DMC from

Booz Allen a week before, collected a copy of the report from Banham's office and flew straight back to Detroit with it. Three days later, on Saturday, he wrote Quigley a fifteen-page reply. The Commerce officials were meeting on Tuesday the twenty-fifth, and time was now precious. By Monday the Penrose letter was in Quigley's hands. It attempted to deal with McKinsey's criticisms and doubts with a mixture of condescension and obfuscation.

McKinsey, Penrose implied, just didn't understand what it was talking about. The analysis was drawn from its "extensive and highly regarded experience" of the U.K. and European Economic Community automotive industry, but a critique "which does not include U.S. perspective may not be balanced or objective." The new DeLorean company was "lean, hungry and aggressive" and should not be compared with the stodgy old companies such as Porsche or BMW that Banham was using as a yardstick. "Digital Equipment Corporation," added Penrose by way of example, "has achieved annual sales of more than $1 billion by pursuing market opportunities that IBM ignored." DeLorean, he implied, could achieve something similar by penetrating markets that General Motors ignored. The DMC management had 276 man-months invested in the program. How could McKinsey analyze it even better than they in eleven days?

Perhaps the most interesting point to emerge from this letter was the reaction to McKinsey's worry about the dependence of the project on one man. Obviously, acknowledged Penrose, DeLorean could suffer a heart attack, die in an airplane crash, or even be killed in an act of terrorism, so the company had taken out a "key man" life insurance policy from Prudential. The sum: $10 million. "Management believes that this amount will be more than sufficient to offset any loss in program momentum which may result from Mr. DeLorean's demise."

Tuesday, July 25: Four days to go before the master agreement is signed and just over a week before Mason himself will be there for the grand ceremony, which is now scheduled for August 2, the press conference to be held a day later. The news is beginning to leak. Mason has bumped into Gerry Fitt in the House of Commons and indicates that he has something special to announce soon for West Belfast. He does not say what it is, but there have been teams out looking at the Twinbrook development.

Everyone knows there are Americans in town, and Belfast is a small place. The *Belfast Telegraph* carries a story indicating that NIDA has something major on the way that will offer thousands of jobs. Mason is busy priming the Cabinet, preparing the ministers through their Permanent Secretaries. He already knows there will be opposition.

By now the basic framework of the deal had been settled. John DeLorean had equity, grants, and loans totaling $106 million. In addition there was another $15-million loan offer to fill the gap left by Oppenheimer. The NIDA cash was a complex mixture, but the key component was £17.757 million (worth $35.5 million) of equity money, or risk capital. That entitled NIDA to 17.757 million votes on the basis of one vote per share. DeLorean contributed $1 million through DMC and got 546,000 shares of Class B ordinary stock, each worth ninety votes. So he ended up with 49,140,000 votes, 73 percent of the total, for an investment of $1 million. On top of the NIDA equity there was $50.4 million in nonrepayable grants and $20 million in loans from the Department of Commerce.

De Lorean also negotiated a so-called "technical assistance" agreement whereby DMC would be paid by the Belfast company for its managerial and technical expertise. This was a generous $290,000 per month—for the next two and one-half years this was DMC's only official source of income. Then there was a complex royalty agreement: NIDA and the Department of Commerce were entitled to $375 for each of the first 90,000 cars sold and $90 per car after that. DMC would have sole distribution rights to the car in the United States, but no cars would pass from the Belfast company to DMC without payment first. Finally, DMC was not allowed to involve itself in any other venture without NIDA's express approval.

The last major issue, an inflation clause, was sorted out the week before.

"What allowance are you making for inflation in your projections?" asked one of the Commerce people of DeLorean.

Neatly, DeLorean turned it back on him. "That's up to you guys, isn't it? You're the government. It's your inflation, not ours."

The officials were nonplussed, but DeLorean would not let up. "You've raised it and I think it's a good question. What do you suggest we do?"

In the end it was agreed that inflation and movements in the pound against the dollar should be taken care of in a special clause added to the master agreement. This stated that the Department of Commerce would "be prepared to consider" the possibility of further financing "if required for the satisfactory establishment of the undertaking at the factory and for the provision and maintenance of the (specified) levels of employment . . . as a result of currency fluctuations, inflation or other causes outside (limited's) control." It was another fateful mistake that would cost the British government dear.

By now the DeLorean team was beginning to build up for the Grand Finale. Strycker was back in Belfast's Europa Hotel redoing the corporate plan originally made for Puerto Rico. With him were Penrose and DeWitt. DeLorean, Brown, Kimmerly, Dewey, and Collins would all be there by the weekend. The officials, lawyers, and accountants were burning the midnight oil, dotting the "i's" and crossing the "t's" of the lengthy, complicated master agreement.

At One New York Plaza, Oppenheimer had had a change of mind. Times were hard on Wall Street, and $2 million was $2 million. "We weren't going to get paid unless something really consummated itself," recalled Hayes. "And we put in a lot of time and effort into the project —a lot of people invested, including myself, you know. We all thought he had a good idea and he could make money."

With the deal all but closed, with Northern Ireland offering approximately twice as much as Puerto Rico and three times as much as the Irish Republic, and with almost no strings attached, Oppenheimer decided Belfast was the place after all. Howard Phillips booked a flight to Belfast to get him there in time for the signing.

By now it seemed unstoppable. Mason was confident of enough Cabinet support to get it through, and indeed he had it. The Commerce officials were responding to his enthusiasm by pushing NIDA, although in truth there were not many critics about.

There was at least one, however. At the NIDA board meeting on Wednesday morning, the august figure of Sir Lindsay Ring, former Lord Mayor of London and a leading financial figure, spoke up. Ring had missed the original meeting that had agreed on the DeLorean deal. Now he had just been given a copy of the McKinsey report, which he told all the other board members he saw as "highly critical." Why didn't they all have it earlier so they could study it properly?

Patiently, Faulkner pointed out that the report had been prepared for Dr. Quigley at Commerce, not for NIDA, and NIDA had received it just as a matter of courtesy. But Ring thought that even without an earlier look at the report NIDA had not been supplied with enough information to make a proper decision. How could they possibly tell, on the basis of what they had seen so far, that it was a viable proposition?

Faulkner and Chief Executive Henderson pointed out that there was a deadline they were working to, that it had been discussed at one monthly and four special board meetings, that the executive had studied three separate consultants' reports and the ones from Booz Allen and Kearney were favorable. Henderson, Hopkins, and Harte had studied those reports in great detail and had concluded that while there were certainly considerable risks, the project was worth pursuing because of the employment prospects for West Belfast and the potential morale boost to the province.

Sir Lindsay Ring found some support from trade union leader John Freeman, who disliked the fortunes being made by DeLorean and various advisers. But Freeman badly wanted that project for West Belfast.

"There are people there in their thirties and forties who have never worked in their lives, people with grown-up children who have never seen their fathers do a day's work. You have to look at those men's eyes to understand what West Belfast is about. There's no sparkle there, no hope."

At the end of the discussion the NIDA board reaffirmed its decision to go ahead with the DeLorean project, subject now only to Cabinet committee approval. The doubts had been allayed by a revised group structure whereby the Northern Ireland company would own the major assets.

It was another mistake. The structure under which DMC sold the cars made by the Belfast company, now called DeLorean Motor Cars Limited, or simply Limited, meant that John DeLorean himself could make all decisions, concentrate profits where they were most suitable to him, and make it virtually impossible for Limited to get rid of him or free itself of his control. All its cars had to be sold through him.

All that remained now was the signing and the ceremonies. DeLorean arrived with Kimmerly. Brown flew in from California; Dewey and Collins from Detroit. The master agreement was signed that Friday, July 28. DeLorean, in high glee, went off house-hunting over the weekend. He had decided to buy a castle, he said, returning in time for the big ceremony on Tuesday when Mason signed the formal agreement. (DeLorean had it framed on his office wall.)

That evening Mason held a dinner for them in Hillsborough with speeches by himself and DeLorean. The next morning they were ready for the press conference. John DeLorean had made the deal of his life.

7

GPD

Pause for a moment and consider DeLorean's position that summer weekend in Belfast. He now had all the money he needed—more than he expected, more than an enterprise that thus far employed fewer than twenty people could ever reasonably have hoped for. There was now every prospect that in two years he would have a custom-built factory on that cow pasture at the far end of the Falls Road.

The car he would produce there was also advancing—Bill Collins had built two prototypes and the dealers seemed to love them. Dick Brown had nearly completed the dealer network; each of the dealers had put up $25,000 in advance and agreed to take at least the first year's production. DeLorean's team was assembled: Collins the engineer, Dewey the finance man, Brown the marketer, who would also be invaluable in building the factory, and Walt Strycker.

He had his Wall Street supporters: Oppenheimer had now agreed to put together a tax-shelter scheme, having magically found a way around the problems that six weeks before had seemed insuperable. The whole strategy was falling into place beautifully. What could go wrong?

There was one thing he had not yet arranged—John DeLorean had not yet gotten any cash for himself out of it. There was plenty of money around for the car and factory, but that was all tied up—or so in their innocence the money brokers thought. A method to channel some of those funds away from the car venture had not yet occurred to DeLorean.

There is no hard evidence that he set out with premeditation to divert some of those investment funds away from the car project. But there is plenty of evidence to show that when the opportunity arose, he diverted in abundance. Some $17.8 million raised for the venture would never be applied to it.

That story, however, lies ahead. In Belfast in early August, John DeLorean had a different problem: how to live up to his promises. He had persuaded the Northern Irish officials that his staff, slim as it was, was ready to go the instant the deal was signed. He had excellent men who had built the most modern auto plants in the United States—Terry Werrell and Marshall Zaun. Dick Brown had built the highly successful Mazda plant, but he would be occupied in California with his dealer network. Now that he had to produce results, John De-Lorean admitted privately that it could be difficult.

The man to whom he confessed was Brown. After the signing he took Brown aside. "You know, Dick, we really have nobody who knows a thing about building a plant." He looked speculatively at Brown. "Could you stay and get it done?"

Werrell and Zaun were probably capable enough, but they had neither the experience nor the seniority that DeLorean claimed for them and he knew it. So did they. They had come to Belfast to help search for the right site.

"Once they got there it was pretty apparent that they didn't have the ability or the confidence to get it done," said Brown. That was no reflection on either Werrell or Zaun—they were simply presented as something more than they were. They soon left.

DeLorean was also talking expansively of another idea. Renault had a division, SERI, that had built car plants all over the world. SERI could do a turn-key operation on the plant, he suggested.

Brown blanched. It was several days before he could get DeLorean to see that it wouldn't work. The whole reason for the Northern Ireland government getting involved in the first place was to create jobs. Six hundred of those jobs would be in building the plant—immediate jobs that would last for two years.

"There is no way they are going to allow a French company to come in and do a turn-key," he told DeLorean. "You know, we are here to develop labor for the Northern Irish, not for France." DeLorean finally got the point.

The same day he asked Brown to stay in Belfast, DeLorean also told him: "We really need somebody who knows the ins and outs of the United Kingdom."

Brown had an idea. "Well, John, my next-door neighbor has a brother who is the director of personnel and administration for Chrysler, Europe."

"Well, could we talk to him?"

"Sure," said Brown. The man he had in mind was Myron Stylia-nides, an anglicized Greek who knew his way around the auto industry in Europe. Brown phoned him, and the following evening, the festivities in Belfast over, he and DeLorean flew to London, where they had dinner with Stylianides.

Stylianides had some news of his own to impart in private to the two Americans. Chrysler, desperately strapped for cash, was bailing out of its European operation. There had been talks for weeks, he confided; the deal was almost complete and would be announced in a day or so. Peugeot-Citroën, France's proudest car company, would take it all over. And he, Myron Stylianides, would be out of a job. If DeLorean wanted someone to look after personnel and administration. . . .

DeLorean did. Stylianides became the first new recruit. DeLorean now went home to New York, leaving the Belfast operation to Brown. It had been his longest visit to Northern Ireland—about three days. He would never be there as long again.

Dick Brown did not mind. He was enjoying himself. His father had emigrated from the province in 1910, and Brown felt he was home again. He brought his wife, his son, and daughter over and they all stayed in the Conway Hotel, a few hundred yards from the factory site. On the edge of the site there was a carpet factory, a new but small building, that he used as his headquarters. It had been built for an industry that no longer existed there—another victim of the deep recession that was hitting Northern Ireland so hard.

Brown soon hired another old friend. Dixon Hollinshead had put up the buildings for Mazda when Brown started that company in the United States. Brown phoned him in California and within a week Hollinshead was in Belfast. He, too, brought his wife with him and he became the project manager for the plant. Hollinshead would stay two years and, perhaps more than anyone else, was responsible for the factory being built almost on schedule. Brown would stay in Ireland two and a half months. By mid-October, the project well under way, he was back in California.

At this point DeLorean had to appoint a new chief financial officer. Dewey had done what he said he'd do: keep the team together until the money was assured. In mid-August he left—and was soon regretting it, though for reasons he could not have foreseen.

Brown explained it like this: "When anybody leaves John De-

Lorean, he has an expression—at least I've heard him use it on a couple of people. 'Now,' he will say, 'we've got to get some shit on his shoes.'

"He's done that with everyone who's left. And after Dewey left he had a couple of job offers and John was called for a reference and he told people that the reason Dewey left was because he had a nervous breakdown." Fortunately Dewey's reputation in Detroit and within the financial community was so strong that DeLorean was immediately disregarded.

To the others, Dewey's departure was quite a shock. But the company seemed to be up and running, and for the moment it could bear it. It was perhaps the biggest shock of all to Dewey's immediate successor: Walter Strycker. Strycker turned up at the Detroit office on the first working day in September and Dewey wasn't there. There was no explanation at the time, until Strycker discovered that Dewey had left a note saying he was gone.

"John asked me to cover and I said, you know, I couldn't do that full time because I had a bunch of other obligations and I would give him priority over what I was doing. And I covered the slot for him because I was the only one who knew what was going on. That's how I got sucked in."

Strycker had been a $75,000-a-year consultant. In his new role as chief financial officer he got $100,000. Within a month Dewey had come back, effectively swapping places and salaries with Strycker, as a consultant at $75,000. It was a bad move, Dewey would admit later.

"It was dumb because I didn't really care for Mr. DeLorean. John and I just were never going to see eye to eye."

It was months before he realized what DeLorean was saying about him. And by that time he was once again locked in with the man. Since no harm had been done, Dewey let the matter slide; it merely firmed his resolve to break free permanently as soon as possible.

During August and September, DeLorean was busy doing what he seemed to be doing from the day he left General Motors: raising money. He didn't need any more—not then, and not if the car could have been built to budget, which Collins, Dewey, Strycker, and the company's hordes of consultants believed it could. But there was all that Oppenheimer limited partnership money. And John DeLorean was never a person to let money pass him by. In this case, however, he seems to have had other motives.

Oppenheimer's Howard Phillips had gone to Dublin with the De-Lorean team. He had also turned up again for the signing in Belfast. NIDA in Belfast filled the financing gap left by Oppenheimer with an offer for a loan of $15 million, but in those last days of July, Phillips negotiated Oppenheimer back into the deal. If it could still put the partnership money together, NIDA would withdraw that loan offer. The amount of money DeLorean would get would be the same, but the mix would be very different. And the way it was spent would be even more different, although it was several years before anyone other than DeLorean or a few of his close colleagues knew that.

On the day of the formal signing in Belfast, DeLorean signed a separate agreement with Phillips, countersigned by Henderson on behalf of NIDA, to indicate his agreement with the arrangement. It was effectively an amendment to DeLorean's sales agreement with Oppenheimer dated March 23, 1978. The limited partnership was officially back in business. On New York Plaza, Mike Hayes got on the phone again.

This same letter also clearly set out Oppenheimer's fees: $2,050,000 —$200,000 at the closing of the partnership, the rest paid at a rate of $100,000 a quarter. Oppenheimer would get its pint of blood—or at least some of it.

After fees, the Oppenheimer money came down to a net $15.5 million. And what exactly did the DeLorean Research Limited Partnership hope to get for its money? For a start, it got the car. And it got the ERM process rights. Neither of these were ever owned by the Northern Ireland company, despite the fact that it would end up paying for everything. DMC contributed all its rights to the DMC car to the partnership and became the sole general partner with a 1 percent interest. In turn, the partnership licensed the company in Belfast to build the car. For that, it would receive either $375 in royalties for every car manufactured and sold or 23.4 percent of DMC's profits.

John DeLorean accepted that extraordinarily expensive money despite the fact that he had a signed offer for a loan for roughly the same amount from NIDA, which wouldn't require dipping into profits. Why should he agree to give away nearly a quarter of his profits when he already had the money he needed? It had made sense for Puerto Rico where Manuel Dubon and his men at Fomento insisted on the money up front. It made sense for Ireland, where he could not have hoped to get the project off the ground without the Oppenheimer money. But it made no sense at all now—unless John DeLorean knew that money would not end up in the car.

There is one further item to be fed into the equation. Bill Collins had been laboring for three years under the impression that he would lead the engineering team that would build the car. He built the nucleus of his group and at the end of August he took his engineering colleague, Alan Cross, over to Britain to start work on what he assumed would be the climax to his years of work on the prototype.

The British car industry in Coventry was in deep recession, and the takeover of Chrysler, which was intimated by Stylianides to DeLorean and Brown, now occurred.

"Chrysler was laying a lot of people off and I'm sure we could have put together a good engineering group right in Coventry. Well, that's what I thought John intended," said Collins.

The Oppenheimer money, Collins believed, would finance the work he would do to take the car from the prototype stage to a pre-production model. It was what he had joined to do. Instead, as he remarked later, "In the meantime John had been talking to Chapman."

So enter Colin Chapman, arguably the best designer of Grand Prix racing cars who ever lived. When the deal with Northern Ireland was signed, no one in Belfast knew that Chapman would be involved. When Oppenheimer put together its limited partnership tax-shelter money, none of the investors had heard of Chapman unless they were Grand Prix buffs.

Strycker, Brown, Collins, and Dewey—DeLorean's key executives —had no idea Chapman would be involved. But all of a sudden, at the end of September, he was on the scene, and from then on would play a dominant role in the design of the car.

To DeLorean aides, he appeared from nowhere. In fact, he had been in the background all the previous summer—tentatively in the early days, more positively as the Northern Ireland deal was signed. John DeLorean wanted a winner on his team, and it was Chapman's string of wins that season that had drawn DeLorean inexorably toward the taciturn, brilliant engineer.

Zolder, Belgium, May 21, 1978. The Belgian Grand Prix was about to get under way. The crowds, the mechanics, the hangers-on who swarmed around the low, flat machines all day had gone. The drivers were now in the cars, strapped immobile in their cockpits, unrecognizable behind their helmets. In pole position on the starting grid was the black and gold JPS Lotus of Mario Andretti, the favorite and leader in the world championship, although it was still early in the season. Behind him was his teammate and second favorite, Ronnie Peterson, a Swede who was generally regarded as one of the most skillful drivers on the entire circuit. They were driving the two fastest cars that world racing had ever seen. Unless they had mechanical problems or made a mistake, they would be virtually unbeatable that day.

Less than a minute later, in a tearing crescendo of noise and burning rubber, the cars leaped away, watched by 60,000 spectators and by millions more on live TV. Andretti started smoothly, taking a lead he would not lose. Peterson took up his accustomed second place behind Andretti and stayed there until the fifty-sixth lap. Then he had to change a tire and dropped to fourth. Gilles Villeneuve chased Andretti for a while but could never really get near him.

Ten laps from the end, the excitement focused on the second Lotus when it began its fight back for second place—which Peterson regarded as his right. He overtook Jacques Lafite's Ligier and then, with some brilliant driving that had the crowd on its feet, caught and passed Villeneuve's Ferrari only four laps from the finish. It was another one-two win for Lotus.

For Colin Chapman, founder and chairman of Lotus, 1978 was his best season ever. He had turned fifty two days before, but he was already a legend in the world of auto racing. He had won his first Grand Prix eighteen years earlier when Stirling Moss drove a Coventry-Climax-powered Lotus to victory at Monaco. That day at Zolder was Chapman's sixty-sixth Grand Prix win, a record topped only by Ferrari, which had been racing much longer.

"It's difficult to know what to do for an encore," Chapman told reporters who gathered around the winning team. "Mario wins with the new car and Ronnie has a fantastic drive for second place after a pit stop. We have the best drivers in the world!"

It was his series of Grand Prix victories that season that drew John DeLorean to Colin Chapman like a bee to honey. Chapman had everything that DeLorean wanted: his own car company; a world reputation as a designer and engineer of genius; a beautiful old home in the English countryside, complete with his own airstrip and two planes; and his car factory beside it. He had wealth, reputation, respect, and the comforts of life. Above all, he had done what DeLorean wanted to do—build his own car company from scratch.

Anthony Colin Bruce Chapman—the ACBC monogram was incorporated into the Lotus emblem—had started from far more humble beginnings than had John DeLorean. He built his first competition car in 1948 when he was only twenty in a garage in Muswell Hill in North London. He based it on a beat-up Austin 7. It was to become the first in a long line of sports cars leading to that superb JPS machine driven by Andretti at Zolder.

Chapman borrowed twenty-five pounds from his then fiancée (later his wife), Hazel, and set up his own business, concentrating on "kit" cars, to be assembled by impecunious but enthusiastic sports car drivers at home. He raced on weekends, basically to advertise the Lotus name. Now he hired the world's best drivers to do the same thing in 1978—Team Lotus advertised the wedge-shaped sports car, which Chapman produced in his factory at Hethel, in the middle of the East Anglian countryside. Now it was a larger—but still precariously financed—operation.

Throughout that summer DeLorean tried to tie up with a partner who would build the car for him. To have tried to build the DMC-12 from scratch on his own, he decided, was impossible. It was always intended to be an "off-the-shelf" car—with most of the major components supplied by other manufacturers—from the Renault engine to the stereo speakers. But someone had to do the basic design work, which meant thousands of pages of drawings and specifications, not only for the components but for the tools, stamping machines, and other production equipment that would make those parts. Then the key parts had to be fitted together and tested under stress and later under road conditions so that they could be refined and precisely put together.

And finally, after all those parts were tested, instructions had to be prepared—again by detailed sketches, drawings, and directions—for the men on the assembly line who would put the DMC-12 together and drive it to the shipping lots. As skilled as Bill Collins and his design team were, they could not do the work in the eighteen months allowed without some outside help. Collins always assumed, and rightly so, that his role would be to oversee and direct those crucial final decisions. DeLorean, however, had other ideas.

DeLorean talked to Porsche about doing the job, but that fell through. He talked to the Jensen sports car company in England, makers of small numbers of $40,000 cars and constantly in need of funds, but that never came to anything either. He moved around Europe that summer, trying with growing desperation to make the right deal.

One top DeLorean executive later recalled, "We just made the rounds looking for someone who would help us. I think John was instantly enamoured as soon as he saw Chapman's setup in Norwich, Maybe he [Chapman] was the type of guy John always wanted to be." But what impressed DeLorean more than anything else were those Grand Prix victories. He still remembered his own races along Woodward Avenue in Detroit, but the enormous excitement of Grand Prix racing was something else. He wanted to be part of it, if only by proxy.

In July DeLorean first found his way to Chapman's head office, home, and factory in Norwich. He had already had preliminary discussions with Chapman, but with the Northern Ireland deal moving toward its successful outcome, his plans had crystallized and escalated. He no longer wanted just a contract with Lotus for the development work on the car; he wanted nothing less than to take over the whole company. There was one obstacle: Colin Chapman controlled Lotus through a series of offshore and nominee companies, and it was his brainchild, his creation, his life. DeLorean worked on a scheme that would tempt him to sell.

"John DeLorean appeared here at short notice," recalls Fred Bushell, then Lotus finance director and long-time confidant of Chapman. "He talked to Chapman in terms of buying him out of Lotus. Chapman listened and wasn't particularly impressed. I believe Mr. De-Lorean had some fairly grandiose schemes as to how he would develop Lotus and he was skilled enough to present his arguments in an attractive manner. But obviously for the founder of a company to contemplate disposing of it is a great psychological hangup. Once he'd gotten through all the charms and the blandishments, the hard-core resolve of Colin Chapman was that this was his business and that's the way it would stay. DeLorean's plan to buy the company and impose his own stamp on it just didn't get a response from Chapman and the conversation petered out."

While DeLorean proceeded to negotiate his agreement in Belfast, Chapman's fortunes continued to rise. In July the French Grand Prix was held at the Paul Richard Circuit near Marseilles in a blinding heatwave. Once again, it was a one-two for Andretti and Peterson.

"Just perfect," said Andretti of his car, decked out in the gold and black colors of Chapman's sponsor, the John Player Cigarette Company.

"Just keep the winning streak going," said Chapman. And they did. It was, said the automobile reporters, the "Year of the Lotus," its superiority clearer than anything in the history of Formula One auto racing.

By August DeLorean had the money he needed and the place to build his car. Now he turned to the pressing problem of the car itself, redoubling his efforts to talk Chapman into doing the development work on it. The racing man was tied up emotionally in the Grand Prix season, pushing himself and everyone else harder than ever as his cars went faster and faster, his two drivers first and second in the World Championship. But despite his successes, Chapman was financially vulnerable. His Lotus Cars, a public company that he kept separate from the racing team, had run into a cash crisis the year before and been bailed out by American Express.

Chapman knew only too well how transitory success on the track was. To keep his team going cost about $5 million a year. His contract with John Player was running out, and the cigarette company had indicated its intention not to renew. DeLorean's car project represented badly needed money. Fred Bushell sets the scene like this:

> Lotus is a business which is always a little fraught and one is always looking to the future, trying to see how a small company this size, which doesn't have any right to exist, is going to continue. And the board, in 1977, faced with the ever higher expenditures that the engineers were demanding, decided that the best thing to do was to seek out contract work. It would enable us to retain a staff of engineers which, frankly, we couldn't afford otherwise. But how do you get contract work? At that time we had no one who could go and bang on people's doors, so we chose to contact a number of long-standing associates of ours, inviting them to act as finders for contract work, particularly in the sphere where we had particular expertise: the application of what we now call our "composite technique" and structures which involved lightweight and high efficiency engineering.

One of the "associates" that Lotus approached was, according to Bushell, the Juhan family of Geneva whom Chapman had known for twenty-five years. Jaroslav "Jerry" Juhan was a Czech motorcycle champion who emigrated to South America after the war, settling for a while in Guatemala.

In the late 1950s Juhan returned to Europe and eventually settled in Geneva. He and his wife, Marie-Denise, built up a series of businesses dealing in automobile components, wine, watches, diamonds, and other products. At one time their Perrin Importeurs distributed Lotus, but according to Bushell that arrangement ceased in 1974.

In 1976 Chapman and the Juhans made another deal. Chapman decided to abandon European distributors and move to a single-tier system for distribution—direct from the family to the dealer. "And we engaged the Juhans," says Bushell, "because they are multilingual and have contacts to find those dealers for us. They also were very useful in organizing local technical clearances in those countries where approvals were required." To do this for Lotus, says Bushell, the Juhans set up a company called L.C.I. SA Distribution Automobile, which sounds as if it might stand for Lotus Cars International, although Bushell claims it stands for "nothing particularly."

In 1977, when Lotus asked the Juhans to find contract work for them, a new company was prepared in Panama, a country with which Juhan had some familiarity from his South American days. The common practice in Panama is to create thousands of little companies to be sold "off the shelf" to foreign interests who use them for their own purposes, usually related to taxes, or the avoidance of disclosure, or both. The Juhans had bought such a company, ILC Inc., to handle their contract-finding work for Lotus.

Chapman, meanwhile, was still very much preoccupied with the Grand Prix season now approaching its climax. It had reached the stage where drivers were maneuvering for places in the next year's teams, and Peterson was clearly tired of playing second fiddle. Nothing could stop a Lotus driver from winning the world championship —the only man who could catch Andretti was Ronnie Peterson.

Peterson, thirty-four, was a tall, pale Swede regarded by his peers as the fastest of all Grand Prix drivers. He finished four times in second place behind Andretti, strictly honoring his agreement to do nothing to jeopardize Andretti's chances to become World Champion. Now he decided to leave Lotus at the end of the season to join McLaren.

But for the Italian Grand Prix at Monza early in September, both Lotus drivers were in top form. Monza is an unpopular track with drivers. The cars start on a wide straight and then funnel into a narrow corner, unlike other tracks that are a similar width throughout. Under the rules in force that day, the cars approached the starting grid from the warmup lap. When they were all in position, a red light came on. Six seconds later it turned to green and the race was on.

The idea was to permit up to twenty-four cars to be spaced out in rows of two, have the cars come to rest, and shift into first gear. That September day some of the cars in the rear were in third gear moving at 90 miles an hour when the light turned to green. So they jumped the start, causing the cars in front to bunch. The result was disastrous.

Peterson started from the third row. His car took off sluggishly and several rows of cars behind shot past before he got to the zigzag turns of the chicane, as it is known in racing. James Hunt's McLaren was right on his tail. Then Hunt was rammed from behind, hit Peterson's car, and caused the Lotus to slide across the track. Vittorio Brambilla's Surtees rammed it broadside. The cars crowding in from behind piled into them. Within three seconds of the start, there was a ten-car smashup.

Peterson's car, its fifty-five gallon fuel tank full, was hurled into a guardrail and caught fire, the driver trapped under the twisted steering wheel. Hunt leaped from his stalled McLaren and with help ripped off Peterson's safety belt and eased him out of the flames and smoke as a track marshal sprayed foam on the wreck.

Both of the Swede's legs were broken and he had suffered burns and lung damage from inhaling the fumes. At first he seemed to be recovering from emergency surgery, but complications set in. The following day he fell into a coma as clots began to block the blood and oxygen supply to his brain, kidneys, and lungs. On September 11 he died.

Andretti was sixth in a rerun race that was won by Niki Lauda—and that was good enough to capture the 1978 world title. But it was a gloomy Chapman who returned to his headquarters in Norwich to pick up the pieces of his business.

Chapman had been there before. He had never fully gotten over the death at the wheel of a Lotus of his great friend Jim Clark. It was Chapman's partnership with Clark that first established Lotus at the top of world Grand Prix racing in the 1960s. When Clark was killed, Graham Hill took over and won the 1968 World Championship, only to die in another accident years later, when he piloted his plane into land in fog. World Champion Jochen Rindt had also died in a Lotus —ironically at Monza as well—eight years before. He was replaced by Emerson Fittipaldi, who also became World Champion in a Lotus. Now Peterson had been killed through no fault of the driver or of the car. Tragedy was a part of auto racing. Drivers died, but the team went on. Chapman would bounce back, he had been a driver himself and knew the score. But it did not make it any easier. It was at this time that he began to negotiate seriously with John DeLorean.

There is still some mystery as to how the deal was revived after its inauspicious start. Bushell's version is that

> The Juhans told us they had ascertained that DeLorean was going around Europe looking for a way to engineer his new car. Wouldn't this be just what we were looking for? And again Chapman was very disinterested. He didn't think it was going to be a viable program and he didn't really think that DeLorean could make it. All we knew about it at the time was what we had read in the press, a very coy statement that the British government were going to provide him with a factory in Belfast. They didn't mention any funding for the car at all.

According to Bushell the Juhans said, "Well, we've spent a lot of money on your behalf in the past year looking for contracts and haven't got very much in return yet. At least talk to the man."

DeLorean went to Lotus twice that summer—the first time in July, the second in September. As far as Bushell recalls, the next time Chapman and DeLorean met was in Geneva at the end of October, at the invitation of the Juhans. Long before that, however, the deal seems to have been agreed upon, if not yet fully consummated.

On September 20, nine days after Ronnie Peterson died, the name of the Panama Company, ILC Inc., was changed to GPD Services Inc. The Panamanian law firm involved told *Automotive News:* "This John DeLorean was part of the corporation." To the London *Sunday Telegraph*, it confirmed that Colin Chapman was also involved. Thus, the vehicle for the two men to do business had been created. From now on, John DeLorean had no doubts about who would build his car for him. It would not be his loyal engineer, Bill Collins, who was now effectively out of a job. It would be Colin Chapman.

Chapman was a trim, pale man with piercing blue eyes and a clipped mustache, his fair hair showing the first tinges of gray. He had a decisive, sometimes grumpy air and a reputation for being difficult. "He was not the easiest man to live with," says Bushell, who was close to him for twenty-five years. "The better things went with the racing team, the harder time Chapman gave the rest of us. When things were going well for the team, he would get the big stick out and beat us for not matching it. When they lost a race, then we had a bit of breathing space." Even to men like Bushell and Lotus managing director Mike Kimberley, Chapman was "a bit of a Jekyll and Hyde." When he left Norwich for a race meeting, they never dared phone him about business decisions. "No bloody way," says Mike Kimberley.

"I couldn't live with him at a race meeting," says Bushell. "That's why I rarely went—he wasn't the man I knew. In motor racing, decisions have to be made quickly; there's no finesse; it's either yes or no; you've only got twenty-four hours before the flag drops. Once he went to a race he just changed personalities—that was probably the secret of his success. And he changed back the minute it was over."

Despite his success and his millionaire status, Chapman was a private, almost lonely figure, with few close friends apart from his immediate family—his wife, Hazel, a son, and two daughters. In more recent years he had developed a weight problem, the pounds going on and off in reverse relationship to his Grand Prix fortunes.

Back in New York, Walter Strycker was getting his first taste of John DeLorean's accounting. Until the deal with Northern Ireland, there was very little money around. As Dewey had discovered, it was going out faster than it came in. In the summer of 1978, Dick Brown had to lend the company money as DeLorean kept up his expensive lifestyle.

"There were some things that came up real quick after I got exposure to the books," said Strycker later. "One was that John gave himself a retroactive raise back to January 1 of 1978, and I also found out that although he said he wasn't taking any compensation, in lieu of a salary he was taking a cost of living allowance for being in New York."

That cost of living allowance would run as much as $150,000 a year. And while DeLorean did not take a "salary" as such, the "consulting fees" paid to his privately held DeLorean Manufacturing Co. would amount to another $375,000 a year in addition to the living allowance payments.

Over the following months, Strycker was to question again and again the enormous expenses of the operation.

"I can't wait the five or six years it will take for the company to perform," DeLorean told him bluntly. "I want to live now."

On October 2 John DeLorean was back in Belfast for what was scheduled to be a big day. He brought Cristina with him. Brown and Hollinshead were right on schedule. Exactly two months after the signing of the agreement with Northern Ireland, the champagne bottles popped for the ground-breaking ceremony. The Northern Ireland minister of state, Don Concannon, Roy Mason's deputy, did the honors, heading up a cast of hundreds, including the Lord Mayor of Belfast, the mayor of the local town of Lisburn, and a host of local politicians, clergymen, and local dignitaries. Ten large bulldozers moved forward to begin churning up the mud. The building of John DeLorean's factory had begun.

DeLorean made a little speech. "We have been working very hard both here and in the States the past sixty days. I must say that our experience and the accomplishments in Dunmurry thus far has only reinforced our conviction that Northern Ireland, with its highly motivated and competent work force, is the ideal place for DMC to assemble our entry into the world's prestige car market."

Beside him, Cristina's elegance and style contrasted with the drab costumes of the local people. But it was all smiles that day. Everything was moving forward.

That day DeLorean chaired the first full board meeting of the new Northern Ireland company. Brown and Collins were both members. So was Stylianides. NIDA was represented by Shaun Harte and Ronnie Henderson. Tom Kimmerly was also a DMCL director from the beginning, although he refused DeLorean's offer to join the board of DMC on grounds of professional conflict.

By now DeLorean had told his directors he was making a deal with Lotus, but no one except perhaps DeLorean himself and Kimmerly was quite sure yet what sort of deal. He told Strycker in New York that he was thinking of buying Lotus, that NIDA would fund it, and that he would create a new Porsche in Britain, offering enginering deals to the auto world.

NIDA was complaining that the cash withdrawal from the agency and from the Department of Commerce was falling behind schedule. So DeLorean obliged by speeding it up.

He had already received a 10p a share first installment—£1,775,000—immediately after the signing. Now, at that day's board meeting, he called for another 15p a share, making £4,439,250, and requested a further £1,775,700 (the pound was then approaching $2.00) by November 15. The money was rolling in very nicely.

The Lotus headquarters where John DeLorean went to negotiate that summer and fall was very different from anything the Detroit man had ever seen, and it filled him with a desire to acquire something similar for himself. It was hidden away in England's East Anglia countryside, approached through narrow country lanes—along which tiny Lotus cars could be glimpsed hurtling around hairpin bends—or by private plane into Chapman's airstrip. DeLorean preferred to fly in—the journey by car took nearly three hours from London.

Chapman's office was in Ketteringham Hall, once an English nobleman's country mansion, later a United States officers' wartime mess, then a prep school. There was an ornamental lake complete with moorhens, and pheasants inhabited the hedgerows. The design studio occupied what was once the chapel. Racing cars lined up in what had been the stables. It seemed a charming place—very English, a combination of Old World elegance and modern technology.

On the edge of the park was a former bomber base where thirty-five years before, Flying Fortresses took off to bomb Hitler's Germany. Now the hangars were assembly plants for Lotus cars, part of the airfield a test track. It was here that Chapman, year after year, attempted a new design in Grand Prix cars when other designers seemed to have reached a plateau of performance.

It was here, also, that Chapman had his main business—although not his chief interest—of designing and building, more or less by hand, his high-performance, high-priced sports cars. Once he had made more than 4,000 cars a year. Now he was down to less than 400, and he was spending heavily on the research and development of a new car, the Turbo Esprit. It would be easy enough to design two cars at once, use some of the same components, some of the same design team—build a car for DeLorean and for Lotus side by side.

Until DeLorean could strike a deal with Chapman, there wasn't even a place for Bill Collins and his team to sit. Chapman put them in the chapel of Ketteringham Hall, and at first they found it a delightful place. "Anne Boleyn lived here," a Lotus man told them. There was supposed to be the ghost of an airman in the rafters of one of the old hangars. But the history and graciousness of the place were no compensation for their growing frustration.

Collins expected to explain his prototype and work to the Lotus people and help them through the next stages. He was, after all, a senior director of the client customer—or the prospective client customer. He was the chief engineer. He was an experienced man with a good record at the biggest auto company in the world, making more cars in a single hour's production than Lotus did in its entire history. There were four years of his work in the car, and he had a good team with him—experienced American car men who knew the DMC-12 as well as he did.

Collins was becoming increasingly uneasy. He could not get to talk to Colin Chapman, who would not even begin to go through the design of the car with him yet.

In the early weeks of October, DeLorean's dealings with the Juhans in Geneva had moved to the point where there was now a draft contract: $12.5 million would be paid by the Oppenheimer limited partnership scheme, which had officially come into being on September 22, its net $15.5 million after expenses and fees now deposited in the Chemical Bank in New York; another £2.5 million would be paid by DMCL in Belfast for the rights to the VARI plastic molding process developed by Lotus. Even at this early stage, and still without serious negotiation with Chapman, DeLorean was prepared to abandon the ERM process that was such an important feature of his original concept.

In mid-October the pace increased. DeLorean had to have someone to build the car and he knew it had to be Chapman—no one else could do it in the time allotted; no one else had the same reputation for the type of engineering he wanted. And no one else was available. On October 17 there was a tiny but highly significant signing ceremony in Panama: the three members of the Junta Directiva (board of directors) of GPD Services Inc.—Rodrigo Arosemena, Eloy Benedetti, and Cecilia Arosemena de Gonzalez Ruiz—gave power of attorney to Mrs. Denise Juhan Perrin, more often known as Denise Juhan. Control of GPD had now officially passed to Switzerland.

A day later, DeLorean turned up in Belfast with the draft of the GPD contract. He convened a board meeting of DMCL to seek approval for the deal. One board member recalls DeLorean's argument like this:

> I had planned to have all the engineering work done in the United States. The sourcing for the prototype is American. But if we're going to build here, that is going to be very awkward. I don't really know this country and I'm not happy about it. The alternative is to get another company to do the engineering work, and with that in mind I've been talking to Porsche and to BMW and to Lotus. Porsche and BMW either want too much money—about $30 million—or they're talking about too long a time—two to three years at best and probably more with all the other work they have. They're not really that interested, which leaves Lotus. Now in my view Colin Chapman is the best designer in the world—he's brilliant. He is this year's designer of the year, a world champion. His cars wiped everybody else off the track.

There was one problem with Chapman, DeLorean went on. He was reluctant to do the work except on his own terms, and that meant through an intermediary in Switzerland. Everyone understood his point. Chapman did not want to pay taxes on the money he received. At that time under the Labour Government in Britain they ranged up to 83 percent. He hinted to DeLorean that he would do the job if the money could be paid in a "tax-efficient" way. If not, then they were in trouble, with little hope of hitting the timetable. "It was absolutely clear in everybody's mind that the deal was being done this way because that was the only way that Chapman would play ball," says one of the men present that day.

The board approved a payment to GPD for £2.5 million. Britain still had exchange controls, so it was not a simple matter of transmitting funds. The Donegall Square West branch of Northern Bank

Limited handled it, filling in a form for "application to purchase foreign currency." Later that day John DeLorean and Myron Stylian-ides dropped by to sign it, each of them twice. The name and address of the beneficiary was clearly stated: GPD Services Inc., European Office, 120 Rue de Lausanne, 1202 Geneva, Switzerland. The amount: $4.9 million. It was not yet a transfer of cash, but the first step had been taken.

Three thousand miles away another check was made out to GPD that day. On Broad Street, at the Wall Street branch of Chemical Bank, a clerk filled in the amount—$12.5 million from the account of the DeLorean Research Limited Partnership. Now one of the DeLorean financial staff turned up, signed the check on behalf of DMC, which was the General Partner, and carried it back across town. It would spend most of the next two weeks in John DeLorean's wallet, carefully folded.

From Belfast, DeLorean returned to New York, picked up the check and by the middle of the following week was back in London again. He had to make his deal with Chapman, and it had to be done quickly.

He assembled some of his team from Belfast in London. Robin Bailie, Harte, and DeLorean went to the Bank of England's Exchange Control division just across the road from St. Paul's Cathedral. The bank had to approve all transactions involving transfer of funds out of Britain. If there was a bona fide contract for a bona fide business, then it was just a formality. DeLorean had the draft GPD contract with him, and Harte agreed that the Northern Irish authorities had ac-cepted the payment as above board. It had been passed properly by the board at DMCL. The bank gave its blessing without fuss.

DeLorean was joined by Tom Kimmerly, and the two went to Geneva that Sunday followed by Robin Bailie. Colin Chapman and Fred Bushell arrived too, checking into the President Hotel, Geneva's best. The serious negotiations were about to begin.

The next few days were neither friendly nor easy. Chapman and DeLorean were not men who could comfortably stay in one place for three days on end, going over the minutiae that were required. De-Lorean had not done it for Puerto Rico, for the Irish Republic, or even for Northern Ireland. No one had known him to stay so long in one negotiation. If anything, Chapman was even more impatient. "He was a man who couldn't sit still even through a meal," recalls a friend. "I remember once at lunch there were no tomatoes. And Colin liked tomatoes. Instead of waiting for the girl to come back in, he went out to the kitchen and sliced them himself. He was the most active man I've ever met." To that extent they were two of a kind.

Fred Bushell recalls who was at the meetings:

> A host of people. Chapman and me of course. The Juhans from time to time, both of them. There were American lawyers. Tom Kimmerly was there. A series of lawyers and other people were wheeled in and out and it was really a marathon that went on quite late in the afternoon. For Colin to be in one room for three or four days was a miracle. He was running the racing program from the hotel, running the rest of the business, and then we would meet again with DeLorean for hours. And most of it was negative.

Bushell recalls that Chapman was negative from the beginning almost to the end. It was Bushell, worried about the Lotus finances, who wanted the DeLorean contract. "Chapman, while he was far-thinking, would not let financial considerations enter into the argument at all. He was concerned about the product, whether it was good for the company image, whether it was good for Colin Chapman's image. But I wanted to prove that we could get that kind of work. I must have saved the negotiations two or three times, because I would go out of the room and talk to Colin and bring him back in and we would lower the temperature and talk again."

The argument was not over the money—the Juhans seemed to have set the rate for the job, according to Bushell. Nor was it over GPD's position. "We had accepted that they had set the job up," says Bushell. It was about the car itself and the tight program. DeLorean insisted the job had to be done in eighteen months. He argued that it was really quite simple, mostly a matter of exchanging American components for European components on a car that was already fully designed and ready to go.

"What you've got there is no more than one stage in a mockup," Chapman told DeLorean at one point. From the ground up, he argued, Lotus would need three to four years to build the car, and it would be a "ground-up" job.

There were long arguments over the configuration of the car, in particular the way the engine was to be mounted. DeLorean wanted the engine in the back. But Chapman produced midengine cars and held the strong view that if you didn't put the engine in the front, it should go in the middle, never in the back. "It can't be made to work, John," he kept saying impatiently at the end of long technical discussions.

From the engine, Chapman turned his attention to another part of the DMC-12 that he did not like. "These gull-wing doors. Nobody does those, they're vintage, they belong to Mercedes twenty years ago. What on earth makes you think they are either marketable or feasible?

DeLorean's strategy, however, was to appeal to Chapman's competitive instinct, challenge him. "Nobody else could do it maybe, but *you* could." And gradually Chapman gave way saying, "Yes, anything can be done, provided you are prepared to pay the price and spend the money on it."

Chapman raised doubt after doubt about DeLorean's dream, and it was Bushell who kept persuading him into a semblance of diplomacy. But the engineer's contempt for the car was thinly disguised. If he was going to do it at all, it had to be his way. "Unless you let me have a free hand, I don't want to do it," he said again and again. Apparently his fear was of failure. Chapman had never been associated with failure, knew he could not afford to be now. And he seemed to equate that prototype of John DeLorean's with failure.

DeLorean gave way on point after point, saying, "I don't care how you do it, just so long as you leave the engine in the back, the gull-wing doors, the stainless-steel body, and enough room behind the passengers for a full set of golf clubs." He also added a few more points until Chapman said, "You are not leaving me enough room."

Chapman had a major worry about the project that kept coming to the fore all the way through. Fred Bushell says:

> We had a mental picture that if anything went wrong with the project we—Lotus and Colin Chapman's personal reputation— would probably be sullied. We would be the patsies in the middle, and that obviously gave us considerable cause for concern. We had to avoid having Lotus in direct contractual obligation to DeLorean. We didn't want John DeLorean being able to lean on Chapman. Chapman said, "He's not going to be able to walk in

here and tell me what to do. I've already said I'm not going to sell him the company. There is no way you're going to drag me into that situation."

Chapman was also concerned about product liability. In his chairman's statement, written only weeks before he died in December 1982, he said, "Our company was initially chary of the implications of this [DeLorean] proposition, involving an American operation and predominantly an American market, from the aspect of possible future problems and product liability. You may recall we were already having some problems of this nature at the time."

One example was then uppermost in his mind. Says Mike Kimberley:

> An eleven-year-old Lotus Europa sold in Britain and imported into Canada before regulations became the norm was then transferred across the border and sold eleven times in the United States. It was eventually converted to a racetrack car with a roll-cage and a different body, and the head was taken off and skimmed. It had a different carburetor and two fuel tanks, one on either side. Then one Christmas Eve, the young chap who owned it was driving home from a party with his girlfriend at two o'clock in the morning on icy roads, doing 75 mph in a 45 mph restricted zone. He lost control on the ice, spun off, hit a curb, demolished a telegraph pole, and slid for 100 yards. He crawled out, but the girl was injured and she sued him. He didn't have insurance so he sued us for millions of dollars. And that was the sort of lawsuit we were suffering under the product liability situation in America.

To an American auto company that sort of lawsuit is part of everyday life. To a small, specialized British car company, it is terrifying.

"Here was a car," says Fred Bushell, "that we weren't very impressed with. We were likely to be involved in its design engineering and we thought to ourselves, 'Lord, the exposure on that for the next twenty years could just about wipe us out.' " A clause was inserted into the contract: "The Partnership and Limited agree to hold GPD and its nominated contractors harmless against any or all claims that may be made in the future by users of the finished product." The partnership would take out insurance for $5 million minimum to cover it, so that hurdle was eventually cleared. In Chapman's mind it was perhaps the most important: "It was only the fact that GPD Services Inc. was the principal contractor and was able to cover the financial and other risks involved that encouraged us to accept the assignment," he said in December 1982 in his chairman's statement to Group Lotus.

On Tuesday, October 31, the Northern Bank in Donegall Square, Belfast, had another application to purchase foreign currency. This time the amount was a modest $250,000, to make the total $5.15 million. This time the signatures were Myron Stylianides and Buck Penrose for DeLorean, but instead of the beneficiary being neatly typed in as it was before, it was written in a hand that uncannily resembles John DeLorean's. Again the beneficiary was GPD. With the Bank of England having approved the overall arrangement, permission was a formality. The Northern Bank now had $5.15 million ready to be wired to GPD in Geneva. John DeLorean had another, and now slightly grubby, $12.5-million check folded away in his wallet. All that was necesasry was a signature on the new contract documents.

November 1 was signing day at last. The contracts were finally agreed upon, and they were signed simply "Juhan" for Madame Denise Juhan, on behalf of GPD. John DeLorean signed on behalf of both DMCL in Belfast and the partnership. Both initialed each page of the ten-page contracts. GPD had a separate contract with Lotus.

For still unexplained reasons, there were at least three versions, typed on different typewriters and individually signed, of the contract between GPD and DeLorean. One was later found in the files of DMCL in Belfast, a second and cleaner version was filed with the SEC, and a third was given to the authors by a DeLorean executive who had not noted the differences. The rougher two are dated November 1, 1978. The cleaner version is marked on the front "Effective November 1, 1978."

There also seems to have been a fourth (and earlier) version that neither Strycker, Brown, Collins, or Dewey recall seeing. But Harry DeWitt, Dewey's original assistant, does.

"The original contract was typed on two sheets of paper, by a very flimsy typewriter, not an electric, obviously a manual typewriter," said DeWitt. "With very bad legal language in it. I don't know who wrote it, but that's the original agreement that came back from Switzerland."

DeWitt also recalls that although the amounts of money in the original contract were the same, the signatures were not.

DeWitt no longer has a copy of that contract. "I had one in my files at home and when I moved, I'm sure I moved those files. When the shit hit the fan, so to speak, I went back to find it and all my files were intact except that particular one." His garage had been broken into and the only thing missing was the GPD file.

The earliest version gave a fictitious address for GPD—a public building in Geneva. It also required "up front" payments of $12.5 million from the partnership and $5.15 million from DMCL. That was later changed to an up front payment of $8.5 million from the partnership, the other $4 million to be paid in four installments through 1979. This actually meant that $4 million was returned by GPD to the partnership and then paid back again, possibly so that it would be tax deductible in 1979. There are apparently minor differences in wording between the contracts that would interest investigators later, but the main provisions and payment schedules in the public versions are the same.

The significance of the various versions of the GPD contract lies not in the differences in wording but in the startling sameness of the important terms. When tied to the fact that John DeLorean was carrying around checks that turned out to be the precise amount Colin Chapman agreed to accept for the project, there is a presumption that DeLorean and Chapman may have framed a rough agreement on the venture even before the negotiating teams arrived in Geneva. Further support for this presumption lies in the details of the final version of the contract.

The contract essentially stipulated that the partnership, now the owner of the rights to the car itself, intended to develop a "prototype sports coupe with 6-cylinder V engine to series production readiness," and that DeLorean Motor Cars Limited of Belfast intended to develop a VRIM (vacuum resin injection molding) "alternative to ERM plastic components." Both the partnership and DMCL desired "to engage the services of GPD for design, test and calculation work" for these purposes.

GPD undertook to complete a product/vehicle layout, with detailed drawings of all the parts that could be used for production purposes. The concern had to provide complete component lists, assembly manuals, tolerances, and material specifications. It had to perform the analytical calculations of design variants, economy, handling, and brakes. It had to make the tools, do the testing—basically build a car "based on existing initial styling work and prototype's technical documents."

DeLorean, for his part, was to make available to GPD "the services of employees . . . to assist GPD in the performance of the services to be rendered by GPD under this contract." In other words, although he didn't know it, Collins and his team were now working for GPD.

On page four of the ten-page contract, Chapman made his first appearance. There it says: "GPD confirms it has retained the services of Lotus Cars Ltd. ("Lotus") of Norwich, England, including the services of Mr. A. C. B. Chapman to assist in this project. It is acknowledged that the personal involvement of Mr. Chapman is fundamental to these arrangements."

The contract was signed before Robin Bailie ever saw a copy, and he raised a serious point with his client. DMCL and the partnership had a contract with GPD, but they had no contract with Lotus, which was to do the work. How could the DeLorean company be assured that Lotus would carry out all the research and development that GPD had contracted for? This point had not occurred to anyone before. Bailie suggested that Lotus guarantee GPD's contract, and Chapman agreed. This meant that a contractor was guaranteeing the work of an agent—a highly unusual procedure and one that indicates that Chapman had by now become very anxious to have that contract.

The result was a letter, written on Lotus stationery and addressed to DMCL and the partnership. Signed by Colin Chapman and Fred Bushell, it read:

> Gentlemen,
> In consideration of DRLP and DMCL entering into an agreement with GPD Services Inc. of even date (a copy of which is attached) and Lotus Cars Ltd., being named a sub-contractor under agreement of even date, we hereby warrant and guarantee to you the timely and full performance of each and every obligation of GPD Services Inc. under your agreement with GPD.

The Oppenheimer Limited Partnership may have been the senior party to the DeLorean-GPD contract, but it had ceased to exert any control over the funds it has raised for the project. On September 22 the Oppenheimer firm deposited $15.5 million from its fund-raising in DeLorean Motor Company's account at Chemical Bank of New York. From that point on, the investment house exerted no supervision over its clients' money and the partners waited in vain for their profits.

Still, it was understood by all the parties involved that Oppenheimer funds would be used to fund all the engineering work and for the research and development of the DMC-12 production model. The price tag to the partners for this work was $12.5 million. Salaries for personnel involved, "who are anticipated to number approximately eighty," were to be paid separately, but most of them were to be paid from the remaining partnership funds.

The DMCL corporate entity in Belfast, on the other hand, was to pay Lotus (through GPD of course) only for work on the VARI (or VRIM, as it was first called) variable resin injection molding process, which was to be used on the new car in place of DeLorean's ERM method. One of the ironies of the car's history is that after taking millions of dollars ostensibly to perfect the ERM, DeLorean agreed to scrap it without much debate.

Lotus was to get $5.15 million immediately for its rights to use its own VARI process on the car. This money from Belfast would later by supplemented by payments for travel and salary expenses by Lotus' DeLorean project staff on a monthly basis—again, with the billings going from Lotus to DMCL via GPD.

Thus, at this point, on paper, the GPD project with John DeLorean involved payments to the Swiss company of $17.65 million for the design of the car and the VARI rights. In the months to come there would be added payments to cover extra expenses and travel—a reasonable total for such a job by industry standards.

But over the life of the contract, Lotus billed DMCL for £12 million (roughly $18.5 million in the volatile exchange rates of the time), a sum that included payments for work on VARI *and* the full engineering expenses and design work on the DMC-12. This means that GPD actually handled a total cash flow of $36.3 million—The $18.5 Lotus billings, the $5.15 DMCL VARI payments, the $12.5 million from the partnership plus several hundred thousand dollars in incidental billings—until the project's collapse in 1982.

Much later the British bankruptcy receivers and other official investigators would establish to their satisfaction that Lotus received only the £12 million it actually billed to the Belfast firm through GPD. It never received the $5.15 million VARI rights payment or any of the partnership money, which eventually totaled $12.65 million. That $17.80 million remained in Geneva and has never been fully accounted for to this day.

One cause of the continuing mystery about the money is the intense secrecy that surrounded the 1978 Geneva talks. It was probably the most secret meeting John DeLorean ever held. None of his directors, including Walter Strycker, knew where he was. Strycker, in fact, had been expressly forbidden by DeLorean from accompanying him when the chief financial officer suggested that perhaps he should be along on such an important financial issue. If there were American lawyers there, as Bushell recalls, they were not members of DeLorean's standard team of lawyers, which knew nothing of GPD either. DeLorean had been open enough about making the deal with Chapman, and had even showed the draft GPD contract around in advance. Afterward, it became a hush-hush subject, deliberately deleted from documents, its name carefully not mentioned in later SEC filings, although a copy of the contract was filed with the SEC.

In Geneva during those few days, Robin Bailie, DMCL's lawyer, never attended a single meeting. He spent his time either sitting in his hotel room or in one of the lawyers' offices. The contract was crucial to the whole future of the company, yet none of the directors were involved in it.

On November 1 John DeLorean took that $12.5-million check and passed it to GPD. The following day Mr. B. H. Menown, an assistant manager of the Northern Bank in Donegall Square, wrote to DMCL's financial controller, D. Tanney, that the sum of $5.15 million, then equivalent to £2,499,258.50p, had been Telex-transferred to United Overseas Bank, Geneva, "for account GPD Services Inc. per instructions of Mr. R. Bailie."

What happened to that money? Who got it? Did DeLorean and Chapman divide it between them, either equally or on some predetermined share? GPD was only a convenient and empty shell used for the purpose of bringing the two companies together. Could it possibly claim a $17.80-million commission on such a deal, for introducing people who already knew each other? It is possible—but not credible. The Juhans are perfectly reputable Swiss business people and there is no suggestion that they kept the money. Presumably they took a commission for their work, paid by Lotus, not by DeLorean, who was awarding the contract. There was an elaborate attempt by certain Lotus personnel to establish that GPD was something more than it was, that its "personnel travelled the world looking for contracts" although it had not even existed until September 1978.

Those close to Chapman believe DeLorean took all the money; those close to DeLorean believe Chapman spirited it away. That one or both of them did so is almost beyond doubt. At the time, Brown, Strycker, and others wondered enough to ask DeLorean. Brown recalls, "We were told that Colin Chapman wanted it done in Switzerland because it was beneficial for him from a tax standpoint and Chapman was supposed to have this GPD thing." Chapman did have a GPD thing, but it was a different GPD—it stood for Grand Prix Drivers and was a company set up in Geneva when Chapman nearly made a deal with Olympus Cameras to sponsor his Team Lotus Formula One cars. The deal fell through. The GPD involved in DeLorean's contract stands for General Product Developments, according to Madame Juhan's letterhead.

To Collins, the GPD deal and the decision to go ahead with the money from the Oppenheimer partnership rather than from NIDA are clearly linked. "Northern Ireland wanted us to go ahead without that partnership. Why would John want to go ahead with it anyway? Ostensibly it was because all those important people in the partnership had already made the commitment and we couldn't back out on them. But then he couldn't have started GPD, could he?"

Later DeLorean was to give two different versions of how the contract with GPD came about—both to the *Sunday Telegraph*. He first said that in the summer of 1978, when he was looking for someone to build the car for him, he was approached out of the blue by GPD, which he'd never heard of, and offered a deal with Lotus on "very good terms." In another interview, however, he told a different story: it was Colin Chapman who insisted on the GPD connection.

Chapman's version was entirely different from both of DeLorean's versions. "DeLorean wanted the deal done like that," he told the *Sunday Telegraph* in November 1981.

But a more logical explanation is that Colin Chapman overcame his initial dislike of John DeLorean and his doubts about the ultimate success of the DMC-12 because of the prospect that he would be able to share in a large sum of money that could be diverted from the project. After all, Chapman was an aggressive strategist in avoiding the crippling tax levies of his own country. Tax havens in the Cayman Islands or the British Virgin Islands are as common accoutrements for the U.K. executive as his bowler hat and umbrella, and Chapman had acquired his refuges years before.

Indeed, the long and at times heated arguments during the Geneva negotiations were not about money—as might be assumed—but about the technical specifications and design features that Lotus was agreeing to provide. Combined with the fact that John DeLorean was carrying checks with him drawn on the final payment totals, the concentration on technical rather than financial details in Geneva and the long-time Chapman ties to the Juhans all impel one to the conclusion that both Chapman and DeLorean had reached a prior agreement to siphon off more money via GPD than was actually needed to do the job. Perhaps they planned to return some of the excess funds if an alarm was sounded; perhaps not.

But the fact remains that Chapman would never have stood for a deal in which Lotus billed for roughly half of the $36.3 million funds sent to GPD and watched while John DeLorean pocketed the rest. Nor would DeLorean have freely handed over hard-won capital just to win Chapman's cooperation.

At the end of 1982 there would be evidence handed over to the investigators for the DMC creditors group that the GPD accounts were held for the benefit of DeLorean Motor Company in New York, thereby strengthening the conclusion that John DeLorean took a probable lion's share of the $17.80 million and used at least $7 million of it to finance his purchase of the Logan Manufacturing Company snow-grooming subsidiary of Thiokol Inc. in the summer of 1979.

Whatever the details—and the last word has not been written—by November 1, John Z. DeLorean and Colin Chapman had a deal. DeLorean had some further agreements to sign and decided to travel up to Norwich and tell his engineering team about it at the same time.

It was an awkward journey in the best of times, but in winter, it could be very tricky indeed. Normally DeLorean used a helicopter or Chapman sent a plane to pick him up in London. That day Norwich was covered in thick fog, and DeLorean came by car. He stayed at the same old brick hotel northeast of Norwich where Collins had settled in.

In the evening the group had dinner together in the dining room:

John DeLorean, Bill Collins, Alan Cross, the other members of the team and their wives.

"John came in and we had some wine and celebrated the fact that Lotus was finally on board," recalled Collins.

Money was now flowing, and Bill Collins' status improved to the extent that Chapman moved him and his team out of the chapel to more permanent quarters—an old barracks on the Hethel air strip. But once there, they sat all day long, doing even less than before. Chapman and his team still ignored them.

To Bill Collins, it was a complete mystery. Here he was at the heart of the most important project of his career—a new car and a new company. Since he joined, he had been working all hours to get it off the ground, trying with all he knew to come up with the revolutionary, ethical car that John DeLorean had asked him to build. Companies such as Porsche took seven to eight years to engineer a new car with an established team. Collins had been trying to do it in half that time. And he had, in his own view, made significant progress. He knew there was still a way to go, but at least he had a starting point. Surely Chapman, as a professional engineer himself, would welcome his input. And surely John DeLorean, as another professional engineer whose name was on the car, would insist on it.

He took the matter up with DeLorean.

"John, I can't understand it. You know I have a guy who has been in the chassis area working on the car. I have a guy in the safety emissions area. I have an electrical engineer. My chief draftsman is here. We've all worked varying lengths of time on this car. I myself have worked on it since 1974, and I know why some of the things are the way they are, and why we've not done some things. Why are we being ostracized?"

"Well," replied DeLorean unconcernedly, "take it up with Colin."

Bill Collins could tell that DeLorean did not care, that he felt the engineer was just being a nuisance. Talking to Chapman, Collins knew by now, was easier said than done. Chapman was busy on other projects, including his new Formula One car for the next season.

There was another, larger, problem brewing. Collins and his Detroit-bred team simply did not do business the way the Lotus engineers were used to designing a car. At Lotus the entire design philosophy was geared to producing limited copies of high-performance vehicles. What this means is that the Lotus engineers did not bother themselves with the staggering mass of documentation, the myriad sketches, drawings, and detailed instructions that are considered essential by any engineer schooled in GM-style mass production. Such detail work was viewed as fussiness by the Lotus designers. To Collins' eyes, there seemed to be a "file-it-down-until-it-fits" attitude that worked very well indeed in the hands of the highly skilled workmen in the Lotus assembly areas. In fact, such on-site fittings gave the car a certain cachet with its owners; each Lotus could truthfully be said to be a handmade, superbly engineered machine.

Collins, however, was horrified. Surely Chapman realized that such apparently individual engineering and designing would prove disastrous if it were tried out on a Dunmurry plant full of inexperienced factory hands. But Chapman was spending very little time on the DeLorean project. He was busy, moving around the world or tied up in meetings. Although Collins represented the biggest contract Lotus had ever undertaken and one that was to contribute nearly half its total revenues for the next two years, he could not even schedule a meeting with Chapman to explain his fears. The car he had worked on from its birth was being torn apart, both physically and metaphorically, by the Lotus engineers, who were now building their own version.

ERM, in which the limited partnership had been asked to invest, was an early casualty. Mike Kimberley says:

> After we were given the job, we assessed the ERM process and we also looked at the car. Utilizing the technology we knew about, our own VARI process, we could produce a body with all its structure in two halves that would meet the American crash regulations. DeLorean decided in the end that he would use the Lotus process because it would assure him of getting the job done in the very critical time limit that was set. That was the fundamental reason for going to the VARI process rather than ERM —the ERM was not proved yet, and it was incapable of giving all the necessary characteristics.

Collins, who regarded VARI as being a generation behind ERM, became more and more bewildered. He kept postponing moving his wife and home to Norfolk—he'd been around long enough to recognize what was happening to him. Yet he was reluctant to go, since the car was very much his baby.

One of the reasons for the gap between Collins and Chapman was the Lotus man's open contempt for the prototype the Americans had delivered. There were now two DeLorean cars in existence, both of them made in the U.S. but by different model shops. One of them had a Citroën four-cylinder engine, and to the Lotus men, used to the fastest cars in the world, it was impossibly dull. They never drove it.

"Look—it's got nineteen welds in the exhaust system," sneered a Lotus engineer.

"That's a prototype exhaust system," argued Collins. "That's the way you make them."

"Well, it's not the way *we* make them at Lotus."

Collins was to hear that refrain again and again. Lotus simply did not operate according to the strict mass-production codes and rules of Detroit.

"One of the first things you have to do in a new vehicle program," he argued strenuously with Chapman, "and I don't care whether it is a sports car or a passenger car or whatever—you start out after the styling is finished and you make a body draft and it is very accurate and it defines all the surface, all the exterior. And we have not gotten that done yet."

Chapman just looked at him.

"That's not the way we do it here," he eventually replied. "We build a plastic underbody. We find out how much it shrinks and then we design the outside around it."

Collins couldn't believe it. Disgruntled, he went away, muttering to himself.

"Going about it this way," he would say, "where you build this fiberglass thing first and find out how much it shrinks and then put the skin around it, to me that's . . ." Words almost failed him. "Well, it's not the way I am used to doing things. Certainly not when you are designing for a 20,000 to 30,000 kind of volume."

Lotus, for all the brilliance of its engineers, of course, had never designed for any sort of volume. It was a problem that was to plague the production people in Dunmurry as they got the assembly lines going, and it meant that almost everyone involved in the project had to do considerable on-the-spot improvisation before the cars began to roll.

Neither Collins nor Chapman was wrong. It was simply a matter, as both were realistic enough to admit, of a different philosophy of vehicle design. Chapman was designing the car in the way he always did—but in a way that was not necessarily ideal for a mass-produced car. Collins knew about designing mass-produced cars but did not have Chapman's genius. The approaches of the two men were incompatible.

Early in 1979, still another engineer came on board. Mike Loasby was a slim, serious-looking, forty-two-year-old Midlander who had headed the engineering team at Aston-Martin, producing some of the world's finest and most expensive luxury sports cars, machines in an engineering and price bracket way above the DeLorean.

He had been responsible for the V8 Vantage, the world's fastest-accelerating production car, and the Aston-Martin Lagonda, a machine that cost more than a Rolls-Royce and was the last thing in sports car luxury. His final contribution to Aston was an amazing car called the Bulldog, which by coincidence also had gull-wing doors—something the DeLorean men, conscious that this was about the only unique feature about their car, were to resent.

Like so many others, Loasby initially saw DeLorean as an opportunity he could scarcely pass up. Here was a new project—a car being built by Colin Chapman at Lotus, a man absolutely at the top of his form. The project had all the government money it needed. It had a brand-new factory going up in Belfast. It had a dealership network. It had a man at the top who was still something of a legend in U.S. auto circles and the American motoring public. How could it miss?

He landed right in the middle of Bill Collins' days of frustration and disappointment. The prototype that the Lotus people were now busily ripping apart was not Loasby's design, so he could watch it objectively at the beginning, although less so as time went by. Like Collins, Loasby soon wondered what he was doing there at all, since the Lotus people were so clearly doing all the engineering and there wasn't room for Collins, let alone him.

Soon the Lotus engineers were busily producing a car that Bill Collins would find virtually unrecognizable. One of the few similarities that remained was the distinctive Giugiaro design, and even that was altered later.

DeLorean had loftily stayed above the argument raging in the Norfolk countryside, refusing to support his own engineering team, almost never supporting Bill Collins' complaints. Collins now decided to try to shake him out of his aloofness.

"John, when you are at General Motors and you have a bum product like the Vega—and we both know that was a bum product—you can still rely on the Seville, the Pontiac, to carry you through," he told him bluntly. "But when you have only one product, you can't foul that one up because you have nothing to fall back on. You should be spending every minute with the thing, and when those engineering changes are being made, you should be aware of every damn change!"

DeLorean was unmoved, disinterested. He went to Hethel once a month, his visits greeted by a flurry of activity by the Lotus people as they prepared the way for their biggest customer.

Chapman, rarely seen by the DeLorean people, was always present if DeLorean appeared. The men who came over from Belfast were to notice the difference on visits when DeLorean accompanied them and when they were on their own.

The hangar would be cleared of Lotus cars, the Esprits that were taking shape alongside the DMC-12 moved out, and DMC's moved in. All the DeLorean cars would be sitting on ramps or in businesslike positions, assuming an extra air of activity.

Collins first, and later Loasby, pointed this out to DeLorean. But nothing changed, and DeLorean wasn't ever interested. It was Chapman's car and would be left to him.

"It's coming out as a stainless-steel Lotus," Collins grumpily told his colleagues. Later the engineers were to remark that if you added a stainless-steel shell to the Esprit, the weight came out pound for pound the same as the DMC-12.

By early spring, Bill Collins had been ignored long enough. There was no place for him. The car being built had less and less of his own craftsmanship in it. It was time to leave. He saw DeLorean one last time to say, as he put it himself, "Adios, John."

DeLorean took it calmly and the meeting was amicable. DeLorean halfheartedly suggested that Collins stay on the board. But by March he had gone to American Motors, and later teamed up with his old DeLorean mate Bob Dewey in starting their own company, Vixen Motor Co., in Detroit, making motor homes.

In their final meeting, Collins again brought up the mystery of GPD. He had been through the contract and he didn't understand it.

"John, this doesn't make sense to me," he told him. "You are paying Chapman this money, but then I think, in here, if I read it right, you also have to pay him time and materials." To Collins it looked like a bad deal.

"Why should we pay him time and materials when we have already paid them?"

"Don't worry about it," replied DeLorean. "That's the way it is."

8

THE DREAM
TAKES A DARK SHAPE

As 1979 opened, everything seemed to be in place for John DeLorean. In Belfast the bulldozers had worked through the winter, starting to convert the boggy fields of Dunmurry into what would become a custom-built, spacious factory, positively luxurious by the standards of the struggling British or European car industry.

Men who had never worked in their lives were enthusiastically seizing the opportunity they thought would never come. From the Catholic housing development of Twinbrook on one side to the Protestant enclave of Seymour Hill on the other, the whole of the area watched as a small river was diverted and the steel framework began to appear.

Three hundred and fifty miles away, in the Norfolk countryside, the car itself was being worked on by the man who stood at the very pinnacle of the greatest career in Grand Prix racing, a man whose superb engineering skills were producing the fastest cars in the world's history.

In the United States, the dealer network was nearing completion —a body of wealthy men across the length and breadth of the nation, whose total assets mustered more than half a billion dollars. They had invested their money, had seen the prototype and liked it, and were now impatiently waiting for the machine itself to arrive so they could begin selling it.

John DeLorean now had money, plenty of it, for the first time since he started the car project. He had enough to build the factory, finish development of the car, and get it onto the market. What's more, he had been able to construct the whole edifice without investing a nickel of his own. The British government had contributed far more generously than he could ever have imagined. The Oppenheimer limited partnership had come through—maybe not the full amount, but close. DeLorean was at last able to look forward to real wealth, and to increase his personal expenditures to even higher levels, never caring that it was British taxpayers' money, designed to create jobs in the poorest area of Europe, that was paying for it all.

His first move was typically extravagant. There would now be income for at least two years—the car, originally scheduled to start production in August 1980, was beginning to slip back. The organization was tiny, with the bulk of the employees either in Belfast or Bloomfield Hills. At the time of the Northern Ireland deal, DeLorean was still working out of his room in the Chris-Craft office. The instant he had money he decided to move.

There was actually no reason why he should be in New York at all, but John DeLorean loved the New York scene, the feeling of being at the center of the fast-changing social modes and fashions. Cristina thrived on it. They were making smart friends there, invited to the right sort of dinner parties, seen at the fashionable clubs and restaurants. DeLorean didn't naturally belong in that world: obsessed as he was with his health and figure, he had no interest in food and was happier with a bowl of zucchini at his desk than lunch at Le Pavillon. He barely drank—a single glass of white wine would be made to last through a long dinner party. He had seen Hollywood as a great new world—faster, modern, progressive after the dull, formal auto town of Detroit—but even Hollywood had begun to wear off for him. New York was more exciting, more vibrant. His reputation there had gone ahead of him, and, in a town of celebrities, John DeLorean stood out. But he needed an office to go with the new image. After all, General Motors had a building in Manhattan, didn't it? And Chrysler? He was not quite up to a DeLorean building yet but he would do the next best thing.

By early 1979 he found what he was searching for: the penthouse suite on the 43rd floor of 280 Park Avenue, just across the street from the Waldorf-Astoria. It was a smart building and an even smarter penthouse. The current occupant was the Xerox Corporation, which had used it as their corporate headquarters. In a cost-cutting exercise Xerox had moved out, leaving behind a modest art collection and some fancy furnishings. It suited DeLorean perfectly. There was an express elevator to the 43rd floor; plenty of space. He had his own private bathroom, and his roomy office in the corner gave him panoramic views over Manhattan. Ironically the General Motors building was visible, even on an unclear day. In one corner he placed a telescope, though no one ever saw him use it. His own desk was a standard burlwood veneer that Xerox had left. He covered the walls with pictures of Cristina, a framed copy of the formal agreement with Northern Ireland, and some of the pictures he inherited.

At the same time he moved apartments, buying a Fifth Avenue duplex formerly owned by the wealthy widow Mabel Dodge, herself a Detroit matron. It was in Cristina's search for help in decorating the hopelessly old-fashioned apartment that she first hired the services of an art dealer and decorator named Maur Dubin, who soon became almost inseparable from one or the other of them. Later Cristina would write of Dubin in her diary on the day her husband was arrested: "He does and does and does everything for you and never asks for anything in return."

In addition to the new Fifth Avenue home, DeLorean showed Dubin the new Park Avenue office. For the decorator it was good material, and with a generous budget he went to work. The lobby area acquired two elegant life-sized dolls on either side of the reception desk. On the white marble floors he put rugs and red water buffalo hide chairs. Behind the reception desk he hung an enormous blown-up picture of the DMC-12 in full glorious color. And having acquired some paintings and sculptures, Dubin began to kindle DeLorean's interest in building an art collection. Soon both of them were busily shopping in the art galleries.

In January 1979 *The Wall Street Journal* did a long piece on DeLorean with the headline: TAKING ON DETROIT; JOHN DELOREAN SAYS HE'LL SHOW INDUSTRY HOW TO BUILD CARS! A wry subheading read: "Was he a pain in the neck?" referring to his GM fracas. The article concluded:

> Mr. DeLorean is moving faster than ever, spending half of each month away from his New York City home, jetting to and from such places as DeLorean Motor headquarters near Detroit, an auto test track in Phoenix and various spots in Europe—often with a stop in Belfast. His car collection has dwindled to a mere 25 vehicles, his two ranches in Idaho and his California avocado farm get scant attention, and he has sold his interest in the San Diego Chargers football team. He retains a small chunk of the

New York Yankees—but his novel, dealing with the nuclear-arms race, remains unfinished and long-neglected.

The novel was nothing more than a thought, now forgotten.

That same article contained a quote from a Wall Street auto analyst, David Healey, that would later echo around the world and become something of a catch phrase: "When people ask my advice about investing in Mr. DeLorean's venture, I tell them to put the money into wine, women and song. They'll get the same return and have more fun." People were to remember that the day DeLorean was arrested.

While DeLorean was concentrating on office furnishings, three thousand miles away there were swarms of engineers working over his dream car. Collins had gone, of course, and with him much of the American flavor of the early prototype. He never did figure out why he was ignored, and why the engineers at Lotus treated him with such lofty contempt. In fact, it had a great deal to do with the Geneva agreement and the terms that Chapman extracted for building the car. But it also had to do with another factor that Bill Collins was ignorant of, and that only now was becoming apparent.

DeLorean had greatly exaggerated the work already done on the prototype. He had persuaded the Northern Irish authorities that it was far advanced and although it required further engineering work, the basic car was already built. Chapman also believed that much more work had been done, otherwise he would have been even less convinced that Lotus could hit DeLorean's eighteen-month target.

It was Mike Kimberley, Lotus managing director and a favorite engineer of Chapman's, who wrote the document that set the tone of the work on the car and determined many of its features. The report was utterly damning of the prototype Doris 1. The body/chassis structure was weak and needed a steel backbone, front and rear suspensions were unsatisfactory, there were no sun visors, ashtrays or space for a spare tire. The door latches and water sealing were poor, the electrical system was incomplete and the rear lights were only mockups. DeLorean had produced written results of tests on the air conditioning, but it had not been connected on the car and would not even fit. There was much more work to be done than Lotus had bargained for.

DeLorean himself was at the meetings at which the basic parameters for the car that Lotus would build were laid down. The discussions were long and professional, seldom heated, although Chapman brusquely attacked some of DeLorean's key points. Several times he told DeLorean he wanted to start from scratch and re-engineer the entire car, but DeLorean held on to the aspects he regarded as crucial: the stainless-steel shell, the rear-mounted engine and the gull-wing doors. Chapman finally accepted these as "important marketing features" but ran a backup program for standard doors just in case the gull-wings caused too much trouble. He took DeLorean around his paintshop, showing him the gleaming colors they could paint the cars in and the superb finish they could produce. "As good as anything in the world," he enthused, and DeLorean had to agree. But he wanted his stainless steel.

There were five other features that DeLorean insisted on including: Pirelli P7 tires on sixteen-inch wheels; his own instrument package that had been expensively designed for his prototype; a rear side window; air conditioning for the American models; and of course the Giugiaro design. There was one other element that DeLorean made much of and would raise again and again until it became a great joke with the engineers. There had to be room behind the driver and passenger for a full set of golf clubs. "This car is aimed at a particular section of the market," he told the Lotus team as well as his own growing organization in Belfast. "The horny bachelor who's made it!"

For the rest he increasingly accepted Chapman's recommendations, and as Lotus now started transforming those specifications into a prototype, more DeLorean features dropped away, including the tires. Goodyears were much cheaper, more available in the United States and were quite adequate although they gave a softer ride. DeLorean accepted that recommendation from his own team, backed by Lotus.

The man who now became DeLorean's most senior executive outside the United States was Charles "Chuck" Bennington, another Chrysler man picked out by Myron Stylianides. A tall thin man in his early fifties, Bennington sported a wispy blond mustache and goatee. Although he still retained his American accent, much of his working life had been spent overseas, building plants and factories everywhere from Cape Town to Turkey. At first the Lotus people did not know what to make of him with his cowboy boots and his turtleneck jerseys. Soon they came to regard him as their closest ally, and the relationship was to outlast the DeLorean project.

Bennington quickly established a reputation as a "workaholic" and insisted that others follow the same arduous schedule he set himself, which meant working at least six days a week and sometimes seven. DeLorean had made him a tempting offer that included share options in DMC and a big salary raise. He arrived in December and set up his office in Belfast, but in those early months of 1979 spent two to three days a week at Lotus. He was the man to whom DeLorean had given responsibility for building and staffing the factory and overseeing the work at Lotus. It was a tall order, but his team grew rapidly: Barrie Wills to head up purchasing, Loasby on engineering, George Broomfield, another American, for actual production of the car, and Joe Daly, an Irishman who had also been with Chrysler, for finance.

At Shoreham on England's south coast, Bennington mocked up the interior while Lotus worked on the rest of the engineering. He brought DeLorean down to see it in the spring and displayed it, illustrating that one key requirement was there. "We actually went out and borrowed a set of golf clubs and threw them in the back, more as a joke to show John they would fit than anything else," he said later.

During this period, DeLorean turned up in Belfast and Norwich around once a month. That suited both Bennington and the Lotus people, who preferred to get on with the job themselves. Once he had sorted out the arrangements with the Northern Ireland government, made the deal with Chapman and agreed on the basic parameters of the car, DeLorean showed less and less interest in the details of both the factory and the car.

The building of the factory could progress without him because there were competent people working on it and the schedule was not as tight as that for the car. Bennington remembers telling DeLorean at a very early stage that he wasn't going to meet his schedule on the car. "I'm inclined to believe you," DeLorean replied. "But I don't think we want to broadcast that until you get more detail on it." In fact, DeLorean never did reveal that information until his program was already late. At this point he seemed far more interested in what was happening in New York than on the other side of the Atlantic.

In Belfast, however, he was a hero. His name was on the factory, and his visits were almost royal events. He had brought jobs and hope and given Northern Ireland its great chance to break into the car industry, something it had always wanted since the pre-war days when Chambers and Ferguson made cars there and a local veterinary surgeon named John Boyd Dunlop fitted out his son's bicycle with the first pneumatic tires and started an entire new worldwide industry.

The center of Belfast may have been a gloomy spot, with its security checks and constantly patrolling armored cars, but Dick Brown soon discovered what all visitors in Northern Ireland find: the IRA attacks were on the whole concentrated on the security forces, and the number of violent deaths in the Province in a year was less than that in Dallas or Detroit. The factory was left alone. Factories usually were— it was not in the IRA's interests to damage jobs.

Compared to Detroit, Northern Ireland was a relatively peaceful place, its reputation far exceeding the real thing. Once the English and American newcomers got used to the sight of armed soldiers and constant checks, it was a remarkably pleasant place.

Soon, as the engineering and production teams at Dunmurry began to come together, they spilled over into a group of Quonset huts set up on the perimeter of the seventy-three-acre site. A large, stately home, Warren House, was taken over too, and work began on converting that into living quarters for visiting royalty such as DeLorean, whom Dick Brown expected to live there more often than he would in New York. A kitchen staff was hired.

Myron Stylianides hired Mike Loasby to head the engineering team, and Loasby in turn began hiring others, eventually creating a production engineering department totaling some eighty people, whose job would be to translate Lotus' work onto the actual production cars.

DeLorean may seldom have gone near the place, but to the men in Dunmurry that was not a problem. They were getting on with the job, making rapid progress through that winter and into the spring. Once the first shovel of dirt had been turned on the factory site, the whole team joined in the site-planning with the keenness of men taking part in an exciting new venture, and in this brief spell that is what it was to them.

In the second week of February John DeLorean was in Las Vegas. It was to be a big time for him—the National Automobile Dealers Association convention was held there. He had one of the two prototypes set up on a stand and he invited his board and his backers. Johnny Carson came along to look at his investment and posed beside DeLorean, looking solemn. Behind them Cristina and Carson's wife,

Joanna, looked bored. DeLorean and his team came to the conven‑
tion, as Edward Lapham, financial editor of *Automotive News*, wrote,
"like plunder‑laden legions returning to Rome."

But despite the Northern Ireland plunder, the team was hard at
work on yet more fund‑raising: with SEC approval DeLorean would
soon begin signing dealer‑shareholders for the project again. He had
raised $5.16 million at $5 a share from his initial offering, but now
with the Northern Irish money behind him, he was in a much more
attractive position. In Las Vegas that week he bubbled with confi‑
dence. The original offering was made at $5 a share, minimum sub‑
scription $25,000. Now he was asking for $10 a share, still demanding
a minimum investment of $25,000. The S‑2 report filed with the
Securities and Exchange Commission showed that his personal com‑
pany, JZDC, owned 64.1 percent of DMC. After the offering, assum‑
ing a full subscription of 400 dealers, he would be diluted down to
58.9 percent. At $10 a share, that still made him worth $100 million.
But it was a paper fortune only—DeLorean could not translate any of
it into actual cash.

He had not only invited Johnny Carson to Las Vegas but also his
other backers from Northern Ireland. Ronnie Henderson and Shaun
Harte turned up. Both men were enthusiasts. Harte's role in the
original deal was more technical than anything else, while Henderson
as the NIDA chief executive was the decision‑maker. But Harte had
been assigned as the NIDA man who would monitor the investment.
The Irishmen stayed for three days in Vegas watching Dick Brown's
marketing team at work presenting the car and recruiting dealers.
Brown had it down to an art and was genuinely good at it. Both
NIDA men were extremely impressed by what they saw, as DeLorean
intended them to be. The figures floating about sounded euphoric—
at the DMC board meeting held in Las Vegas that week, DeLorean
concluded that the dealers seemed to be suggesting the car be priced
at $20,000. And 100 units per dealer annually would not even meet
demand at that rate—that was what the dealers were saying, he
stated. Henderson and Harte reported these figures enthusiastically
back to NIDA in Belfast, although in the revised corporate plan that
DeLorean presented to the board at Las Vegas, the selling price of the
car was taken to be $14,000 and sales were projected at 7,000 cars in
1980, 21,000 in 1981, 25,000 in 1982, and 30,000 in 1983. Both
men returned from Nevada reassured that the British government had

made a wise and shrewd investment. Thirty thousand cars a year? NIDA would be the toast of Belfast.

In the spring, the euphoric, pioneering atmosphere was beginning to deteriorate in Belfast. A war was brewing between the engineers in Dunmurry and the engineers at Lotus which would continue right through the whole project. Lotus understood that they had the contract to engineer, design and develop the car to make it ready for production. Mike Loasby in Dunmurrry felt that he and his growing engineering team should be involved in the conceptual stages too, rather than the more mundane job they were assigned. Loasby's role had not been made fully clear to him. He had joined with the idea that he was the chief engineer, a successor to Bill Collins. Neither Bennington nor Lotus saw it that way and soon it gave rise to friction. The first skirmish was over the design that Lotus was working on in the spring of 1979. Loasby had a certain sympathy for Collins, and felt his prototype could have been developed as easily as the Lotus version. In fact, he felt it should have been used because of the tightness of the timing.

The most experienced of the DeLorean engineers was Ted Chapman (no relation to Colin Chapman), who had been in the automobile industry all his life. Now nearing retirement age, his great value was that he had been through several new ventures in his career, and the younger men on the team (Loasby was nearly twenty years his junior) looked to him to anticipate problems and find solutions.

It was Ted Chapman who produced the first major contretemps at Lotus following Collins' departure. In the spring of 1979 the engineers in Belfast designed body sections to incorporate everything they would need when it came to mass producing the body—all the little tricks that Ted Chapman, whose specialty was body engineering, had learned through the years. The designs allowed for metal adjustment, door sealing, and other features that the engineers felt would be essential when it came to getting the gull-wing doors to fit properly on the production line.

In May Ted Chapman took these designs along to Colin Spooner, the man at Lotus who was in overall charge of the DeLorean project. Spooner brushed them aside. The Lotus team had it all under control.

Not as far as he was concerned, retorted Chapman. It was his job to make sure that what Lotus designed would work on a production line, and he must be involved in the design now. Lotus, he challenged, was going to do the design itself, then present the team in Belfast with a *fait accompli.*

The two became so angry that Spooner telephoned both George Broomfield, the production manager, and Chuck Bennington in Belfast. Ted Chapman, he told them, was making a nuisance of himself and could not get on with his engineers. Would they kindly keep him away from Lotus?

Reluctantly, Chapman had to accept this, but he bluntly declared that this meant that "I cannot fulfill my obligations to DeLorean Motor Cars Ltd."

There were a number of similar battles as the car took shape, but the decisions were made by Chapman, Kimberley and Colin Spooner at Lotus and agreed to by Bennington and DeLorean on his monthly visits. The car that was now emerging bore little resemblance to Collins' prototype, now gathering dust in a neglected corner of one of the hangers. ERM, of course, was gone before the project ever got under way, although dealers in the United States as well as the Oppenheimer investors were still assuming it would be used. Chapman and his team now designed a car with a steel backbone welded to two subframes in the shape of a double Y. The rear subframe would support the engine because Chapman had given up hope of persuading DeLorean to go for a midengined car. The gas tank went in the notch of the front Y, where it was well protected but small. Chapman redesigned the luggage space, although he was unhappy about the tiny amount available. He managed to get the spare tire under the front hood, still leaving space above it for another set of golf clubs ("In case the bachelor's girlfriend plays," remarked one of the engineers cynically).

Feature by feature the car was becoming a different model and concept from the one that DeLorean launched three years before. Chapman used more and more standard parts, knowing there was no way that special parts could be designed in time. Standard parts were easier to fit and work with, but they made the DMC-12 an increasingly ordinary car. Chapman himself put none of his genius into it. He was involved in the major decisions, but to him the DeLorean job was a moneymaker and no more than that. It would keep his company from dying from lack of funds as it almost certainly would have without the DeLorean contract. Colin Spooner, a competent engineer, did put everything he had into it, working the same hours that Bennington had set for himself. But in eighteen months he could not produce a Porsche or a Ferrari.

The airbags for the driver and passenger had long since disappeared after some horrendous tests with dummies, although DeLorean himself retained his belief in them. GM's testing program revealed that the bag tended to squash passengers so that limbs or other parts of the body were forced sideways through the doors, and could be sliced off as the doors were forced shut again by the impact. GM abandoned the airbag, and DeLorean was dependent on the car giant's development work.

His original plans had talked about a front-end structure devoted solely to "energy management," jargon for absorbing the impact of a crash. Originally, too, he had talked of a foam-filled rear structure that would provide similar crash protection. The car that emerged had a number of useful safety features and was certainly in a "crash-sense" safer than many cars on the road, but the features were really nothing new or special.

Instead of the originally planned Pirelli tires, it was decided to change to Goodyear, largely because Goodyear offered a better deal and the engineers thought the tires were more suitable. The Pirellis had a "hard" ride but showed up all the bumps in the Lotus suspension. The Lotus engineers liked it that way—they felt it produced a more sporty feel. Loasby and his team thought it was wholly wrong for the market they were aiming at.

The high sill that had been part of the original prototype was gone, no longer needed because of the backbone chassis. The dash and instrument cluster remained substantially unchanged, but more European parts were used, mainly because DeLorean had spent a large amount of money having it designed and tooled in the first place.

The computer featured on some of the mockup models was never used, nor was the Craig overhead audio system. The DeLorean engineers were very keen on the Craig system.

That spring another event was shaping up that would have a major impact on the future of the DeLorean project. Britain was heading toward an election. The previous October Labour's Jim Callaghan seemed to be sitting comfortably in Number Ten Downing Street, all set to be re-elected prime minister. He made the fateful mistake of delaying the elections, figuring things might look better in the spring. Instead the British unions, normally militant at the best of times, turned the following months into one long battle with the government and employers. It became Callaghan's "winter of discontent," and by the spring, with time running out for him, he was slipping in the polls. Margaret Thatcher and the Conservative Party were making a comeback. On March 30, however, Mrs. Thatcher received a deep personal blow that would also have a significant impact on John DeLorean.

The Conservative politician with special responsibility for Northern Ireland was Airey Neave, probably Mrs. Thatcher's closest friend and confidant in the party. He had persuaded her to run for leader in the first place, organized her campaign, tirelessly drummed up support for her, and in the end helped her defeat former Prime Minister Edward Heath for the top position. Neave also acted as her eyes and ears in the parliamentary party; he was her political strategist and close adviser. He had taken a keen interest in the DeLorean project and was critical of it—early in March he told colleagues he was going to press the Government for answers to a number of issues. He never got the chance. On March 30, as he was driving up the ramp from the underground parking lot in the House of Commons, his car exploded and he died immediately. A bomb had been placed on the car outside his home that morning, and was triggered by a tilt mechanism as he drove up the ramp. Both the Provisional IRA and the Irish National Liberation Army, the military wing of the Irish Republican Socialist Party of Northern Ireland, claimed responsibility.

His replacement was the gentler Humphrey Atkins, a tall, former Royal Navy man. He had been Chief Whip, the MP with responsibility for making his colleagues vote the way the party leader wants them to. Atkins had been a competent enough Whip. As a minister he was to prove no match for John DeLorean.

Callaghan finally set May 3 as polling day and lost heavily. The Conservatives were now in power and Margaret Thatcher took over in Number Ten with the avowed aim of "rolling back the State frontiers," which meant cutting back sharply on government involvement everywhere. That did not bode well for a project dependent on government money, but at the time it looked as if DeLorean probably had enough to get the factory and car built. Few would guess how wrong that estimate proved to be.

John DeLorean turned up in England in election week with a new member of his team. Eugene Cafiero was another auto wunderkind who had gotten to the top of Chrysler before Lee Iacocca took over as president. Cafiero was bumped upstairs to the position of vice chairman. In November 1978 Cafiero, a slim, good-looking fifty-two-year-old Italian-American, quit his $310,000-a-year job and began looking for something else. He found it with John DeLorean. "I thought it would be fun to go with a small company where there was no history, no built-in constraints. I wanted to start with a clean piece of paper." He became president and chief executive of DeLorean Motor Company, which technically made him senior to DeLorean himself. DeLorean himself quickly squelched any thought of that: "Gene is the boss but he answers to me."

Cafiero accompanied DeLorean on a tour of the plant and the Lotus works before deciding to take the job. DeLorean left him in Belfast and went on to Italy with Dick Brown, who was feeling somewhat out of joint: he had wanted the presidency, and DeLorean quickly explained that Cafiero had become available from Chrysler and it was an opportunity not to be missed. Cafiero did not lose in the transaction—in fact he did very well. DeLorean gave him a five-year contract at $375,000 a year plus cost-of-living adjustments, pension rights, a $164,000 interest-free loan to compensate him for any loss of pension rights at Chrysler, and a car. Soon Cafiero was installed in the office next to DeLorean's at 280 Park Avenue.

On that floor he joined another recent recruit; in October 1979, William F. Haddad had been recruited by DeLorean as his public relations adviser at $125,000. Haddad had known John DeLorean since the mid-1960s when he contributed a ghosted chapter to Haddad's book on development of black business enterprise. Haddad was a journalist with a long involvement with the Kennedy family. He was born in Charlotte, North Carolina, in 1928 to an Egyptian-Jewish father and a Russian-Jewish mother, grew up in Florida, took a physics degree at Columbia, and was soon involved in liberal politics, becoming an aide to Tennessee Senator Estes Kefauver, who won the vice-presidential nomination from young Massachusetts Senator John F. Kennedy in 1956.

Haddad later worked for Kennedy and became deeply involved in the Peace Corps, the plans for which he would later say "came out of my typewriter." He married Kate Roosevelt, a granddaughter of

Franklin D. Roosevelt and an adopted daughter of John Hay Whitney. Haddad went to work as a journalist with the *New York Herald-Tribune,* owned by his father-in-law, before going back to Washington to a Johnson administration job in the ill-fated Office of Economic Opportunity. Later, John V. Lindsay put him on the New York City Board of Education, where the *New York Times* attacked him in an editorial as "Haddad the Heater," accusing him of making "grossly intemperate remarks." He was a prize-winning investigative journalist, a skilled public relations man, and a person who knew his way around Washington and the Democratic party. More to the point, Haddad regarded himself as something of a DeLorean friend: he had been at DeLorean's second wedding, had helped set up the National Alliance of Businessmen office that DeLorean headed after he left GM, and DeLorean had consulted him about Puerto Rico, where Haddad had some business interests. For DeLorean in his new grand style, the fifty-three-year-old Haddad was an ideal choice as vice president in charge of planning and communications. The team was getting bigger and more expensive.

It was June when Chapman and Spooner questioned one of DeLorean's cherished fixed instructions for the car, the Giugiaro design. To them it looked old-fashioned and would look even more out-of-date by the time it hit the market. Chapman suggested getting Giugiaro to "freshen" or "tweak" his design, and DeLorean and Cafiero saw the point. Chuck Bennington went to Milan to have it done.

Giugiaro sent back his changes in August. He did it cleverly: half the car was the old design, half the new one. The differences, which subtly softened the original shape, were small but quite startling. Mike Kimberley recalls: "Gene Cafiero and I looked at Giugiaro's styling and there was no doubt about it. Although we were both concerned about what it would do for the timing of the program and the cost, Gene and I both decided it was a hell of an improvement. It took the car into the eighties."

It also meant that ten months into an eighteen-month program, the whole exterior of the car had been redesigned. DeLorean was still not admitting it publicly, not even to NIDA in Belfast, but the program was steadily slipping, and a change of styling would now delay it several months. Although to the casual observer the changes seemed slight, the alterations meant that every body drawing had to be redone.

The pressure was now intense. The next step involved making a body stack, which is a wooden body actually carved by draftsmen to the engineer's design and from which moldings of items like windows and body panels, that cannot be drawn, can then be taken. Visioneering in Detroit got the job and Chuck Bennington and Colin Spooner began commuting on weekends to Detroit.

Through July and August the gap between the Dunmurry engineers and Lotus widened, with Bennington angering Loasby by continually taking the Lotus side. On July 23 Loasby complained bitterly to Bennington that the engineering department has received "about six assorted drawings, mostly out of date; but these represent . . . such a small proportion of the total available." In the purchasing department Barrie Wills had more drawings than Loasby, and this was rapidly becoming a major bone of contention. Loasby and his engineers were convinced that the project was heading for major engineering problems. They kept pointing out that Lotus had never engineered a mass-production car, and they were going about it the wrong way, starting with the doors and windows and working outwards to the corners. "You have to start at the corners and work in," Loasby insisted.

But on August 28, when Loasby asked Colin Spooner if he was ready to incorporate the body sections suggested by Ted Chapman in mid-May, the real explosion came. They were not going to use those body sections, replied Spooner. He and Mike Kimberley had already reached an agreement with DMCL about it. An agreement with whom? asked Loasby. With Bennington—the three had decided to discard those body sections and leave all the work to Lotus.

Spooner, a slight, intense, serious engineer, had his own ideas on the body. He respected Ted Chapman, whose comments were down-to-earth, practical and to the point, but there was a fundamental difference. Ted Chapman's expertise was in sheet metal and the DMC-12 underbody was to be fiberglass. Lotus prided itself on having greater experience with fiberglass bodies than any company in the world. And Ted Chapman, good as he was, could not easily absorb the new ideas and concepts that Lotus specialized in. "He was of the old school and was not used to doing things in the new Lotus way," said a Lotus engineer.

This was a major philosophical difference that dogged the project. Many of the engineers at Dunmurry were older men, steeped in conventional auto industry procedures. Building a stainless-steel body shell and then designing a plastic underbody to fit inside, and working from there to the chassis—from the outside in—was incomprehensible to them. Even Lotus objected to it, but DeLorean insisted on it being done that way. "It was not a conventional car," says Colin Spooner. "Hell, it was a completely different concept to anything that had been done before."

Back at Park Avenue DeLorean took an Olympian attitude about the Battle of the Engineers. He was moving on to other things. At the end of May he and Cafiero were "too busy" even to make it to Detroit for the annual meeting of DeLorean Motor Company. Dick Brown handled the meeting, explaining that his two superiors were both in New York preparing for another trip to Belfast. But at that stage DeLorean seemed to be keener on negotiating a new business venture: to become sole U.S. importer of Alfa-Romeo cars as well as Suzuki four-wheel-drive vehicles. It was to see Alfa that he had gone to Italy with Brown earlier in May. Brown would be in charge of this one, and had already taken an option on a building in Marina Del Rey, near Los Angeles, to act as the distribution center.

DeLorean was also planning to become a bus manufacturer. This was an ambitious venture that died like many others, and cost both time and money. In May he organized a task force, which included Bill Haddad, to develop a prototype of a modified German bus, called the DMC-80. It was, he said, an "Americanized version of a German bus, but it would be lighter than conventional U.S. buses, have wider aisles, a twenty-two-inch floor, and be available with a ramp for wheelchairs or a door-lift device." His task force included Otto Schultz, head of the German bus-maker FFG, and his son Rainer. The prototype Transbus was shown at the American Public Transportation Association in New York in September, but at a press conference DeLorean had to admit that it did not meet the Department of Transportation safety standards. It would be brought up to standard, he promised. But it never was. The bus project never got off the ground, although it cost the company money.

The Alfa-Romeo venture came to an end soon too: in Milan the Italian automaker announced it had not been possible to harmonize differences in emphasis attributable to DeLorean's focus on his upcoming new sports car and Alfa's desire to expand the U.S. market share of its entire range of automobiles.

But it was in Belfast that John DeLorean was making his most ambitious pitch yet. He now decided, with everything on the surface going so smoothly, that it was time to tap the British government for more money. He wanted to build another new car, a sedan with two large gull-wing doors, to be called the DMC-24. And the contractor he wanted to build it for him? None other than GPD Services Inc. Early in July DeLorean instructed Bennington to ask NIDA for the money, having done what he could to clear the way first with the still enthusiastic Shaun Harte. On July 10 Bennington wrote a formal letter to Harte and NIDA and to McCann at the Department of Commerce.

He started with a glowing paragraph about how a sedan model would "solidify our distribution organization" and protect the company from "the obvious hazards of a single-model production line." These would, he said "contribute greatly to increased profitability for DMCL." In Milan Italian designer Giugiaro was already at work and the plan was to introduce the sedan into production eighteen months after the sports car. But the engineering work would again have to be done outside Belfast. Coolly ignoring the experiences of his engineers, he then wrote:

> Approaches have been made to both Porsche and GPD Services Inc., to carry out the detailed engineering development program. While cost estimates provided by these firms are comparable, it seems reasonable to contract the services of GPD and Lotus because our present relationship with respect to the development program for the DMC-12 has been totally satisfactory. This experience leads me to believe that the most effective route both technically and as regard cost effectiveness would be to develop our program based on their continued involvement. In addition, the personal brilliance of Colin Chapman's engineering is a vital additional ingredient.

This request is almost breathtaking in its audacity. GPD had already been paid approaching $18 million and had passed none of it on to Lotus. Every bill, every cost that Lotus incurred was paid for month by month from the Belfast company out of funds provided by the British taxpayer. Now DeLorean, through Bennington, was going to ask for more. Bennington was an unwitting party to it all—almost certainly the letter was drafted by DeLorean, who felt it might come better from the man on the spot.

GPD, Bennington went on, had already been approached and "have indicated a willingness to undertake the development of the sedan series." That was scarcely surprising in view of the money involved. But, he added—and here we get to the crunch—"as they have been approached to design and develop a line of prestige products for one of Europe's leading automotive manufacturers, they are insisting on an early commitment on our part." GPD, as we well know, had no design capacity and there was no big contract in the offing. DeLorean was simply putting the pressure on. Then Bennington got down to money. GPD, he said, proposed "a similar arrangement to that entered into in respect of the DMC-12 with an initial prepayment of £10 million." With a bit of negotiation the payments could probably be phased, he added helpfully. He then enclosed seven pages of detail on the sedan.

Harte recommended to NIDA that the agency give the company further guarantees of up to $22 million to build the sedan. NIDA, however, was beginning to worry about Mr. DeLorean and his odd accounting habits—it was not getting the information and progress reports that were part of the agreement. The board decided to let this one pass—it could wait, even if the busy GPD, with its profitable workload, could not. There is no evidence GPD ever did get another contract.

At Dunmurry that summer the atmosphere among the engineers and production men continued to deteriorate. On August 29 Broomfield and Loasby wrote a joint memo to Bennington. They marked it "personal and confidential" and put on record for the first time their serious doubts about the project. If the Northern Ireland authorities, who were supposed to be monitoring the project, had even caught a hint of it, they would soon have lost their composure.

The two men protested the decision, which they had only learned about from Colin Spooner at Lotus, to drop their work. They had learned that the sections in question had actually been completed nearly two weeks earlier and "were hand-carried to Visioneering by Messrs. Peacock and Parker to be incorporated in the flanging details of the master model." (Visioneering, a Detroit firm, was producing the master model, as it had done one of the original prototypes.) It was now obvious, they wrote to Bennington, "that the design is a *fait accompli*.

"Based on the Lotus proposals, the vehicle parameters cannot be achieved," they concluded gloomily, recommending that "a complete review be made of all body sections prior to finalization and inclusion in the master models."

It was quite a blast, and Bennington was in no mood for it. He and Loasby were increasingly at odds. Bennington felt Loasby was too much of a perfectionist, a superb engineer if you gave him seven years to design a car, but on an eighteen-month program where speed mattered more than design, he was proving to be an irritant. The constant friction between Colin Spooner and Loasby was annoying, and between Loasby and Barrie Wills, who had become Bennington's closest ally. Loasby kept accusing Wills of taking "discussion only" drawings from Lotus and going off to component makers to have them tooled up. As the summer wore on, the friction got worse. In November Loasby came back from a trip to Visioneering and accused Wills of having had the front and rear fascias (façades) and all the pieces of glass made from drawings instead of the proven system of taking models from a finished body stack.

Loasby shot off an angry letter to Wills. "If the window glasses and fascias are manufactured in isolation from the body stack we cannot, in any way, ensure their proper alignment with the bodies in our assembly."

It was a fundamental point and as in so many cases involving the car, both men were right. But Wills argued that unless he anticipated final designs, there would simply be no car. He had to take something rough to component makers, get them to quote him a price, decide on who would make it, and then place the order. Many parts would have to be retooled with the design still not "frozen," but Bennington decided that was the only way to keep the program within sight of even the (privately) revised timetable. That was anathema to Loasby, who increasingly felt that the whole engineering function was being pushed into the background.

Early in November John DeLorean was back in the news again. Late in the afternoon of Tuesday, November 6, a new book suddenly appeared on bookshelves all over Detroit. Within hours it was the talk of the auto world. It was published by a firm no one had ever heard of—Wright—which also was the name of the author, J. Patrick Wright. *On a Clear Day You Can See General Motors: John Z. De-*

Lorean's Look Inside the Automotive Giant had finally hit the market after four years of vacillation. And Wright, a thirty-eight-year-old automotive journalist, had published it himself.

The story of the book is an extraordinary one. Wright sets it out this way: "In February of 1974, John Z. DeLorean asked me to write a 'no nonsense, no bullshit book' with him about his life and experiences at the General Motors Corporation. The work would 'open up the board room from the inside,' he said, adding, 'I know you have to name names and talk about specific decisions.' "

DeLorean, according to Wright, handed him a large "stack of material which contained personal papers, memos from GM, business analyses he had prepared, rough drafts of several chapters, his handwritten notes about items and sections to be included in the manuscript and his correspondence with several literary agents and publishers. 'Here,' he said. 'You're the doctor.' "

Wright and DeLorean prepared a detailed proposal and received a $45,000 advance from Playboy Press. By Labor Day 1975, Wright had finished and presented the manuscript to the publisher, who he said was "ecstatic."

> John DeLorean was not. He refused to let the book be published. His objection as expressed to me was that the book we'd written would anger General Motors executives who he said would make it difficult, it not impossible, to build and market an "ethical sports car" which he was developing. He admitted that this consideration was a latter-day influence on his plans for the book and was not a part of our original discussions or agreement on the project.
>
> Despite his objection to publishing the book, he praised it on several occasions, including one time during a meeting in New York called by Bill Adler, executive editor of Playboy Press, to try to resolve the book crisis. It was February 6, 1976 and John said flatly to Adler, Philip Spitzer, our agent, and me: "Pat has done a fantastic job. . . . The book is what should be said about American business. The book is what should be published. It really is the only book." But he also reiterated his fear of reprisals from GM if the book was printed. A month later he added, "I've got to play with the system for another 18 months. Then I can say this stuff."

Rather than flatly ban the book, DeLorean vacillated and stalled Wright for the next four years. "At times he said he was eager to get the book published. At other times he was adamantly opposed to it. And at still other times he offered to help me do my own book about General Motors, provided I leave him out of it."

Twice DeLorean told Wright he would repay the Playboy advance and cancel the contract. But he refused to sign a cancellation agreement when Playboy submitted it: "Before terminating the Playboy contract he first wanted me to sign an agreement with him not to publish the book on my own or write anything about him without his permission. He also wanted me to turn over to him all of the documents, notes and tapes used in writing the book. In return, he would give me $5,000 and 20% of the author's revenue of any 'DeLorean General Motors Book' that he might write. This proposal was unacceptable to me and thus the book remained tied up into 1979."

Wright finally decided to publish it himself at a cost said at the time to be $50,000. No publishers would take it. It proved to be fortunate for Wright, for by publishing it himself he probably made $250,000 to $300,000. Despite his unhappy experiences, Wright remains a DeLorean fan. Referring to the book: "It is not a dispassionate overview of an industrial giant. It is one man's heartfelt story about the business world about him as he worked his way toward the summit, and then found that the climb was not worth the reward. In this case, that man is one of the most successful and talented executives in the post-World War II automobile industry."

Soon the book was headed for the bestseller list. John DeLorean found himself a hero throughout. He told about how the ill-fated Corvair's "questionable safety" was well known and debated inside GM before its introduction; of management blunders in which hundreds of millions of dollars were wasted; of how GM executives stifled initiative; of his own battles with them over his lifestyle and much else. "John DeLorean's story," said the jacket blurb, "is more than an exposé." It was "a personal account of one modern executive's struggle with big business management."

Wright continued: "As the antithesis of the traditional, stodgy, dark-suited GM executive, DeLorean operated with flair and panache. He openly criticized his company and his industry when he felt they deserved it. He avoided the corporate social scene in favor of a cadre of friends that included professional athletes and movie stars. And he dated models and actresses who were often younger than the daughters of his fellow executives."

He chronicled John DeLorean's version of how he got to near the top at GM and then found that: "Life at the top was a disappointment. DeLorean found his job on executive row to be boring. Moreover, he began to question GM's management system which he felt often promoted mediocrity, sometimes produced illegal and immoral business practices, and stressed personal loyalties to the detriment of the corporation. His efforts to push for change from within were fruitless. To these frustrations was added the startling revelation that resentments inside GM had been formed into a campaign to destroy him. So he quit."

In short, what Wright took down and wrote was certainly, as he said, John DeLorean's own story. Wright is a first-class journalist. His role originally was to be little more than a ghost-writer, using his professional skills to turn DeLorean's writings and jottings into a readable book. The book is in the first person, and Wright's sole original injection into it was the foreword—about the only part that has not been questioned since. The book brought about some interesting reactions, but only very muted ones from the GM men whom DeLorean savaged. That was not the way things were done at GM.

Thomas A. Murphy, GM's president, who was characterized in the book as an understanding man, was asked for his reactions at a Detroit press conference. He replied by reading a telegram sent in 1973 by DeLorean to a Detroit newspaper publisher in which he protested that he was not dissatisfied with his life at GM and that his seventeen-year career had been "very happy and satisfying."

DeLorean himself at first expressed surprise and disappointment when the book came out. But when the highly favorable reactions began to build, he changed tack and called it an accurate portrayal of the information he had given Wright. He said his objections had more to do with tone than with content. "I am not disavowing the book at all."

But while On a Clear Day did much for DeLorean's image with the outside world, it also generated growls of dissent from within Detroit's automotive industry press corps, which knew him better than anyone else—with the exception of his former colleagues at GM.

The most telling critique came from veteran Detroit journalist Robert W. Irvin, who had leaked DeLorean stories back in 1972. Irvin reviewed the book in his popular "Irvin at Large" column in *Automotive News* on November 26: "DeLorean spares no one but himself. He criticizes fellow executives for pettiness and playing office politics. He tells us about a conspiracy among some top executives to force him out of GM—even using the press to discredit him. Yet DeLorean did the same things in his career at GM—engaged in office politics to further himself or hurt others and tried to use the press to further his own ends."

Irvin then went on to blast DeLorean's penchant for taking credit for the advances made during his time at Pontiac and Chevrolet and he correctly credits Jim Wangers for his GTO ideas. ". . . DeLorean liked his perks too. He liked his hotel suites stocked with fruit and drinks when traveling. And he complained when he found he didn't rate a driver on the 14th Floor, where he was just another vice president."

Noting that the book was coming out in embarrassing coincidence with DeLorean's efforts to launch the DMC-12, Irvin made a dark prediction: ". . . GM, meanwhile, is preparing a second assembly plant in Bowling Green, Kentucky, to increase production of its Chevrolet Corvette, America's only production sports car. . . . Then in late 1982, GM will bring out a redesigned Corvette to be built in the new Bowling Green plant. Any way you look at it, this is going to be tough competition for DeLorean from GM's Corvette. Some people, mindful of DeLorean's book, will probably be working extra hard on the new Corvette project."

Irvin never lived to see how true his prophecy would be. He died in 1980.

Earlier in 1979, even though he had promised in writing to NIDA to restrict his business efforts to the car company, DeLorean was determined to gain control of the Logan Manufacturing Corporation of Logan, Utah. The firm made the track vehicles that scrape and pack the snow for ski resorts, and in the early months of 1979 Logan, then a division of Thiokol Corporation, had about 80 percent of the U.S. market despite competition from Canadian and West German snow-grooming equipment makers.

In its annual report to the Michigan corporation commission filed in November 1978, the assets of the DeLorean Manufacturing Corporation—DeLorean's privately held company—totaled just

1

2

1. The house where John DeLorean lived as a boy. *Detroit Free Press*
2. DeLorean was defeated for student council president in 1947. *Lawrence Institute of Technology*   3. John DeLorean (front row, third from left) poses with his first love at Lawrence—the Lawrence Tech Band.   From the 1942 L-Book. *Lawrence Institute of Technology*

3

4. In 1968 a chubby John DeLorean posed with the new Pontiac Grand Prix designs his division had created. The car boasts "the longest hood in the industry" among other styling advances. *Detroit Free Press* 5. Despite the smiles, DeLorean's marriage to Kelly Harmon was beginning to break up in 1970 when this photo was taken at a dance. *Detroit Free Press* 6. The 1973-model DeLorean, his chin line extended by cosmetic surgery and his touched-up hair now at avant-garde length, posed for this preview photograph of the Chevrolet Vega, in the background. *Detroit Free Press*

5   6

7

7. *and* 8. Freed of the constraints of the GM dress code, DeLorean now lived out the part of the maverick business tycoon to the hilt. In these December 1973 photographs, he was openly emphasizing his outside business interests, including the San Diego Chargers and New York Yankees, a horseracing track and his Grand Prix of America miniature car tracks. *Detroit Free Press*

8

It's life's illusions I recall...

9. Never shy about promoting himself or his new laid-back lifestyle, DeLorean had this still photograph from a Chevrolet promotion film, featuring him and infant son Zachary, printed into a color poster as a holiday gift to friends and the Chevrolet dealer network. *Detroit Free Press*

10. With its spectacular view of mountain ranges, DeLorean's 400+ acre ranch at Pauma Valley, near San Diego, was one of his early General Motors years investments. Here he joined the eccentric social circle that surrounded computer wizard Fletcher Jones, a group that included his future wife Cristina and pilot Morgan Hetrick. *Glasheen Graphics* 11. Even though his career at General Motors was coming to an end in a matter of weeks, DeLorean kept up a good front at his engagement party for bride-to-be Cristina Ferrare. *Detroit Free Press*

12. The happy couple at their new home in Bloomfield
Hills, Michigan. *Detroit Free Press*   13. Cristina gets to
know her new son, Zachary. *Detroit Free Press*

13

14, 15, and 16. Members of the DeLorean Motor Company
Team: William Collins [14], Robert Dewey [15], and William
Haddad [16].

17. The interior of the DMC-12.
Despite the much-publicized emphasis on
safety, DeLorean paid far more attention to
cosmetic details such as the matte finish on
the surfaces of the instrument panel and
dashboard. *DeLorean Motor Company*
18. Compared with the competition, from
left to right: a Corvette, an early DMC prototype,
a Mercedes-Benz and a Porsche. *Detroit Free Press*
19. The Car, *DeLorean Motor Company*

20. The Belfast Team. Seated: Shaun Harte, DeLorean, Eugene Cafiero, Chuck Bennington, Brian Beharrell. Standing: Tony Hopkins, Alex Fetherston, Myron Stylianides, Joe Daly, David Adams, George Broomfield, Mike Loasby, Robert Donnell. *The Daily Telegraph, London* 21. John and Cristina are all smiles at the groundbreaking festivities at the DeLorean factory in Dunmurry, Northern Ireland.

22

23

22. DeLorean with (left to right), Don Concannon, Don Lander and Roy Mason. 23. Humphrey Atkins, secretary of state for Northern Ireland until 1979. *British Central Office of Information*

24. James Prior, secretary of
state for Northern Ireland, 1981
to the present. *British Central
Office of Information*
25. Adam Butler, Northern Ireland
minister of state, with Shaun Harte.

26

26. Members of the Lotus Team: Mike Kimberley, Colin Chapman and Tony Rudd.

27. The Dunmurry factory was a state-of-the-art assembly plant
where the newly trained workers turned the DMC-12 into
reality. (a) Workers assemble the unique double-Y chassis,
which moved by robot carrier (b) through each phase, adding
on the rear-mounted engine and stainless steel body, to the final
testing and checks (c) before being shipped to the United
States. *DeLorean Motor Company*

27c

28. John DeLorean, his hands manacled behind his back, en route to arraignment on October 20, 1982, on charges of conspiring to distribute cocaine.

$650,000—obviously not nearly enough to cover the $15 million asking price Thiokol wanted for Logan. DeLorean began a much publicized selloff of his private real estate holdings as a means to raise the money. First to go were three plots of ranch and farmland in Southern California, which netted him $4.6 million. Then DeLorean was contacted by a real estate investor named Kurt Kuennecke with an offer for his luxurious Pauma Valley estate. DeLorean wanted $2 million; Kuennecke offered $1.5 million in cash.

Kuennecke is a refugee from Hitler's Germany who emigrated to Calgary, Canada, and prospered as a real estate investor and speculator. He and his wife fled the Canadian winters in the early 1970s and settled near San Diego, where he has continued his investments. When he first approached DeLorean, Kuennecke and his wife suddenly found themselves being included in the DeLoreans' glamorous social life, and they spent a long weekend as guests at Pauma Valley. The deal was agreed to orally, as Kuennecke recalls:

> I offered Mr. DeLorean $1.5 million cash with delivery of clear title for the property because I didn't want to have a mortgage on the house. At first this was fine and dandy with him, then the deal was changed and he asked if he could—for tax reasons —take 29 percent down, a little less than $500,000. I agreed to do that and to deposit another $1 million in a certificate of deposit that would pay him $200,000 a year over the next five years.
>
> The next thing I know I get a telephone call from Mr. DeLorean's banker informing me that Mr. DeLorean had tried to borrow $1 million against my certificate of deposit and the bank wanted me to cosign the note. I refused. I told them that Mr. DeLorean's security was the property and that I had offered payment in full.
>
> And then the banker said, "Well, John needs the money and he wants to borrow the million against the certificate—that way he can defer the taxes." And I said I had no intention of giving Mr. DeLorean a mortgage on the property for $1 million and then cosigning a $1 million promissory note to the bank—that's some sort of double indemnity because Mr. DeLorean can take the money and not pay off and leave me to pay twice.
>
> So that died out and after a couple of weeks I was called by

Henry Bushkin, a lawyer in Los Angeles for Johnny Carson, and he had another similar deal going with Mr. DeLorean and wanted me to sign a note. I refused. But Mr. DeLorean still refused to deliver the property under our earlier agreement and so I sued him for delivery.

The suit prompted a handwritten note to Bill Haddad about Kuennecke: ". . . have him checked out—he is suing me maliciously—a Canadian—is he an undesirable alien?"

By mid-June Haddad had a report from a private investigation firm that DMC regularly used to check on prospective employees. After listing the Kuennecke's family and business ties to Calgary, the report concluded, "There is no known derogatory information as concerns Mr. Kuennecke and he is not known to Canadian police authorities insofar as any criminal record is concerned." However, DeLorean did not stop at a mere private eye search for possible "SOS" material to use as a lever against Kuennecke.

"I started hearing about a man named Nesseth, a friend of De-Lorean's. There were never any direct threats, just friends of ours would relay warnings. And finally a friend brought to my attention what had happened in Puerto Rico—the double dealing there—so I just dropped my suit and bought some land in Valley Center," Kuennecke says.

"It's all very sad. I'd never experienced anything like the shenanigans that DeLorean put us through; saying one thing and then contradicting himself in the next fifteen minutes or sending a telegram that refuted what he had said. I told him at the time we called the deal off, 'John, you are a man on the run. I don't know what you are running from.' And he said, 'Kurt, you don't know what you are talking about.' "

With Kuennecke's money out of reach, DeLorean tried other abortive ways to raise funds including a deal through Henry Bushkin, who tried to convince his client Johnny Carson to put up more money by buying DeLorean's avocado ranch so he could complete the purchase of the Logan company. Carson backed off from that deal, however.

Suddenly, the deal with Thiokol went through, even though De-Lorean was by most accounting short of the purchase price by $4 to $8 million. At the time, Walter Strycker remembers DeLorean bragging about "a Swiss bank loan he had secured at less than the prime rate going in this country. I asked him about that because that was when the prime rate had been around 16 percent and was still pretty high, but he suddenly got very coy. I concluded that he must have quite a bit on deposit there because the Swiss won't lend below market to anyone unless it is heavily secured—probably by an equal amount of cash."

As with most of DeLorean's business investments, the Logan company quickly began to lose market share not only to the neighboring equipment made by Bombardier in Canada but also to a West German producer, Kassbohrer Fahrzeugwerke GmH. Again, in April 1980, DeLorean relied on his favorite tactic of sniping. A memo to Haddad ordered, "Please check Kassbohrer—are any of them Nazi collaborators, guilty of war crimes, etc. See if your Washington contacts can come up with anything at all."

Haddad responded six days later, "Kassbohrer comes up clean. Intelligence files list no present or previous negative information."

But DeLorean was not satisfied and in November 1980 filed an unfair trade practices complaint with the U.S. International Trade Commission, charging Kassbohrer and other competitors with unfairly pricing their products to beat out the DMC's snow-groomer in the American market. After examination, the ITC staff recommended no action be taken; they reported that the company's market share problems were due to management deficiencies, not unfair trade inflows.

DeLorean's business dealings were now being questioned by Edward Lapham of *Automotive News*, who took the DeLorean financing deals from the first corporation all the way through the NIDA contracts. The article dated February 5, 1979, was titled "Analyzing DeLorean's Project: Is It Just a Paper Empire?"

In painstaking detail Lapham worked from the beginning. He disputed DeLorean's claim of having put $4 million of his own money into the project. The claims, he said, were "fuzzy and undocumented." At each step from the formation of DSCP through the DMC stock offerings to the new offering for the DRLP, the piece showed how DeLorean's stake and control over the project and its rising capital holdings grew without any real contribution from him. Interestingly, even at that early date Lapham had tracked the connection with GPD, but he confused the Swiss account with a legitimate design firm in Ferndale, Michigan, of the same name.

Finally Lapham concluded, "Some critics say the only weakness in the plan is the ERM process which hasn't proven itself enough for a production run. Others claim there is no market for such a vehicle and as the S-2 [SEC document] admits, 'the success of the company depends to a large degree on the efforts of a few individuals'—De-Lorean, C. R. Brown and William Collins.

"And some critics still believe the entire DeLorean enterprise is an elaborate scheme to enrich a few individuals at the top."

Years later, Lapham muses on just how close he came. "I take a lot of pride in that article. It stands up pretty well over the years," he says. But as usual, his thorough research and troubling questions were studiously ignored by the Detroit dailies and the general news publications in New York, which had such a vested interest in the De-Lorean image by now.

9

CRISIS AND CONFUSION

As 1979 progressed, the Northern Irish officials were not unhappy with their investment. They may have had a few doubts here and there, but the basic attitude was that they were dealing with professional men who believed in the project. While the team was working six to seven days a week to make things happen, DeLorean himself was seldom seen, although everyone had fully expected him to be more or less sitting on top of the project. The officials knew nothing about the worries of the engineers and production men and the battles raging at Lotus. Shaun Harte continued to report back enthusiastically, particularly after a visit to Lotus on August 3, when he found that despite the plant vacations, work was still proceeding on the DMC-12. The first wholly produced Lotus version was running, he told the NIDA board, and initial reactions were excellent.

But while Loasby and Broomfield were worried about their own technical difficulties, NIDA was starting to worry about DeLorean's finances and his money-spending habits. A special DeLorean monitoring committee had been set up in August with both NIDA and Department of Commerce people.

The committee held its first meeting on September 23. It included Shaun Harte and local businessman Alex Fetherston, the two NIDA nominees on the DMC board. From the Commerce Department, Frank McCann was appointed the senior Department officer responsible for the DeLorean project. The monitoring committee was chaired by Tony Hopkins, who had taken over as NIDA chief executive from Ronnie Henderson after he departed that summer, proving to be something short of a dazzling success.

Hopkins was tougher, shrewder, more ambitious than Henderson.

With the new Conservative Thatcher government in power, there was also a different attitude toward public expenditure, although Northern Ireland continued to be acknowledged as a special case.

By the time Hopkins took over, euphoria over John DeLorean was beginning to turn to disillusionment. Promised business plans were not turning up despite repeated requests. Memos and letters were going unanswered. The extravagance of DeLorean's lifestyle was becoming apparent. Why did he need that expensive office? the NIDA board asked. No one had any answers. DeLorean was not under control, they began to realize. And there was very little they could do about it except write their letters and send their Telexes. The monitoring committee sounded impressive, but it was a watchdog with no teeth.

Part of the July agreement between DeLorean and NIDA specified that he would provide the agency with a detailed plan of operation that set out the timing and goals for production and, more important, employment. But it was October before the DMCL office presented the final plan, and NIDA officials found it anything but reassuring. Harte was the man who had to dig it out of the Dunmurry management, and it gradually dawned on him, too, that the financial controls were poor to say the least. Government money was flowing without anyone worrying too much about how it was spent. It was going to Lotus in far greater quantities than anyone ever expected, because of course no one realized that none of the Oppenheimer partnership money, which went to GPD's Swiss bank account, was getting through to Lotus at all.

Back in New York, the man theoretically responsible for financial controls was complaining about them too. Walter Strycker was the chief financial officer, but he was an increasingly reluctant and rebellious one. Like Dewey, he decided to go—but he was no mouse and did not creep away quietly. By the time he left at the end of the year, Strycker would no longer be on speaking terms with John DeLorean —and DeLorean had come to hate Strycker for the trouble he stirred up with the accountants, with NIDA, and with his own legal people.

Strycker became chief financial officer after the deal was made with Northern Ireland. Until that time he had gotten along well with DeLorean—having only seen the better side of his nature, he remarked later. But once he went to work for DeLorean, things changed:

It really was like the difference between night and day, before we got funded and after we got funded. John was a whole different person. Looking back on it, he had to do a lot of things that were personally distasteful to him. He didn't want to be out talking to all the dealers and hustling them for money to become a part of his dealer program. He hated them and he didn't like talking to the investment bankers. He didn't like raising money. He didn't like working with Oppenheimer and the others. So the minute that was over, why, he had to forget about it. After we got funded, he turned all his attention to promoting John and Cristina and he hired a PR firm that was paid $10,000 a month plus expenses just to promote John DeLorean. The ironic thing was that it was the same firm that had promoted Bricklin.

Strycker had a series of confrontations with DeLorean, one of them over the acquisition of the snow-grooming company. DeLorean used many of the people paid for by the British government on that project, and Strycker questioned DeLorean once again about the costs: "Hey, you've got to keep records and you've got to reimburse the company for using other people's time."

DeLorean used three lawyers on the payroll for that job, but as far as Strycker could see, there was no reimbursement. According to him, Buck Penrose and a consultant "spent most of their time on the snow company. And there was no attempt to reimburse the company. When I said he ought to keep separate records, I got all kinds of shit thrown at me."

The more Strycker examined the way money was spent, the more uneasy he became. "The use of the government money was all wrong. The salary levels and type of compensation paid out were not justified for the initial stage of a start-up company. DeLorean was paying himself $500,000 directly, and another $500,000 indirectly via people hired to do work for him that had nothing to do with the company."

For example, Strycker found on the books a consultant in Detroit who was supposed to be doing systems work for the company. Strycker never met him, nor could he identify exactly what he was doing for the company.

"He gets $3,000 a month," Strycker complained to DeLorean. "What's it for?"

"Just pay him," replied DeLorean. Strycker never learned what the man did.

Then there were two servants on the DMC payroll, a practice that Strycker objected to. Jonathan Mazzone was supposed to be a driver and "supplemental supply clerk" for the New York office. Strycker calculated he spent less than 10 percent of his time working for the company. He acted as personal chauffeur for Cristina, kept Maur Dubin's books, and took his orders from Cristina and Dubin, not from any executives at DMC. Then there was Edward Chasty, a personal servant and driver for the DeLorean family, who received his entire salary from DMC.

Strycker kept straying upon items that he feared could involve the company and himself as chief financial officer in serious trouble with the SEC. Strycker was well aware that financier Victor Posner and Gulf + Western's Charles Bludhorn had just recently been criticized by the SEC for similar improprieties.

Maur Dubin was not only using company employees for his own private business with DeLorean's blessing, Strycker discovered, but he was also using company property. DMC kept a van in the underground garage and when Strycker went down one evening to use it, he found that an employee of Dubin's was driving it. Later he discovered that the van, driven by Dubin's man, had been involved in an accident on December 6, 1979.

There was also $75,000 a year paid to a man out on the West Coast who worked on DeLorean's private ranch and property. "He acted as John's manager and the company paid for him," Strycker said.

But it was DeLorean's own personality that disturbed Strycker as much as anything else. He had seen how DeLorean forced Collins out once the Lotus deal was completed, in spite of all the sweat and effort Collins put into the early design work. He watched as DeLorean continually hatched plans to develop other companies. He was astounded one day when DeLorean told him quite casually of his great new idea:

"Walt, I'm going to take over Chrysler." Oppenheimer was to be asked to put together a $2-billion limited partnership. At that stage the car company was at its lowest ebb and Lee Iacocca had not yet achieved its resurrection. DeLorean figured he was the man to do it —presumably turning Chrysler into another subsidiary of the DeLorean Motor Company. It is interesting to speculate on what the

British government would have thought about this particular fantasy —Chrysler's red-ink U.K. operations had cost them many millions already. Fortunately for everyone, Chrysler escaped. But Strycker had had enough. Like Dewey before him, he decided to leave.

For Strycker, DeLorean Motor Company had never been a full-time job. He agreed to join part-time only with the idea that as soon as the company was running properly, he would leave or revert to consultant status. He was still running a venture capital fund, a vineyard in Lake County, California, and a strip-mining operation in eastern Kentucky. Each of these enterprises was taking up a portion of his time.

In Belfast, at the insistence of a now agonized NIDA, the local DMCL finance director, Joe Daly (the former finance director for Chrysler Europe who had been hired for the Belfast operation by Myron Stylianides), had been given responsibility for preparing and issuing a formal updated business plan—but he still had not seen the DMC business plan. The company was running increasingly out of control, and DeLorean displayed the same contempt for administrative work in his own company that he had shown at Pontiac. In any case, that was the responsibility of Eugene Cafiero. The company was getting into a mess.

And what was Cafiero, president and chief executive, doing at this time? He now features briefly in the saga—as centrally as he ever does. For such an obviously able, tough professional, he remained peculiarly obscure and distant in his nearly two years with DeLorean. He worked in the offices on Park Avenue but did not seem to be part of the inner circle, which was essentially DeLorean and Kimmerly with Nesseth coming and going randomly.

But on September 27 Cafiero accompanied DeLorean to Belfast for a meeting with NIDA. Dennis Faulkner was there in his capacity as chairman, so was Tony Hopkins. The two Ulstermen wanted to sound off about their serious worries: the overall financial control was not satisfactory and NIDA needed a proper flow of information; and the role of chief financial officer in New York was not being properly filled. DeLorean and Cafiero promised they would correct both.

Faulkner and Hopkins were increasingly worried about Bennington. They had nothing against him personally, but felt that no man could work for long at the pace he set himself, and unless he had more support, the project would get further behind. DeLorean now agreed. From now on Gene Cafiero would spend half his time in Belfast.

That sounded better to the NIDA men—if Cafiero was good enough to get to the top of Chrysler, he should be able to cope with the situation at Dunmurry.

Faulkner and Hopkins brought up another couple of points: regular board meetings of DMC must be held, and the two NIDA men on the board, Harte and Fetherston, must be supplied with discussion papers in advance. They had been attending without first receiving an agenda.

Finally, Faulkner and Hopkins insisted that the DMC-12 project be given priority over all other projects being run out of New York—they were horrified by the venture into the Transbus. DeLorean and Cafiero accepted that, although DeLorean would slow his search for outside businesses only when he began to run out of money the following year.

On October 19 Cafiero was in Belfast again and appeared at NIDA for another meeting with Faulkner and Hopkins. Again the NIDA men went over much the same subjects; Cafiero agreed that there must be "substantial improvement" in providing control information. What NIDA wanted was something better than a revision of the budget plan every three months—they wanted to see actual spending compared to budget spending, with a full explanation of variances. That was normal practice and made it easier to monitor—but DeLorean was not doing it. Cafiero agreed to put that right, too.

Cafiero finally undertook to put the whole financial control and information systems through a major shakeup and to provide NIDA with a full business plan for 1980, incorporating the Ulster and U.S. operations, that would be capable of being measured month by month against performance.

Now there was another move that would later raise eyebrows and about which, even at the time, the NIDA board had mixed feelings. DeLorean offered Shaun Harte a job as director of planning, with responsibility for coordinating the production program between Dunmurry and Lotus. Harte wanted to accept—it would mean a significant increase in salary for him, and he was still enthusiastic about the car project. DeLorean had gone out of his way to be charming to Harte, in the way he originally had with Strycker and Brown and any of the others he wanted to join him.

At forty-one, Harte was a bright accountant whose greatest fault, perhaps, was his naiveté. But it was not difficult for an outsider to become enthusiastic about John DeLorean and his dream—after all, Cafiero had become excited, and he was an older, more experienced hand than Harte, whose business experience had been largely confined to Northern Ireland and Canada.

Hopkins was dubious, however; it would not look good if the NIDA man, who was essentially responsible for monitoring the agency's biggest investment, were to join the recipient of that investment less than halfway through the program.

On October 29 he raised the issue with DeLorean at a meeting between the two. DeLorean argued that while NIDA was complaining about the coordination and information aspect of the project, he and his team were really just interested in building the car, which was all that mattered. Everything else was just administration and paperwork. If NIDA wanted information, who better to provide it than their own man?

Hopkins put it to a NIDA board meeting on November 28. The trade union leader John Freeman objected. He thought it was all wrong and should not be allowed. But the NIDA board finally agreed, primarily on the basis that Harte had been providing information from the outside until then, but could now provide it from the inside. They also hoped Harte could discover what exactly was happening at Lotus —the whole program seemed to be slipping badly there. Hopkins was planning to go to a board meeting at Lotus on December 17 to find out for himself. On December 1, Shaun Harte joined DeLorean Motor Cars Limited. He would stay on until the bitter end. It was Harte who courteously and generously opened the gates and allowed the authors into the plant on the day of John DeLorean's arrest—and amiably chatted while the authors test-drove the last cars off the production line.

At this stage NIDA genuinely believed it was getting somewhere in its efforts to control DeLorean. Cafiero seemed to be the key. One last effort and they might be able to get some proper controls, although they felt there had been a visible improvement in the last few months of the year. It was still far from satisfactory, though—in fact, by normal standards, it was appalling with such large amounts of taxpayers' money at stake. Hopkins decided to increase the pressure still more.

Two weeks before Christmas, Cafiero was again in Belfast—honoring DeLorean's promise that he would be there half the time. On

December 13 Faulkner and Hopkins met with him and again empha-sized, as they were tiring of doing, their dismay at the meaningless quarterly revisions of the plan without reconciling the figures with the original budget.

They had to have budget figures in one column, actual expenditures beside them, they complained. Only then could they see clearly where the money was being spent—or misspent. And they needed it monthly.

Cafiero, however, said he had been at work—the integrated group plan for 1980 was ready. He had promised it for December and they would have it in December. He would get approval of it from the DMCL board at a meeting on December 17. What is more, he prom-ised, the plan would not be altered during 1980, which meant no requests for further money, and perhaps of even greater interest, a replacement for Walter Strycker as chief financial officer had now been identified.

Hopkins had known for weeks that Strycker was going. He and Faulkner were dismayed—to some extent it was because of Strycker that they had been so generous to DeLorean in the first place. They did not blame Strycker, but it made them even more unhappy with John DeLorean, whom they were now beginning to wish they had never heard of.

Hopkins decided he could not ignore Strycker's impending depar-ture. At a NIDA board meeting on December 19, he presented a long, detailed paper on DeLorean. He outlined his battles to persuade DeLorean and Cafiero of the need for financial controls in the group, and his optimism that things might now improve. But he also recom-mended that Faulkner, as chairman of NIDA, should write to De-Lorean setting out the agency's unhappiness and insisting on further improvement in the supply of information. It was to become some-thing of a historic letter. Unfortunately, Faulkner took nearly a month to write it and it was eventually sent on January 17.

By then Walter Strycker had become the second chief financial officer to leave John DeLorean. The final straw was the snow-groom-ing company. Strycker was excluded from the auditing and record keeping on the company, he says, which he had found particularly disturbing.

"John let it drop that he had refinanced some of the monies for the snowmobile company and that it came from a bank in Switzerland.

And so I in turn went to Arthur Andersen—because they were doing the audit and handling the bookkeeping for both companies—and I suggested that they look very hard at the source of money and make sure they were satisfied that there was no connection and that those monies had nothing to do with GPD. And they did and came back and said that as far as they were concerned, it was okay."

Strycker believed the auditors had been far too easily satisfied. "You know, John can look you straight in the eye and tell you that black is white and I sat there while he gave Arthur Andersen a bunch of discrepancies, and they just believed him."

The man at Andersen's to whom Strycker complained was Dick Measelle. He had been performing the DeLorean audits for several years. Strycker brought with him Harry DeWitt, the young accountant who was hired as Bob Dewey's assistant and who was now feeling similarly nervous about the way the money was being spent. Together, they were the finance division of DMC.

Strycker and DeWitt raised a series of points they believed the auditors should look into. It would still be nearly eighteen months before any revenues would flow from the sale of cars, but the DeLorean operation in the U.S. was now costing more than $800,000 a month, and in projecting the cash needs forward, the finance men could see DeLorean was running out.

"We had people working on the bus," says DeWitt. "We had people working on a four-wheel-drive recreational vehicle. We had people looking into other projects. We had lots of people not working on the car at all. We were concerned with corporate expenditures for travel and reimbursement. And we were concerned with the GPD contract."

DeWitt could not see the point of the GPD contract. Like Collins, it remained a puzzle to him why DMC should pay a Swiss company to get Lotus to do the work. GPD had by now become a talking point among Brown, Strycker, and Bill Haddad, but DeLorean gave them all the same answer: "Chapman wanted it that way, it's a tax scam for him."

Why did Measelle and Arthur Andersen accept the DeLorean version rather than that of his financial officers? "Remember," said Strycker, "this is 1979 and at this point John is riding high. In the U.S. press and the business world, why, he's a hero. We would get on airplanes and people would come up to John and say, 'Aren't you

John DeLorean? God, I really admire you! You are doing a fantastic thing and I wish you all the luck.' "

Strycker, however, no longer admired him. "I would say that he is probably one of the better salesmen, con men, that have come along." To prove his point Strycker offered this example:

> Two of the things that were on the list to be discussed with Arthur Andersen were automobiles that were in Los Angeles that were owned by the company. One of them was a $54,000 Mercedes and Dick Brown had delivered the car to the Golden Door* with a red ribbon around it. John had ordered it for Cristina to drive around in Los Angeles, and so Dick took it over there. The only people who ever saw the car were Cristina and Cristina's family. Nobody else in the company ever saw it.
>
> And then they had a Mazda that was delivered to Cristina's brother, who drove to USC in it—it was his personal car. The auditors went and talked to Dick Brown and Dick told them Cristina got the car to go to work and the kid is driving the other car to USC. And so they came back and they had a list and they say, "John, what about this car in Los Angeles? Who is using it?" He said, "Oh, that's a test car. We are testing the sedan because we are manufacturing a luxury sedan and we are testing all the quality sedans that will be competing with it."
>
> And they said, "Okay, fine." Crossed that off. They said, "What about the Mazda? Cristina's brother is driving that." He said, "Well, he's taking that over to USC and letting some fraternity brothers drive it and fill in some questionnaires on the car so that we could get a feel for competing sports cars." They said, "Oh, okay," and crossed that one off.
>
> And I thought: "Oh, shit. I don't belong here."

At that point Strycker went to see Al Cohen, who had been the leading lawyer at Paul Weiss, Rifkind, Wharton & Garrison on the Northern Ireland deal. Strycker told him his story and asked for his advice. Cohen was worried.

"Walt, the best thing to do is try to get out and get away from it as fast as you can without turning it into a mud-slinging match where you would lose. He has the media and you don't."

Strycker gave DeLorean notice that he was leaving at the end of

---

* The posh California health spa frequented by celebrities.

the year and they hammered out an agreement whereby Strycker would remain as a consultant, but he would be in California, not New York. It was an arrangement that lasted thirty days. On December 15 Strycker went on vacation. And DeLorean began his old process of "SOS."

Within weeks Strycker received two calls from people in New York. Both were friends and both said the same thing: they were sorry to hear that Strycker was having a problem.

"What problem?" asked the astonished Strycker.

"Well, we heard that you were being indicted for fraudulent activities in delivering coal to a Kentucky buyer in West Virginia."

Strycker had never been indicted for any such thing. Nor was he even involved in a dispute. John DeLorean's imagination was hard at work. Fortunately, just as he failed to blacken Bob Dewey's name, DeLorean was unable to damage Stryker's reputation within the financial community.

Over a year into what was supposed to be an eighteen-month program, the schedule kept slipping. The original timetable had to be crunched into nine months. Even before it realized the full extent of what it had to do, Lotus never believed it could build the car in eighteen months—its own critical path analysis showed two years. Bennington and Wills were desperately trying to cut months off that estimate by taking "discussion only" drawings away to be tooled up, but for every month they gained they lost two because of further changes to the car itself.

Lotus' role was expanding all the time as new jobs were added. The engine was a major addition. Its fuel economy under EPA conditions turned out to be 18.6 miles per gallon, which meant that DMC would have to pay a penalty of $5 for every $\frac{1}{10}$ mile per gallon below twenty-two on each car imported into the United States for failure to achieve the minimum standard. Improving it should have been the job of the engineers in Belfast, but DeLorean asked Lotus to do it.

He kept making additions, too. On one visit to Lotus he noticed the rear louvre designed for the new Lotus Esprit Turbo. It was eye-catching and modern. "Let's have that on the DMC," he told Chapman. Then there were electric mirrors that had not been planned, electric door locks, a new instrument package and wiper system, and many others either not on the prototype and the original specification, or added and changed later, usually by DeLorean. For the most part they improved the car, and Lotus was impressed by DeLorean's observations and his eye for detail. But the changes meant further delays, only partly made up by the extra engineers, who now occupied the sealed-off area allotted to DeLorean at the Lotus plant.

Hopes that Cafiero would relieve the pressure on Bennington were being only partly realized. Cafiero's exact role remained a mystery to those in the company. "I don't think Gene was ever allowed to contribute as much as he was capable of doing," says Bennington. "He and John were not getting along terribly well in New York. A lot of things that Gene wanted to do, John didn't want and he had his way."

Walt Strycker says, "Cafiero was supposed to be responsible for manufacturing. My feeling was that John hired him to be a buffer between him and the people of Northern Ireland—be the presence *he* said he would be. He was afraid somebody would shoot him, so he got someone else to stand there in his stead."

Cafiero's standing in Belfast and Norwich was not improved by statements he seemed to be making in New York. "I'm not afraid to be the SOB who has to go over there and tell them 'No' after they've been working on something for months," he was quoted as saying in *Auto Week* in February. The engineers hoped he might side with them in their dispute, but he never involved himself in it, for which Bennington at least was thankful, although Loasby was not.

In January 1980 Cafiero took a party of journalists to Dunmurry to show them the factory. It was still a muddy construction site, but the buildings were rising fast. The speed at which the project was running at Dunmurry was impressive by any standards. The 263,000-square-foot assembly plant, the heart of the complex, had been finished by the end of the year. Work had begun on the 200,000-square-foot body-press plant, a 50,000-square-foot marshaling building, a 50,000-square-foot fabricating building, and a boiler/pump house.

A half-mile proving track had also been finished, although the journalists were not to know that this too had been a project of some controversy, with the engineers designing the track they wanted only after a struggle.

There had been some lighter moments to break the tension that affected everyone. Dixon Hollinshead, the American building contractor who was invaluable in the early days in putting the plant together, was fond of relating the incident of the "fairy tree."

The Northern Irish are no more superstitious than anyone else, but they were prone to attempts to convince the Americans that there were still some who believed in leprechauns. (Contrary to legend, it would be difficult to find anyone in the whole of Ireland who has ever truly believed in leprechauns. But many an Irishman has earned a drink with a good leprechaun story. At Dunmurry it was no different.)

Someone told Hollinshead that there was a local legend that if a tree in the middle of a field survives the elements, there is something special about it—it must be protected by leprechauns.

"Somehow, this one tree didn't get knocked down by the dozers," Hollinshead related to Edward Lapham of *Automotive News*. "So one cat operator decided to have some fun and said he couldn't knock it down because it was a fairy tree. Naturally, all the other operators joined in—no one would knock down this damn fairy tree."

The tree was right in the middle of the assembly plant site, and it was getting to be beyond a joke.

"I thought about transplanting it or building an arboretum or something. But that just wouldn't have been the same. It got to the point where I started spreading the word that there was a $100 bill buried under the tree, but there were no takers. Finally one day a woman who works here said she knew someone who would cut the tree down. A few days later it was gone."

There was some ribbing that Hollinshead had crept out at night and chopped it down himself, but he denied it stoutly.

"It just disappeared. I guess the little people decided to move it."

The Catholic area of Twinbrook had a reputation as a housing area of last resort, and as many as 10 percent of the population were estimated by the security forces to be either IRA members or sympathizers. It was not really the sort of place where there was much local folklore of any kind, but there was not much violence either. On the other side of the factory was the Protestant enclave of Lisburn and the small village of Deriaghy. The factory was giving the area a status it had never enjoyed before, with ministers and television crews coming in regularly.

"Mr. DeLorean has a great chance to do good by doing well," said John Simpson, an economist at Queens University, Belfast. Even as the factory was emerging from the field, there were clear signs it was beginning to bring the communities together. An air of hope hung over them, although Catholics and Protestants still had their separate entrances: the Catholics from the north side, the Protestants from the southeast.

There was not much levity on the penthouse floor of 280 Park

Avenue, however. DeLorean was stepping up his SOS job on Walter Strycker. The opportunity for the blast had been unwittingly provided by Dennis Faulkner, who on January 17 had finally gotten around to writing his letter to DeLorean as directed by his board on December 19. Courteous, formal, and firm, it infuriated DeLorean, provoking a blast of Telexes between New York and the agency that were to sour relations irreparably.

"I would like to express firstly that the Agency fully recognizes the scale and complexity of the project which you and your colleagues have undertaken," wrote Faulkner politely. He also recorded the agency's "recognition of the very significant progress" that had so far been made. Then he got into the points he really wanted to raise: "We have criticized the financial control within the group as a whole and with particular reference to the function of the Chief Financial Officer of the group where we felt that the task was not being adequately performed. You had indicated that you hoped to fill this position with an individual having sound financial experience in the automotive industry by 1 January 1980. I would be grateful to know when you expect to make this appointment."

Faulkner then went through the various control procedures and better information flows that he and Hopkins had taken up again and again with both DeLorean and Cafiero. He said he was "pleased to note from our most recent discussions that you have brought to completion a reporting system which, we understand, will enable effective measurement of results and cash flow on a detailed departmental basis against the December 1979 Plan. We are also pleased to see that the necessary information is now to be made available in advance of the monthly Board meetings."

Shaun Harte's transfer, Faulkner added, "will enable more attention to be given to the critical aspect of the timing and coordination of the various activities necessary to enable the project to be implemented on schedule."

None of that should have been too offensive to DeLorean. The next paragraph certainly was:

> We have also discussed the question of the group being involved in activities other than the DMC-12 project. I appreciate that these other activities may assist the Company in the United States environment in its relations with the U.S. Government

and its image in the market place and may therefore assist the DMC-12 project itself. I am sure you will agree, however, that between us we must ensure that the DMC-12 project has total managerial priority and that the financial resources are employed solely on the DMC-12. I know that you have indicated a willingness to drop other activities if NIDA should so insist. At this point, I would welcome an assurance from you that other projects will not be undertaken without prior discussion with us and that in no case will other projects be considered if they cannot clearly be shown to be entirely complementary to the DMC-12 project.

This letter, which forevermore would be known as the "Faulkner Letter" at 280 Park Avenue, arrived on January 25. It caught De-Lorean in a foul mood.

When something went wrong, DeLorean always found someone else to blame. When his rich Saudi backer, Ojjeh, had backed out in 1977, it had been First Boston's Cookie Gibb he complained of (although never to). When the auto dealers were not rushing forward to subscribe for his shares, he blamed Brown. Collins and Dewey innocently received blame for other things that misfired.

Now John DeLorean's wrath turned on Strycker, although he must have known that Faulkner was not even referring to Strycker. After storming around the office for some time, DeLorean pulled out his usual engineer's log paper and wrote a memo, ostensibly to Eugene Cafiero and Tom Kimmerly, with a copy to Haddad.

> The attached letter from Dennis Faulkner reiterates politely the very strong NIDA opinion that Walter Strycker was not competent to perform the Chief Financial Officer function in DMC.
>
> Dennis and Tony Hopkins also told us privately that Strycker would spend all of his time in Dunmurry on the telephone handling personal business back in the States, much to the chagrin and disappointment of our staff there. In addition, Joe Daly and Bob Dewey have found that Harry DeWitt completely botched the accounting job in Detroit, in spite of his large staff.
>
> I must also confess, I was deeply hurt by Dick Measelle's comments that he had not seen such disloyalty and insidious treachery in all of his years in Arthur Andersen; when Strycker and

DeWitt asked for a private audience with Arthur Andersen and then revealed a number of nonexistent breaches of propriety. Obviously, Strycker was building a case to show that his dismissal was on grounds other than his incompetence and NIDA's dissatisfaction with him. He was also trying to hide his own $40,000 misappropriation of funds by accusing all others. I was also startled by Dick Measelle's comments that when they got around to checking Strycker out a month ago, they found he had misrepresented his experience and qualifications—and that if we had checked his background we would never have hired him.

I, of course, take full responsibility for his hiring. It seemed expedient at the time. The lesson to be learned is that this time around we need the best of the best as a Chief Financial Officer; one that checks out completely and also receives NIDA's endorsement.

In the meantime, Joe Daly and Bob Dewey have decided that no one in the Detroit financial staff is worth keeping. This is in line with Arthur Andersen's comments that the rotten apples have spoiled these people anyhow.

I will prepare an answer to Dennis Faulkner's letter which both of you can review before it is sent. I would appreciate any suggestions you might have.

The memo was vintage DeLorean, SOS. The fabrication served an important double purpose that overrode the certainty that none of the three executives who received the memo could possibly believe a word of it. Most important, DeLorean was able to ventilate his own frustrations by blaming someone else. And even if the recipients did not believe the memo, it might prove valuable in the future when it could be pulled from the corporate files; DeLorean thus was creating his own version of corporate history as he went along.

Again, fortunately, Strycker remained unaware of the memo for years and even afterward it was no more than an irritating reminder of his frustrations with John DeLorean.

February 1980, an important date: the first showing of the new prototype. Visioneering, Inc., of Fraser, Michigan, built the car just in time for the National Auto Dealers Association convention in New Orleans. Originally it was to be ready by the end of 1979, but as it turned out, it was a race against time and Visioneering just made it.

Ostensibly it looked the same as the Bill Collins model, which the dealers had already seen. The styling was softer, but it was still a stainless-steel, gull-wing, luxury sports car. Underneath, however, the frame had changed completely.

DeLorean had brought his board, plus their wives, and was regaining his momentum.

"We think Ireland is an excellent place to do business in," he remarked for the record.

Off the record he was less formal.

"If Northern Ireland can build the *Titanic*, they can build this car."

Away from Lotus and Dunmurry, more dark clouds gathered over the car, problems that many of those present at the New Orleans meeting were to suffer as well. The second great oil crisis, ushered in by the revolution in Iran and the exit of the Shah, had already caused sales of luxury sports cars to peak and go into sharp retreat.

The Corvette sold 42,247 cars in 1978; it sold 38,631 in 1979 and was doing even worse in 1980. The Porsche 924 was selling at $16,000 —$2,000 less than the price then planned for the DMC-12—yet its sales had also fallen sharply, down 3,000 in 1979.

And the design was already beginning to look dated. Rear-mounted engines were going out, front-wheel drive was now the rage. Even Porsche had moved away from the rear-mounted engine.

But the car still had its admirers. Said *Auto Week* of the DMC-12: "It has the performance characteristics of the Porsche 911 and a Renault Alpine, a ride similar to the Mercedes-Benz 450SL and the power train punch of an unfederalized BMW."

Back in Belfast, the engineers did not know what the magazine was talking about. They were at the point where they could see only problems, and there were more than enough of them to obscure everything else.

On February 13 DeLorean wrote out another memo on the subject of Walt Strycker. This was "To File" and was DeLorean's version of a conversation he had with Harvey Hament of Resources for Industry, a small venture capital operation in New York. According to this memo, Hament came into DeLorean's office, closed the door, and said he had been visited by Strycker. The former DeLorean executive, said Hament to DeLorean, told him not to raise any money for De-Lorean, "since we were not honest and honorable people. He said we were dishonest and were cheating our investors and employees. He said that the directors had severely criticized me at the New Orleans meeting for activities other than the car (notably Transbus) and that they accused me of losing interest and being bored with the car project in favor of other activities."

There was more along the same lines. "Strycker said our entire executive staff felt that they were being cheated and that I could not be trusted and that most of our executives were looking for jobs." Hament had also gone on to say, according to the memo, that he and his colleagues did not want to deal with Strycker anymore "because he would keep them waiting up to half an hour at a time while he handled personal phone business related to his coal mines, etc.— several times they were inclined to walk out."

The final paragraph was the most damning, showing the true depths of what DeLorean saw to be Strycker's betrayal of him: "Hament said that Strycker said he was going to tell the same thing to all of our investors, investment counselors, and bankers."

He marked the memo, "cc: Cafiero, Kimmerly and Haddad."

The following day DeLorean and Kimmerly met with Alan Cohen of Paul Weiss Rifkind Wharton & Garrison. DeLorean showed Cohen his "memo to file" on Strycker who had, as DeLorean put it, "bad-mouthed me and the company." He added that Stu Sieger of Javits and Javits had told him that Strycker had appointed his personal company as general partner in the STS Stirling Engine Limited Partnership, a new DeLorean venture that was to do for the Stirling hot-air engine (a 150-year-old British invention for an external-combustion engine) what the Oppenheimer Limited Partnership was to have done for the DMC-12.

Strycker, DeLorean complained to the lawyer, had "set up the finances such that he was to collect a retainer of $85,000 per year plus expenses, as well as a percentage of the gross revenue amounting to some $16,000,000 over the life of the partnership. He became very upset," went on DeLorean, "when I told him this had to be paid to the company, not to him personally, and that none of us could live with the conflict of interest created by his collecting these high fees." DeLorean was accusing Strycker, in effect, of "doing a DeLorean."

By now he had worked himself into a state of utter loathing for his former financial officer.

"Strycker was a regular dinner guest in our home and I treated him as more of a friend than an employee, never once sensing that he was stabbing me in the back with a series of self-serving memos and accu-sations," he told Cohen.

The memo to file that he wrote the next day about his meeting concluded:

> Alan Cohen had the distinct impression in his last meeting with Strycker that Strycker had gone off the deep end. This would certainly seem the case. In order not to hurt Strycker's reputation we had contrived a consulting arrangement paying him $10,000 per month plus expenses for ten days' work per month. We were prepared to say that Strycker preferred to live in San Francisco as a reason, rather than surface the UK Govern-ment's demand that he be terminated on the grounds of incom-petence and inattention.

This memo to file was also marked for copies to go to Cafiero, Kimmerly, and Haddad—but DeLorean never signed it.

The exercise was another proof of the effort DeLorean was prepared to invest to build a favorable corporate historical record. Many of the people cited in these and other "memos to file" deny ever making the comments that are quoted; others, such as Haddad and Cohen, recall having vastly different conversations. The message about Walt Strycker that came through loud and clear was not that he engaged in any corporate misdeeds but that he was on the loose, warning potential investors and lenders that there was something wrong inside the DMC financial structure. DeLorean would stop him any way he could.

Two weeks later, on February 28, a Western Union telegram ar-rived from Strycker from San Francisco. It read, RESIGNATION FROM DELOREAN MOTOR COMPANY BOARD OF DIRECTORS EFFECTIVE 31, DE-CEMBER, 1979.

Kimmerly got it and scribbled on the top righthand corner: "Bill, what about DMCL? Tom" and shot it along to Haddad. Strycker seemed to have forgotten that he was a director not only of DMC but of the Belfast company as well. Kimmerly played around with a draft letter of resignation, suggesting that DeLorean and Strycker would agree "not to cast the other's participation . . . in an unfavorable light" and that Strycker would not solicit DMC investors for his own private interests. In full settlement, Strycker would get $24,000 for the January and February period that he had still been working for DMC.

Strycker refused the "soliciting DMC investors" provision, but accepted the rest, although it was reworded to read that he would "refrain from derogatory descriptions." He honored it for a few months only. DeLorean does not seem to have honored it at all.

In February 1980 both DeLorean in New York (along with Cafiero) and Bennington in Belfast were insisting that production could begin by July and that the car would be on the U.S. market by the fall.

"I'll build this car on schedule," Bennington told *Automotive News* in November. "I may miss it by 30 days, but by no more than that."

DeLorean kept up his public image because he still needed to raise money. The schedule meant pilot production in May and Job One in July. It was not even remotely possible. By May, not only was the car not in pilot production, but the target date continued to recede as new technical problems came up. Now it was the window.

The window became one of the more crucial marketing drawbacks of the car. Originally, DeLorean had promised his public electric windows. But the shape and design of the gull-wing doors ruled out a reasonably sized dropping window. Bill Collins had an early version of a sliding window that could be pushed back far enough to allow the driver to crawl out if the door jammed shut—he even had a photograph of himself hauling his lanky frame through just such a window on one of the early prototypes. His ultimate aim was to add an electric motor to it.

Ted Chapman came up with a similar solution, and Loasby was also a "sliding window" man—he had designed one at Aston Martin. But Bennington and Spooner produced a dropping window that really was just a small inset into the larger fixed-in-place window—an opening only large enough for an arm to reach out to pay tollbooth fees and parking lot tickets. It was a solution that no one was entirely happy about, but Lotus calculated that the sliding glass window would delay the project by several months and did not have the right image for an expensive automobile.

For all their self-assurance, the Lotus men (other than Chapman, who kneeled to no man on earth) were overawed by DeLorean and his reputation. They were a small car-company stuck out in the back of nowhere, almost unconscious of their own world reputation, but very conscious of DeLorean's. "He'd say, 'I've got to go now because I'm having dinner with the Chancellor of the Exchequer,' " says Fred Bushell. "And frankly, we were impressed. He would arrive here with his helicopter and his entourage, and then suddenly Cafiero, the ex-president of Chrysler, turns up. Even if Chrysler is in the doldrums, the man who controlled it is no slouch. If he wants to throw in his lot with John DeLorean, who are we to tell him what he should put in his car?"

Thus, DeLorean would arrive roughly once a month, look at the work done, agree with some of it, suggest changes in other parts, and sometimes insist on changes that caused considerable anguish since they slowed the program further. After a while DeLorean and Chapman seldom spoke about anything other than technical matters. But DeLorean could still side with Chapman against his own staff. Bennington recalls one incident. "Chapman wanted to go for fixed-alignment front end. I disagreed. I convinced John we should stay with a plan that allowed some adjustment. Then one day he and Colin were on one of their tours and this subject came up and John immediately agreed with Chapman. I lost the argument so we ended up with a fixed front."

In May there occurred the most vicious argument yet between the two sets of engineers. Ken Bunker had just joined the Loasby team to work on the suspension, which was his specialty. He was an experienced, professional engineer, but in the three weeks he worked for DeLorean he alienated Lotus more than any other individual. On May 17 he wrote a farewell memo: "When I joined DMC I realized the situation in respect of product engineering was not good but I had no idea that it would be as bad as it appears." In his view the emphasis was entirely on producing a car that could be assembled by hand rather than mass-produced. Bunker criticized just about every aspect of the car: it was considerably over the design weight and now weighed more than 3,000 pounds against DeLorean's original (and hopelessly optimistic) estimate of 2,200; its steering was very close to being unacceptable; the suspension was designed in such a way that all components would have to work harder than necessary, thus negating the DeLorean principle of a long-life car; there were no design parameters, no properly organized team; the drawing situation was disastrous. Bunker believed the whole project could only end in failure, and he was not going to stay around for that.

He himself, he concluded, had been employed by DMC "as design and development manager and I can see no way of fulfilling that function. Lotus Cars are contracted to design and develop the DMC-12 and my input at best is advisory. Had I known this situation, I would not have exposed my family and myself to such a risk. I therefore wish to terminate immediately my contract with DeLorean Motor Cars Ltd."

He signed his name, "K. J. Bunker" and departed, leaving behind an engineering department even more worried than before.

Bunker's letter went to Loasby, who passed it on to Bennington, who in turn sent it to Mike Kimberley at Lotus. If there was any truth in it, then the project was indeed in deep trouble. At Lotus, Kimberley and Spooner were enraged. Who was this man Bunker? "He was never even introduced to me," stormed Spooner. Bennington was apologetic. It had been done stupidly, he acknowledged. Loasby should have brought him over personally. But what about the changes he made?

Kimberley wrote a four-page letter back, rebutting Bunker's comments paragraph by paragraph. "You have had many individual and team experts into Lotus in the last 18 months studying, assessing, analyzing etc., all of whom, to the best of our knowledge, assessed the situation diametrically opposed to the view of Mr. Bunker," he concluded. The Bunker affair died there, but the taste lingered.

DeLOREAN'S PEN

Let us consider for a moment the world in which all of this was happening. In particular let us consider the world of Northern Ireland, where the focus now lay. John DeLorean's dream was going to live or die depending on the events now shaping up around the factory: the building of the car, of course, but more important, the chances of getting more money from the British government. And that would be determined to a large extent not by DeLorean himself, but by the pressure of outside events, notably the continued desire of the Conservative government to go to considerable lengths to keep a factory that would help reduce those horrendous employment figures.

In Northern Ireland outside events intrude abruptly into the business world in a way that would be wholly untypical of, say, Detroit or Coventry. The big battle in Northern Ireland was against the men of violence, and although John DeLorean was highly conspicuous and no doubt felt that his requests and whims should be noted above all others, the British government saw it in a different light. DeLorean was using the British; but the British, too, were using him as part of the drive against the men of violence.

When Roy Mason took over from Merlyn Rees as secretary of state in 1976, he had pursued a two-pronged policy designed to end what was then an eight-year conflict in the Province. His strategy was to combine a tough security policy designed to wipe out the Provos with a massive program of overseas investment to provide jobs and wean the young away from violence. When John DeLorean's project came onto the scene it appeared to be the answer to Mason's prayer in his effort to win more—and the right sort of—investment for the Province. Mason had launched a billion-pound plan to stimulate Northern Ireland's competitiveness, and the DeLorean project, taken at face value, was a perfect fit. With that project in West Belfast, Mason was hoping to show the Catholic community that if they continued the path of peace and spurned the IRA, he would deliver jobs and prosperity for all—or at least for some.

When DeLorean arrived, Mason was recording some visible successes. The use of undercover Special Air Services (SAS) teams, a generous allocation of resources to the Royal Ulster Constabulary, and expansion of the police reserve were beginning to pay dividends in terms of the number of IRA men arrested or killed on "active service" in the 1977–1978 period. The number of bombings and shootings declined noticeably and there was a general lessening of tension, although in the summer of 1980 the IRA was far from a spent or defeated force, as Britain still knows to her cost.

But in crude terms, the IRA did not have to attack factories, even if it wanted to. For the world recession in 1980 was dealing the Province a far greater blow than any bombs of less than several megatons could have done. Factory after factory was still closing. Only John DeLorean's factory and a few others were going up. It was desperately important to keep it going.

Thus, when DeLorean emerged in the spring of 1980 with a request for a major new injection of money, Mason's successor, Humphrey Atkins, had to take it very seriously indeed. The request was based on the clause in the Department of Commerce's formal letter to DeLorean offering additional money if the original amount proved insufficient because of currency fluctuation or inflation. That silly little clause was to cost the British government at least £14 million. The NIDA team may have been boiling with rage and frustration at the way DeLorean was spending money, but they were not in a strong position to complain to Atkins' ministers. They had recommended the investment, although they would probably have constructed a better deal if Mason had not applied pressure, but it was their job to monitor and control the project after that and they were only too aware that they were not succeeding. Nobody in Belfast had ever encountered anyone like John DeLorean before, and reports from New York that DeLorean was boasting he had them "over a barrel" only brought from them a grudging admission that he did. They had few weapons.

They did have one, however, and they were deploying it with a tentative but growing skill through the early summer. DeLorean wanted more money, and if he did not get it, there would be no factory and some £54 million would be down the drain. But that argument could be turned against him, too. There would be no more money unless DeLorean reformed, cut his expenses, stopped flitting about on other projects, and put all his efforts and money into the car. To ensure that he did so, there could be a major renegotiation of the master agreement, giving NIDA a larger vote, untying the absurd clause in the agreement that gave DMC sole distribution rights (so that one DeLorean company in Belfast was required to sell all its products to another DeLorean company in New York) and generally tidy up the arrangements that NIDA was beginning to bitterly regret leaving so untidy in the first place. Some good might come out of the crisis.

As he set the scene for a new demand for money, DeLorean decided to be conciliatory to NIDA, probably under pressure from Cafiero. His Telexed reply to the Faulkner letter in January had been an angry, insulting effort and for two months NIDA and DeLorean had swopped nasty messages. It was March 20 before DeLorean formally answered Faulkner, and the letter was deemed so important that Cafiero hand-carried it and delivered it personally to Faulkner in Belfast. DeLorean may have seen it as an olive branch, but he could not avoid filling it with classic DeLorean braggadocio: HAVING HIGH-CALIBER DEDICATED PEOPLE IS WHAT IS BRINGING THIS VERY CHALLENGING PROGRAM NEAR TO FRUITION. OUR VERY LEAN ORGANIZATION HAS MADE OUR RESPONSE RAPID, THOUGHTFUL AND DECISIVE IN OVERCOMING MANY DIFFICUL-TIES WHICH WOULD HAVE SWAMPED A LESS EXPERIENCED GROUP OF AUTOMOBILE PEOPLE. And there was much more of that: except for Daly and Dewey, no financial officer was coping; Shaun Harte was making a great contribution. Toward the end DeLorean allowed him-self a little homily:

> One hears critics ask, for example, why didn't the large auto-mobile companies look ahead? Why didn't they see the energy crunch? Why didn't they do more about safety and pollution? This company is trying to do those things because being new and vulnerable it is even more necessary that we look to the future. A successful launch of the DMC-12 alone will not ensure survival in today's unpredictable world.
>
> A total concentration solely on this one vehicle we don't

consider to be a sound and thoughtful management approach,
therefore when we tell you, e.g., we are exploring the possibili-
ties of a small 4-wheel drive utility vehicle that can get 50 miles
to the gallon—this is not a frivolous diversion of time from the
DMC-12 project but rather a management response to the possibility that the U.S. and other governments might find it necessary to tighten fuel economy standards drastically and it may
be necessary to have such a vehicle in order to average our fleet
fuel economy to continue selling DMC-12's.

If such a scenario were to come to pass I guess we would be
criticized if we had no response ready for such an eventuality.
Therefore, I assure you that all of the so-called other activities
we have engaged in, do have a direct bearing on the success of
the DMC-12 and our company. We have attempted to explain
the reasons for these undertakings; however, I assure you that
other projects will not be entered into without prior discussion
as to their relevance to the DMC-12 success.

The response did little to improve Faulkner's impression of De-
Lorean, even though Cafiero had been sent to the NIDA meeting to
placate the agency. Faulkner and Hopkins were getting increasingly
tough with DeLorean, but they were still not rolling him back an
inch. Protests that he was spending too much were either ignored or
he had some new and wonderful explanation. They were chipping
away, however. In June DeLorean sent Hopkins a Telex, beginning
"Dear Tony," which was unusually friendly in a Telex. He had, De-
Lorean said, now got the accountants to quantify DMC's out-of-
pocket, nonreimbursable costs on non-DMC-12 projects. He listed
them: $106,571 on the Transbus, $39,210 on the DMC-44 four-
wheel-drive vehicle, $14,016 on the Stirling engine project, $49,600
to prepare the study to take over Chrysler, and $69,581 on the project
making replicas of old cars. Total: $277,978. It was a very selective
bit of accounting. But DeLorean, beginning to feel nervy about his
claim for extra money, was still conciliatory: WHILE NOT CLEAR FROM
YOUR TELEX I UNDERSTAND FROM GENE CAFIERO IT IS NIDA'S INSTRUC-
TION THAT THESE ACTIVITIES BE ELIMINATED FROM DMC IMMEDIATELY.
THIS HAS BEEN DONE. I'M CERTAIN GENE HAS TOLD YOU WE ARE CON-
SOLIDATING ALL OF OUR ACTIVITIES ON THE 35TH FLOOR AND HAVE
REDUCED OUR MONTHLY U.S. EXPENDITURES TO LESS THAN 50 PERCENT

OF THE MAY 12, 1980 BUDGET SHOWN IN YOUR COPY OF THE BOARD OF DIRECTORS REPORT.

This too was nonsense. DeLorean was still spending as hard as ever. He was actually expanding on the 35th floor, which he had taken in addition to the 43rd floor penthouse. He did not move off the 43rd floor, despite threats and entreaties from NIDA, until after his company went bankrupt. Nor did he cut out those other activities. They were always around, although not many came to fruition.

June 18, 1980, was an important day at the Lotus works near Norwich. By now there were nearly 300 people working round the clock, seven days a week, on the DeLorean project. The pace and pressure had reached a peak, the engineering and design problems were now coming to a climax. Many of the Dunmurry engineers, including Mike Loasby, had moved over from Belfast, and the hotels and private houses within driving distance of the factory were filled with DeLorean men. Bennington, under pressure from Loasby and Broomfield, had taken on extra men, often semiretired American auto draftsmen, to help with the flow of drawings. Lotus didn't want to release drawings until the specifications were complete; Bennington and Wills decided not to wait. But the backlog was huge and every day counted.

From early morning on there had been a noticeable edge to the atmosphere. Busy men became even busier. Colin Chapman was very much in evidence, checking progress, sending men scurrying around to finish off jobs and others to tidy the drawing offices and factory floor. Some of the Esprit Turbos, built alongside the DMC-12, were rolled out and DMC prototypes were wheeled in.

If they had not known it already, both teams of engineers would have recognized the signs. The Big White Chief himself was paying a visit to the Lotus works. It would be a crucial one, with a whole series of decisions to be made. Chapman used DeLorean's visits as benchmarks to measure the progress of the project; certain things had to be accomplished in time for a visit, and that morning he was making sure Lotus was as close to schedule as could be.

As usual DeLorean had come in overnight by Concorde. An early car took him to the Battersea Heliport on the Thames in West London and by shortly after ten he touched down in front of Lotus' gleaming modern plant and was then driven in a Lotus to the older hangars that housed the DeLorean operation. Chapman brought him through every drawing office, with Spooner and Kimberley doing most of the talking and explaining. But it was Mike Loasby and some of his team who wanted to draw their worries to his attention that day.

Peter Allinson, the DeLorean engineer in charge of safety and emissions, was increasingly concerned that the car was not going to make it through its federal certification tests. He had pulled together some Lotus figures and pointed out to Loasby that there was a steady increase in weight of the prototypes. Lotus was now up to D-7, and each of the preceding six cars was heavier than the one before. Once it was fully fitted out, the D-7 was going to have a weight, without passengers, fuel or luggage (in auto industry jargon this is "dry curb weight") of 2,614 pounds, which was considerably more than anticipated. If the weight crept up, then fuel economy was creeping down. And if the weight got really high, then the car might be in a test-weight category beyond the capacity of the rolling road (a set of rollers on which the car can simulate normal speeds while actually remaining stationary) at Lotus. Loasby said as much in a Telex to Lotus earlier in May. There would be problems with California's stringent emission tests.

The DeLorean sales literature was citing a weight of 2,400 pounds, something the car never really was. That day, DeLorean could not avoid the weight problem, but he could fudge it, and he did.

At first, however, there were a few pleasantries at lunch in Ketteringham Hall, which he envied Colin Chapman. He was still trying to buy something similar. He asked Chapman how the Grand Prix team was doing. It was a sore point. Chapman's new car, with its revolutionary aerodynamics, was having problems. It had not won a Grand Prix, and the Lotus team had been out of the winning stakes since Peterson was killed. He was also having trouble with his own weight again. "You know, Colin, we only use Lotus because you're world champions," said DeLorean in a lighthearted rejoinder, which fell flat.

In the afternoon, with both DeLorean and Chapman present, they went through a series of points. Weight was the first and major one. The problem was presented and DeLorean seemed to take it all in without reaction. As usual, he doodled, drawing out surprisingly artistic shapes on his pad but also noting the figures that Loasby had prepared for him. The dry weight was now 2,471 pounds, and the vehicle needed to be less than that to make the 2,750-pound inertia weight class at which it would be certified.

They went through a series of items: leather trim and new upholstery cloths, the leather-covered steering wheel, and so on. Then they moved on to controls, the switches and knobs in the car. DeLorean produced his pen and held it up. It was black plastic, a very fine matte finish, expensive. "I want them similar to the finish on this Lamy pen," he said. The pen was reverently passed around the table and stopped again at the end. Later, it was to be placed on a cushion and borne around as if it were the crown jewels.

"That damn pen," the engineers called it as they tried to copy its finish for their switches. It was to prove yet another extra little problem. The finish was so fine that the switches scratched easily and all too often had to be rejected or replaced.

On his way back to New York from that meeting, DeLorean wrote out his version of it. He had it typed up and sent to Bennington in Belfast with copies to Cafiero and Mike Kimberley "summarizing my understanding of our meeting at Lotus today," he began, before going on to "emissions."

This concerned the weight of the car, and DeLorean clearly had been doing some thinking on the Concorde home. He started off with that dry weight figure of 2,471 pounds. Under it he wrote a list of eight items originally planned as standard features of the car that he now proposed to make theoretical options on "at least the first few thousand cars." He wrote a column headed "delete" and then started with air conditioning (115 pounds), tool kit (a modest 3 pounds), spare tire (40), louver panel above the rear window (18), the stereo radio (22), sound package (43), righthand mirror (3) and the central locking system (8). That came to 252 pounds, but DeLorean added it up to 192 and then deducted it from the original weight of 2,471 pounds to get 2,279. Despite the faulty mathematics, he was delighted with the result. "On this basis," he concluded triumphantly, "you could leave the louver panel in and still be under 2,300 pounds."

It was a cynical exercise that astonished those who saw that memo. For five years DeLorean had been making the point that his great "ethical" car would be fitted with these features. Without air conditioning, the car, with its tiny side windows, would be unbearable. The vehicle could not be marketed without a spare tire; it would look absurd without that louver panel, an essential part of its styling; the stereo radio and sound package were standard items on a luxury sports car.

DeLorean knew as well as everyone else did that a car sold without these items, most of them standard equipment on expensive cars, would be a disaster—particularly at the price he was proposing to offer it. He was not seriously intending to sell it that way. He was just going to make these items "100 percent options" in order to get over the weight problems for emission-control certification.

In his eagerness to fiddle with the figures, he missed one extraordinary factor. The starting weight of 2,471 pounds already allowed for the deduction of these items. In presenting him with the figures, the engineers had done the same calculation he was now doing, except that their "net" figure was his "gross" figure. They had deducted his 192 pounds for the same items. DeLorean was double counting!

Unconscious of the discomfort he was causing, DeLorean went on remorselessly to recount eleven points of discussion at Lotus. Point 8 showed he was at least still conscious of some of his original concepts, although it also showed that he was trying to evade them.

"We will look quickly at a gull-wing door passenger belt system that will also serve as the gull-wing door pull down strap. I'd like to see a mock-up of this within the next few weeks. We are publicly committed to safety and air bags. This is an important but small pallative [sic]."

DeLorean raised other points such as the seats, for example, which were proving uncomfortable. "I don't know the experts but we need the best. This could be a fatal flaw." The Craig stereo system: "Like everyone else, they must be competitive in both performance and price."

DeLorean had a knack for focusing on detail as fine as the trim and the windshield wiper system and a dozen other points mentioned that day. Loasby and his engineers felt he had ignored the more important problems with the car, although Lotus thought they were now over the hump and unless DeLorean insisted on further major changes, their part in the car would be completed by the end of the year.

In Belfast from June onwards there was a flood of memos from Loasby and his staff setting out problems. Bennington, Wills and Shaun Harte accused the engineers of being too fussy, of destructive criticism and of watching out for themselves and ignoring the project itself. Spooner at Lotus welcomed the Bennington/Wills approach, although he was still nervous about allowing unfinished drawings out. He too accused Loasby of not "joining the team" and of criticizing from the outside.

If DeLorean was aware of the ill-will developing between members of his own team, and the dislike between his director of project engineering in Belfast and the Lotus staff, he remained aloof from it. Whenever he appeared he so dominated the normally blunt and outspoken professional engineers that they only spoke when spoken to. And Bennington wasn't the sort of man to go running to DeLorean with his problems.

Now, in the summer of 1980, when the sports car should already have been in production, the launch date was slipping further and further away. There was no lack of activity. Most of those involved, including Bennington, were working six- or even seven-day weeks. Shaun Harte, in his capacity as project coordinator, was drawing up flow chart after flow chart, each one showing the dates gradually slipping back, although Harte himself stayed among the optimists. His "activity chart," as he called it, dated April 19, 1980, which NIDA received for its meeting on April 25 and didn't believe, showed series production beginning in September. Even that was optimistic.

NIDA had retained the McKinsey group to provide a monthly independent analysis of how the DeLorean project was progressing. In its May report, McKinsey assumed that production "would build up steadily from October onward, with sales of nearly 1,280 units by the end of December and almost 3,900 by the end of March." Now, at the end of July, as Humphrey Atkins was persuading the Cabinet to put in the additional money that DeLorean was requesting, McKinsey reported to NIDA that "present DMCL plans call for the buildup of volume production to be delayed until February 1981; and only 1,000 units will have been sold by the end of March 1981."

The engineers knew that even that was still overoptimistic. The design had been changed yet again, and there was hardly a part of the car that was not presenting some problem or other, mostly to do with quality control rather than Lotus' designs. The engine was not meeting the EPA tests; the fiberglass in the body molds was not setting properly; the gull-wing doors were not fitting; and almost no testing had been done. The factory in Dunmurry was nearly two months behind its very tight schedule, but that did not matter anymore—there would be no car to build in it for some months yet.

On July 22 DeLorean, Cafiero, and Bennington went to Lotus again after their own board meeting in Belfast. Everyone by now was preoccupied by the looming cash crisis. It began to look as if the British government would not come up with the amounts needed, and money was draining away very fast indeed. Lotus, under considerable pressure, had come up with a revised development-program schedule at the end of June and was promising all necessary information and drawings by the end of July.

Bennington, in his managing director's report on July 21, was optimistic. Prototypes D-8 and D-10 were being prepared in Dunmurry for the 50,000-mile certification test that would start later in the week. Six additional technical consultants had arrived from the U.S. and taken up residence in Norwich. They were experts in body, power train, sealing, and doors and hoods. Lotus had allocated another twenty-two people to the DeLorean team.

This was the hopeful message that DeLorean took in during his brief visit. The car was a distraction from the main problem of keeping up the pressure for that extra money. Again, the other problems were either ignored or brushed aside. He accepted the good news, rejected the bad.

Through July DeLorean and his senior men were explaining away the delays to the dealers and other interested parties in the U.S. The latest delay was a "stretch-out" of the final pre-production and training phases, said Eugene Cafiero in his capacity as DMC president. This stretch-out would allow the company to commence pilot production in November (it had previously been May), after the vehicle finished its 50,000-mile EPA endurance testing.

Cafiero told *Automotive News* that the company had hoped to do just the 4,000-mile test and "piggyback" on the Volvo 262 50,000-mile test because both cars used the same power plant. "We made certain changes to the engine which greatly enhance mileage, and the EPA told us we would have to do the 50,000-mile test after all," he said, adding that the mileage was now twenty-two mpg.

Then Cafiero went on to say that "the emissions work was essentially done, with very comfortable margins," and he gave figures that apparently showed the DeLorean vehicle well within the 1981 standards.

"The stretch-out will allow us to really ingrain into our work force the need for quality," he went on. "That way we also won't be entering the current soft market in the U.S., and we make sure we don't get into trouble building cars before our EPA tests are completed."

Soon afterward, John DeLorean himself addressed the *Automotive News* World Conference, a prestigious event on the auto calendar. He intended to give the world the latest optimistic picture of the DMC project, but typically, he went on to turn his address into a plan for concerted action to save the entire North American auto industry: tax code changes that would "provide stimulus for capital formation" needed for the modernization of the industry; a revision of the regulatory process that would include "simultaneous consideration" of the "interaction" between health, safety, environmental considerations, fuel economy, and other standards; "incentivization" of research and development through an investment tax credit; a cohesive energy policy and much else, full of jargon like "prioritize national goals."

On the future of his own company, DeLorean got carried away. Capacity at the Dunmurry plant, he said, was "120,000 to 150,000 units a year" and more if the company used outside sourcing. That was pure bunk. He might make them, but where would he sell them?

Any day now the British government would be deciding whether to give him more money, so DeLorean put in a few kind words for Mrs. Thatcher: "Mrs. Thatcher is a significant world leader. She has the potential to do for England what de Gaulle did for France." The Dunmurry work force, he went on, was "superb"—there were now nearly 400 of them, and the absentee rate was 1.2 percent. "Do not let anyone convince you that the labor in Belfast is torn by industrial or religious strife—it isn't."

It was at this meeting that DeLorean repeated an idea that he had been bouncing off some of his own people for several weeks. Take the first 1,000 cars off the production line, test them all for 5,000 miles, and then sell them, perhaps in Japan—he had planned, he said, to approach Nissan, which made Datsun—or in the Middle East.

To his staff in Belfast, the idea seemed totally weird. The sheer logistics of testing 1,000 cars for 5,000 miles, with all the test drivers and track that would be needed, were impossible. At one of the board meetings in Belfast, DeLorean had mentioned the Renault track but had been told that was not available. Then he thought of Goodyear, but no company, whatever its goodwill, could possibly lend its track for the amount of time it would take.

The cars would be lining up for weeks on end, following each other around the track. The project would take six months, put the whole operation back until near the end of 1981, and would achieve very little. The engineers wanted testing, but properly organized rig testing and track testing under conditions they could fully control. The company could not even build a single car for the October motor show in Britain, to be held that year in Birmingham—where were these 1,000 cars to come from?

By the end of July the tension had really mounted. Hopkins felt he might have DeLorean at bay. DeLorean needed new money desperately, and although the NIDA people knew there was little doubt he would get some, they were intent on not giving it away without something in return. How much? Every time DeLorean asked, the amount escalated. "This is not an inflation clause—it's a hyperinflation clause," remarked one of the officials after a long session. "Highway robbery more like," sourly remarked his colleague. DeLorean had started by asking for £2 million, which soon became £5 million, then £12 million, and now even more. It would not be new cash—the Commerce Department would provide a government guarantee that DeLorean could use to borrow from a commercial bank. But it would still qualify as government spending and would need Cabinet approval. Humphrey Atkins was not sure if he would get it.

On July 18, 1980, McKinsey had produced yet another status report. The launch date of the car, it announced, had been postponed. It would now be February 1981. Furthermore, there was bad news. J. D. Powers, the market research analysts, had done a new survey. And it showed that at the new planned sticker price of $24,000, no more than 8,000 to 10,000 units could be sold. With its overhead, the company could make nothing but losses at that level. But worse news still: "DMCL will run out of funds during the third week of August and the cumulative funding gap will approach £14 million by February 1981." Disaster was once again approaching. The New York operation would soon face an even bigger cash crisis, warned McKinsey: its only known source of income was the handsome $290,000 a month management fee for its so-called "expertise" that the Belfast company was paying. DeLorean could certainly cut back in New York, concluded McKinsey, and save $324,000 a year just by shutting the 43rd floor—but there was "a real risk that planned expenditures reductions in North America will prejudice the effectiveness of the sales launch by cutting into vital sales and marketing 'muscle' rather than overhead."

The crisis was rapidly building to a climax. It was now up to the government. Would Margaret Thatcher agree to more money for DeLorean? The House of Commons was under the impression that the amount of new assistance, if it were given, would be no more than £8 million, and even at that level many members were already rearing in indignation. Giles Shaw, the unfortunate minister of state, was being pressed about it week after week. Politicians from opposite poles of the political spectrum combined to make his life a misery.

On August 4 Atkins brought up the subject of DeLorean at a Cabinet meeting. It was a late one—ministers were overdue on their holiday break and the Cabinet normally never met in August at all. Telling only a select few the result, Atkins took his ministerial plane to Belfast that evening. DeLorean was waiting on tenterhooks for the news that he knew would either make or break him.

Hillsborough is a small linen town on the Dromore-Lisburn Road, five miles south of Dunmurry. Ulster's hero, King William of Orange, had stopped at the old fort there on his way to the Battle of the Boyne, which permanently stamped the history of Ireland, in 1690. The fort had been built by the Hills family, whose most famous member was Wills Hill, First Marquess of Downshire, who had become George III's exceptionally stupid and implacable secretary of state for the American Colonies. It was Benjamin Franklin who said of him, "His character is conceit, wrongheadedness, obstinacy and passion."

On the morning of August 5, sitting in the very house that Wills had built, another secretary of state was thinking similar thoughts about John DeLorean. Atkins had chosen to give DeLorean the news there rather than in his office in Stormont, on the other side of Belfast. At 9:15 DeLorean's car rolled into the castle forecourt and DeLorean and Gene Cafiero stepped tentatively out. They still had no idea what to expect. Had they got the money?

There were three people in the room they were ushered into: the tall figure of Atkins, Giles Shaw, and Atkins' senior civil servant. No NIDA people, no one from the Commerce Department. Atkins was making this deal directly, cutting the agency and officials out of it. The meeting lasted half an hour. It was the first time Atkins had met DeLorean. What he saw was a tall, thin American whom he disliked in advance. The Cabinet committee had met the night before, he told DeLorean. They had considered his request for more money. They had been made aware of the McKinsey report indicating a cash shortfall of £14 million by February and more if the program slipped further. It was the government's policy to restrict public expenditure but at the same time there was an interest in creating and preserving as many jobs in Northern Ireland as possible. Under the circumstances, therefore, he had obtained Cabinet approval for the Department of Commerce to guarantee bank loans of up to £14 million. This would cover the extra costs incurred because of the rapid rise in the British inflation rate, now running at 20 percent, and the rise in the pound as a result of the new oil crisis. But there would be conditions —a reorganization of the royalty arrangements on the car, and, most important, an agreement that this would finally and fully discharge the government's commitment to DeLorean. There would be no more money after this. He was providing enough to see the project through and that would be that. Not a penny more—whatever happened.

If DeLorean was pleased or surprised, he certainly did not show it. He gathered his thoughts as Atkins spelled it out. Now he protested. "If we're going to get those conditions, then, you know, I think we should have more," he finally said. "Well, you won't get it," snapped Atkins coldly. Behind the façade Atkins may not have been the most effective minister in the Cabinet, but with his gray hair, his tall, slim figure and military bearing, he looked the part perhaps more so than anyone else. And he had not been a Chief Whip for nothing. He was fully aware of the storm that was going to break around him from NIDA, from the Department of Commerce, and in the House of Commons, and he was in no mood for cheek from this nasty American.

But DeLorean had done it again—he had gotten his money. And what is more he had slipped out of the chains Tony Hopkins thought he was about to bind around him. The NIDA people were furious with Atkins. But Hopkins was a civil servant, and the politicians ruled. He would have to start all over again, although there was a certain relief in the feeling that now at least DeLorean should not be back for more money. That was to be one of the greatest of all the mistaken assumptions.

It was some months before the money would come through, and DeLorean was short. How short is emphasized by an incident just before he left for his meeting with Atkins. Dick Brown was sitting in his office in California talking to Bob Dewey on the telephone in the New York office. In Brown's secretary's office a paper was coming in over the telecopier—a resolution from DeLorean. Brown's secretary laid it on his desk and as he was talking to Dewey he idly started to read it. It was a board resolution sent to him for his signature. De-Lorean Manufacturing, John DeLorean's 100-percent-owned private company, would lend DMC $600,000. But in return for the loan, Brown saw, DeLorean wanted to collateralize all the assets of the Motor Company, including any future receivables. Brown's casual interest had become intense.

"Bob," he said into the phone, "I'm reading this resolution. Do you know anything about it?"

"No," answered Dewey, who was not on the board. "What is it?"

"It's a resolution to borrow $600,000 from John's personal company and assign all the assets of the company as collateral for the loan," replied Brown. "I'm not going to sign this: $600,000 will last us thirty days. What happens thirty days from now when the $600,000 is gone and John gets all the assets?"

Brown then called Gene Cafiero. "Gene, did you sign this resolution?"

"I did," replied Cafiero. "But I wanted all the directors to sign it rather than just do it through the executive committee."

"Well, Gene," said Brown, "I'm not going to sign it." And he explained why. There was a strangled cry at the other end of the phone. "Oh, my God," said Cafiero. The ex-Chrysler man clearly had not thought through the implications of the resolution.

"If you want, Gene," proffered Brown, "I'll get my attorney to verify what it says." He hadn't yet checked with his lawyer and wasn't entirely certain his quick interpretation was correct. But the idea appealed to Cafiero.

"I'll tell you what, Dick. If you get your attorney to look through it, I'll pay half the cost." According to Brown, he then checked with his lawyer "and he verified in spades what I suspected, and Gene never paid me half the costs!"

By that time Brown was in a long dialogue with Kimmerly and DeLorean on the phone. There were four or five other telephone conversations on this matter, which Brown carefully documented. Wendy, his secretary, took his side of the conversation in shorthand and after the conversation he filled in the other side.

"It was ugly. Messy. And I told John, 'Why can't you be man

enough or executive enough to live up to your responsibilities? You are the chairman of this company. You founded the company. You are the 84-percent stockholder. Do you mean to tell me you would not loan this company $600,000 without pledging all the assets? Is that all the confidence you have in this operation?' And then it got very ugly."

The conversations went on for hours:

> And I just told him I wasn't going to sign it, period. But Cafiero had signed it. Henry Bushkin had signed it. Edward King had signed it. Then Bushkin found out my position and he called me and said, "Thank God somebody in the company was thinking," and he and Edward King withdrew their signatures. Before I would sign I requested an opinion letter from Kimmerly saying we had authority to do this and that it conformed to all the applicable SEC regulations and other regulations governing corporate activities in the states of California and Michigan. When the opinion letter finally came forth, it said that they didn't have the authority to do it and they nixed the thing anyway and the loan fell apart.

By then Atkins had come through and the loan was no longer needed. But this incident was to have an extraordinary sequel, one with major consequences for the DeLorean Motor Company.

Consistently, Brown was the one man who could seriously challenge John DeLorean. Collins, although he probably had more to complain about than anyone else, had avoided confrontation and left quietly. Dewey's protest had been to leave, only to experience the humiliation of having to come back. Strycker was more vocal and had gone to the auditors and the lawyers—but he too had lost as he knew he would. Brown, however, was not easily replaceable, because he had signed up the dealers and his job had yet to come—selling the car once it came off the production line, which was now scheduled for only six months ahead.

Brown was no sycophant or toadie, nor was he a weak character whom DeLorean could easily browbeat. He was 47 years old, had owned and run his own business, started Mazda in the U.S., and introduced the car in what was a classic launch of a foreign car in the American market. Brown also had the advantage of being removed from the politicking and maneuvering going on in 280 Park Avenue —he had his own separate DeLorean operation in Irvine, California. At one stage he was so incensed about DeLorean's attitude to the factory in Northern Ireland that they suggested giving it to him—let him make the cars and take charge of the whole Northern Ireland operation—but he would still have to sell them through the DeLorean distribution system.

In the middle of August, with the financial crisis past, Brown was summoned to New York for a staff meeting on Monday, followed by a full board meeting on the following Wednesday. It was only weeks after his battle with DeLorean and Kimmerly over the loan. He went to the staff meeting, where temperatures were chilly. The following Wednesday was the date of the board meeting, and the British directors, Bennington, Harte, and Daly, plus NIDA representatives Hopkins and Alex Fetherston, were due in. For some of them it would be their last DMC board meeting.

In Norwich the engineers had decided they must make one final try to bring to the whole board's attention their worries over the emission problems. That day, Harte got a Telex from Loasby stating simply: RE TELEX FORWARDED TODAY, PLEASE ENSURE YOU HAVE COPY OF SECOND PART SENT TO CKB. "CKB" was Bennington, but Harte knew it was not Bennington that Loasby was trying to get to. He wanted the whole board to see this.

The main Telex was an attempt to go over Bennington's head and reach DeLorean himself. It was read out loud at the board meeting. Loasby began, "I am very concerned with the situation in the emission area of Lotus. . . ."

There followed a detailed complaint that, although target figures for the normal performance of the engine had been established on July 3, "we have had one set of results within the target figures and no repeat tests of the same specification." To ensure certification by January 1, the 4,000-mile tests would have to start by September 1— that was the very last date, "and we have not yet defined a specification."

Lotus, he added, was concentrating on "other investigations" for which Loasby clearly did not have much use but which were "allegedly at Mr. Bennington's request." Loasby was not pulling his punches or mincing his words. "It cannot be overemphasized that time is being apparently frittered away, for whatever reason, pursuing frivolous investigations at the expense of establishing a reliable base calibration which can be reasonably expected to give satisfactory results when tested by EPA at EPA."

This was a fair point. DeLorean had asked Lotus to re-engineer the standard engine to improve its fuel economy and escape federal penalties. Loasby believed there was no time for that and with such a tight program they should stick with what they had. But the "frivolous investigations" he was complaining about were actually John DeLorean's policy decisions, on the whole supported by Lotus. Loasby feared that unless they concentrated on getting the existing engine certified, they were going to miss the dates altogether. He was already desperately concerned at the lack of testing time that would be available for the final production car. Normally it would be three to six months, but here it would be nothing at all the way the program was developing.

DeLorean had now decided to push Bennington aside, fire him if possible. The excuse was that he had done his job, created the factory and the team, got the car to the point where production was about to begin. But it was probably for other reasons. "Chuck said no to John once too often," says Barrie Wills. When Loasby's message arrived, DeLorean sent Bennington back to Hethel to sort things out.

When Bennington finally got back to Lotus, he was exhausted, jet-lagged, and looking ill, with bags under his eyes. "God, Chuck, you look dreadful," someone remarked. "Your eyes are bloodshot." Bennington still had enough spirit to quip, in the immortal words of Lee Marvin, "You should see them from this side."

It was during this week that DeLorean decided he would brook no more opposition from his own board. He would reconstitute it, stack it with people who were tied to him in some way or were not the type to raise their voices in anger. He could be exceptionally rude about some of the men he would keep on it: Chuck Bennington, for instance, wasn't up to the strain of Belfast (more accurately, Bennington wasn't up to the strain John DeLorean imposed on him). He kept promoting Joe Daly, too, largely because the Irish accountant barely opened his mouth in DeLorean's presence unless he was spoken to, but even DeLorean hesitated before putting Daly on the DMC board, although he was still acting chief financial officer.

On Thursday, the day after the meeting, Brown was sitting in an office in 280 Park Avenue when DeLorean sauntered in. He perched himself on the arm of a chair and looked across the desk at the solidly built figure of Brown. "Dick, we didn't think you were too comfortable on the board and we're making some changes, you know, bringing in some new people." He had had a shareholders meeting and "we have reconstituted the board." Brown was off it.

"John, don't give me that crap!" stormed Brown. "Everybody knows what you've done."

"What are you talking about?" asked DeLorean innocently.

"Seriously, John—last Monday night after I got here you and Kimmerly had a shareholders meeting in Kimmerly's office at ten o'clock at night and you reconstituted the board. In other words, you stacked the board."

"What do you mean?" challenged DeLorean, rocked by the other man's knowledge.

"You put all your insurance guys on the board and you put your wife on the board. You've got everybody on the board who will say yes to you."

This is precisely what DeLorean had done. He had brought on eight new people, including Cristina, who was now listed as "businesswoman" in company documents. Off went Brown—he had been appointed, without knowing about it, vice president for North American operations. And off went Shaun Harte, also without knowing it. He didn't mind too much—he was really only on the board as the original nominee of NIDA and was relieved to be out of the firing line in New York. There was enough fire in Belfast.

Brown, however, refused to let DeLorean off the hook. "I know what you've done here and it doesn't bother me. The only reason I stay in this company is because of the people I've brought into it. I recruited the people. I built your company. I brought in a lot of investor money and built the Northern Ireland operation and now you pull something like this. But I'm going to stay, even though you may try to get me to leave. I'm going to stay here to protect their interest. I'm telling you, John—Nesseth and Kimmerly are going to be your nemesis in the final analysis."

DeLorean just looked at the floor before saying, "There isn't going to be a final analysis."

Finally, when both men had talked themselves out, DeLorean proffered peace. "Let's you and I start over and forget all this."

"So that was that," said Brown. "I continued. I wasn't on the board here in the United States, but I was on the board in Northern Ireland." DeLorean had won again, but Brown had scored a few points.

On that date at Lotus, Loasby and two of his engineers, Peter Allinson and Joe Hillebrand, were making their own attempt to get things sorted out. The design of the car, even now, was still not "frozen," and they decided to pin Lotus down and agree on the basic points.

The three DeLorean engineers held a meeting with Lotus senior engineer Tony Rudd, and it was Rudd himself who dictated the minutes. It was a single sheet of paper, and the DeLorean engineers regarded it as a major breakthrough, although to an outsider it is meaningless. "Below is the agreed job one specification for DMC-12," it starts. Then there are three subheadings: automatic transmission, manual transmission, and engine specification. The automatic, they agreed, would have middle-of-tolerance change speeds, the same Renault torque converter now on development car D-3, and the same gear ratios as standard Renault transmission. The manual would have the same unit now used on D-8 and D-10, and the engine would be the 1981 Californian Volvo base engine.

That was all. The document was dated August 21, 1980. Hillebrand, Allinson, and Loasby signed it, but although he had agreed to it at the meeting and it was his document, Rudd would not. There was too much intracompany politics in all this.

By now the McKinsey consultants were gathering information for their reports for NIDA. They apparently saw everything and talked to everyone, but the engineers were under instructions to "be positive," keep their doubts and friction to themselves and show them only problems that had been solved and the progress they were making. McKinsey knew nothing of the worries over emissions or of the batteries of Telexes that flew between Bennington and the Lotus engineers.

The division between the engineers and the purchasing department had also widened, and the two departments were barely on speaking terms. Over and over again, the engineers pointed out that unless parts were tooled up to final specification, they would not fit and would have to be tooled again; not only was that more costly but in the end it would also take longer. The purchasing people, under Barrie

Wills, supported by Shaun Harte, felt there was no time for these niceties and that unless they did a bit of engineering ad-libbing here and there, there would be no car.

By now parts were arriving in Belfast, and Broomfield was trying to set up his production line. Although they had missed the eighteen-month schedule (which was never *their* schedule, but DeLorean's), Lotus was producing a car in under two years, an extraordinary effort by any standards. There were still plenty of problems to solve, and there were still considerable tensions, but Lotus was beginning to allow itself a feeling of modest pride. The worry now was not their own standard of work, but the quality of the work that would be done at Dunmurry. The emphasis was beginning to switch back from Norwich to Belfast, where Lotus' development work now had to be translated into a workable production line. And Lotus had grave doubts about how it would emerge.

NIDA was beginning to hear more encouraging news about the progress on the car, in contrast to DeLorean's continual money problems. But in July McKinsey listed nine problems with the vehicle.

McKinsey actually generated great confidence in that report. "The design was frozen 10 days ago," it said on July 18. The design, in fact, was still very hot. It was still being changed six months later. In September McKinsey barely touched on the technical problems of the car. The report focused almost entirely on the funding problem, which was becoming worrisome but "appeared to be manageable." By October the report was quite optimistic, saying that although the DeLorean company now "accepts that there are development problems still to be solved," it was satisfied they could be overcome. It was late in the day, but the car was finally nearing completion.

By the fall, as dealers in the U.S. were told they could not expect delivery until the spring, there was further agitation over another factor: the price of the car.

Don Lucas, a dealer in California, for instance, was quoted in *The Economist* as saying he spent $100,000 buying four DeLorean franchises and invested another $25,000 of his own money. He was told, but not guaranteed, by DeLorean that the car would sell at $18,000. Now it would be $25,000, and that, he believed, would scare off half his customers. The Corvette was only $17,500, and the Porsche between $17,000 and $20,000. Another Californian, a San Francisco dealer, was also quoted in the same article, saying that he would need to sell the car at $30,000 to compensate for the delay and to get back his promotional costs.

The Economist cited the weak dollar (or the strong pound) and "teething problems." Britain's Lotus, it said, had spent months redesigning the car after prototypes proved hard to handle. That was not quite the way the engineers back in Dunmurry saw it, but the price increase was a new factor, which should have been triggering alarm bells by now, but was not.

In its July report, McKinsey had included an estimate of sales at different prices, prepared once again by market research analysts J. D. Powers. This showed that at $16,000 to $18,000, the company would hope to sell around 20,000 units per year, which was the planned production level. At $21,000 the forecast sales dropped sharply to 13,000 to 16,000 in the first year, and at $24,000, which by then was the planned sticker price, an estimated 8,000 to 10,000 vehicles would be sold. Powers also included an estimate for a $28,000 price tag and calculated 4,000 to 5,000 cars in the first year, which in the light of events was astonishingly accurate.

Nonetheless, McKinsey was content to warn that planning should be done on the basis of no more than 15,000 vehicles a year, although "the prices for components were originally negotiated on the basis of sales volume of 30,000 units a year."

By September, then, the DMC-12 design was moving toward production but was still far from complete, with many problems still to be solved, tests still far from complete, an unhappy and worried band of engineering and manufacturing people barely on speaking terms with their own purchasing department and with the men at Lotus responsible for designing the car.

The new bunch of American engineers had speeded up the flow of drawings, but road tests in the fall were throwing up new and unexpected difficulties: the manual car was only doing 7,000 to 8,000 miles on a set of tires against the originally estimated 30,000; and on a head-on-crash test, the hood crumpled into the windshield.

On the other hand, the standard engine had passed EPA requirements on its 4,000-mile test, and although it would have to be retested by the EPA itself to see that it passed the twenty-two mpg requirement for 1981, that had cheered people up. Unfortunately it could not repeat those figures and failed the next tests, plunging everyone back into gloom.

The price was still creeping up, further delays were looming, cutting into the precious quarantine time needed to make sure the first marketed cars were of a roadworthy quality, and the company was again running out of cash.

As the company lurched from crisis to crisis, people began to wonder just what DeLorean was doing with his future and their dreams.

11

A DAY IN THE LIFE

"I can hate the sin and still love the sinner, can't I?" asks Arvid Jouppi. "Well, that's the way I feel about John DeLorean. I may not approve of all the things he's done in his life, but I have to stick by him now because he is one of the few genuine geniuses our industry has ever produced. And what he accomplished—nearly—was monumental."

Arvid Jouppi is a rare combination among corporate securities analysts of authority, expertise, integrity, and good humor. He is *the* financial and marketing authority on the American automobile industry and he can chide it with the love that comes only from devoting a lifetime to watching its companies stumble and falter. As the unquestioned dean of his craft, Jouppi consults for leading brokerage houses as well as advises scores of the industry's top executives. People may listen when "E. F. Hutton talks . . . ," but when Arvid Jouppi talks about cars, the impact is felt from Detroit to Wall Street.

Unlike most industry-watchers, Jouppi admits to having been a long-time admirer of John DeLorean's drive, even when he disagreed with some of the end results.

"You can't understand how exciting it was to watch John shaking things up around here twenty years ago. Sure, things were said about him, about his personal life. Some of them were pretty weird. But even if they were all true, the fact remains that John tried to do something that had not been attempted in nearly fifty years. Not since Billy Durant has anyone tried to start a major competitive large-production car company in this country."

Jouppi is a rumpled senior cherub who loves to talk about his industry as much as he does to puzzle through its balance sheets and production schedules. Presiding at a luncheon table at the Recess Club atop the Fisher Building in Detroit, Jouppi keeps a running account of the top industry executives as they enter this private sanctuary; there are none he cannot call by name, and few fail to stop by his table to greet him. He is proof that integrity, respect, and affection are not mutually exclusive goals; indeed, the contrast between this gentle, generous man and John DeLorean is all the more difficult to understand.

"I didn't say I *liked* John. We were never social friends, if that's what you mean. But the lack of competition, the trend to consolidation, were killing the industry long before the oil crisis. And John DeLorean was trying to do something that would have reversed that trend. He came up with a good concept, he raised the money, he put together a good dealer network and he built the car. Every step of the way people were waiting for him to fail. Well, now he has failed and you have to ask yourself whether we are any better off for his having failed. I think not."

Jouppi was not alone in his admiration for DeLorean's adventure. It is an important factor worth remembering at this time. For even though there were warning signals, the DeLorean public reputation was at a high-water mark in the autumn of 1980 and into the spring of 1981. During this period, John DeLorean could argue with some effect that he was doing what he said he would.

In fact, with the capital injection from the British government, he had done even more. He had not only raised more than $160 million for his venture in the previous five years, but he had also welded together a dealers' network, which, along with the money, gave him a potential economic clout of about half a billion dollars—America's fourth largest car producer, American Motors Company, had a working capital of only $236 million at the time.*

And, without putting too fine a point on it, John DeLorean was viewed by many people as a political symbol, proof that the failures of American big business and big American government were not inevitable. Life could be changed for the better here in these United States if someone could, as DeLorean was always saying, just cut through the bullshit and get on with the job.

And who cared if Detroit did not like John DeLorean? Detroit had failed America by pushing the public into a generation of gas-guzzling,

---

* Moody's Handbook of Common Stocks, 1983.

substandard junkers. So the public had every reason to applaud De-Lorean's attempt to stick a thumb in the eye of the established automobile industry.

Inside the DMC executive offices in New York, the feeling of us-against-them steadily intensified as DeLorean's setbacks and failures mounted. Top executives such as Collins, Dewey, and Cafiero brought their own desires to show former Detroit bosses and colleagues a thing or two, but the high level of personal commitment extended well down into the staff, where it was embodied in and directed solely to the person of John DeLorean.

"I'm a real flowerchild idealist of the seventies, an antidraft counsellor when I was in college during Vietnam, all that. And I had plenty of job opportunities at the time but I chose to work for DMC because I wanted to work for John DeLorean. I wanted to be part of what he was doing."

The speaker is another who shares Arvid Jouppi's persistent admiration for John DeLorean's dream. Beginning as a low-level clerical employee, this loyalist stayed on through the final days of the DMC and became a close personal aide to DeLorean himself at the end.

He continues:

No one worked harder than John DeLorean. He was all business. This nonsense about a jet-set lifestyle was just media hype. I'm pretty bitter about the news media generally and the car enthusiast magazines in particular. They made John. They made an image to suit themselves and then hoped he couldn't live up to it. David Davis and people like him never gave John a chance; all we ever heard once the car began to come off the assembly line was that it had this fault or that or that it wouldn't be as cheap as a Corvette. They never wrote that the new edition of the Corvette was kept off the production line for a full year because GM was having so much trouble with it.

And this crap about John being a swinger. I can truthfully say I never saw John DeLorean take a drink in my life. He was too much of a health freak to involve himself in booze or drugs. If I wanted to set him off, all I had to do was leave a candy bar on my desk—I'm a chocoholic of sorts—and he was good for a fifteen-minute lecture on what I was doing to myself.

I wasn't part of the inner social circle, but I don't think either he or Cristina were big on parties. They both watched their diets, and from what I could see, their idea of a good time was a small dinner party at home with close friends. I was at their Christmas party at the Bedford Springs farm in December 1982, after John was released from jail. They had neighbors and their children in and the punch bowl was just fruit juice.

As for his personal life, it was really inseparable from the company in those days. We got in together at about the same time, around 8:30 in the morning, and often I wouldn't leave until 7 at night and he would still be there. He rarely ate lunch out of the office—invariably it was a tuna fish sandwich and a diet soft drink—and the rest of the time it was phone calls, memo writing, and reading, reading, reading.

The portrait is apparently an accurate one. Other DeLorean employees, former secretary Marian Gibson included, confirm DeLorean's almost legendary capacity for working long hours without complaint. A normal working day begins at 6:30 A.M. with DeLorean, by all accounts, slipping out of bed in the couple's Fifth Avenue apartment and going to a separate room that he and Cristina had fitted out with exercise equipment for a minimum half-hour rigorous workout.

The DeLorean mania for a youthful appearance remains unchecked. Although he no longer dyes his hair an unnatural black and has stopped posing for magazine layouts lifting weights and flexing, shirtless, for posters, John DeLorean is more concerned than ever about appearances. His leanness appeared almost skeletal in the days after his arrest, when his face was so thin that the outlines of the plastic chin-extender implanted by a plastic surgeon fifteen years earlier stood out in sharp relief in the news photographs.

But for the moment the workouts give DeLorean the energy to continue his hectic schedule. After taking a shower and dressing for work, DeLorean sits in on breakfast with Cristina, young Zachary, and their still toddling daughter, Kathryn. He eats little, often experimenting with vitamin, malt, and fruit juice concoctions done up in a blender.

It is an important family time and one that the couple apparently kept as part of the regular routine whenever their two schedules permitted. No one has ever disputed DeLorean's affection for his children, or for Cristina for that matter. The marriage of John and Cristina DeLorean has survived a decade of tumult and pressures that would have wrecked many another couple, standing in stark contrast to his previous record of failed relationships and sexual odyssey.

That the marriage has survived is one more proof of DeLorean's increasing ability to keep his life in almost hermetically sealed separate compartments. He kept his family in one—a very calm island where the pleasures were simple and low-key. Then there was the public image of the glamorous, still-swinging corporate executive and his famous ex-model wife and their Studio 54 coterie of friends. In truth, this part of their life was the greatest sham. And of course there was DMC itself, but even there his career was fragmented between the car company's problems and his growing desire to break free into other business ventures that would create the DeLorean empire he dreamed of—only then would he be truly free.

That DeLorean was able to walk from compartment to compartment without losing his way is further proof of the driving forces inside him. Indeed, he could not have been much of a swinger and have survived as long as he did. During the period from 1979 right up until the end, every minute of his life was spoken for.

After breakfast, DeLorean's personal routine rarely varied. The maid and houseboy have by now arrived and are bustling about their appointed chores; the live-in maid has taken Kathryn in charge and seen Zachary off to school. Cristina is planning her day of calls to photography studios, fashion houses, and magazine offices. DeLorean himself finishes up his morning newspapers and then selects one of the dark, modest, print neckties that are as much a part of his unchanging wardrobe as his dark, French-cut, three-piece suits and blue shirts with the elongated collar points. Even here the myths about his $700-custom-made suits were an exaggeration; to be sure, he had his suits custom-tailored because of his height and slender frame. But $400 was the most he would pay for a suit, and he often marveled at the reports that they cost more. In a rare personal joke, he wondered aloud whether people thought the suits looked so good on him that they must have cost $700.

On most mornings DeLorean walks to the office. The route seldom varies: down Fifth Avenue to 51st Street and into St. Patrick's Cathedral. Although he had been baptized a Catholic, his father was never active in the Church and his mother experimented with several Protestant affiliations throughout her life. DeLorean freely conceded that he was not an actively religious person and certainly not denominational. Yet every now and then he sought the sanctuary of a church, both in New York and in London.

After leaving St. Patrick's, DeLorean would walk briskly over to Park Avenue and then farther south to 280 Park Avenue, where a special elevator stood apart from the bank of elevators for other tenants; an express that stopped once at the 42nd floor at a private club called the Boardroom before going on to his offices on the 43rd floor. The sun shines through large windows looking out over Park Avenue from the DMC suite which occupies half the floor.

DeLorean steps briskly through the foyer dominated by a huge glass table and four water buffalo-hide chairs on either side of the room. Pictures of the DMC-12 in various poses dominate the corridors through which he sweeps every morning on the way to his office. If a receptionist or secretary is in at that early hour, there is no greeting, not even an acknowledgement.

"All the girls complained that he walked straight past them," recalls his English secretary, Marian Gibson. "He was so tall and imposing but he never said a thing. Once, in the early days, I was in the elevator with him and I was carrying a basket of flowers for my birthday and he didn't say a word for forty-three floors."

Another secretary recalls an office legend: "It was Christmas Eve in Detroit one year. He put his coat on and walked out. And everyone said, 'Well, that's nice. Isn't he even going to wish us a Merry Christmas?' His secretary then was named Colleen O'Neill, and she had worked day and night to help get this thing on the road. So she called him later in New York and said she was very embarrassed for him because he hadn't wished anyone a Merry Christmas. He made some excuse, but he was really indifferent to it and never improved. That's not really nice when you've got a small crew of about eight people working for you, but he was just indifferent."

The loyalist aide agrees. "You had to get used to it. That was his style. No small talk at all."

DeLorean's spacious office is on a level with—and directly opposite —the twin towers of the Waldorf-Astoria and their green copper rocketlike heads. There is a framed photograph of Cristina on the desk, perched between two telephones, and there is an even larger picture of her on the wall. He sits in a high-backed chair to begin the day.

Marian Gibson brings in the morning mail. It is voluminous. De-

Lorean has installed a General Motors-type system of communication, which means that everything is written, even within the office. "I felt sorry for him," Gibson says. "Without exaggeration it was two feet thick. And it wasn't just like insurance fineprint, it was worse. It was emission standards and newsletters from Detroit and Washington and material on the cars and he read through it all and dropped it on the floor."

The morning's pile also included magazines like *Country Life,* advertising fine country houses in England or New Jersey. DeLorean still had the house-hunting bug. "He was bidding for everything," says Marian Gibson. "You know, Sutton Place, Paul Getty's old place, came onto the market and we sent away for the material on that. It went for millions of pounds! He was looking for estates in Ireland too, and I think he was trying to emulate Colin Chapman with that boys' school of his. Looked at estates all over England, a few in Ireland. He would constantly rip these things out of *Country Life* and other English magazines and our backup secretary, Barbara Bates, would write off and follow up with the correspondence on the houses."

There was seldom any material in the morning mail related to Belfast—in fact almost nothing on it. "Everything transmitted between the New York and Belfast offices must have been oral because I saw only a few letters," says Gibson.

Having worked his way through the mail, DeLorean then begins his interminable memo writing. Many of the memos go to Tom Kimmerly, who is only ten yards down the corridor. DeLorean pulls out a pad of high-gloss engineering graph paper and starts writing in his large, angled scrawl (often he would sign documents at a 45 degree angle). These memos are then dropped on Gibson's desk. She types them and walks them down to Kimmerly's office. From her office outside his, she can keep her eye on DeLorean by her own private method—she catches the reflection of his gray hair in the gray-tinted mirror glass that lines the halls outside. If she can see the hair, she knows his head is down, he is writing—as he always seems to be.

Then there are phone calls. DeLorean has a habit of not taking the calls as they come in; Marian Gibson intercepts them, promises her boss will call back, and a few minutes later he does. He is efficient at returning calls, even unwelcome ones. And there is a steady stream of people coming in to see him now—Haddad, Kimmerly, perhaps visitors from outside the office. He works hard all morning, setting a pace that the office has to strain to match. The DMC-12 and the factory in Northern Ireland, however, scarcely figure in the daily routine, which is mostly work on outside ventures—the snow-grooming company, the idea for Bausch & Lomb sunglasses to go with the car, or an expensive suede DeLorean jacket that Maur Dubin has designed, and many others.

Often DeLorean stays at his desk through lunch. He doesn't eat much—perhaps Marian Gibson will send down to the Cowboy Restaurant in the building for a bowl of chili and a soda. No alcohol. At other times he will walk back along Fifth Avenue for lunch with Cristina and the children, but most days he is too busy to go home so he eats his chili and keeps going. The afternoon is spent much the same way, except there is usually a lawyers' meeting. DeLorean is thinking about floating a new company, although he hasn't yet told anyone other than Kimmerly, who is designing the structure. Kimmerly is the only one he allows close to him, trusting him as much as he has ever trusted anyone. The slight, bespectacled Michigan lawyer repays his trust with a doglike devotion.

Some of the memos that DeLorean exchanges with Kimmerly are bizarre, grandiose. Marian Gibson recalls one: "Will you find out how I can buy the Harrod's name? I want to use it to distribute in the U.S." At this time he is also trying to set up a test track in New Jersey that would cost millions of dollars.

At 5:30 DeLorean leaves his office for the day. He has made no decisions that affect the DMC-12 sports car and the factory in Northern Ireland, although he has talked to Dick Brown out on the West Coast, now working at full blast for the expected arrival of the cars in the spring. DeLorean takes the elevator to the ground floor and walks home. Sometimes he and Cristina go out to dinner parties, but with increasing rarity, for he does not particularly enjoy them, dislikes the mad social scramble of New York. "You have to remember," says a former employee, "these people were Detroit, not New York. They had only been in New York two years and their whole mentality, their whole corporate game plan, was Detroit. In New York they were gauche, awkward. They just were not streetwise. They thought so, but they never were."

DeLorean now arrives back at his Fifth Avenue home. Does he plunge into a frenetic evening at Studio 54? A wild party organized by Maur Dubin and his friends, where he'll meet Frank Sinatra or

Raquel Welch? A film premiere? Surely at least a smart dinner party given by his friend Sheldon Tannen, one of the owners of "21," or Don S. Hewitt, executive producer of "Sixty Minutes"? Or a cocktail party at the apartment of independent film producer David Brown and his wife, Helen Gurley Brown, editor of *Cosmopolitan,* with dinner afterward at La Côte Basque?

No, he does not. John DeLorean, after an initial flurry on the fringes of New York society, has given way to his own better instincts and stays home whenever he can. He is never fully at ease in the circles he has aspired to—actively disliking and discouraging dinner parties, where he has no small talk and often feels at a loss. The DeLoreans will have a Halloween party later this month and Cristina will amuse everyone by clowning as a witch, which she does with style and humor. And they will throw a party for Herb Siegel's birthday. For this party Cristina will call in her mother from California to help her prepare dinner for fifty of the Chris-Craft chairman's friends. "There was pasta, salad, a fancy dessert and gobs of caviar," a guest will later relate. "She did a fish covered with carrot chips to look like scales. But John was abstemious. He ate very sparingly. I don't think he cares much for food."

DeLorean has more than enough time away from home already. At this stage he is traveling to London for torrid meetings with the Northern Ireland office, or to Belfast for more meetings there. He is jetting to the West Coast for meetings with possible investors in his project; he goes to Utah to see his Logan snow-grooming company; he gives speeches and lectures from time to time out of New York, requiring an overnight stop. Although the DeLoreans are spending large sums of money making further improvements to the beautiful house in Pauma Valley, near San Diego (they have installed an eight-person hot-tub and over the next year they will extensively remodel and redecorate the house), they are spending very little time there either. Cristina likes to have a good time, but she too is happy to stay at home. Friends will say they think of her as being "in jeans, a woman of simple tastes."

So this evening they are both happy to stay home. John makes some phone calls, mostly to California. He is negotiating for an injection of new capital—he is always negotiating for that. And he spends hours on the phone persuading the would-be investor what a splendid opportunity he is passing up. The unfortunate fact is that although plenty of people express an interest, no one will give him money. And increasingly he needs money—again.

On that note we send him to bed. He does not read a book—he cannot concentrate or sit still that long. He watches TV for a while, perhaps his friend Johnny Carson. But he has no interest in that either. His mind is active, constantly leaping about. Perhaps this is why he sleeps so little. But we eventually lower him into a restless and slightly troubled sleep.

12

DELAYS AND INDECISION

By the fall of 1980, only months after Humphrey Atkins had agreed to the extra £14-million loan, DeLorean was running out of money again. In August he had accepted Atkins' money on the promise and understanding that this would be all, the very last drop of British taxpayers' money. In September, however, NIDA in Belfast received yet another nasty shock: McKinsey delivered a bombshell. "Despite the commitment of £14 million by Her Majesty's Government . . . the funds gap by April 1981 is likely to be in the range of £2 million to £14 million, with a 'most likely' level of some £9 million." The report noted that the cost of supporting the New York and United States operations was running at $900,000 a month "and is planned to rise to $1.5 million in February—although thereafter expenditures will be reduced by revenue from car and parts sales." NIDA had known, even as Humphrey Atkins was excluding Hopkins from the Hillsborough meeting with DeLorean, that there would still be a funding gap. But not as large as this.

McKinsey wasn't altogether gloomy. The gap, it reported, was bridgeable. For John DeLorean had a plan: New Court Securities, part of the New York office of the Rothschild empire, had prepared a proposal that could raise $20 million in two portions, the first $10 million by November, the second by early 1981. The first part therefore could come in time for a key accounting date at the Belfast subsidiary: for DMCL had lent DMC in New York about £4 million to finance the lavish expenditures and salaries of the American operation. By the end of November, which was the DMCL year-end, £3 million was due to be repaid. If the loans were not repaid, the British Inland Revenue had intimated it would consider the loans as a paid-out dividend, and DMCL would be required by British tax law to pay

£1.7 million of advance corporation tax on them. That little item was already setting teeth on edge at NIDA—not only was it having to support John DeLorean in New York, but it was having to pay taxes for the privilege. Of course it was all government money, and would simply involve taking it out of one pocket and putting it into the other. But it still came out of the Northern Ireland budget.

McKinsey had high hopes for New Court Securities' $20 million, and John DeLorean continually raised these hopes. Rothschild in New York, however, never saw the proposal as more than an outside possibility and was astonished to learn eventually how centrally it featured in the finance plans. It was yet another example of wishful thinking, or exaggeration, by DeLorean. But he kept the prospect of this Rothschild money at the forefront of his talks with the Northern Ireland authorities for months to come. By now Tony Hopkins was not easily misled, however. At the end of September he reported to his board that while McKinsey felt the funding gap was manageable, he himself was "skeptical of this evaluation" even if New Court did come up with the money.

On September 23 DeLorean flew in to Belfast for a board meeting, full of optimism about his financial plans. He had not yet worked out his strategy for asking for more money. Although Hopkins was half expecting it, the subject didn't come up. All was cheerful: Lotus, reported Chuck Bennington, had virtually completed the transfer of the production drawings on the car. There was good news on the 50,000-mile certification test: it was no longer required, at least not for the 1981 model. The performance of the Volvo engine had now improved measurably and was averaging twenty-three miles per gallon, manual and automatic taken together, compared to the 1981 official requirement of twenty-two. The Volvo engine, widely used in America on other cars, would get the benefit of a "carry-across" and would not have to undergo the rigorous testing they thought.

DeLorean himself reported on the good news on financing: Rothschild was working on its $20-million special loan "which will have conversion rights and will be secured by way of a warranty fund"; a complex plan involving the creation of a $1,650 mandatory warranty payment which would be added to the price of each car. To those sitting at the boardroom table, the car seemed expensive enough without burdening it with another cost. DeLorean brushed that aside. The Oppenheimer limited partnership, went on DeLorean cheerfully, as though this were even better news, was being revised to find more money for the sedan version. Hopkins resented the partnership very much, with its rights to 23.4 percent of DMC's profits in return for funds that had gotten no nearer the car than Switzerland, although Hopkins did not know it at the time.

DeLorean was in such a confident mood that he even raised the subject of the Transbus again. He wanted, he announced, to seek the board's view (he meant NIDA's view—Hopkins was glowering at him from down the table) on whether the Transbus could be completed within the legal framework of DMC—or "should we float it off to another company?" Everyone looked to Hopkins for the reply, and, controlling his anger, he gave it. NIDA, he reminded DeLorean, had a formal agreement that had been agreed by both the DMC and the DMCL boards and which stipulated that "all activities not directly relevant to the launch of the DMC-12 car" had been stopped. If the project had nothing to do with the development of the car, and therefore with employment in Northern Ireland, NIDA would take an extremely dim view of it. Hopkins was firm, barely polite.

Day by day the men at NIDA were growing nearer to despair with John DeLorean. Hopkins bore the brunt of it, although Faulkner and Freeman fully supported him. They were now reaping the bitter harvest of the badly negotiated master agreement and Humphrey Atkins' move back in August to give DeLorean money. Atkins genuinely believed he had an agreement that DeLorean would not ask for any more than the £14 million he had given him. The men at NIDA knew differently. What they could not know yet was how DeLorean intended to get that money. If they had seen the papers which DeLorean carried with him in his slim briefcase, they would have been even more dismayed. This and subsequent meetings were only part of DeLorean's softening-up process. He was preparing his major offensive for the new year and had set it all out in New York only two days before in one of his interminable memos to Tom Kimmerly. This one was also marked "cc: E. A. Cafiero, W. F. Haddad."

It is perhaps the most revealing memo in terms of DeLorean's long-term plan for getting money out of the British government. There is nothing subtle about it. Rather, it is a sledgehammer approach, with some rough blackmail as part of the deal. Dated September 21, 1981, the memo stated:

In developing our strategy for collecting the balance of the money due us from the UK government, I think we should do these things:

1. Get statements from all involved in Master Agreement Meetings confirming the £8 million [over $19 million] obligation in relation to royalty NIDA is getting. This has partially been accomplished.

2. Develop, from outside counsel, a legal opinion citing the responsibility and obligation each of the officers and directors incurred as a result of telling our investors we were getting the inflation adjustment in the identical manner to original funding (50% grants, 25% equity, balance, loans, more or less) and that NIDA would give us the £8 million when and if we needed it since we were paying them the royalty for providing this money.

This opinion should include the statement that to minimize personal and corporate liability, the company and its officers and directors are obliged to take all necessary legal remedies, including litigation, to enforce this agreement. Otherwise dealers and investors can demand their money back and money damages— potentially devastating to DMC.

3. We should have our UK counsel prepare but not file our case demanding the specific performance from NIDA, DOC [Department of Commerce] and the UK government. We will then front it to the government with the legal opinion in paragraph 2. This presentation will be on the basis of a mutual problem— we don't want to sue—it would destroy the credibility of NIDA —but our lawyers tell us we must.

This memo is almost breathtaking in its boldness. Only six weeks before, DeLorean had been offered a loan of £14 million by Humphrey Atkins on the clear condition that all British government obligations were now discharged. Yet DeLorean is now preparing his case for more money due from the UK government. What is more, he is actually proposing to sue the British government, which has already given him nearly £70 million!

DeLorean's "ideal outcome" was this: ". . . the government has cited their royalty income many times as the factor that makes DMC a good deal for them, they never once mentioned their equity ownership publicly. When we get through rattling the saber we would hope they would return their stock to us to fulfill their obligations."

In other words, DeLorean was now trying to persuade the British government to surrender its modest equity interest in the venture as well as some more money.

"Obviously," he concluded, "this is an idealized scenario fraught with potential pitfalls and problems, but one we must pursue aggressively. We should be ready to spring this in January 1981, about the time they are ready to take the bows for the success of the project.

"This proposal requires careful planning from a government relations and public relations standpoint."

This last was Bill Haddad's job. The money involved meant very little to Haddad at the time—he was not particularly good at figures. What he was good at was presenting a case, and that he understood full well. He was still in the honeymoon period and had not yet begun to have serious doubts. It was perfectly logical that if you needed more money, and genuinely believed the British government owed it to you, the time to ask for it was when they were feeling most favorably inclined toward you, and when they were in no position to say no. To Haddad and DeLorean that pointed to January, when the car would be in production. No one would dare pull the plug at that point.

In November DeLorean acquired his third chief financial officer, nearly a year after he first promised to replace Walter Strycker. James G. Stark was fifty-two, a Canadian who had spent some years with Northern Telecom, where he had been chief financial officer from 1974 to 1979. DeLorean was increasingly in the mood to pay out large and lavish salaries despite the growing financial plight of the company: he paid Stark $300,000 a year, although Strycker made only $100,000. Stark moved onto the 43rd floor, but took some time to get used to the setup. NIDA hoped he might tighten the financial strings a little, but Hopkins was not optimistic. By now he knew all too well who ran the company.

Later that month, however, there was an appointment that did make a noticeable difference. NIDA had indicated earlier in the year that it thought the pressure on Chuck Bennington was too much, and DeLorean admitted freely that Bennington was no longer up to the job. It was outside all his experience and the pressures were too intense. He had to contend with his squabbling engineers, who complained about Lotus, and with Lotus men, who complained about his engineers; engineering and purchasing departments in a state of open warfare; problem after problem with the car, the plastic molding process, the production line, design and parts, and testing; money; and a thousand and one other things. He was trying to cope with DeLorean's erratic instructions and was the buffer between his employer and NIDA. He had to organize the material given to McKinsey and worry about their reports. He was trying to recruit and train a work force that would total 2,500 people within a year. "Chuck was very much of a loner by inclination," says Shaun Harte. "He would be happiest in the Sahara with a bunch of natives building an early-warning system. Without doubt not a man to build a management team, but he *is* a man to put bricks and mortar together." Bennington, like Collins, had served DeLorean's purpose and had worn himself out.

Now DeLorean shoved him aside and brought in the man who would get his car built, late as it was. Don Lander had plenty of experience running an auto company held together with British government money. He had been managing director of Chrysler U.K. from 1974 to 1976, and far from creating enmity among British government officials, as DeLorean was doing, enjoyed considerable respect in those circles. He was yet another of what came to be known as the Chrysler "Mafia"—Cafiero, Bennington, Daly, Stylianides, and now Lander all came from the struggling Chrysler.

In contrast to Stark, who was floundering, Lander hit his stride instantly. He settled into the Conway Hotel (later he moved to the caretaker's flat in Warren House) and began to pull the program together. Gene Cafiero was supposed to spend half his time in Belfast but he never did. And with Lander's arrival Cafiero was seen there less and less often. "Lander was a super guy," says one of the Belfast executives. "He really made things begin to happen."

And what of the car? Its problems had not mysteriously vanished —far from it. There were considerable problems in the body shop, trying to get the fiberglass material to set properly. The angle strut on the gull-wing door was breaking under testing, and the sealing on the door was still not right. Part of the front chassis cracked during rig testing, and when development car D-11 was sent down to the south of Italy and back on a road test, it developed problems in the back suspension. The latest development cars, D-14 and D-15, had completed only 4,000 miles of their planned 50,000-mile tests, and already the engineers were aware that design modifications were needed.

It all meant the car would be late on the market—there was no way there would be enough units to ship to the United States before April, which would mean first sales by June. John DeLorean could not survive financially until then. Lotus was still eating DeLorean money —£600,000 a month was flowing directly from Belfast to Norwich, although the original program stated that Lotus should have finished the car some months before. By June he would need an extra $50 million.

The tension in the months of November and December 1980 would have been too much for most men. DeLorean deliberately sought more. While his men in Belfast were now working around the clock seven days a week in a desperate effort to get the bugs out of the car and the production line, John DeLorean turned again to his Transbus. He refused NIDA's instructions to abandon it, and Hopkins could only grin and bear it. DeLorean had learned a useful lesson from playing off Northern Ireland against Puerto Rico, and now applied the same formula to his Transbus. He went to riot-torn Liberty City, a Miami neighborhood, and offered to become a large-scale local employer with a package deal whereby the city would give him forty acres at a low rent, lend him money to build a plant, and then help him apply to the federal government, which under the Carter regime put up 80 percent of the money when a local community decided to purchase new buses. Again he was thinking big: he would, he told Miami officials, employ 4,000 people and build a $120-million project. He scorned objections that most of South Florida's unskilled workers had never been inside an auto plant. "We expect to train our workers," he said dismissively. "We have never failed at anything."

He was offering almost exactly the same package to the South Bronx in New York. His executives in Park Avenue were spending hours working out the details, putting together the packages. Yet the only source of income in that office was the management fee of $290,000 a month paid by the Belfast company, plus large loans flowing from Belfast to New York that were never repaid.

On December 3 the first DMC-12 came off the production line and the men gathered around it in the forecourt for a ritual picture. It was hardly a smooth production process. Parts were being filed, bent, forced together, even bolted where they did not fit. But Don Lander had brought a sense of order and purpose to the production line, and the men were learning fast as they went. There were some horrendous mistakes made in those early days, but this is understandable in any new auto venture. Even at GM changes were always being made at the last moment. In this case, however, all the safety margins had been used up, and there was little proper testing, which is much less excusable.

There was another side to the apparent chaos. Mike Loasby would later write:

> Throughout all this the sense of achievement was immense and fully justified. A car was made and produced, more or less on time and by any standards extremely quickly, in a factory which is a showpiece, and also built in an extremely limited period by enthusiastic workers, often in appalling weather. Support from the local community was never stronger than during the 50,000-mile road endurance running carried out in Northern Ireland. First cars off the production line were driven round the clock by members of the Ulster Automobile Club, recording an average of 800 miles per day until the required mileage was completed. Some 40 drivers were employed, so the complexity of the required organization can be imagined as they drove, two to a car, in four-hour shifts: the enthusiasm can be judged from the minimal number of late starts recorded and no shifts were missed due to driver absence.

It was all very much an ad hoc effort, with men solving problems on the cars as they were inching their way along the production line, new tooling arriving halfway through the process, parts not fitting and then being reordered. But the miracle had happened: there was a car. By the spring there would be enough for a shipful. John DeLorean's dream was a reality.

The dreamer himself wasn't thinking very much about his car. From the very first day he started the venture, it was raising money that preoccupied him. Now it was no different. During these months he was working on plans for yet another public issue of shares. A larger one this time, which would make him personally much wealthier and at the same time free the company from tiresome cash restraints. It would be timed for the launch of the car so as to get maximum publicity for both car and company. With all the risk now taken, and some $200 million of other people's money spent, it would be a very different issue from anything he had tried before. No begging this time. Wall Street would be begging him.

But first he had to batter NIDA into accepting his proposals. He had done it for two years now, and he anticipated no great trouble in doing it again.

Belfast, December 17. There were a few brave attempts to hang Christmas decorations around the city and in the NIDA office where John DeLorean arrived to begin one of his most important meetings in Northern Ireland. He brought Jim Stark with him, giving the Belfast officials and his own team their first look at the new finance director. He also brought Bill Haddad, who would be needed for that tricky public relations job, one which Haddad himself was beginning to resent. How do you persuade a government it is in their interests to deprive them of their equity in a venture that has been kept alive by them?

DeLorean was not going to wait for January. Two to three cars a week were coming off the production line, and although not even DeLorean, with all his flair for hyperbole, could claim they were fit to go into dealers' showrooms, they gave him an extra bargaining edge. The time to spring it was now, and he did. It had a devastating effect.

The NIDA people knew by now that he was going to ask for more money, and that the financial position of the DeLorean companies was more serious than ever. But nothing had quite prepared them for DeLorean's extravagant demands that day. He wanted that £14-million loan converted into a nonrepayable grant—it was the company's clear contractual understanding that the money given for inflation should have been a grant and not a loan. This was the case with all NIDA-sponsored firms and should be the case with DeLorean. He was, he pointed out humbly, only doing his duty by the company in demanding that the agency honor its contractual commitments. "We don't wish to appear to be biting the hand that feeds us nor, I expect, would NIDA wish to appear as failing to honor contractual obligations."

He then went on to the $15 million that NIDA was to advance in place of the Oppenheimer money but never had to because Oppenheimer came back in. Now, he told the NIDA board, he wanted that money—he was due it and NIDA must either advance it or cancel its royalty agreement.

He appreciated that NIDA might have "cash constraints" just now, so he had a proposal. If the £14 million could be converted into a grant, that would make it easier for him to raise new money through the offering of new shares in his company. Then DMC would redeem NIDA's shares (for nothing)—in effect this shareholding would be canceled. NIDA didn't want it anyway, he pointed out. They only had it because of some silly SEC rules that had required a conversion of the original deferred shares into real equity.

Then he went on to point out how easy it would be politically for this package to be presented inside the United Kingdom. No one in Britain even knew this NIDA shareholding existed. The master agreement was still a secret document; the terms of NIDA's support for DeLorean had never been disclosed. The redemption of NIDA's shares wouldn't even be noticed—it was a "painless solution for NIDA."

Hopkins and the NIDA board were stunned. But worse was to follow. DeLorean now turned from cajolery to threats. The alternative was to go to arbitration—he would sue NIDA, which he was entitled to do under the master agreement. His London solicitors had assured him he would win, and the entire £14 million would be awarded to him as grant, whereas now he might even settle for half grant/half loan. It all must be settled quickly, otherwise he wouldn't be able to raise money in New York with his new offering. It was up to NIDA, their responsibility. Then he threw in his bombshell. Until the situation was resolved, he had no option but to withhold royalty payments to NIDA (£185 on each of the first 90,000 cars produced and £45 per car after that). How could he do that? asked a shaken Hopkins. "We simply won't pay it," said DeLorean.

While the NIDA men reeled from that one, DeLorean quickly followed up. This would all have to be disclosed under SEC rules in the United States. Think, he warned, what the press was going to make of the story: DELOREAN WITHHOLDS NIDA ROYALTY PAYMENTS. That would make NIDA look a bit foolish. Now the argument became heated to the point where DeLorean insisted that NIDA was not entitled to any royalty at all and that he was not going to pay any. Hopkins insisted DeLorean put that in writing to the agency—tell NIDA categorically that the DeLorean company was not going to pay NIDA the royalty that it had agreed to in the master agreement signed on July 28, 1978. If DeLorean had legal opinions saying this was his right, then NIDA wanted to see those too. But as soon as DeLorean put it in writing, NIDA would be seeking its own legal opinion.

It was the stormiest meeting yet between DeLorean and NIDA. Hopkins could scarcely believe it. DeLorean was unruffled. For him it had gone more or less as planned, except that he had expected Hopkins to cave in more easily. But the man probably more appalled than anyone else was a member of DeLorean's own team: Bill Haddad, his public relations expert. Haddad was a newcomer to corporate PR, but he was a specialized lobbyist, and there really was very little difference between lobbying a United States government department and a British one. It was very clear to Haddad that DeLorean's way of doing things was not going to win friends and influence people.

Haddad had other reasons for becoming disillusioned. While in Belfast he had talked to the engineers and heard the first doubts about the quality of the car. None of these had percolated back to New York at his vice-presidential level, and they had been glossed over on his previous Belfast visits, when he had been with DeLorean. The atmosphere in Belfast for a DeLorean visit is described by engineering chief Mike Loasby: "Reading On a Clear Day one is immediately impressed by the many similarities between the GM John DeLorean describes and his own DMC compared particularly in the political and personnel relations areas: the team approach as described by 'Himself' was very much in evidence, spectacularly so on John's visits when the alacrity with which certain personnel snapped into line had to be seen to be believed. Opinions and views uncannily agreed with John's on that day, whether they had or not beforehand. John's was always the first opinion stated, those that followed generally agreed."

On his last trips to Belfast, however, Haddad departed from the normal procedure and began talking in earnest to others outside the immediate Bennington/Daly/Harte circle. One of the people he talked to at length was Mike Loasby. "I liked him very much," says Haddad. "I thought that he was a straight arrow. He opened up to me once he realized that I was not John's eyes and ears. And he opened up to me about a problem. Loasby was disgusted at the way they were cutting corners." Haddad had brought it up with DeLorean, not mentioning Loasby's name, and been brushed aside. Now, after a week in Belfast, he returned to New York without DeLorean, to brood on events. He and DeLorean were barely on speaking terms, and Haddad did not go into the office in those days before Christmas.

He even missed the Christmas party in the penthouse. DeLorean, back from Belfast, suddenly decided there should be an office party and deputized Marian Gibson to organize it. But he had left it too late and Marian could not find a place that was not already booked. "Let's have it here," said DeLorean, gesturing at the broad, elegant spaces of the 43rd floor. She organized the party and it went well, but Haddad did not appear and DeLorean noticed, mentioning it to his secretary.

Haddad wasn't deliberately shunning DeLorean—he didn't like parties, particularly office parties. He had taken the opportunity to spend some extra time with his children in his house in New Hampshire after a spell away from them in Belfast. Over the Christmas weekend he became seriously worried about the last weeks in Belfast and the events now taking place in the company.

Like most professional journalists, Haddad thought best over his typewriter. Christmas was on a Thursday that year and the office was closed for a long weekend. On the day after Christmas, known to the British as Boxing Day in deference to the Victorian tradition of "boxing up" the Christmas leftovers and distributing them to the servants, Haddad sat for a long time over his typewriter before starting the memo that would become known as the "Boxing Day memo" or more commonly as the "gold facet memo." That day he had no conception of the central role it would play; he just wanted to put down for John DeLorean's attention a summary of all the doubts and questions that had come up in the traumatic last month.

> I continue to be concerned about our efforts to set up a scenario under which the British relinquish their share of equity in the program. I just don't think it will work. And, if it does work, it will only follow a storm of public protest which will reach from London to Detroit to Washington.
>
> Perhaps I don't understand the reason for the push at this time. I don't see how it can help our cash flow problem. So I assume the action is taken in conjunction with our plans for a public

offering. If that is the case, while it may enhance the DMC equity position and, consequently, what people are willing to pay for the stock, the public outcry may reduce the attractiveness of the offering and even require the postponement of the offering.

This was a good point and very true. Wall Street investors would be far more influenced by the political stink involving the company than by the figures in its balance sheet. DeLorean should have been thinking about that. But even if he wasn't, Haddad was doing his job as official company PR man in pointing it out.

This was only part of Haddad's concern. In New Hampshire that day he decided to unburden all his worries to DeLorean. He wasn't in the company at the time of the 1978 agreement with Northern Ireland and wasn't in the best position to judge the legal argument now raging. But he had seen enough to know that DeLorean's case was far from being airtight. "For the purpose of this memo," he wrote, "let's assume our position is legally correct." Even then, there would be problems. Haddad went on:

> I know you believe the power of the logic and the facts presented to the British in a closed room will create the conditions for them to relinquish their equity position. However, I don't believe that any action of this magnitude can be decided below the ministerial level, the Whitehall level, and that, of necessity, given the British system, will produce, I am convinced, a violent Parliamentary outcry and a mandatory Parliamentary inquiry. Given the Fleet Street nature of the British media, and the cynical attitude toward private enterprise (and DeLorean in particular) exhibited by the BBC, I think you and the company will be painted in the blackest of terms.

The tautology was not Haddad at his best. "Fleet Street" is a generic term for the British media, and includes the "heavy" newspapers such as the *Telegraph, Times* and *Financial Times,* as well as the more sensational newspapers. Haddad's phrase was the equivalent of saying, "Given the Madison Avenue nature of New York advertising." And until this point the British press and TV had been remarkably kind to John DeLorean, with one or two notable exceptions. But as Haddad often said, "You have to exaggerate to get John's attention."

While he had that attention (he hoped), Haddad was going to bring up all the matters on his mind:

> I am also worried about what a Parliamentary inquiry will uncover about our expenditures on both sides of the ocean. There are the "official" complaints which can be sensationalized even though Arthur Andersen, SEC, et al, will give a clean bill of health. The Strycker picture is a highly personal one of John Z. DeLorean milking the company for his private profit. Some of the discredited Strycker charges can be succulent journalistic morsels for the Fleet Street crowd never overly concerned about separating accusation from fact.

Until this point Haddad had not taken sides over Walter Strycker; he had arrived too late to be involved. But now all the doubts raised by the Strycker incident were fitting into a different context. His eyes had been opened to a new John DeLorean, although even now he was not wholly ready to admit it. But as a former journalist he had come to see how the Strycker picture could be presented by someone not sympathetic to DeLorean. Everything would come out, and he might well be washed away. Haddad went on to list some of the other little matters that might be revealed.

> As you know, I am also troubled by some of the Bennington actions regarding the house and some of the expenditures which appear to have been "fuzzed" (like a 10,000 pound expenditure at Harrod's for gold faucets,* etc.). I recently learned, for example, that we may have hidden some of the capital expenses of the house in expenses for the project. In short, the books were altered. Silly, because the house can be justified.

The house he referred to was Warren House, beside the factory in Belfast. Chuck Bennington had, in the view of a number of people in Belfast, gone overboard in doing it up, apparently with the idea of housing visiting dignitaries. Again Haddad was exaggerating: the renovation of the house had certainly been absurdly expensive, but there were no "gold facets"—there were some gold-*colored* taps, and they

---

* His secretary would mistype this as "facet."

were not from Harrod's. But he was right: expenditure on the house had been mixed in with expenditure on the factory.

In recent weeks Haddad had strayed upon something of much greater importance although he did not yet know what it all meant: GPD. He knew none of the details but there were whispers that disturbed him. "GPD was not a word in the company. Nobody ever heard of GPD, nobody ever saw GPD. We always dealt with Lotus. John told me that GPD was a Colin Chapman idea and that's why they used that device," Haddad said later. As with the other items, his concern was essentially in how the press might play it.

> The Lotus situation troubles me too. I know everyone approved it, but, no matter the hero status of Colin Chapman, hidden Swiss accounts to avoid British taxes may be viewed differently in the media than in the courts or in the higher circles of sophisticated government bent on getting something done quickly and efficiently.

Of course not everyone had approved it. But when Haddad raised GPD with DeLorean, he was able to point to the fact that Arthur Andersen had queried the original payment from the Belfast company and insisted on drawing it to the attention of every member of the board. The payment got exchange-control approval from the Bank of England—a formality, since there was an invoice, a contract, and an apparently above-board deal. For reasons best known to themselves, the NIDA people never queried GPD seriously either. Haddad's point was that even if it were a perfectly legitimate tax-avoidance scheme, it would still look bad for British taxpayers' money to be used in that way. He was more deeply troubled than that about GPD, but in this memo he confined himself to the publicity risks.

> There is also the problem of moving so quickly. I understand from my University contacts that it is fairly well known that the architects made a small fortune on us (so did Lotus!). They may have deserved it, but what are the small items which made up this fortune? Did we monitor closely enough? Why wasn't JZD there to oversee everything? Was he, as Strycker charges, pursuing other interests?

If we were in production, and the British could taste the recovery of their money, the contrast between these items and the general state of their economy would not be so dramatic. After all, any of the higher expenses will cost us as well as them, and we, in the end, are not only repaying their investment, but with a dividend in people off the dole and 2,000 new jobs in one of the most unpopular areas of the world (their goal in providing us the money). Perhaps, due to the offering, we were legally *required* to take this unpleasant action. I know the counterarguments.

The story which could emerge, however, is that DeLorean (it is your name on the door), who got £60,000,000 * of British taxpayers' money, is so greedy that he wants to take more and deprive the British of their rightful equity.

No matter your legal briefs, the accurate comments of those present at the time, that is the story which *could* emerge: The 1980 American robber baron image, enhanced by Fleet Street's love of the spectacular. And the British are on record, as you know from the recent Belfast interviews, as stating they owe us no more money.

Until now Haddad's comments had been reasoned, professional. He could have been writing a memo to Ted Kennedy or the governor of New York. He was identifying, very shrewdly as events were to prove, the sensitive areas on which the media might focus and where DeLorean was most vulnerable. But like many Americans and even British, Haddad wholly misunderstood the nature of the politics of Northern Ireland and of the IRA in particular. He now went on to set out what he told DeLorean were the areas that worried him "deep down":

We are *not* now a target of the IRA because we have "good will" on our side. On my last trip to England I met with one of the producers of the BBS show where you were surprised with questions which they had promised not to ask. The producer said he tried to halt this line of questioning during the show, but the presenter kept pushing. However, he did say that *never* in his experience did any show produce such a negative response from the audience. He was literally flooded with angry letters com-

---

* Haddad was underestimating: it was already £68 million and DeLorean was trying to get another £20 million.

plaining that the presenter was harassing a man who only wanted to do good for Ulster. You are a hero in Ulster, untouchable by the IRA or any of the more loosely organized terrorist groups.

If that attitude changes, and they paint you black, and it sticks for even a short period of time, and evokes a local response, the IRA could put us on the list. They won't go for the factory, they will go for you. In Belfast or, just as easily, and more dramatically, here in New York.

Those are the stakes. That is what worries me.

The IRA had no interest in John DeLorean. His quarrel with the British government was of no concern to them. Although investment in his factory in West Belfast was perceived by Roy Mason as part of the anti-IRA campaign, the IRA never seemed to concern itself with this aspect of foreign investment in Northern Ireland. Whether John DeLorean thrived or failed, employed 2,500 or none, hired more Protestants than Catholics or vice versa, built a world-beating car or something that was not even roadworthy, mattered not at all in their calculations. The IRA campaign at this time was just moving into a new gear, aimed at winning the hearts and minds of Irish-Americans and of world opinion. Nothing could have been more disastrous for the IRA than for John DeLorean to be blown up or gunned down in Belfast, unless it was his slaughter in New York. Haddad may have been trying to jolt DeLorean—he knew already his phobia about Belfast and the IRA—but he possibly detracted from the more pertinent message in the rest of his memo. After that bit of drama he finished lamely:

I just want these views factored into any decision you make.

As I said, I don't know the rationale or the urgency, but I do worry about the potential consequences if we continue down this road.

And don't shoot the messenger, just review, carefully, the message.

Haddad finished typing at last—four and a half pages of memo. Then he called a special messenger and had it run into Manhattan, where his secretary was ready to retype it. Later there would be controversy over whether it was ever delivered to DeLorean's office. Haddad claims he has written proof in the shape of a signed affidavit that it was.

DeLorean was not in New York that weekend. He and Cristina had taken the children and entourage to the house in Pauma Valley and stayed there over the New Year. The renovation was not yet complete, but it now had six marble baths, a skylighted family room with an aviary wall by the fireplace, and a large, sunny breakfast area. La Cuesta de Camellia occupies a knolltop overlooking John DeLorean's forty-five-acre estate, which includes seventeen acres of citrus groves, and across Pauma Valley to Mount Palomar. The estate contains two guest houses, each with its own private garden, plus the main house —a nine-room adobe building with 7,000 square feet. On the valley side there is a terrace onto which glass sliding doors open from all the main rooms; it ends in a screen of thick flowering shrubs and the main new feature of the ranch, an eight-person hot-tub. There is also a forty-one-foot swimming pool and a five-room house for the ranch manager. By any standards it is a magnificent place.

Bill Haddad was almost certainly not at the front of the DeLorean mind that week in California—the battle with NIDA was. Before Christmas he put his proposal in writing as Hopkins insisted. But he pulled back, as Hopkins must have thought he would, from the categorical statement that he would not pay any royalties. He stated instead: "In the meantime we are forced to withhold our royalty payments to NIDA until this matter is cleared up." But he still added the rider that under U.S. laws he would be obligated to disclose these details in the prospectus he was currently preparing, and when that was published it would "no doubt be a major news item." Hopkins replied by telling Jim Stark and then Telexing DeLorean directly in New York that the agency had no intention of foregoing the rights attached to its shareholding, nor its rights under the master agreement to receive royalties. NIDA was proving unexpectedly stubborn. And at Dunmurry, after the first few cars, the problems had proved too much for the production line and it was almost at a standstill. There were only half a dozen cars produced so far. From his idyllic spot near Escondido, DeLorean would soon have to return to the firing line in Belfast. It could not have been a prospect he relished.

The opening days of 1981 were gloomy for all those involved in the DeLorean project. At his board meeting at Dunmurry on December 17, DeLorean had approved a budget for the new financial year which showed a cash flow shortage of £766,000 by April. That was absurdly optimistic. On January 5 it jumped to £5.7 million and a week later was over £8 million.

The options were running out. "Despite the high confidence of DMCL management expressed to us in September, New Court Securities (Rothschild) has not produced a single investor to date. DMCL now considers that it will not produce the funds anticipated," reported McKinsey. New Court now faded from the picture—in reality it was never seriously in, except perhaps in John DeLorean's imagination. DeLorean was now casting his net even wider. An investment bank named Hambrick and Twist, reported McKinsey, was a possible source, but "it is highly unlikely that private investment capital will be attracted to the project until the company has launched a quality car in America." There was only one source of funds yet again: the British taxpayer.

Throughout January Tony Hopkins and NIDA considered their options. They had little choice. Without more money from the British government there would be no project—that much was now all too clear. Her Majesty's Government was the only source, and NIDA could not really refuse DeLorean, not at the point where the car was finally coming off the production line and would soon be in dealers' showrooms. But Hopkins would not give in to DeLorean's blackmail: NIDA would keep its shareholders' rights and its royalty rights. Hopkins felt DeLorean could get by on £5 million to £8 million, but in return for that extra assistance, he was going to screw DeLorean to the floor: strict rules on the way board meetings were conducted; controls over his expenditures in the U.S.; a renegotiation of the transfer price mechanism, whereby DeLorean in Belfast would effectively be able to sell to DeLorean in New York at whatever price he wanted; "categoric clarification and reacceptance" of NIDA's royalty rights; and reaffirmation of DeLorean's obligations as to debt repayment, employment, and all the other factors that NIDA in its innocence thought had been settled in July 1978. Unless DeLorean agreed to all these, and more, there would be no extra money.

January 21, Dunmurry. John DeLorean folded his long body into a DMC-12 at the end of the production line, reached up to grasp the leather strap on the gull-wing door, pulled down the door, and drove the car out in the forecourt of the Dunmurry factory. He was in Belfast to personally deliver a formal request for "short-term working capital," the face-saving formula Hopkins had worked out. But he did get a bit of publicity for the car at the same time. "We aim to get about 700 cars into the States by the end of April for a coast-to-coast market launch early in May," he announced to the journalists outside. Yes, he admitted, there had been delays. But as always DeLorean was turning them to his advantage. "It is fortunate there have been a few delays, because the United States market has been dull but is reviving again. We will hit it at just the right time."

Production of the car was speeding up—three a day were now coming off the line—still a desperate crawl. By now there were 865 people working at Dunmurry, the number having doubled in a month as production got under way. Recruits were being taken on forty to fifty at a time and given basic training. The workforce was quick to learn. There is a long industrial tradition in Northern Ireland, and although many of the new men had never had jobs, some had been mechanics, garage workers, or had worked in the Grundig factory nearby, at the shipyard, or in one or other of the factories now closed. Commenting on the numbers employed, DeLorean made the statement: "By the end of this year we will have 1,500 working here, and 2,000 by the middle of next year."

On the same day he made his formal request to the Department of Commerce: he needed £10 million urgently, which could not wait for the legal battle over his other demands to be resolved. It would just be a short-term loan. He had banks standing by willing to lend the money if the department would provide a government guarantee. The ministers in Westminster would be able to present it as "short-term assistance," although it was still another £10 million of government money. But Hopkins was determined he was going to impose his conditions on DeLorean, who was gradually giving way, surprised by the opposition to demands that by now he had persuaded himself were entirely reasonable.

Back in New York a few days later, he exploded in anger over breakfast in the Fifth Avenue duplex. He was reading *The Wall Street Journal* when an item caught his eye: DELOREAN MOTOR CARS ASKS BRITAIN TO PROVIDE $24 MILLION MORE IN AID. It was a short, five-paragraph story, but for DeLorean it was more than enough. Later in the day he discovered the *Financial Times* in London had run a similar story, and the *Detroit News* had picked it up. Bill Haddad was still in

Belfast, conducting the tricky job that DeLorean had assigned him of improving government relations. The following day Haddad and finance director Joe Daly got a DeLorean Telex, marked prominently ATTENTION FRANK MCCANN, the man dealing with DeLorean at the Commerce Department.

The Telex read:

> AN INVESTMENT BANKING FIRM WHO HAD TENTATIVELY COMMITTED TO HANDLING A PUBLIC OFFERING FOR US HAD THEIR INVESTMENT BANKING COMMITTEE MEETING TODAY. THEY DECLINED TO RAISE FUNDS FOR US BECAUSE OF THE ARTICLES IN THE WALL STREET JOURNAL AND ONE IN THE DETROIT NEWS SAYING WE COULD NOT MAKE PAYROLL AND WERE BACK TO THE GOVERNMENT. DOC AND NIDA MUST UNDERSTAND THAT THIS "LEAK" OF THEIRS HAS CLEARLY COST US OUR PUBLIC FINANCING. IT IS UNCONSCIONABLE THAT SUCH CONFIDENTIAL INFORMATION BE LEAKED TO THE PRESS. IN ADDITION THIS LEAK HAS SERIOUSLY INJURED OUR DEALER CREDIBILITY AND PERHAPS OUR BANK LINES. REGARDS, JOHN Z. DELOREAN

He sent copies to Gene Cafiero, Tom Kimmerly, and Jim Stark in his own office, and Frank McCann and Tony Hopkins in Belfast. It was several days before the puzzled but outraged McCann sent back his reply:

> I WAS DISMAYED BY YOUR TELEX OF JANUARY 29. YOU MAY BE ABLE TO SUBSTANTIATE YOUR STATEMENT ABOUT THE WITHDRAWAL OF A TENTATIVE COMMITMENT AND ITS CLEAR EFFECT OF YOUR PUBLIC FINANCING BUT THE FACTS ON THIS SIDE OF THE ATLANTIC ARE THAT THE MINISTER OF STATE IN ANSWER TO A SPECIFIC QUESTION IN THE HOUSE OF COMMONS CONFIRMED THAT DELOREAN MOTOR CARS LIMITED HAD APPLIED FOR THE ASSISTANCE OF THE DEPARTMENT IN RESOLVING A SHORT TERM WORKING CAPITAL REQUIREMENT. NO ADDITIONAL INFORMATION WAS GIVEN IN THE HOUSE OR TO THE PRESS. THE DEPARTMENT MADE NO FURTHER COMMENT AND WAS NOT RESPONSIBLE IN ANY WAY FOR THE PRESS SPECULATION WHICH OCCURRED. ENDS

DeLorean may have had an investment bank "tentatively committed" to handling a public offering for him at that time—Bache Halsey

Stuart Shields was certainly on the scene shortly afterward. But there is no evidence the so-called leak damaged his position any more than the ordinary inquiries any investment bank would conduct damaged his public offering. More likely this blast was another part of his softening-up process, throwing the blame and responsibility onto NIDA. If NIDA had spoiled his chances of raising money from outside sources, then NIDA was going to have to come up with that money.

By early February, however, the story of John DeLorean's fresh demands and his written statement that he would withhold royalties had leaked. The *Belfast Telegraph* picked it up first, and again DeLorean hit the roof. In New York he denied the story and then ordered Bill Haddad to serve a writ for libel on the *Belfast Telegraph*, whose story was based on British government documents. It was, as Haddad advised him, the worst possible move. The *Belfast Telegraph* is a powerful voice in the local community and in the early days had been as enthusiastic about the DeLorean project as anyone. In recent months, however, reporters Alan Watson and John Kane had learned about the battle with NIDA, and in the first week of February carried three long and informed stories, soon picked up by other papers. They had the effect of reversing the pressure back onto DeLorean, although Hopkins was angry enough to initiate a hunt to find the leak. After another few days of heated Telexes flying across the Atlantic, DeLorean reluctantly retreated. He was rapidly running out of money and needed that £10 million "short-term assistance." With ill-grace he assented to Hopkins' terms. On February 11 he wrote to Northern Ireland's new minister of state, Adam Butler, formally saying so, personally handing the letter to Butler that day in Belfast. It was another terse meeting, with DeLorean going back over all the old arguments and Butler holding Hopkins' ground—no more money unless he accepted the conditions. He would be making a statement to the House of Commons the next day. They had to agree now.

Thursday, February 12, the House of Commons. Humphrey Atkins finished his stint at answering questions, and as he sat down, Butler, his number two, stood up to field a battery of questions on DeLorean. The two men he feared most were in the House: the left-wing Labour MP, Bob Cryer, and Jock Bruce-Gardyne. Bruce-Gardyne belonged to the same party as Butler; he had developed a grave suspicion and dislike of the DeLorean project, attacking it both in the House and in his *Sunday Telegraph* column. His first question asked why, in view of Atkins' statement in August 1980 that the government's obligation to consider further financing to DeLorean had been discharged, he was now considering a further application.

Butler could cope with that one. He had his answer ready to the effect that the application was for a government guarantee for a commercial loan "to help the company resolve a short-term cash problem and take the DMC-12 car through to market launch." He had, he announced, agreed to a time-limited guarantee of up to £10 million, subject to DeLorean's accepting that neither NIDA nor the Department of Commerce had "any financial obligations towards the company and which confirm that royalties remain payable as agreed." He made no mention of DeLorean's other demands, knowing all too well what Bruce-Gardyne's reaction would be. But the back-bench Tory MP already had enough for a fair-sized broadside, which he now delivered at Butler.

> Does not my honourable friend realize that those undertakings were given to the House six months ago? Is there not a danger that my right honourable friend [this latter referred to Humphrey Atkins] in his dealings with Mr. DeLorean, will come to resemble the young lady from Riga who went for a ride on a tiger? Is my honourable friend aware that Mr. DeLorean apparently has a T-shirt on which is emblazoned the slogan, "I am a con-man"? Would he consider sending him a character reference? Can he seriously give the House the assurance that it needs that we shall have the opportunity to debate the matter and vote on it before any further money is given to that con-man?

This is unusual language from a Conservative Member of Parliament, even in the privilege of the House of Commons, where Members cannot be sued for libel or slander. It clearly rattled Adam Butler, who despite his ill-treatment by DeLorean never classified him as a con-man. In this instance his indignant reply was misleading. "My honourable friend does not help his cause," he told Bruce-Gardyne in the archaic but required language of the House, where you are an "honourable friend" if you belong to the same party, an "honourable gentleman" if you belong to the party opposite, and a "right honourable friend" or "right honourable gentleman" if you are or have been a senior minister. Thus Adam Butler was Bruce-Gardyne's "honourable friend," but Humphrey Atkins was his "right honourable friend." Proper names are not allowed in the House. In this particular case, neither Butler nor Bruce-Gardyne displayed the slightest sign of friendship for each other. "It is a serious matter," Butler went on reprovingly. "In fact, no more money is being provided but purely a government guarantee behind commercial loans to help the company to launch a car that it believes has good market prospects. The obligations were removed in the agreements last summer but, because of certain press statements about the beliefs of one or two parties to the arrangement, I felt it necessary to come to a firm written understanding with Mr. DeLorean that no such obligations now exist."

In view of all that went before, this was not quite the whole truth. Butler was adopting the old adage of "if there's no one else, blame the press." In the rest of the debate he repeated that there would be "no more selective assistance" for the DMC-12 project, that he was perfectly happy with the information the company was providing, and he and his opposite number, Don Concannon, ended up with a little burst of mutual self-congratulation on their joint determination to support the project. It is cruel to subject Butler's performance to the test of hindsight, but even then his remarks sounded fatuous and out of touch to those taking part in the debate.

DeLorean's tally of British government money by this date stood at £78 million, £24 million of it from a Conservative government that was supposed to be cutting all State spending savagely. When he got his original £54 million from Labour's Roy Mason, he did so on the basis that he would ask for no more. When he got the extra £14 million from Humphrey Atkins, he agreed there was no further obligation and would ask for no more. Now he had another £10 million and was promising he would ask for no more. He had yet to sell a single car, or repay the British government its first penny, except insofar as his growing band of workers in Belfast paid taxes.

The car project was now moving rapidly toward its crucial test, the climax of seven years of planning, money raising, hiring, firing, and intriguing: the launch of the car. By sheer hard work, plus a great deal of inventiveness and innovation, the men at Dunmurry were producing cars off the production line. They were months behind schedule, the cars were relatively untested, they should have had months of quarantine for the early bugs to be sorted out—but there was no time for any of that. By the end of February production was running at twenty units a day—enough to begin preparing a shipload. And so on February 20 the first cars began arriving on Belfast docks, ready for their journey across the Atlantic. John DeLorean's dream was heading for the market at last. But not, alas, without problems. The engineering difficulties had not simply gone away. In the last months before production, and even while the car was coming off the production line, Mike Loasby and his team, plus the Lotus people and anyone else who knew anything about engineering, had been trying desperately to make good the defects.

On February 17 a memo from Peter Allinson, one of the more experienced engineers, painted a worried and gloomy picture of various aspects of the car. When he got to its certification in the United States, however, he voiced his real concern. Because of the "shortcomings" he believed the car "currently being certified will not be acceptable. . . . There is now a serious question with regard to vehicle weight which has not yet been fully recognized. Cars are being built to a different specification from the one they are being certified at."

Allinson's fear was that the cars now being loaded at Belfast docks were not actually certified for use on the American roads, that the certification had been done for a different weight car, with different emission specifications, and that the engine was not performing up to the standards the EPA had been led to believe. If his fears were confirmed, the project was heading for disaster even now, because there was no time for recertification.

Early in February, after much argument and some initial failure, two cars were tested by the EPA in Michigan and approved, the automatic on 21 miles per gallon and the manual on 23, giving a rating of 22.5 miles per gallon. Allinson was still concerned that there had been so many changes to the car even on the production line, that the certification might not cover what was now being produced. His discussions with friends in the EPA increased his doubts. "Lotus has said that the Fuel Economy Label is approved. EPA has advised that it is not." By now he and Loasby were reading something more sinister into it all. Chapman's cash-flow problems had become so apparent at Lotus that they believed he was deliberately spinning out the DeLorean program to keep the money coming in. At this stage the DMC project accounted for nearly half its revenues.

Allinson wrote:

> The current political situation between Lotus and D.M.C. is delaying completion of the programme.
>
> 1. I believe Lotus are deliberately withholding information that would prevent us from completing our programme. I have requested information on the specification details on at least six occasions, without obtaining the information. I have been told that the fuel economy label info is in the post—it has not arrived.
>
> 2. I believe that we will not see a certificate of conformity if the political situation is not resolved. It is a too-powerful bargaining tool.

His point was that once Lotus passed over that certificate, the Chapman firm had no further role in the DMC-12 car. There would be no more cash. While the certificate was still in the pipeline, the payments still flowed. But as Allinson wrote this and sent a copy to Don Lander, the cars were winding their way out the factory gates, through the streets of Belfast, to the docks beside the giant crane of the Harland and Wolff shipyard, where once the *Titanic* had come down the slipway. They were already on the way to the United States. A memo as powerful as this from the manager of safety and emissions, Allinson's position, should have given someone pause for thought. Instead the cars were loaded hastily into the ship and it weighed anchor four days later. It would be up to Dick Brown to sort out what problems he could at the other end before the cars found their way into the showrooms and eventually into the hands of customers. It was not a prepossessing sendoff.

13

BOBBY SANDS

On April 20 the first batch of 400 DeLorean cars set sail for Long Beach, California, well behind schedule. Adam Butler sent a message of congratulation, but pointed out too that the company's task now was to demonstrate to both taxpayers and private investors that "their faith in the project has been justified." Gene Cafiero in Belfast made a little speech to the effect that "the effort of the work force has been outstanding." There were now over 1,000 men in the Dunmurry factory, and under Don Lander's experienced hand the production line was beginning to settle into some sort of rhythm. But everyone, management and workers, Catholic and Protestant, was increasingly listening for news coming out of the hospital room where the IRA man Bobby Sands lay on a waterbed covered in sheepskins, lifesaving equipment standing by should either he or his family request it.

Sands had already become a hero to the Catholic population. Soon he would be what the IRA needed badly: a martyr. His fame was spreading into the circles the IRA wanted. Senator Edward Kennedy called on Britain to make "new and urgent efforts" to halt the hunger strike. Former U.S. Attorney General Ramsey Clark arrived at the Maze prison but was refused permission to see Sands. The Pope sent his personal secretary, Monsignor John Magee, and he saw Sands twice but could not persuade him to end his hunger strike. Prince Charles, on a trip to Venezuela, was handed a petition by eleven U.S. Congressmen asking him to use his "good offices as heir apparent to the throne to intercede." Soon, however, nobody could help Sands —he went into a coma and in the early hours of May 5 he died.

It was just after 1:30 on that Tuesday morning when the news reached Twinbrook. At first there was only the banging of a single garbage can lid. Within seconds it was a pandemonium of noise and blazing lights as the entire Catholic population of the housing project on the edge of the DeLorean factory poured out onto the streets. The noise of clanging garbage can lids spread on toward central Belfast, through Andersontown and the Falls Road until the whole of the capital was awake. Around the Province the same scene was taking place in Londonderry, Strabane, Newry, and every other town or village that had a large enough Catholic population to make itself heard. Protestants bolted their doors and stayed inside. They dreaded and feared what they knew was about to happen.

No one in the whole of Northern Ireland that night needed to be told what the noise meant. It was the signal for which the Province had been waiting for days: Bobby Sands, twenty-seven-year-old IRA man and Member of Parliament for Fermanagh and South Tyrone, had died after sixty-five days on hunger strike in the Maze prison. For the British security forces, it was one of the worst setbacks they had suffered in a decade of fighting the IRA, bringing as it did a new wave of bombings, shootings, and civil unrest; for the IRA it was a major propaganda victory, demonstrating to the world what the IRA had failed to do until that moment—that its members believed in their cause sufficiently to die for it. For John DeLorean it was an irresistible opportunity to ask for more money for a factory that had become more caught up in Northern Ireland politics than ever.

The death of Sands was of special importance for the work force at the DeLorean factory. If the IRA man had a home at all other than the Maze and the streets of Belfast, it was Twinbrook. His mother lived there, within sight of the car factory. Sands himself had spent some of his teenage years there. He had friends, relatives, and supporters, many of them on the DeLorean payroll, living in Twinbrook.

That night the DeLorean factory was locked and silent, the security guards keeping out of sight so as to provide no provocation. For weeks the management had been preparing for this very night, taking what precautions they could. "We knew that the center of the demonstration was going to be fairly close to us," says Shaun Harte. "But we felt, and I'm sure retrospectively we were right, that the target of the fury wasn't going to be the DeLorean factory, but rather the situation in which this had happened in Twinbrook. And the first thing that comes up in their sights that isn't theirs is good for a target." It was to be less than an hour later that the factory came into the rioters' sights. Already in the distance from central Belfast and the Catholic areas, the violence had taken root. The sounds of spontaneous riots in the Falls Road, New Lodge, and Antrim Road areas of Belfast could be heard (and seen) above the tumult in Twinbrook. By 2 A.M., forty-three minutes after the final flicker of life had passed from Sands' emaciated body, swathed in bandages to prevent his bones from piercing the skin, the whole of Belfast seemed to be caught up in the worst blaze of violence it had seen for years.

The main gate of the DeLorean factory was formidable enough to turn back the first halfhearted onslaught. The security men were out of sight and reach, and there was nothing inside within gasoline-bomb throwing distance that would burn. The gate on the Twinbrook side, however, was a flimsier affair. A bunch of the more hotheaded rioters broke away from Twinbrook, grabbed an old car, and drove at high speed at the gate. The lock gave and the mob was inside the DeLorean compound. Not very far inside, however. The factory had been well designed and it presented a formidable obstacle to any such incident. It had two fences—the rioters were now inside the outer one. The inner gate, made of sturdier stuff, held. But just inside it was a row of temporary wooden huts, occupying the approximate area of two tennis courts. A few weeks later, when the main buildings were complete, these huts would have been gone, their occupants and contents housed in the comfort of properly constructed buildings. That night they made an irresistible target for the youths. Within seconds gasoline bombs, mixed with paint to make the blazing mass adhere better to the target, were being lobbed over the fence to land on the flat roofs of the huts. "They burned like fun," says a DeLorean executive. No one in the factory had a hope of putting it out. The fire brigade was called out, but by the time it arrived, the fires had taken hold and the wooden buildings were burning well. The violence of Northern Ireland had finally entered the world of John DeLorean.

The press soon descended on Northern Ireland. For the next few days, the death of the first IRA hunger striker dominated world news and the Belfast riots were echoed by demonstrations from Irish-Americans all over the United States. The focus of it all was Twinbrook, a modern and well-laid-out housing project perched on a small hill which ran down to the edge of the seventy-two-acre DeLorean site, where the Sands family lived. As John DeLorean observed the angry mood spreading through the United States, a plan began to crystallize.

When he heard the news just before midnight at home, at first he appeared shaken, his almost pathological fear of the IRA confirmed. He was in the office early the next morning to read the first damage reports. It was some hours before his old trick of turning every disadvantage to an advantage came to his rescue.

At 8:30 that morning Shaun Harte walked into the Park Avenue office to learn of the fire damage to the factory. He was in New York on business unrelated to Bobby Sands, but DeLorean quickly summoned him to a conference. All the engineering drawings had apparently been lost, said DeLorean, who had just heard from an unruffled Lander. How serious was that for the car project? he asked Harte, who was the coordinator of the whole program. Not serious, said Harte instantly. "There is a set at Lotus and I know where they are— we can get them. In any case we took the precaution from the beginning of keeping a spare set filed away offsite. That's no real problem." From the information that had so far arrived, Harte thought it was the prefabricated huts on the edge of the site that had been destroyed —the factory itself would not burn easily. What else was kept there? DeLorean asked. Harte tried to recall. There were personnel records —that would be a nuisance because they were busy interviewing new recruits as the factory rapidly expanded, and all the forms and records would almost certainly be in the burned huts. There was a computer terminal too, he remembered, but not the computer itself. More seriously, there were purchasing records and much of the systems work— that could all be reconstructed but it would be an irritant.

Harte recalls that DeLorean still appeared grim that morning, but at the end of the fairly reassuring assessment, he relaxed a little. "How quickly can we get things moving again?" he asked. Harte couldn't tell from the limited information available, but he was optimistic. DeLorean's mind soon turned to costs—was the factory insured? Could they claim damages from the British government? During the day, his plans became steadily more ambitious.

By the following morning the full extent of the damage had been analyzed and it was much less than first feared. The huts were lost, but they were only temporary structures anyway. There were some word processors and a computer terminal, filing cabinets, and other office furniture. All the personnel records had been lost, but that did not affect production. The records of job interviews had been burned and the interviews had to be repeated. But not all the huts were burned to the ground—only the ones nearest the fence; the others were still half standing. Mike Loasby's office was badly damaged, the door burned right through, but many of his papers were no more than singed. George Broomfield's production engineering department had already moved out, although some of their records were destroyed. The purchasing department had its own set of drawings in Coventry, and Loasby now reclaimed them. "It really didn't cause more than a hiccup," said Loasby.

For DeLorean it was enough. The damage could be made to sound very serious indeed. He watched the groundswell of anti-British feeling build up around him in New York, dominating the news broadcasts. The British, he decided, were in their weakest position ever. No one was going to argue with him now. Bobby Sands was just being buried when he laid out his plan to his team of Cafiero, Stark, Kimmerly, Lander, and Haddad, followed up in a May 7 memo to Haddad: "Today DMC is faced with the greatest opportunity of your corporate lifetime. With the troubles in Twinbrook/Belfast for the first time in our tenure there, *no single person in UK begrudges us the $160,000,000 we got from the government! Most today think we've earned it!"*

For DeLorean there was no tragedy—only an opportunity to press his claim for more money. "The government who dealt with us in bad faith, and in effect made us borrow $50,000,000 that they owed us, is in a position where they must become responsive to our needs."

A few months ago Hopkins had turned the tables on him. Now it was his turn:

> We should become the industrial heroes of the UK—bringing jobs and prestige to an area all Britains now agree is uninhabitable. The government should throw money at us to expand and continue. Our failure today would doom Northern Ireland industrially forever and cost the government another billion or two dollars. We have a chance to become competent, professional benefactors in the eyes of our customers throughout the world. An image worth more than an infinity of advertising. In short, this is the single, great opportunity to give our company the ultimate shining image and provide all of the finances we will ever need—but 60 days from now it will be too late.

He was right. At that moment the British government was in a mood to give him anything, as the world protest gathered pace. On the day of Bobby Sands' funeral he dispatched Haddad to Belfast. "Upon due consideration you should plan on moving to Belfast for at least the next six months. Take your wife and child with you. Plan to stay there and help get this job done."

Bill Haddad had been in and out of Belfast since the hunger strikes started and had developed his contacts in Queen's University in Belfast and in the city's political world. He had some understanding of the political tension the Sands death had created. But this was something more than a strategic decision. It was punishment. DeLorean himself hated and feared Belfast and would have done a great deal to avoid the fate he was now ordaining for his public relations man.

The reasons for his annoyance with Haddad were similar to his reasons for falling out with Strycker: Haddad was making a nuisance of himself by querying and objecting to his new master plan. Most of the other directors were objecting to it too, but Haddad was the most outspoken—in fact he seemed to have become the spokesman for the others. During the hunger strike Haddad had been in Belfast often, spending weeks at a time there. He brought back with him the complaints of those who would be affected by the new plan, and that basically included all the senior men.

DeLorean himself was very pleased with the plan. He had decided he would not issue more shares in DMC after all. He was still annoyed that NIDA had shares in it, for one thing. So he decided he would float an entirely new company, a holding company that would be the new parent for DMC. Haddad had 100,000 options in DMC—they would now become worthless, since the shares would never be issued. Gene Cafiero had 500,000 options worth a potential $5 million that would also become worthless. Stark had options, as did Lander and Bob Dewey and most of the others. It had been DeLorean's method of tempting them in: big salaries but also options on shares in the business. Now he was proposing to take them all away.

He had finally found an investment bank that would handle the issue for him: Bache Halsey Stuart Shields, one of the biggest houses on Wall Street. The new company would be called DeLorean Motor Holdings and it would buy out the Oppenheimer limited partners, issuing them shares in the new company. And it would give John DeLorean himself well over half the shares. Bache was already estimating $12 to $14 a share, which would make DeLorean personally worth $120 to $140 million. Oppenheimer would get another fee of

$2.4 million (on top of the $2 million they already had) for organizing the buying out of the partners. The dealers, on whom the whole project would soon depend as the cars arrived in the U.S., would be left in DMC. And so would the British government.

Haddad became the spokesman for the others, not unwillingly. He was the man with the easiest access to DeLorean when he was in New York, and he was less awed by him than the others, less bound by the Detroit tradition that you don't argue with the boss. Haddad's initial protests were met with technical explanations that it was very difficult to get new equity into a company because the Oppenheimer partners had a lien on 23.4 percent of the profits, that it was impossible to get the DMC balance sheet into the right shape for a flotation, and that this method was cleaner, better for everyone. Haddad switched his attack to the position of the auto dealers who had bought shares in DMC and would not be brought into the holding company.

"They are going to open up the paper," he told DeLorean, "and see that DeLorean is going public, and then they are going to realize that they have been motored, just at the time when the car is coming over and we need their excitement. John, we need their anticipation and their excitement. The dealers really like you, there is no two ways about that. But this is a bad idea."

DeLorean was hearing the same from others and eventually he acquiesced, deciding to offer the dealers shares in the new DeLorean Motor Holding Company in exchange for their shares in DeLorean Motor Company. Haddad, however, still pursued the issue of the senior executives, who would be left out in the cold with their worthless options.

Haddad commented:

> That really created a furor in Belfast. The auto industry is very much like the Japanese—you work for only one company. A lot of these guys gave up a lot to come and work for him and they were very talented people and they were very upset. Everybody was. In New York too. These guys were ruining good careers and giving up pension plans. They took a risk with John and now he was depriving them of their equity. And they all talked to me privately, and I became the spokesperson for that group. Everybody regarded me as eyes and ears for John, an extension of John, and at first I was getting stripped-down versions of what was

happening. But being a fairly good newspaperman, I slowly penetrated deep enough.

It was only days before Bobby Sands died that Haddad, just back from a trip to Belfast, where he had again picked up a chorus of dissatisfaction, had a major confrontation with DeLorean. He had already sent him a memo, and DeLorean had not bothered to reply. Now they had it out face to face.

"First of all," DeLorean told him, "what we are doing is legally necessary. We've been through all that before. Secondly, you are misrepresenting the attitude of everyone. You say they are all upset. Well, they are not upset. You know, Bill, you are full of shit. It's you who are upset. You're the only one who's upset."

Haddad held his ground. "Guys worked like hell over there," he told DeLorean. "And they really are very upset. I've talked to them. You've destroyed their morale."

In the aftermath of Sands' death, DeLorean decided to kill two birds with one stone. Sending Haddad to Belfast would keep him out of harm's way in New York and it would almost certainly get him out of the company altogether. No one, he believed, would stay in Belfast for long—and certainly not Bill Haddad, accustomed as he was to the high life of New York and Washington. At the same time Haddad could be used to follow up the advantage the IRA man's death gave him. The scenes of the funeral that day convinced him the British government would put up no serious opposition to a request for more money.

In Belfast between 50,000 and 70,000 mourners turned up by train, bus, or car to honor the dead Republican. The funeral service was held at St. Lukes in Twinbrook, only 200 yards from the small whitewashed row house where the Sands family lived, and not much farther from the DeLorean factory. A third of the DeLorean work force did not report that day, the highest absentee rate the factory ever had.

Outside the church nearly every house in Twinbrook flew a black flag, most of them clearly visible from the factory. It was another miserable day of driving rain and wind which relentlessly swept the battered Province. A masked bugler and two pipers marched in front of the coffin as it wended its slow way to the cemetery of Milltown, a two-mile procession following behind the hearse. The IRA provided the guard of honor, seven sinister men in battledress, hoods, and black berets. Sands' own black beret and gloves rested on top of the coffin, which was draped in the Irish tricolor.

That was the scene American viewers saw on their TV screens that night. John DeLorean's request for more money had already gone to the British government. This time there was no real opposition. In the climate of Northern Ireland and particularly of West Belfast, the threatened closure of the factory would have been unthinkable. "We lost 60 percent of our offices, our vital engineering records, our MOS data, our NP purchasing records, and our employment records," said DeLorean. "Enough to put any business on its knees. We lost the equivalent of two or three weeks' production, with more losses to come, as a result of the violence and unrest." It was nonsense—his excuse for the claim. Within two weeks he had his money—£7 million more, bringing the total to £85 million.

Again it was Adam Butler who announced it. "For some while following the fire, manning and productivity levels were severely reduced because of disturbances in the vicinity of the factory," he told the House of Commons on May 22. "The disruption of production and shipment of cars had adversely affected the company's cash flow." So, to help out, the government agreed to provide another "time limited guarantee" of £7 million to overcome this problem. Again he faced the anger of Jock Bruce-Gardyne from his own benches and of Bob Cryer from the Labour benches across the other side of the House. But the Sands episode had thus accomplished for DeLorean what months of steady attrition had failed to do. Once again NIDA felt undermined by the ministers, who took the decision over their heads. The British government had not exactly thrown money at DeLorean as he had predicted, but it had been exceptionally generous on grounds that were spurious at best. Hopkins complained bitterly that Atkins and Butler had not even asked for NIDA's view on the matter before agreeing to give DeLorean the money, and made no attempt to extract further conditions from DeLorean himself.

Three weeks after the death of Bobby Sands everything had returned to normal. There were further incidents as other hunger strikers followed Sands and died in the Maze, but they weren't from Twinbrook. The factory by now was better protected. The top gate, where the rioters had broken through from Twinbrook, was welded up and never used again for vehicles—pedestrians could still get in and out during working hours. A heavy steel beam was welded across the doors of the assembly building low down, so that the low-slung DMC-12 cars could get out underneath it, but a heavy truck would be decapitated if it made an attempt to smash through into the plant itself.

In the days following Sands' death, the more dedicated trouble-makers became better organized. Their aim was always to cause enough of a nuisance to bring out the Army and the police. On the day of the funeral, for example, Northern Ireland's own patented slingshots came into their own. Late that evening a group of youths gathered on an empty knoll on the edge of the plant. They hammered two stakes into the ground and slung a pair of pantyhose between them. Then bottles full of the gasoline-paint mixture were fitted in the crotch, pulled back, and sent whizzing off into the night, high over the wire fence of the factory. The plant was pretty safe from this form of attack, the bombs falling harmlessly on the test track or smashing off the concrete walls or asbestos roofs. As the days length-ened—and in Belfast in midsummer it is still bright past eleven o'clock—the attacks slackened, their effect wearing off. The Army stayed clear, for the most part preferring to avoid provocation, and the security guards and management also stayed out of sight. "Once when the bombers got a bit obnoxious, the Army came in," recalls Shaun Harte. "But mostly what they did was to lob their bombs onto the test track where they had a good flame-up for a while and then the whole thing died down. If we brushed the glass off before we tested the cars the next day, there wasn't much problem." There were a few shots in the air during this period too, but no evidence that anyone was ever singled out to be shot at—just stray bullets from minor battles elsewhere in the area. Says Harte, "It was pretty edgy around Belfast particularly at night, for the next three weeks. And after that it went away altogether." It was to be John DeLorean's only real encounter with violence in Northern Ireland. By the time it had run its desultory course he had his money.

While DeLorean was successfully negotiating the new cash injec-tion from the British government, an almost unnoticed but nonethe-less major event occurred in California. The first shipload of cars arrived—379 of them. There were references to the project's "acid test." The lawyers working on the prospectus for the complicated stock issue could now see the car for themselves and test consumer and industry reaction. The dream was not only built, but it was ready to be driven. Well, not quite ready. In fact, as Dick Brown soon discovered, it was very far from ready.

Brown had set up two Quality Assurance Centers—in Bridgewater, New Jersey, and Santa Ana, California. He organized the operation well: the cars were either delivered to Wilmington, Delaware (cost $370 per car), or sailed through the Panama Canal to arrive in Long Beach ($470 per car). They were subject to import duties, but only modestly: less than 3 percent. Just outside Wilmington, on a thirty-acre site, Brown organized a third 40,000-square-foot facility. The cars were brought to these centers, thoroughly checked over, and then shipped by truck to the dealers. The idea was not just to give them a predelivery check, but to road-test them, safety-check them, and give the stainless-steel shells a good polish. Brown was apprehensive before the first cars arrived, anticipating that the inexperienced work force in Belfast, working against the clock, might not have produced the quality a $25,000 car was expected to have. Nothing, however, prepared him for the reality.

"If you were a dealer and you had seen the cars as they came in initially," he said later, "you would have—you know, if you didn't have faith in this guy, you would have just walked out the door and said, 'Hey! We can't sell this shit!'

"And that's exactly what it was. Shit. I'll tell you what it looked like. It looked like somebody put a hand grenade in the front seat and the back seat and then set them off. All the guts were out. You couldn't ride in them. You looked in the window and all the components were just stuffed in. They weren't built in, they were stuffed in. Doors wouldn't function. Electronics wouldn't function. We had to redesign and retool some parts here just to make the car salable."

Brown hired teams to rebuild the car more or less from scratch, though as the work force in Belfast gained experience, the cars were better made. In June and July Brown's team sometimes worked around the clock. He was only too aware of what would happen if any of the cars went out to dealers and customers as they had been delivered.

The cost of the operation was enormous. Nearly $700,000 was spent in June—$2,178 per car. In July it was $2,914 a car, another $746,000. In August it dropped just below $2,000 a car for another $1 million. In those three months alone, the company had spent $2.5 million just for quality control on cars that should already have been up to standard.

When the cars got to the auto journals for testing, they did not have a smooth ride either, althouth in retrospect the DMC-12 got off surprisingly easily. Don Sherman, technical director of *Car & Driver*, wondered whether "the firm will exist a year from now" because of the quality-control problems, although he praised the car's handling and the "boldness" of John DeLorean's whole project. Sherman, one of the United States' most respected auto journalists, complained that he felt "entombed" when he first sat in a DeLorean car. He had tested it in Belfast earlier in the year and thought those early models were "abysmally short of any commercial standard of acceptability." He went on: "Switches popped loose, parts fell off, the rattles had squeaks, doors jammed shut, doors refused to latch, and windows fell out of their tracks. What's worse, there wasn't a single car, either in our entourage or up and down the long assembly line, that you could point to and say, 'this is a perfect (or even acceptable) door-to-body fit.' "

Sherman was fairly sympathetic. He pointed out in DeLorean's defense that the first 500 units had been pressed out on prototype tooling—the production tooling had not yet arrived. If the car's problems could be solved, Sherman told an *Irish Times* reporter, the DeLorean firm would have a bright future. But if the car turned out to be deficient in a U.S. market in which high quality was vital, it would run "the risk of being cast into oblivion within a short time." On Park Avenue, Mike Knepper in the public relations department was busily countering the Sherman article, insisting that there had been "considerable refinement to the car" since Sherman tested an early model.

Sherman's doubts, and those of other auto critics, did not affect the sales of the car in those early days—at least not badly. There had been so much publicity and so much talk about it over the years that buyers could not wait for it. By early July, when Brown reluctantly allowed the first cars out of his Quality Assurance Centers and sent them to the showrooms, some dealers were reporting waiting lists of from two months to a year or more. One dealer reported more than 200 names on his list, although he would receive only twenty cars by December. Brown was trying to get cars to all the 345 dealers as soon as possible, but he knew he could not release any without doing substantial work on them first. By the first week in July, the 1,000th car had rolled off the line in Belfast. Dealers all around America were reporting that the cars were commanding a premium—in many cases up to $5,000 and sometimes even more.

It was a euphoric beginning to the sales campaign, brushing aside for a while the gloom that had haunted the engineers and production men in Belfast and causing even Brown, still desperately worried about quality, to relax a bit. In its August 13 issue, *Automotive News* surveyed the sales scene, talking to dealers around the country. The picture seemed to be the same everywhere—supply could not keep up with demand. The DMC-12 was a roaring success. "Our list is so long that even with a good deposit the wait will be two to three months," said George Attelt, general manager of Jerry Goodwin Dodge, Fullerton, California. "We're only expecting about twenty more cars through the end of this year, after which the supply will be better." *Auto News* quoted Wayne Jones, sales manager for Melrose Ford, Oakland, California, as saying that his dealership had more than fifty DeLorean customers on its waiting list, each of whom had put $5,000 down even though some of them faced a ten-month wait. "Before McInnis Peterson Chevrolet in Baton Rouge," said *Auto News*, "had advertised the DeLorean, it had a list of ten customers who each deposited $3,000." On the West Coast, where most of the early cars had been delivered, new DeLoreans were reportedly fetching $30,000, with actual prices at individual dealerships ranging from $25,950 to $31,000. The DeLorean sales team was worried about the premiums. "There's nothing we can legally do to hold down the prices," said Jack Fearer, one of Brown's team. "We set the manufacturer's suggested retail price at $25,000 and that's about it." Fearer reported some customers using the long waiting period for personal gain by selling their places on dealers' waiting lists.

In that same issue *Auto News* carried a little boxed item that epitomized this brief period of euphoric sales. The first secondhand DeLorean turned up on the used-car lot of Ellis Motor Company of Maplewood, a suburb of St. Louis. Its price: $33,900. It is the highest recorded price asked for a DMC-12.

The cars were being built, shipped, rebuilt again by Dick Brown, and finally sold. It seemed the project was a success. It was actually working after all that sweat, worry, heartache, and battling. NIDA even got a royalty check—a modest £205,000, representing £185 a car on the first 1,100 cars sold to dealers. Cars were now coming off the line at 175 a week, the factory in Belfast employed 1,600 people, and in the United States dealers were reporting that just having a DeLorean in their showroom meant that their "floor traffic was fantastic."

All seemed to be well with the DeLorean dream. Or was it? Where was DeLorean during this phase? Once again he was busy with activities that occupied him during the entire project, from the first day to the last: raising money. But he was also doing some spending—some very extravagant spending.

While Bobby Sands was starving himself to death and new IRA hunger strikers were joining him in this new form of protest in the Maze, DeLorean was busily shopping for yet another new home for himself, Cristina, and the children. He was moving up again, intent on getting into the best social set. For over a year he scoured his favorite magazines for a suitable house, bid for several, and went to see others. In the late spring of 1981 he found it: 430 acres in Bedminster, New Jersey, with a three-story, twenty-five-room mansion. It was a beautiful place and DeLorean paid big money for it: $3.5 million. But he wanted changes, and a landscape architect named John Smith was contracted to produce a "grand design" complete with swimming pools, tennis court, fountains, gazebos, and a stone boathouse.

Cristina later claimed the house was bought principally with her money. It wasn't. It was bought by an offshore corporation named TK International. The initials stood for Tom Kimmerly, and Kimmerly later admitted that TK International was a "personal corporation" which purchased the Bedminster estate so that DeLorean could make a tax-free exchange of other property. What property? And why did he need to avoid taxes so much at that stage since his only source of income was his salary from DeLorean Motor Company? Where did he suddenly get another $3.5 million?

TK International assumes an extra degree of significance for this reason: at the end of 1980 Bill Haddad claims to have strayed upon evidence indicating that roughly $9 million of the money that went to GPD was funneled back again into TK. Haddad certainly believed that the purchase of the New Jersey house was made with GPD money. Kimmerly, however, denied it, insisting no GPD assets were involved.

At any rate, the DeLoreans had a new home, although not without a haunting echo of other days. In a lawsuit, the architect John Smith charged that DeLorean did not pay him for his landscaping. DeLorean claimed that Smith had gone over budget. "My original impression was that he was a gentleman with great ideas and expectations," said Smith later. "I liked him. At first."

The new house was only a sideline, a minor pleasantry in the serious business of getting the new DeLorean Motor Holdings launched despite the obvious and growing antipathy from his own executives, voiced openly by Haddad, but more keenly by Cafiero, who would lose options valued at $5 million in the deal. Now Tom Kimmerly, already close to DeLorean, came into his own.

It was Kimmerly, the small-time Detroit lawyer whose three-man firm—Kimmerly, Gans, and Shaler—was still based in Bloomfield Hills, who took charge of the enormous job of preparing the legal documents and SEC prospectuses. The fees on this project were high by any standards—except, it seems, Kimmerly's. "I started Mazda U.S.," said Dick Brown, "and my fees for outside counsel were about $10,000 a month. DeLorean's were about $1.5 million a year. I thought the Paul Weiss fees in particular were astronomical." Kimmerly disagreed: "I use a rule of thumb that one-half percent of a company's gross should be spent on professionals. Since we were start-up, I cut that in half. Bear in mind that we were looking for a $400-to-$500-million annual gross."

Even at the time of peak sales for the DMC-12, John DeLorean was spending more on lawyers fees than he was on advertising. In this period the car may have been selling at a premium, but once Dick Brown's Quality Assurance costs, plus extra interest charges and other costs directly related to the delay in getting the car onto the market, had been added on there was still only a large trading loss. But DeLorean was going for his biggest deal yet, his eyes now intent on the flotation that would show the world his paper worth of $120 million.

The issue taking shape under Kimmerly's organization was a complex one. The new DeLorean Motor Holdings would be an umbrella parent corporation, but at the same time it was floated, the DeLorean Research Limited Partnership put together by Oppenheimer would be bought out and so, now, would all other holders of DeLorean Motor Company stock—the dealers, NIDA, Wood Gundy, and of course Johnny Carson. All would exchange their stock in DMC for new stock in the new company. Options on stock in DMC, which is what had tempted Cafiero, Haddad, Lander, Stark, and others into the company in the first place, would be worthless. Complex it might be, but from John DeLorean's point of view it would make his corporate empire considerably tidier and consolidate his own position at the top of it. Although NIDA was fighting to retain its rights as laid down in the master agreement, some of the original restrictive consents, so niggling to DeLorean, would inevitably be diluted or disappear.

DeLorean would also be freed from royalty payment obligations to the original Sports Car Partnership investors, and the Oppenheimer partnership's right to 23.4 percent of profits would end, albeit at a high price. The figures show just how expensive this money had become: the 125 partners found by Oppenheimer put in $18.7 million. This became a net $15.5 million after Oppenheimer's $2 million fee, Javits and Javits' legal costs, and DeLorean's own charges. Of this, some $1.3 million went, according to the Holdings prospectus, to "ERM process work." The rest went to GPD. Less than three years after that money, which was not needed anyway since the Northern Ireland government had offered to fill the gap with a cheap loan, was put up, DeLorean was now proposing to buy out the partners and offering them a total (assuming a price of $12 a share) of nearly $50 million. On top of that, Oppenheimer would get another fee of $2.4 million if it could persuade all 125 partners to accept. If the original Oppenheimer money had actually gone into the car project, which it never did, DeLorean would still have raised $15.5 million and repaid it three years later at a cost of over $52 million. Yet even then there were very few who suspected John DeLorean might have had a different motive for raising that Oppenheimer money. It never entered the mind of Mike Hayes or the sophisticated, market-hardened men at One New York Plaza, where the Oppenheimer men were blinded by the charisma of John DeLorean (or was it by the size of the fees he brought with him?), to question that motive.

Paul Weiss Rifkind Wharton & Garrison, the large New York firm which had been at the center of DeLorean's deal with Northern Ireland, was the lead counsel in the new offering. But Alan Cohen, who played so central a role in the original Belfast negotiations and to whom Walter Strycker had turned for advice, had gone, suddenly withdrawing his partnership after the Strycker affair. American Lawyer reported that one associate who worked closely with him said that associates knew nothing about the decision until a departure memo was circulated the day he left, although Paul Weiss corporate partner Seymour Hertz said, "It had nothing to do with DeLorean."

A formidable battery of New York's best-known lawyers worked on the prospectus through that summer. For the modest little lawyer from Detroit, it was exceptionally gratifying to be surrounded by "attorneys from some of the most sophisticated and prestigious firms in the country." Kimmerly recalled later: "There would invariably be thirty to forty people in the conference room for these sessions, most of them lawyers." Oppenheimer of course was back in the picture because of the proposed buyout of the limited partners and it was represented by Carl Bornmann of Cahill Gordon & Reindel. Bache Halsey Stuart Shields was the underwriter, and it had retained Sullivan and Cromwell, represented at the meetings by Norris Darrell, soon characterized by the others as a "stickler" about disclosure, at one stage causing a DeLorean man to remark that he was "single-handedly jeopardizing the venture."

That was the basic team working on the prospectus, but they all had assistants, deputies, partners, and helpers. The team met regularly in the conference room at 280 Park Avenue, Kimmerly always present. For the most part, despite Darrell's continual probings, there was a mood of something more than ordinary optimism. The car and John DeLorean were big news. It would be a big issue.

There were, of course, some intrusions to jar the air of euphoria. Bill Haddad, more and more opposed to the issue, got his own legal opinion suggesting that the draft prospectus he had managed to get hold of violated Rule 10-b-5, the SEC regulation requiring disclosure of all material information. He sent a copy of his memo to Paul Weiss and to Bache. Darrell acknowledged he had seen a copy (Hertz of Paul Weiss said he did not recall ever seeing it). Haddad later charged that he was fired by DeLorean for calling the prospectus false and misleading and stating that it made serious omissions concerning safety deficiencies, lack of quality control, and "possible wrongdoing in the engagement of GPD Services."

There is evidence that the Haddad memo was discussed by the lawyers as they worked on the prospectus. Their principal concern appeared to be safety. Haddad had found an ally in Mike Loasby, or perhaps it was the other way around—Loasby thought he could get some of his concern across through Haddad since he had failed to do so in every other way. So Haddad picked up some of the concern among the engineers in Belfast and in Norwich, but he barely scratched the surface of it. However, cautious Darrell, the biggest skeptic among the lawyers, called on a DeLorean dealer and test-drove the car. Brown's Quality-Assurance Centers were reassuring factors, and the lawyers gradually accepted that early problems were being rectified (which to some extent was true, although design faults remained). The prospectus eventually included a meaningless criticism of the car to the effect that "commentary to date . . . has included criticism in respect of certain aspects of the DeLorean, such as the driver's field of view and the acceleration rate."

The early draft prospectus showed a simple corporate structure with the new Holdings company at the top, DMC directly underneath as a wholly owned subsidiary, and then two arms from DMC off to the Belfast company and to Composite Technology. Some of the lawyers became concerned by the GPD allegations and by the fact that the principal shareholder in the new company would not be John DeLorean personally, but the DeLorean Manufacturing Company, which in turn was wholly owned by a Nevada-registered company called Cristina. DeLorean owned 100 percent of Cristina. Those ramifications appeared in later prospectuses.

While all this was going on, John DeLorean was making life harder and harder for Bill Haddad. Haddad had gone to Belfast just after the death of Sands and had stayed there most of the time since. He was ill with stomach trouble much of the time he was in Belfast, but DeLorean did not let up. "John kept the pressure up," recalls a DeLorean official. "He sent him a memo saying, 'You came back Concorde although you shouldn't have. We will charge you!' "

DeLorean would later say that one of the reasons he fired Haddad was that he wouldn't go to Belfast. "I practically lived in Belfast," says Haddad. He initially resisted going, since his job was obviously in New York. But DeLorean insisted, "and in the end I said, 'Yes, I will go to Belfast,' and took the family. That shook him up. I decided to call his bluff. But he had us all over a barrel." It was only a matter of time before his leading critic would depart, and DeLorean knew it.

At the end of May DeLorean summoned Tony Hopkins to New York to tell him and the other directors about the issue. Hopkins immediately raised objections, all of which were settled after arguments that went back and forth over the next month, except one point. Hopkins insisted that DeLorean agree not to sell his own shares in the new company for two years. It seemed simple enough: if the company was so great, why would he want to sell them? DeLorean exploded and there were furious communications across the Atlantic.

In the NIDA office, the more DeLorean protested, the more determined they became not to give in. If he was making such a fuss, clearly he *did* want to sell his shares. And if he wanted to sell them after the issue, something must be wrong. On June 23 DeLorean broke off negotiations altogether, saying he was going ahead regardless of NIDA.

It was a letter from Ken Bloomfield, the cool, able Permanent Secretary of the Department of Commerce, that brought him back to his senses. At the end of July Bloomfield wrote, "I'm sorry you've broken off negotiations. In these circumstances it will be difficult for the Department to pay over the £3.5 million still outstanding." DeLorean had received only half of the £7 million agreed upon after Bobby Sands' death. The other half was due any day. Hastily he resumed negotiation but it was too late. He had missed the summer window and would now have to wait until the autumn for his issue to go ahead.

In Belfast that summer, the calm professional hand of Don Lander was having its effect. Workers were learning their skills on the production line with only a few weeks' training, but Lander, Broomfield, and the others had installed checking systems and higher standards of quality control. Everyone was still working six or even seven days a week as the work force increased, production was steadily stepped up, and the quality of the car got better. It was still a long way from ideal, but Lander felt that given a bit of time it would shake itself down. The factory was first-class; the production processes, particularly in the body shop, were worked out more or less as the car passed along them, but in a way that made them better rather than worse. The working conditions were ideal and the work force enthusiastic.

From Belfast Haddad kept up a steady flow of memos to DeLorean. He had few replies and was often not even sure DeLorean read them. He proposed a new DeLorean scholarship for Catholics, which he told DeLorean would "solve that problem." The British security forces must have wished it were as simple as that. DeLorean scrawled an OK on the memo and sent it back. Haddad had raised his objections to the new company and lost. Now he concentrated on the safety aspects. But he also, unwittingly, perhaps, fed DeLorean's neurosis about Northern Ireland:

John, I have been here when an angry mob (confronted by police firing plastic bullets into a crowd of teenagers) has tried to rip our gate down, and seen them hurl fire and acid bombs within feet of our executives. I have seen our executives retreat to the manufacturing building to keep things going. I have watched them leave in their unprotected individual cars, passing alongside the unpredictable areas. (And we know that steel tipped sniper bullets have ripped into this place). I have watched them work away under these conditions to try to maintain schedules and meet C.R.'s [Brown's] parts orders, even when the security has repeatedly advised them to evacuate a building.

This was pure fiction of course. Haddad was not even there on the night of Sands' death, which was the only time the gates were really threatened. And no executives were anywhere near them.

In between the rhetoric about the IRA, Haddad did make some good points. He was hearing more and more from the engineers worried about quality. And he was the only executive to raise the issue seriously with DeLorean. Because he was not an engineer, nor even an industrialist, he was actually the least-qualified person to do so, but he did at least listen to the professionals doing the job. At the end of July he wrote Delorean:

With regard to quality, that is not a theoretical question, but one that lends itself to a factual conclusion. Either the cars coming off the end of the line now are of saleable quality or they are not. What began as creative tension between the field and the manufacturer, has now degenerated into an emotional presentation. My suggestion is that the team of you watch Tuesday's production. Carefully examine the cars, determine their strengths and weaknesses, set a program and an authority to deal with the solutions, monitor them in the same manner, and let it lie. If this is not done, you can retard the progress of the company and stall its growing momentum.

Now this was not bad advice. DeLorean and Cafiero were about to arrive and tour the plant with Lander and Broomfield. All were experienced auto men. Why not use that experience to sort out the problems on the line?

DeLorean was not interested in quality at that time—in fact he had a plan that would considerably reduce quality and perhaps contribute more to the bankruptcy of the company than any other decision he ever made. Now that the car was coming off the line, he was impatient with the small numbers envisaged. After all, at Chevrolet he had made over 3 million units annually; in his last year at GM he was in nominal control of 7 million. Against those numbers, what was 20,000 a year? Sometime during this summer he decided that he must go for something more ambitious, more worthy of his new company. At full speed and with enough skilled men working around the clock seven days a week, the production line at Dunmurry could produce far more cars than the 400 a week now planned as the maximum over the next year or so.

Cafiero was opposed to the idea, feeling that the company should not run before it could walk. But he seldom crossed his employer openly, preferring to urge others to do it, watching quietly at board meetings while his own questions were raised by Haddad or NIDA's Hopkins. When DeLorean first raised the question of producing more cars, Lander was violently opposed and that was more serious. He was the man who would have to make them and was now an essential cog in the wheel.

By July, however, DeLorean's plans had taken root. He would double the work force immediately—there were plenty of people available, so there was no problem finding workers, although they would be wholly untrained because all the skilled men had already been hired. The plan had two advantages. First, it would look very impressive in the new stock prospectus—an indication that the prospects were so healthy that the work force, planned at 2,500 after four years, would hit that figure a year after production started. The second advantage also had to do with money—if DeLorean employed 2,500 people in West Belfast and possibly the same number indirectly making components in the rest of Britain, he could exert immense pressure on the British government. When he needed more money for his sedan and for his expansion, he would get it. How could they refuse? It would be as good as the Sands affair. DeLorean seemed to feel that under no circumstances would he be closed down.

It still took some persuasion to get Lander to go along. In fact, he probably never was fully persuaded. From California Dick Brown was reporting that he could sell all the cars he could get. In Belfast the executives felt they were licking the quality-control problems, and were bitter about the money Brown was spending redoing the cars. "He's taking every wheel off just to check if the nuts have been put on," one manager remarked. "All he has to do is kick the wheel." The Dunmurry men felt that Brown was deliberately exaggerating the need for extra work on the cars; he was not universally popular with the Dunmurry management, although the NIDA officials liked him (his Northern Irish ancestry helped).

Later Lander remarked, when the others asked him why he had given in and agreed to increase the work force: "I've said my piece. DeLorean has control of this company and I can now either resign or do what he wants." Lander was not a poor man, and with his reputation he could have easily found another job. But like so many other men in this story, he too gave in.

By late summer DeLorean's stock among the Northern Irish (outside NIDA circles that is) was even higher. It was still a tense time in the Province, but the deaths of the hunger strikers were losing their impact. The British government was gradually regaining the initiative as the public became inured to the awful suffering the IRA men chose for themselves. However, in the context of steadily rising unemployment, another 1,000 jobs at Dunmurry immediately was difficult for anyone to argue with.

Lander accepted the plan to almost double the work force; he also swallowed his annoyance over the flotation of the new Holding company, although he too would lose his options. Cafiero was deciding during this period that he had better get clear; so was Stark who, like previous chief financial officers, was beginning to realize what sort of man he worked for. Cafiero's position remained a mystery, and still does since he has not cared to explain it. Stark's role was less central, but perhaps even more obscure. DeLorean hired him on the basis that Stark would be reporting directly to him. When he arrived he found he was reporting to Cafiero. His health was poor too (he had a spinal injury) and that summer he wore a neck brace much of the time. In Belfast the NIDA officials saw only a little of Stark and were not overly impressed by him. It was nothing personal; they simply realized he was not going to make a stand against DeLorean and help them in their battle. Like Cafiero, he became irrelevant.

By the end of July the New York office was a hotbed of intrigue. Haddad was almost relieved to be out of it in Belfast, where he could send DeLorean his steady flow of memos. Things were looking up in Belfast now and he was feeling it. He wrote DeLorean on July 30: "I instinctively believe we can make it here. We need to isolate this place from the intrigue of New York (please don't ask me to explain, it would take weeks and I would be repeating myself). We need to isolate normal creative tensions between field and manufacture from emotional outbursts and manipulations, and we must avoid the great temptation, even in the name of creative tension, to avoid utilizing those manipulations."

Then, early in August, the whole internal turmoil began to come out into the open. The catalyst was the revelation in the *Sunday Telegraph* of the proposed flotation of DeLorean Motor Holdings— plus the details contained in the prospectus, which opened the way for the first examination of the relationship with Lotus, of GPD, and of so many other aspects that had been secret.

The paper was already regarded by John DeLorean and his team in New York and Belfast as their strongest critic. By this stage there were many angry DeLorean executives, cheated of their options in the unmarketable DMC shares, and damaging documents began to leak out. The medium chosen was the *Sunday Telegraph*. On Sunday, August 9, the *Sunday Telegraph* disclosed DeLorean's plans for selling 2.25 million shares to the American public at between $12 and $14 each. More shares would be issued to buy out the limited partners; the dealers would exchange their DMC shares for Holdings shares; but at the end of the exercise, DeLorean himself would still have 9,950,000 shares, 50 percent of the company. The amount of money to be raised was really very small: by the time Oppenheimer had received its new fee, Bache Halsey had taken its slice, and the lawyers' hefty fees had been covered, there would be no more than $10 to $15 million. This money was supposed to finance the sedan, but that would have cost $80 to $100 million. So DeLorean would still have to ask NIDA and the Department of Commerce for more money—much more. And the prospectus indicated as much. The story was picked up around the world and there was a spate of publicity the following week, much to DeLorean's discomfort. The *Sunday Telegraph* began probing the relationship with Lotus, which was staying as far out of sight as it could. "We are not allowed to divulge confidential details of contracts with clients," said finance director (later chairman) Fred Bushell. The paper also picked up the annoyance and anger among the executives —on August 16 it warned "there may be a mass departure of key executives" unless DeLorean did something about their options.

In the penthouse on the 43rd floor of 280 Park Avenue, everyone seemed to be waiting for someone else to make the first move. Who would go first: Cafiero, Stark, or Haddad? Who would bring out into the open the doubts and accusations they were all making privately? By September Stella Shamoon of the *Sunday Telegraph* had discovered GPD, and stories on it began to appear, causing panic at Park Avenue and heightening tension even more. Soon someone would break. It was not any of the men whose options on DMC stock would be made valueless by the new issue. The real danger to DeLorean came from an entirely unexpected source. It was not even a senior executive. In fact, it was not a man at all.

14

MARIAN GIBSON

Marian Gibson was speeding north through the English countryside. It was Tuesday, September 22, 1981, and she had caught an early train from London's Euston Station to Macclesfield, a large industrial town in northern England, south of the sprawling city of Manchester. She expected to be met there by a British Member of Parliament whom she had never heard of until a few weeks before, but on whom she was now planning to rely heavily.

Gibson, personal secretary and office manager for John DeLorean, was now determined that her former boss must be stopped. Her instrument was to be Nicholas Winterton, the Macclesfield MP, who still had no idea what he was straying into.

She had come to hate DeLorean as she had never hated anyone in her life. When she landed the job as his administrative assistant at $30,000 a year in September 1979, she was delighted. She knew little about the man, but had vaguely heard his name. She was too experienced to be attracted solely by the glamour, but the job, DeLorean told her in her interview, would be considerably more than just personal secretary. She would be working for the president of a new company and operating out of plush offices. That was fine with her.

Marian Gibson was forty-one, single, blond and attractive. She still spoke with the distinctive English accent that is such an asset for secretaries in Manhattan. Her accent was more London cockney than Oxbridge, but no one seemed to notice.

She was born in Paddington, London, and worked for a few years in the garment industry on Oxford Street. When she was twenty-one, she went to New York for a six-month stay and never returned. She worked in the cut-throat garment industry on Seventh Avenue and then went on to the more fashionable Fifth Avenue trade. At one point in her career she was a buyer at Gimbels.

In late summer of 1979 John DeLorean was looking for a private secretary for the new offices he had taken over from Xerox. Gibson had heard about the job from a friend who knew someone at De-Lorean, and she applied. She suited DeLorean perfectly in manner, ability, and experience—and he picked her out in a final selection from two.

She was aware that DeLorean chose her because of her English accent. His deal with the British government was less than a year old and phone calls were constantly coming in from officials in Northern Ireland. The officials also occasionally appeared in DeLorean's office, staring with astonishment at the expensive furnishings and art collection, and beginning to make what seemed to DeLorean unnecessarily carping comments about the money lavished on salaries and offices in New York when funds were so badly needed for the factory in Belfast. An English secretary, thought DeLorean, might help to soothe them.

The chain of events that led Marian Gibson to her final defection had started three months before, in June 1981. For a year after she joined the company, John DeLorean shared with her almost every business secret—perhaps not consciously, but through his habit of communicating even to his closest staff in memo form. Gibson typed hundreds of memos—to general counsel Tom Kimmerly, the memos "setting up" Walter Strycker, occasional letters to NIDA, and the Northern Irish officials.

It was a six-day-a-week job for her, sometimes seven. No one got to John DeLorean without seeing Marian Gibson first. Bill Haddad called her "the door"—unless you got through her, you didn't get to DeLorean. She made out his checks and he signed them. She kept his log. She organized the office Christmas party.

Marian Gibson had other secretaries to help with the typing and filing while she concentrated on installing efficient systems. DeLorean brought with him from Detroit the full General Motors system and installed it in his own tiny operation: stationery styling, filing systems, the habit of writing everything out even when it was quicker and easier to walk across the corridor—the full modern and efficient procedure of a major corporation. She was an essential cog in it. And for the first year she was intensely loyal. Yet DeLorean never allowed her to become close in a personal sense—no one, not even Tom Kimmerly, was truly close to him.

Marian Gibson was far more than a secretary. She had been in New York for more than twenty years, and she found DeLorean, for all his cosmopolitan lifestyle, still a Detroit boy at heart. He was surprisingly gauche in the circles to which he now aspired. Gibson knew people he did not and she was only too pleased to share them. She took DeLorean to visit various Arab friends and former employers, especially when DeLorean was seeking money, as he constantly was. There was one group for whom she had worked, coincidentally, in the General Motors building. DeLorean wanted to meet them and she arranged it. Ironically, DeLorean would have to see them in their offices on the 14th floor.

"Can't they come over here, Marian? You know, I'd kinda like them to see the spread here." DeLorean was very proud of the penthouse office at 280 Park Avenue.

"Well, perhaps they'd like you to see the spread there," she replied.

Later, when DeLorean returned, he announced, "You know, I'm just bowled over by that office." But he wasn't pleased that someone —anyone—had a grander office than his.

In October 1980 Gibson's position at DeLorean changed. She later claimed it was a promotion, but DeLorean said it was just the opposite. Her new title was deputy administrator for DMC, which really meant office manager.

She could still walk into DeLorean's office to have, as she put it, "a nose around his desk." He didn't mind, and never seemed to notice. For all his tangled business deals, he was curiously open about letters and files. One day he walked in as she was leaning over his desk and he just remarked casually, "Hi, Marian, how're you doin'?"

She was still protective of him then, breaking in his new secretary, doing her best to make things work more smoothly. She would pass back to him the mood she detected in the office.

"You know," she said one day, "you have a lot of enemies." DeLorean was unimpressed. "Is that right?" he asked.

But increasingly, like so many of the others who were to leave, Marian Gibson gradually came to see John DeLorean in a different light. The doubts originally implanted by some of the memos she read or typed began to crystallize. Strycker's departure left a sour taste; so had the objections of Brown and more recently of Bill Haddad.

She started to contrast the casual attitude in the Park Avenue office toward spending company money with what she knew was happening in Northern Ireland. She might have left Britain twenty years before, but she still thought of herself as British. She began to follow the

battle the NIDA men were having with DeLorean, seeing them totally outgunned and outmaneuvered, and her latent patriotism began
to stir. It was all very vague at the time, but it was enough for
DeLorean to sense that she was no longer wholly on his side, and so
he replaced her with a new secretary.

In June 1981 DeLorean moved Gibson again, this time a definite
demotion. She was sent to the public relations department with the
clear implication that it was only a temporary stopping place. De-
Lorean wanted her out, just as he also wanted her new boss, Bill
Haddad, to go. She suspected that the new man in the department,
Mike Knepper, was under orders to make things as unpleasant as
possible for her.

She decided she was not going to go quietly. Her friend and lawyer
Clarence Jones proposed the course of action that many other women
had taken in such circumstances: a civil rights suit for women. Jones,
a tall, elegant, articulate black man in his fifties, had been one of
Martin Luther King's advisers and knew all about civil rights suits.
She began collecting her material in preparation for such a case.

In that curious way he had of ignoring minor matters that no longer
concerned him, DeLorean sought her help as if nothing had changed.
By July 1981 he was once again running out of money. The officials
at NIDA were grinding their teeth in frustration as they tried to
restrain the outflow of money from the Northern Ireland company to
New York. For more than a year they had winced at the extravagance
of that Park Avenue office, insisting it was far too lavish for a company that still made no profits and had such huge debts.

The officials believed they were getting nowhere with John De-
Lorean, but in truth, they were. One day Marian Gibson had a call
from the 43rd floor penthouse. "Are you alone?" asked DeLorean.
She was, but pretended not to be—making a show of saying goodbye
and closing the office door. Finally she told DeLorean she was ready.

"Do you know a rich Arab who might be interested in the 43rd
floor?" he asked her. "The pressure from Belfast is getting pretty
intense and they're insisting we move out of here. We have to make
a pretense of it, but without losing face."

Gibson quickly concocted a scheme that she proposed to her boss.
She had an Arab friend, a Saudi, whom she thought would be inter-
ested. She would ask him. "Let's unload it at whatever it costs us.
These redwood doors and marble floors should go down well," she

suggested. "Meanwhile I'll put out the story that we'll be moving to a joint showroom and office on Park Avenue similar to the one Mercedes has. I'll be sufficiently vague about it so that people won't be able to ask the exact spot—I'll say we can't say exactly where yet."

"Okay, Marian, do it," said DeLorean. Gibson went ahead and put the story out, with the intention of saying the deal on the showroom had fallen through once they all moved down to the 35th floor. But DeLorean didn't move for another nine months—when the company was already in receivership.

During the summer of 1981, Gibson's resentment turned to hatred. In the public relations department, Mike Knepper assigned her a job he thought she would despise—going through the Hansard reports of proceedings in the House of Commons and picking out all the references to DeLorean. There was a huge bundle of the reports piled on the floor.

Although neither Gibson nor Knepper ever dreamed it at the time, no job could have served John DeLorean worse. Two streams in Gibson's discontent were now coming together. Jones was still advising her on the preparation of her civil rights case, and her anger at everything she saw going on around her—heightened now by a very discontented and worn-down Bill Haddad, whose health was visibly suffering—was being fed by what she read in those Hansards.

Gibson became familiar with the names of the MPs who persistently questioned the project. The loudest and most frequent critic was the left-wing Labour member for Keighly, Bob Cryer. During the entire DeLorean episode, he was to ask by far the most informed, perceptive, and penetrating questions that were to receive blind and naive answers from equally uninformed Labour and Tory governments. Britain had a history of sending her worst politicians and civil servants to Ireland. In the late 1970s, little had changed.

There were other critics of course: the Tory Michael McNair-Wilson, and from May onward, the doughty Jock Bruce-Gardyne, who soon became the biggest Parliamentary foe of the DeLorean project. Bruce-Gardyne used a double-barreled weapon—his oratorical prowess in Parliament and his literary skills in his weekly column in the *Sunday Telegraph* of London. All that year, Bruce-Gardyne and Cryer, from opposite ends of the political spectrum, had increasingly pressed the hapless Northern Ireland minister of state, Adam Butler, with question after question. The thrust of the inquiries was immediately apparent to Gibson, who now saw them in a different light—the bland answers of the politician becoming all the more irritating.

She could see that Cryer knew a great deal; he had asked about GPD within months of the signing and had pressed on the deal with Lotus. He questioned the role of the DeLorean Research Limited Partnership put together by Oppenheimer. He knew about ERM. Time after time Butler evaded him although he had nothing to do with the original idea.

One cannot read through the Hansard reports without catching other significant items. References to DeLorean were usually included in Northern Ireland debates that often consisted of ministers reading long lists of casualties in the battle against the IRA; of the horrendous unemployment the Province was experiencing; of companies going out of business for lack of funds.

Around her in the office high above Park Avenue, no one could comprehend it. In 1980 there had been less violence in Northern Ireland than in any year since 1971. There were fewer murders, fewer injuries caused by terrorist violence, fewer explosions, and fewer shooting incidents. And 1981 had started just as promisingly.

But then came the hunger strike, and the Province had exploded again. Marian Gibson was now rediscovering it all through the debates recorded in Hansard. In her emotional state the figures became real for her, something more than dry statistics. Bob Cryer was alleging that the money that went to DeLorean had become available only because of cutbacks in spending on education and housing. Bruce-Gardyne was insisting that the new Tory government think again before "we lay on any extra saunas, sun-parlors or anything else for this extraordinary affair" that he wanted demolished from "the foundation upwards." Emotive prose it may have been, but in one disillusioned and upset employee on the 35th floor of 280 Park Avenue, it found a responsive chord.

The other stream of Gibson's discontent, essentially DeLorean's poor treatment of all who worked for him and his treatment of her in particular, was being handled by Clarence Jones. Bill Haddad offered to help.

"I've got some papers Clarence might like to look at," he told Gibson one day. They arranged a meeting and Haddad turned over a copy of his "gold facets" memo. He also had copies of other memos that had come his way, and many he had written to DeLorean, and he outlined his doubts about Lotus and the GPD deal. Gibson had never seen these papers and Haddad did not show them to her then. Nor did Jones immediately.

"Bill has told me a lot of things in confidence," he said to her, but he did not elaborate and she did not press him at the time. A few weeks later, however, she saw Jones again to discuss her case and the torment she felt about what was happening inside the company.

"These issues are far bigger than just my personal interests," she said. "These are issues of national importance." DeLorean must not be allowed to get away with it, she vowed, but she was afraid he *would* get away with it if he could get the flotation of the new DeLorean Motor Holdings off the ground. That worried her more than anything.

But other DeLorean employees were looking at their boss in a different light: if he was worth $120 million and the stock market was going to value the whole thing at $240 million, then perhaps it was not the empty shell they assumed. How could a guy worth $120 million be wrong?

Jones listened to her tirade, then calmly told her, "Since you feel so strongly about it, I want you to have a look at this." He handed her a copy of the gold facets memo. It was the final bit of fuel she needed to put her on the course that would finally impel her to get on that train to Macclesfield.

That evening in her Manhattan apartment, Marian Gibson began organizing her notes. What to do with them? Her first instinct was to go to Bruce-Gardyne—she felt she knew him best, both from his *Sunday Telegraph* articles and his speeches in the House.

The next day was Saturday, but she was accustomed to working on Saturdays. She had slipped into the habit of lunching at the Cowboy with Kimmerly and his assistant, Jackie Feddock. Sometimes DeLorean came, too.

At lunchtime Gibson took the elevator to the 43rd floor and looked for Jackie. She noticed that DeLorean's office door, which was invariably open, was closed.

"Is Tom coming to lunch?" she asked Jackie.

Jackie gestured at the closed door. "They're in there."

At that moment the door opened and Kimmerly walked out. As the three rode the elevator down to the ground floor on their way to the Cowboy, Kimmerly suddenly blurted out in an uncharacteristic burst of candor, "We're going to sue the British government!"

"Sue?" echoed Gibson. "How can you sue a government?"

"Yeah," said Kimmerly. "Take them to the Paris courts."

It provided yet another bit of impetus to her plan of action.

After lunch she slipped across Park Avenue to the Waldorf-Astoria. In the foyer she turned right, then left, as she walked through the plush carpeted corridors with their boutiques and bars. On the left was a row of pay phones that had the advantage of being in booths with doors. She entered one and dialed the Park Lane Hotel. Her friend Eddie Koopman was staying there.

The Dutch-born antiques dealer from Cheshire, whom Marian Gibson had met eight years before in New York, was a regular visitor to the Sotheby-Parke Bernet art sales and was attending one now. He had no interest in DeLorean and had heard more than enough from Gibson already. "What do you think, they're so stupid over there?" he shouted. "You think they just give away their money and then forget it? You think they don't even check where it's gone?" She explained that she and Clarence Jones had some papers she wanted Koopman to see. Would he meet them?

"I don't want to see a thing," exclaimed Koopman. "I don't want to be involved in any of it!"

"Eddie, I have a problem," she insisted. "I've got to get past the mole DeLorean has in the Northern Ireland office. It's really important. I really would like you to come along and meet Clarence and me."

Koopman, drawn reluctantly into a matter that had nothing to do with him, agreed. They met in one of the cafés in the United Nations building—neutral territory for all, and well out of the way of DeLorean moles.

"Eddie, I'm going to Bruce-Gardyne. He's the most vocal on this issue," Gibson began.

"No, you don't want to do that," said Koopman. "I've got a better man, very reliable. He's in Macclesfield and he's a friend. We could meet at my house. If you're going to go through with this I'll make an appointment with Nick Winterton."

It meant going to England: the cost of the airfare, the inconvenience, and trouble. But Gibson had now made up her mind. Jones approved the plan and agreed to follow her to England to support her.

That Saturday evening she rang Haddad at home. "Bill, I'm taking a vacation." Haddad did not object. He was only too aware that the skids were under both Gibson and himself—he had not been paid since July.

She took a shopping bag and went into the office. From the shelf where they had sat for a year she took down two notebooks, each about four inches thick. They contained copies of almost all the letters and memos she had typed for John DeLorean in the thirteen months she was his executive secretary; she had filed them with no purpose other than the instincts of a trained, efficient secretary. But when DeLorean had moved her out of his own immediate area to Haddad's department eight floors down, she had taken them with her and parked them on a shelf for all to see.

The deeply ingrained philosophy of Detroit men such as Collins, Dewey, or even Cafiero was that you might object, but you did so privately—you never washed your dirty linen in public. Brown and Strycker, to a lesser extent, shared the same fear of making a public fuss. Marian Gibson proved to have fewer inhibitions.

The black binders also contained copies of memos and letters she had seen on Haddad's desk. When she finally decided to make the jump, she gathered together all the papers from her own desk, put the two big binders in a bag, scooped up everything else she thought might help make her case, and left. She slipped into Haddad's office and made copies of some of his files. She knew the risks she was taking, but she needed the documents as a trigger.

By Tuesday she was back on her native English soil and by Saturday was journeying north to Macclesfield for an initial and exploratory talk with Winterton. She had not brought her files to the meeting— she would not entrust them to him until she had gotten to know him.

It was a fine September day, and the English countryside contrasted favorably with the concrete corridors of Manhattan. Winterton was at Koopman's home with his wife, Ann, and Gibson was immediately impressed with the blond, fresh-faced cheerful man with the little Union Jack (his trademark) on his sweater. They strolled on Koopman's grounds for half an hour, but she had not come all this way, as she said to Koopman, for "a social occasion." Koopman led the way to the dining room and they sat down across the table.

Winterton saw a middle-aged woman, visibly worried about the story she started to pour out. However emotional she was, Marian

Gibson still had the ability to marshal her facts and arguments, clearly setting out her allegations and the reasons for an investigation into the way British taxpayers' money was being spent. She described DeLorean's lifestyle and the way it was supported by money that should have gone into Northern Ireland.

Ann Winterton and the Koopmans chatted in the living room while for an hour and a half Winterton went over Gibson's story. He was puzzled by her reasons for blowing the whistle—was she a spurned mistress of DeLorean's? He soon rejected that idea, but at the same time he was convinced that she was once trusted by DeLorean and should therefore know what she was talking about. Finally he stood up.

"Look, Miss Gibson, it's clear you've made some very serious allegations," he said formally, cutting her off. "I take them very seriously, but I don't think you would expect me to take action unless you provide some documentary evidence to support the allegations you've made."

Marian had mentioned several times that she had documents with her in England and would show them to him at another meeting.

"Well," he said, "we must meet again."

Marian wanted to set it up for early the next week. She was already resentful that she had been in England for five days and only now had seen Winterton for the first time.

Winterton suggested the same time and place the following week. Marian was horrified—it would be too late, the Bache issue would have gone through, and there would be no stopping DeLorean. Even her own civil rights suit would have been better than this, Marian thought. It might have held up the issue while the prospectus was redrafted to include mention of it. Marian had no understanding of the busy schedule even a back-bench MP must keep, although Parliament was then in recess, and Winterton did not appreciate her feeling of urgency. The following Saturday it would have to be, with Gibson hoping to have the support of Clarence Jones by then. The following Tuesday she phoned the lawyer in New York. When was he coming over? Unfortunately, he told her, he couldn't. Something else had cropped up and he couldn't make it.

She was feeling increasingly vulnerable and alone—just her against DeLorean with all his support from the British government, Wall Street investors, and rich, powerful men. She did not enjoy the role of whistle-blower and the conviction that she was alone against the world.

Her flight home to New York was booked out of Heathrow for the following Sunday, September 20. Her appointment with Winterton was set up for the day before that. Now she decided she would board that plane without seeing the Tory MP again. It was all too slow and too late.

She phoned Koopman, told him of her decision: she was going home, taking her binders with her. She told him repeatedly, "I'm just disillusioned." Why couldn't Winterton make it sooner if he were really interested? "What blasted whist drive is he at today?" Koopman laughed at Gibson's cutting characterization of the trivial social life of a country Member of Parliament—a whist drive is a card party for charity—and she laughed with him. But for most of that week she was nearer tears than laughter.

"Eddie, Winterton doesn't understand this thing. Bruce-Gardyne understands it. I wish I'd gone to him." During the week that she arrived, however, Bruce-Gardyne had been drafted for higher things by Mrs. Thatcher. He was now watching the nation's purse strings—including spending on DeLorean—from his office in the vast Treasury building in Great George Street. Marian Gibson had read about the appointment two days after she arrived. She figured Bruce-Gardyne was now inaccessible, so she canceled the Sunday flight and rang Haddad in New York.

"Bill, I'm going to be late in getting back. I won't be back until Wednesday." She felt curiously guilty about that. She was at the point of delivering what could possibly be a fatal blow to her employer, removing from him the $120 million fortune that was within his grasp —yet she was worried about being a couple of days late for work. The habits of a lifetime die hard.

She now arranged to see Winterton on Tuesday—this time with her files. On Tuesday morning she journeyed into London and across town to Euston Station. Clutching her shopping bag with the precious papers in it, she paid the extravagant fare of £23 for her ticket and boarded the train for Macclesfield. She was apprehensive and afraid, not knowing what she had stepped into, and she was still in awe of DeLorean, fearful of his reaction once he learned of her intentions— as he inevitably would. She was also not yet entirely certain about Nicholas Winterton, and rehearsed again how she might convince him to help her.

She went over her documentation. On top she placed three pages of her own notes, written late at night in her apartment as she tried to make sense of the information and material she had compiled in the two years she worked for DeLorean. She had copies of the memos Haddad gave Clarence Jones, including the gold facet memo.

There were copies of checks, both corporate and personal—De-Lorean was not fussy about the distinction—for everything from art work bought from Christie's or Sotheby-Parke Bernet to expensive jewelry from the shops along Fifth Avenue. There was even John DeLorean's private address book, listing the telephone numbers of his family and friends and of his favorite restaurants, hotels, and clubs in New York and London—all in a neat little book designed to slip into the pocket of a well-tailored suit without disturbing its lines.

Marian Gibson's own notes contained some half-formed yet pointed allegations that she hoped the memos and other materials in the binders would support. She charged that instead of the $4 million that DeLorean often said he had put into the car project, he had actually invested only $750,000, and that was Cristina's money. She claimed that the money DeLorean received for gasoline bomb damage to the Belfast factory after the Sands hunger strike was excessive: only a few shacks were damaged. She also linked this payment to the purchase by DeLorean of his estate in Bedminster, New Jersey—the timing of the two coincided and she claimed they were connected. She sus-pected that the money approved by Humphrey Atkins and paid by the government through the Department of Commerce had not been sanctioned by NIDA—she had seen letters from Tony Hopkins and knew of his continuing attempts to put pressure on DeLorean for tighter controls.

And there was more. Her notes laid out how she thought but could not prove that DeLorean had diverted British government money into other private ventures of his own: the Stirling engine project, the Transbus, and others. Dick Brown could list eighteen; Marian knew of only half a dozen but even that was enough. She had also strayed upon the well-kept and tightly guarded secret of GPD, mostly from conversations with Haddad. She did not know what it meant, but to her, no legitimate deal was done through a Swiss-based, Panama-registered company that was deliberately excluded from public docu-ments by both parties.

The blue and white British Rail train rolled into Macclesfield Sta-tion just before lunchtime. Winterton met her on the platform, took her to his car outside the station, and drove to Eddie Koopman's home.

Koopman himself was away that day, but his wife, Kit, whom Gibson knew well because she often accompanied her husband to the New York art sales, was there. Kit prepared lunch for them. Gibson was still nervous, but there was something reassuring and very familiarly British about Winterton.

She had never voted in a British election, having left London when she was only twenty. But if she had, she would not have voted Conservative. Of course she was no left-winger either—politics simply did not concern her much. But Winterton's very Britishness was now important to her. She had come to perceive the situation in terms of the British taxpayer being cheated, and she believed that the more obviously British the person, the more easily he would see that.

They spent three hours in the Koopman dining room that afternoon, sitting opposite each other at a large mahogany table on which she had spread out her papers. Winterton went through them with mounting interest: here were details of John DeLorean's travel itineraries worked out in extraordinary detail—down to telephone numbers of everyone he might conceivably want to telephone or see on his trip. Each itinerary was pages long, even when the trip was only a few days. There were accounts relating to purchases from the showrooms and, of course, the memos. From the detail of the items, Winterton could instantly assess the close working relationship that Marian Gibson once had with DeLorean. She was not likely to be exaggerating.

Winterton was less sure of his ability to properly assess the material itself. He was keenly aware that his neighboring MP, Bruce-Gardyne, was something of an expert on DeLorean, and while Winterton had followed him as an interested observer, DeLorean was not strictly his subject.

"You know, I'm no expert on this. I'm not an accountant or a lawyer—I'm a small businessman by background and I don't pretend to be a great expert on motor car companies. I don't really feel competent to assess the true value of these papers. But"—he paused for a moment before resuming more vehemently—"they certainly merit investigation!"

That was all Marian Gibson wanted to hear. The only question that now remained was how to go about that investigation. Whom to give the papers to? The ministry involved was the Northern Ireland office, but she convinced Winterton that DeLorean might have a mole there. She told him about Nesseth, too, and he could see how worried she was by DeLorean's hulking heavy, although they both presumed he was at least 3,000 miles away. This was a matter too big to bring to a mere department; it touched the whole government. Winterton finally decided to take it right to the top.

"It would be best," Winterton told her, "if we went straight to Margaret Thatcher with this."

Gibson caught the train back to London and then took a taxi to her cousin's home near Heathrow Airport. Winterton took photocopies of a few of the more pertinent documents, including the gold facet memo, and returned the original material to Koopman. The next day, September 23, he wrote a letter to Ian Gow, the prime minister's Parliamentary Private Secretary and a fellow Tory MP. He did not mention DeLorean.

"I am afraid at this stage I cannot be specific," he wrote cautiously, "but information has come to me which leads me to believe that the British government is being misled and deceived, and the taxpayers' money misused in a substantial project with which the British government has been involved for some little while." He had the necessary papers, he added, to substantiate that view. "The problem is that I cannot refer this matter to the Secretary of State concerned because, of course, it would be handled by his officials, and inquiries would be made, and I say with some regret that there are moles within government departments and the perpetrators of the fraud and deception would inevitably be advised that inquiries were in hand." He asked Gow to arrange a meeting with the prime minister "some time in the not too distant future" so he could discuss the matter with her personally.

On the same day he wrote that letter, Marian Gibson flew back to New York. But even while Winterton's secretary was typing out the message and Gibson was aloft, back in New York DeLorean was in the process of firing Haddad. Yet another big name, one of John's more visible specialists, was leaving the ship. Of course neither DeLorean nor Haddad knew what Gibson was doing, although Haddad knew she was in England.

The two events were not connected, although John DeLorean later refused to believe there was no conspiracy between his head of public relations and his former executive secretary. Haddad later said he could not fully understand why Gibson had done it. And if it was a surprise to him, although he and Gibson had often discussed their suspicions and worries for hours, it was a bombshell to DeLorean.

Marian Gibson herself found it difficult to explain later—or at least to make people understand. In a sense, her betrayal of her boss was the turning point in DeLorean's career. Doubtless, events would still have caught up with him, but without her move, the Bache Halsey issue of stock in the new holding company would have gone ahead. The alarm bells might not have rung until much later. And the British government might have gone on putting money into a factory that was already producing cars at twice the rate they were selling. The crash would have been all the more severe when it came.

15

SCOOP

If Marian Gibson had brought the papers with her the first time she went to see MP Nicholas Winterton, the next few weeks might have evolved very differently. It would have been different both for Winterton and herself, different also for DeLorean and all who sailed with him, and different for the Northern Ireland officials.

Things would have been different if Winterton had canceled his visits to the local mills, been less diligent in his duties to his constituents, or seen Marian Gibson earlier the second time. She feared the delay would permit the DeLorean Motor Holdings issue to go ahead. At it turned out, however, the delay had entirely unexpected consequences.

Winterton's letter to Ian Gow arrived at the prime minister's office on Friday, September 25. It was opened by Gow's secretary, Tess Jardine Patterson. Gow was on a trip to the Middle East and Australia and would not return to Number Ten Downing Street until October 9. He was accompanying the prime minister to the Commonwealth Prime Ministers' Meeting in Australia, the whole party visiting various points in the Middle East en route. Jardine Paterson wrote a polite letter back to Winterton on September 30, pointing this out and adding that "the Party Conference begins the following week, so it may not be possible to arrange a meeting with the Prime Minister or Mr. Gow until after the Conference."

Once back in New York, Gibson relaxed slightly since she believed, if erroneously, that events were going to move faster now and that the British Fraud Squad or some other police department would be calling her any day. The documents required explanation by someone who knew them. At first glance they were just a bunch of disconnected memos and checks. It would not take her long, she thought, to explain their significance to a keen-eyed British bobby.

It required all her nerve to return to her office at DeLorean Motor Company. She was not reassured by Haddad's greeting.

"You know, our phones are tapped—yours and mine," he warned her. "It's only a matter of time."

From across the street she called Koopman. Where were the files? Koopman said he had wrapped them up tight and had them under lock and key.

That was not what she wanted to hear. Why hadn't the prime minister received them? What was going on? She had mentally worked out a likely timetable on her flight back to New York, and had calculated that the effective date, four weeks from the date the Securities and Exchange Commission gave its go-ahead for the issue of the new company stock, had already passed. She would be too late.

Returning to the office after talking to Koopman, she noticed a stack of cartons. "What are those?" she asked Denis Patouhas, one of DeLorean's more recent recruits in the accounting department.

"They are the old prospectuses," he replied gloomily. "They all had to be reprinted. There were errors in them. Cost us $46,000."

There was still a chance! She phoned Koopman again. *"Where are those binders?"* They were still in his cupboard. No one had asked for them yet, nothing was in motion.

Bill Haddad sat in his office, equally on edge, although for different reasons. He still did not know that Gibson had lit the fuse. He was definitely on his way out of the company, but there were still a number of points to be resolved, not the least of which was his final compensation.

Gibson felt she was walking a tightrope, just waiting to fall off. Any moment now the ax would drop, and although it was she who had sharpened the blade, she was still in the office and in a position where it could hit her, too. For the rest of the week she sat there, waiting and phoning Koopman. By Friday evening nothing had happened— DeLorean seemed to be going about his business undisturbed. The prospectus was ready to go. DeLorean was visibly taking pleasure in the $120-million fortune it would provide him. He was going to get away with it.

Saturday, still nothing. Tess Paterson was not to send Winterton his polite note from Downing Street until the following Wednesday.

On Sunday, at about five in the afternoon, Marian Gibson received a call from London. It was not one she expected nor even wanted, and it sent her into such a nervous state that she called the phone company the next day to have her service cut off. This was to make things very awkward in the following days, but she wanted no more calls of that kind.

The caller was a free-lance journalist named John Lisners, an Australian who had gravitated to Fleet Street several years before and who now made a living writing stories for the "pops," the tabloids that tended to pay more for sensational stories.

Lisners knew Koopman, an acquaintance dating from the time Lisner's child and a Koopman grandchild had been born in the same hospital at the same time.

Lisners had just arrived from Australia. From Koopman he learned that John DeLorean's former secretary had a story to tell, and if she couldn't get a police investigation going quickly, she might be prepared to start moving another way, such as through a newspaper story.

The official investigation—until now, that was what she wanted—into Gibson's charges was moving at a snail's pace. By contrast, the hound of Fleet Street sensed something big and was onto it instantly. It was ten o'clock in the evening London time when Lisners phoned her in New York. Would she tell him the story? Very definitely not, was the reply.

Monday morning brought her back to 280 Park Avenue. Still no news from London, still no sign that DeLorean or anyone else in the office knew what was building up.

By Wednesday she could stand the tension no longer and called Koopman. What was happening? She didn't dare use the office phone since she was convinced it was tapped, so during the day she used the booths in the Waldorf-Astoria and in the evening, the public phone on the corner of Sutton Place and East 55th Street, around the corner from her apartment. When she ran out of coins, she used Bill Haddad's credit card number.

"Eddie, it's been three weeks now. There is a time factor on this, you know. Do I call that journalist friend of yours or not?"

Koopman tried to calm her. "Don't worry, Marian, they'll handle it. They can't do anything because Margaret Thatcher is in Australia."

"Eddie, are those papers still in your cupboard?" They were, and she finally snapped, "Eddie, I may not be much, but I'm all that country has got. If they're still sitting in your cupboard, then it's too late. I'm going to talk to the journalist."

Thursday morning before dawn, Marian Gibson went down to the corner phone and called Lisners. It was ten in the morning in London.

She was terse, unfriendly—but willing to talk. "Listen, I have a story for you. But there are conditions. You come over, I'll give you the full story, but you print nothing without the approval of my lawyer, Clarence Jones."

Lisners caught the first plane out of Heathrow, grabbed a taxi at Kennedy, and by eleven that evening was at Gibson's apartment.

No time for jet-lag, no time for sleep. Lisners didn't even check into a hotel. The two worked through the night, showered and changed early in the morning, and before anyone was around, went down to 280 Park Avenue.

With some trepidation, Gibson pressed the button for the express elevator that took them straight to the penthouse. She took Lisners in, showed him the layout, the two life-sized dolls standing at each side of the spacious marble-floored foyer, the giant pictures of the DMC-12 behind the reception desk, and the red buffalo-hide chairs. She pointed out the art work, some pieces inherited from Xerox, others bought by Maur Dubin in his capacity as keeper of the De-Lorean art collection.

Right turn at Kimmerly's office, along the corridor lined in gray smoked glass. A left turn, past the office where Cafiero once whiled away his day, and in front was the door to the office occupied first by Walt Strycker, then Bill Haddad, and now Denis Patouhas. On the left was DeLorean's private bathroom, with its shower and red-tiled walls. On the right, the door open as usual, John DeLorean's own office with its panoramic views of Manhattan. The telescope stood in one corner; there were pictures of Cristina and the car. The Northern Ireland agreement was framed and mounted.

No one else had come into the office, and they went down to the comparative haven of the 35th floor and Gibson's own office. Soon Bill Haddad came in and she briefly introduced Lisners without directly identifying him as a journalist. "He does what Ellen's boyfriend does," she said obliquely. Ellen was Haddad's secretary, and her boyfriend was a journalist. But Haddad either didn't get it or didn't want to.

At eleven Lisners met Clarence Jones in the Brasserie restaurant in the Seagrams Building and they talked for an hour. Gibson joined them for lunch. Jones needed to get away—he had personal problems of his own—but one look at her face and he knew he couldn't leave her. She was now finding the tension nearly unbearable. But she made it back to the office after lunch; it was the last afternoon she would work for DeLorean. They had decided over lunch that at five she would leave and not go back.

By Sunday Lisners' story would be breaking in London, complete with pictures of Marian Gibson and quotes from her. The offices at 280 Park Avenue would be no place for her after that.

She decided she would not even stay in New York, but would ride out the storm in the more friendly surroundings of her native London. Lisners had already sold the story to the *News of the World*, Britain's most sensationalist newspaper, whose circulation numbered some 4 million. It specialized in what Fleet Street called "tits 'n' bums," carrying photos of as many bare-breasted females as it could cram in, interspersed with the occasional naughty clergyman or "wife-swapping parties in the suburbs" stories.

The newspaper was owned by Rupert Murdoch and was Murdoch's leap from the relative obscurity of Australian newspapers into the bigger time. Income from the paper helped finance his later purchases of the *New York Post*, the *London Times*, and the *Sunday Times*.

Lisners was not offering the paper any sex, but rather "gold facets" from Harrod's, secret memos of Swiss payouts, hints of government money for the IRA, and John DeLorean himself. It had all the makings of a good, old-fashioned scandal.

The *News of the World*'s editor, Barrie Askew, who prided himself on his crusading journalism, had been hired by Murdoch from the *Lancashire Evening Post* after a series of stories involving corruption and brutality in a mental hospital, the exposure of malpractice by the police, and a story that led to the investigation by Scotland Yard into alleged corruption among public officials in Lancashire.

Askew's long hair and cocky manner, in the brief interval since Murdoch put him in charge of his big British moneymaker, had become something of a legend, with constant references to the cot he had moved into his office for purposes other than sleeping.

Murdoch had assigned Askew a new approach: news and investigation would replace the old formula of sex scandals and massage parlors, which the Australian proprietor had decided was out of date and had been responsible for the decline in circulation by several million over the past decade. The story that Lisners offered from New York fitted the new formula perfectly, Askew decided.

Friday afternoon in New York (late Friday evening in London), Haddad began to suspect something was going on, but he still didn't know what. Lisners went off to the Associated Press office to file his story and send photographs through—at lunchtime he had photographed Marian Gibson and Clarence Jones standing together.

It would be the lead story, with a follow-up feature inside, Askew told him.

Marian quietly packed her things, knowing she would leave in just a few hours, never to return. Eight floors above, DeLorean was still blissfully ignorant of what was happening. In London Askew briefed a few select journalists on the story, including his assistant editor, Bob Satchwell, who was now handling the story there.

There would be quite a few points to firm up before going to press, but they would have to wait until Saturday morning. Premature inquiries would trigger interest by the other papers and the story might be out before the *News of the World* hit the streets.

The main point to be established was the prime minister's reaction: at that stage Lisners was writing the story on the basis of the documents having been sent to Number Ten, which made it a "Mrs. Thatcher Gets Secret File of DeLorean Papers" story, listing the allegations made in those papers. A "Mrs. Thatcher Orders Police Investigation of DeLorean" story would be better still. But as yet there was no investigation. The prime minister, in Australia, was as ignorant of the file of documents in Eddie Koopman's locked cupboard as John DeLorean was—or at least so they thought.

Jones called Haddad in midafternoon. "You know, Bill, Marian has been speaking to a journalist."

Haddad was at the height of his own personal battle with John DeLorean. But now he could not get to see him, even to resolve his severance terms. He knew DeLorean would never believe Marian Gibson had done it all on her own; he would believe Haddad had put her up to it. Haddad's anger and frustration had been public knowledge around the office for nine months now. He made no secret of it, and now he knew what DeLorean's reaction would be.

"You know, I'll get the blame for this."

What no one in the Park Avenue offices or the *News of the World* realized was that events were finally moving in the vast Whitehall machine, too. The Winterton-inspired investigation was at last clanking into gear.

Jones had phoned Winterton on Thursday, October 1, to tell him the news: Haddad had been dismissed and was going to talk to the press (this was not strictly true, but was an extra lever). Furthermore, Marian Gibson was talking to John Lisners, an independent journalist who was writing for the *News of the World*. Jones said he believed that the *News of the World* would carry a story the next weekend, on Sunday, October 4.

It was fair warning and Winterton was appreciative. He phoned Number Ten and asked for the prime minister's private office. She was still away, would not be back until Monday. But he reached a private secretary, Michael Pattison, one of five bright, ambitious civil servants culled from other departments around Whitehall and detailed for a spell at Number Ten. The DeLorean business, Winterton explained, was about to break and the government could be made to look silly if the *News of the World* were to break it first. Pattison instantly saw what Winterton meant and went into action.

He knew he must brief the prime minister herself, though she was half the world away in Australia. That night the Telex machines buzzed between Downing Street and the British embassy in Canberra. By Friday morning, even before Gibson and Lisners had visited the DeLorean office, Mrs. Thatcher sent back her decision: order the attorney general's office to begin a police inquiry into the allegations.

The attorney general, the Cabinet minister with responsibility for the country's legal affairs, was Sir Michael Havers; he passed the order on to his deputy, the solicitor general, Sir Ian Percival, and Percival phoned Winterton at home. Winterton was out; his wife took the message: could the MP call him as soon as he got in?

Winterton phoned at 6 P.M., while Gibson, Jones, and Lisners were still at lunch in New York. He briefed the solicitor general in detail on everything that Gibson had told him, laying out the allegations as clearly as he could.

First, Winterton said, instead of the $4 million that DeLorean had often boasted he put into the company in Belfast, the real amount was only $750,000. He continued: the contract with GPD for the building of the car and the placing of sums of government money in a Swiss bank account needed some investigation, and money was being spent on projects that had nothing to do with the DMC-12. Winterton listed some of them: the bus, the gasahol engine, and DeLorean's idea, related to him by Gibson, of turning the company into what she called a "boutique," with DeLorean sunglasses, made by Bausch & Lomb, DeLorean jackets, DeLorean scarves, and all the rest of it. Winterton reminded Percival about the pending flotation of De-Lorean Motor Holdings that, he said, would enrich John DeLorean at the expense of British taxpayers.

Those were the allegations. There was plenty of supporting material, but those were the areas on which Winterton suggested the police focus their investigation. Percival told him there was indeed going to be a police investigation, that the prime minister had ordered it personally, and that the director of public prosecutions, Sir Thomas Hetherington, would be contacting him.

The director of public prosecutions (DPP) is the prosecuting arm of the Law Officers' Department and comes directly under the attorney general. It was the first Winterton knew of the actual investigation he himself had set in motion.

The DPP had already been trying to contact Winterton, and after talking to Percival, Winterton called the DPP. Hetherington had asked Scotland Yard's Serious Crimes Squad to carry out the investigations, he told Winterton. The man in charge would be Detective Chief Superintendent John George. George had been asked to see Winterton as soon as possible, which would probably be the next morning, when he and his assistant could get themselves up to Cheshire, where the papers were located. Could Winterton meet them, give them the documents, and tell them all he knew? It wasn't so much a request as an order. The full weight of the law was grinding into action.

At five o'clock in New York, Marian Gibson left her office for the last time. It was not the way she had always intended to leave, with proper farewells to her friends. It was quiet and without a word to anyone except Bill Haddad.

Emotionally, she was in turmoil. She had arranged to meet Jones and Lisners on the ground floor of 277 Park Avenue, an office building across the street. Jones was there, but Lisners was late—stuck in traffic.

Gibson expected that at any moment DeLorean or Kimmerly—or

even Nesseth—would appear; she was jumpy and very upset. Jones, normally calm and collected, wasn't in much better shape. He had been a friend of Marian Gibson's for some years, but just now he was involved in a personal crisis of his own. Every second spent waiting for Lisners seemed like years.

Eventually Lisners appeared, his grin of triumph contrasting with Gibson's and Jones' misery. His story was on the wire; Bob Satchell was highly pleased with what he had got. In the morning the *News of the World* reporters would begin their follow-up phone calls—to Downing Street, to Winterton, to Bruce-Gardyne and Cryer, to Haddad, and perhaps to DeLorean himself. It was going to be a beauty.

The trio went across the street to Harry's Bar in the Waldorf-Astoria and each had a glass of red wine. They went on to El Parador, a Spanish restaurant on East 34th Street. Jones had had enough by now; he couldn't eat, drank three margaritas, and suddenly left—but not before he passed on the news from London.

He had talked to Winterton: the prime minister had asked the police to investigate.

"You've got what you want, Marian. Remember, it was when the police started to investigate the Watergate affair that the whole thing began to come out."

For Marian Gibson it was both good news and bad. She was relieved that it was all happening at last. But now that the police investigation was going ahead, she no longer wanted Lisners' story splashed across the *News of the World*. There was still the condition that his copy had to be cleared by Jones.

Lisners played the situation carefully. His story was gone, was already on the editor's desk waiting for his arrival in the morning—the front page and page three were laid out, reporters briefed, and photographs prepared. He knew—or thought he knew—that nothing could stop it now. They went back to Gibson's apartment, where Lisners' suitcases were still parked. He had been working on her typewriter and she left him to it, went to her bedroom, and lay down, still sleepless. She had not slept properly for weeks and neither of them had been to sleep the previous night.

She could hear the sound of Lisners typing in the living room. Every so often he would go out the door and let himself in a little while later. Since there was no phone in the apartment, Lisners was using either Gibson's well-established communications center—the public telephone on the corner of East 55th Street—or else one at the back of the apartment building near the doorman's quarters. He had given the *News of the World* the doorman's number and it rang so often that the man was now answering it with a facetious, "Miss Gibson's secretary speaking."

Finally suspicious, Gibson followed the journalist downstairs and heard him dictating more copy into the phone to Bob Satchell.

Furious, she snatched the instrument from Lisners, shouting into the phone, "There's no story, do you hear? No story! You better hang up now because there's no story!"

Back in her apartment, she and Lisners had a blazing fight. "Clarence has not cleared it!" she shouted at him.

"Sometimes you can't stop these things," he replied.

Now it was her turn to use her communications center again. She called Koopman, reversing the charges. It was two o'clock in the morning in New York and five hours later in London.

"Eddie, what the hell are you doing sending me this cheap hack? You never told me he was Australian! I'd never have agreed if I'd known he was Australian! I have enough problems already trying to make the British see the American problems and the Americans see the British. Now I've got an Australian hack!"

Under the circumstances, Koopman showed remarkable patience. He was not a young man, wanted no part in the events that were raging about him, and had done what he could out of friendship for three people: Marian Gibson, Winterton, and Lisners.

But he knew she had been through the wringer. He calmed her down and she returned to her apartment, where she and Lisners now forged an uneasy truce. Later in the night, however, she heard him tapping away again on her electric typewriter.

"I don't know why you're bothering. I told you—there's no story!"

Lisners turned from the typewriter. "Look, Marian, it's very difficult to stop a story like this," he repeated.

That sent her into a fresh paroxysm of fury, and again she dashed for the corner telephone to call Koopman. Then she tried to phone Winterton collect, only to hear his wife on the other end decline to accept the charges.

It was 5:30 in the morning and she felt friendless and even more alone. In desperation she ran to Clarence Jones' apartment—all the way to 68th and Second Avenue—running in the middle of the street since New York at that hour was no place for a woman to be out alone.

"Clarence, he's called the story in!" she gasped when she arrived.

Jones had regained his characteristic composure. "Don't worry, Marian," he tried to reassure her. "Maybe we can still control it."

Later that morning he took her back to her apartment. Jones stood a head taller than Lisners, and without threats or raising his voice, settled down to get Lisners to produce an approved version.

Jones knew almost as much about the DeLorean situation as did Gibson. In preparing her suit, he had talked to a number of disaffected former employees, as well as to others such as Bill Haddad. He had talked half a dozen times to Winterton and been a major factor in the MP's determination to press ahead with his demand for an inquiry.

"He was very articulate, very delightful over the phone," Winterton recalled later. Now Jones was able to reach the compromise he wanted for Gibson quite quickly.

While they were talking, Bill Haddad called. The *News of the World* team in London had been unleashed: first stop, DeLorean; second stop, Haddad.

"They've been in touch with DeLorean and they've been in touch with me," reported Haddad. "I've said I'm not firing the bullets. But it's getting pretty hot."

At that moment, Marian Gibson's doorbell rang and her maid, Alnora Sharrie, came in to say it was DeLorean's interior decorator and confidant, Maur Dubin. DeLorean had sent him to ask why Gibson was doing this. She would not see him, so he sent up a note written on gold letterhead. "John is not angry or bitter," the note read. "He just wants to know why you are doing this, Marian. He just wants to talk to you."

But she did not want to talk to DeLorean.

Later there was another caller: George Hayward, who worked with Kimmerly. Gibson was fond of Hayward, but wouldn't see him either that morning.

"Tell her John DeLorean is not angry," Hayward told Sharrie. "He just wants to talk to her. Please will she talk to him?"

Gibson would not.

But Lisners did. The *News of the World* was chasing DeLorean, leaving messages for him to call back. But the switchboard in the office was unmanned because it was a Saturday morning.

DeLorean was in the office. Haddad had talked to him there that morning. Lisners knew the layout from his surreptitious visit the day before. Clutching his tape recorder, he took a taxi to 280 Park Avenue, caught the express elevator to the 43rd floor, and walked into the office.

There was an electric eye at the door that instantly alerted those inside of a new arrival. But Lisners hurried past the empty reception desk, past the empty offices of Stark and Kimmerly, and walked straight in on John DeLorean. For twenty minutes or so he asked questions and DeLorean answered them, with Lisners all the while expecting to be leaped upon by heavies. But DeLorean, despite the abrupt intrusion into his private office, was surprisingly polite, at least at first. Finally he asked Lisners to go.

The journalist gleefully played back the tape in the taxi he shared with Marian Gibson on the way to the airport until she made him switch it off—she could not bear to hear the voice of her former boss.

Once at Kennedy, she took the journalist to dinner. But three days without sleep finally caught up with him and Lisners slumped over and fell asleep in the middle of it. His elation had given way to dejection by then because he'd discovered he was no longer going to be on the front page. A final phone call to check with the news desk had brought the bad news.

"Sorry, John, they've killed your story." No one would tell him exactly why, just that the decision had come from Murdoch himself.

Murdoch was not often in London, even less often personally present at the *News of the World* news desk. But he was there that night. Why did he want the story squelched?

Events in London that day had moved as briskly as they had in New York. Chief Superintendent John George and Detective Inspector John Hefford set out early in the morning for the long drive up to Macclesfield and Winterton's house. In the meantime Downing Street was getting its first phone calls from the *News of the World* and calls were going out to other parties who might shed some light on the situation.

By midmorning Askew had his confirmation: the prime minister had indeed ordered the police to investigate. It was now a "Prime Minister Orders Police Probe" story—and the *News of the World* still had it all to itself.

Winterton was out on constituency business, and his wife, who

answered the phone call from the reporter, made no comment. Winterton later drove over to Koopman's house and collected the folders
of Gibson's papers, tightly wrapped and sealed by Koopman.

Just after noon, Rupert Murdoch called his editor. That was his
invariable habit, no matter what part of the world he was in. Whether
it be from Australia or New York, every Saturday he phoned Askew
to discuss the main stories with him in considerable detail.

Murdoch was in Oxford that Saturday morning, lunching with the
imposing figure of Lord Goodman, Master of University College, Oxford. Goodman was one of the best-known figures in British life, not
just because of his extraordinarily memorable features—his huge eyebrows, enormous forehead, and generous girth—but because of his
unequaled range of contacts and friends.

In the past twenty years, Arnold Goodman—made a life peer by
Prime Minister Harold Wilson—seemed to have been at the center
of every major dispute, every problem, every big legal battle. He was
not involved as the cause, but as the man who produced the solution
or compromise.

Lord Goodman had served as chairman of the Arts Council, chairman of the Newspapers Publishers Association (all the Fleet Street
newspaper owners), senior partner of the law firm Goodman Derrick,
and friend and conscience to a legion of politicians, artists, real estate
tycoons, and newspaper barons. Murdoch, naturally, belonged to the
last category.

When Murdoch's call came through, Askew was excited about the
DeLorean story as he briefed his proprietor on it.

"That's one hell of a story," Murdoch told the editor. "I hope you
have proof of it."

By coincidence, Murdoch knew DeLorean. They did not know
each other well, but Murdoch's New York apartment happened to be
in the same apartment building on Fifth Avenue as the DeLorean
duplex. "I have never been in Mr. DeLorean's company more than
five minutes at a time," Murdoch later recalled, "and I cannot claim
to know him even slightly, let alone his wife, whom I have only met
in an elevator." Cristina was a noticeable figure around the building,
and John could scarcely be missed either. Later, the coincidence was
to be misinterpreted in Fleet Street bars as word spread that the *News
of the World*'s DeLorean scoop had been killed by Murdoch.

At lunchtime that Saturday, October 3, Rupert Murdoch was just hearing about the DeLorean story for the first time, and his editor, at least, was convinced that he liked the sound of it. Askew explained the inquiries they were making in New York, London, and Australia, where he had a reporter trying to get a direct quote from Mrs. Thatcher.

Sunday newspapers have an early deadline. The Fleet Street presses, the largest in the world, start to roll at six o'clock, which means last copy must be in by four. They can replate for later editions, of course, but that usually happens only when a late story breaks. This was not a late story and it was all running smoothly. Lisners was constantly calling from New York with updates; Downing Street had made the necessary confirmations. They had not reached Winterton yet, but there was still time.

Winterton was greeting the two detectives, George and Hefford, who arrived on his doorstep early in the afternoon after their long drive. He went through the papers with the men from Scotland Yard in his drawing room.

George asked him to outline the allegations that were made to him and that he had passed on to Downing Street. Winterton also relayed his conversations with Clarence Jones as further support. The detectives stayed about an hour, then left with the files, heading for the nearby police station.

Just after they left, the phone rang again. It was Director of Public Prosecutions Sir Thomas Hetherington, who wanted to speak to the two policemen.

"They've gone down to Congleton Police Station," explained Winterton. "If you hold on a moment, I'll get you the number." He put the phone down and looked up the number, but when he came back it was dead—the DPP had hung up.

Soon afterward the News of the World reporter caught him. "We understand you've sent a telegram to the prime minister on the question of DeLorean," said the reporter. The MP confirmed he had contacted Downing Street and that he had seen the police.

By now the Sunday Telegraph picked up the story, too. They knew nothing of Marian Gibson, but learned that Winterton had made certain allegations and that the prime minister had ordered an investigation. But the Telegraph had not seen the documents. They were now at the Congleton Police Station, being puzzled over by a bemused pair of detectives who until the day before had barely heard of De-

Lorean and who, lacking Marian Gibson's guidance, could make little of most of the items in the file. They immediately seized on Haddad's gold facet memo, although the names mentioned meant nothing to them.

By midafternoon the *News of the World* had laid out its two De-Lorean pages and they were being set in type. Murdoch arrived from Oxford and parked himself at what Fleet Street papers call the "back-bench," the area in a newsroom where the senior editors and subeditors sit and where the basic shape of the paper, evaluation of stories, pictures, and policy are handled.

The Australian began examining the DeLorean material meticulously. The paper's legal manager, Henry Russell Douglas, was not on duty that Saturday, but his deputy, John Hinchcliffe, was there. Hinchcliffe had a few doubts. So did Murdoch himself.

Murdoch knew DeLorean's willingness to sue and press his suit all the way, and there seemed more than an outside chance the paper would get involved in a costly writ for defamation of character on this one. Murdoch was also worried about the main sources: newspaper editors have an inherent and well-founded distrust of stories presented by dissatisfied employees. Marian Gibson clearly fitted that category.

Haddad, although not a direct source, figured centrally in the story because of the memos that Lisners was quoting. Murdoch knew Haddad, too—he had worked for him at the *New York Post* for several months and they parted, according to both Haddad and Murdoch, "on friendly terms." Askew recalls Murdoch instantly drawing back at the sight of Haddad's name and saying, "He's a left-wing nuisance." Murdoch denies that. "I may have referred to Bill's love of conspiracy theories, or even called him an 'unguided missile.' "

It was time to seek higher legal opinion. Charles Gray, an eminent counsel and the *News of the World*'s top legal adviser, was summoned to the office and arrived fifteen minutes later. He supported both Hinchcliffe and Murdoch: the story was not safe enough.

Askew argued for rescuing parts of it—the fact that the prime minister had ordered a police investigation seemed safe enough. But now they were running against the clock. If DeLorean wasn't going to be the lead story, they had better find something else quick. Murdoch, Askew, and the lawyers debated what other bits of the Lisners story could be resurrected to support the bald statement of a police inquiry. There were not enough to make sense.

Askew surrendered; he pulled the story out. Fortunately for him, there was a news story breaking that was not too bad a lead. IRA HUNGER STRIKERS SURRENDER was what *News of the World* readers got for breakfast the next morning instead of DeLorean. On page three, the follow-up feature was replaced by a story of a little girl who prayed every day for Idi Amin's right-hand man as he went on trial in Uganda —he was her father.

Nobody outside the paper noticed a thing. But Askew had lost an important battle with his proprietor. He had been editor for only six months and did not stay much longer.

When Lisners and Gibson landed in London Sunday morning, October 4, Lisners quickly grabbed the newspapers. There was no mention of DeLorean or Winterton other than a single paragraph in the *Observer*. Soon, however, the story began to come out, first on the radio but soon after in newspapers. By the next day, every paper carried the story on the front page.

16

THE STORM

Until now there was a possibility, perhaps even quite a good one, that John DeLorean could have pulled it off. No one had yet put all the details together, or thought too deeply about the General Motors background and the years since, or looked too closely at the product DeLorean was selling to the American public.

True, Northern Irish officials were annoyed and upset with him, but they were far from rejecting him completely. The British government—at least the prime minister and some of her key ministers—thought him a con man, but they had no proof, and their feelings for him were based on little more than personal conviction and dislike. There was a growing feeling in Britain that the taxpayer had been had, but that too was vague, unproven.

Up to this point, if DeLorean had turned around, gone to London, and said, "Look, I've been neglecting you people and I'm sorry. I've just had so many things on my mind. But now we've got a car, we're employing 2,400 people directly in Belfast and another 2,400 making components. We're almost there and I'm going to reform and give it my full attention," then he might even have gotten more money. It would have been a hard fight, but if he had been able to come up with another, say, $20 million, then it might still have worked. But the time for that had passed.

The prospects also dimmed in the financial community. DeLorean had dealt with a wide variety of banks and brokers, both in London and on Wall Street. There was Oppenheimer, from whom he had parted company after it raised $18.75 million, but with which DeLorean still remained on friendly terms. Just a few weeks before DeLorean was arrested, an Oppenheimer executive said, "I would love to be an investor in the rebirth of this company, and if they come back for money, personally I would be a player." But he emphasized the "personally." After the Gibson revelations, he could not have put together a prospectus even if he had tried.

Bache Halsey Stuart Shields, no small investment house, was still putting its name and reputation behind the prospectus for DeLorean Motor Holdings. The issue was ready to go any day. The SEC had just given its approval, all the documents had been signed, and if it had not been for the Gibson revelations and the ensuing storm, the offering would probably have been a success.

There were many banks and other institutions behind the scenes toying with the idea of investing. DeLorean had cast his nets wide, and although he had not yet landed many, there were plenty of big fish swimming inside them. Bank of America was already in for $25 million. Citibank lent to the group and so did Barclays. J. Henry Schroder Bank and Trust Company acted as trustee. In New York, Rothschild's subsidiary New Court Securities spent months trying to raise money for DeLorean from insurance companies and other groups.

None of these entities had learned anything more about DeLorean or his dealings than the British government, at least not initially. Through that week in October 1981, the glamour image still held. The DMC-12 had arrived in the United States, and although after the initial euphoria it was not a runaway best-seller, the common belief was that it was not a failure either. Considering the machine its own engineers thought it to be, the automotive press, though critical, had not been too unkind. Many of the faults were due to early production problems—soon they should be worked out.

Also still holding was the view of John DeLorean as innovator and entrepreneur, the man who understood what the American public wanted in its automobiles and who, when he wasn't allowed to make it at General Motors, made it himself. His image still stood high as the man who designed the "ethical" car that would last a generation. And the public, impressed by the man who made his dream come true, was still buying that dream—until Marian Gibson had her say.

In the worst moments of crisis John DeLorean kept his head. The tide had turned against him and was going to come in with increasing force until it swamped him. But in early October 1981, the swell was some way out and there were still a few sandbars it had to clear. He would try to hold it back.

During the weekend that Marian Gibson and John Lisners were traveling to London, DeLorean was already preparing his counter-blast. He was not yet fully aware of what was in the files Winterton had handed to Ten Downing Street. All he knew was that they contained material compiled from the files of both his former secretary and his former public relations chief, Bill Haddad. Neither of them knew the full picture, they had never been on the inside, and they could only be guessing about events of which they had no firsthand knowledge. He could dismiss that as the speculation of two disgruntled employees who had been fired.

DeLorean knew nothing about Winterton, but a quick phone call or two calmed his nerves a bit. No great following or power there, he learned. By a stroke of good luck—one of the few he was to have—Marian Gibson had chosen a maverick Member of Parliament to champion her cause.

The British police would soon be arriving, John DeLorean now learned. He would have to deal with that, too—it would be difficult but not impossible. The police would not be skilled in accounting, and he could show them the figures that were fully audited by Arthur Andersen, a name as well known and respected in British financial circles as it was in American.

Plan to show them everything—that had to be his strategy. Bamboozle them with figures and his openness, convince them they were dealing with the complaints of a couple of cranks and a gullible MP, and maybe apply some pressure from the London end.

DeLorean would start by discrediting the two main witnesses against him, particularly Marian Gibson. On Monday morning *The Daily Mirror* carried Lisners' story with quotes from her: "I don't want people to think I am doing this for revenge. I was quite happy with my job, and I was well paid." She was, Lisners quoted her as saying, "concerned most with the British investment of over 80 million pounds, he would come out on top and the British would lose control. It concerned me as a patriotic subject."

That Monday morning DeLorean took the offensive. He called a press conference, making sure the British press was well represented. Marian Gibson's character was about to be assaulted. In London Winterton was claiming she was an executive of DMC, which was an exaggeration. Now DeLorean verbally kicked her down the employee status ladder. She was a minor secretary, he said; she was then demoted to clerk, and then to typist in the PR department. How low can you go after that? his tone indicated.

What about those charges that he was short-changing the government? someone asked. "That's a completely stupid and asinine question!" he snapped. But it gave him the opportunity to launch phase two of his counterattack.

For a start, he said, he didn't even know what the allegations were. "But no company in the world has been subjected to more scrutiny than this one. We are constantly monitored by Revenue, auditors, accountants, consultants, and there are two directors from the Northern Ireland Department of Commerce on the Board." That was to be a major theme for him.

His contract with the British government was a matter of public record (it wasn't) and "we have more than fulfilled that contract—we are now employing 2,500, three years ahead of the time stated in the contract." He went on: "We are the most successful thing that has ever happened to Northern Ireland. But if I were a banker and somebody made these kinds of charges, I'd cut my credit line off tomorrow. If our banks and financial institutions elect to do that, we're going to close the plant tomorrow because we have no choice."

He was pleased with that. He had shown that if the allegations continued, there would be nothing left in Northern Ireland and it would all be the fault of those who were throwing around silly accusations. It was a powerful argument and would win him more time.

A few other points were made at that conference about which he was not so happy. He had to answer questions about his initial investment, which he again claimed was $4 million and which, he said, was made at the research and development stage before Belfast came into the picture. And on the government inquiry, he took a tone of sympathy with the position of Margaret Thatcher: "It is like anything else; when there is an allegation, the government must listen to the story."

All in all, it had not gone badly. The newspapers the next day carried the headlines he wanted: ALLEGATIONS STUPID, DELOREAN SAYS (*London Times*); DELOREAN ANGRY OVER ALLEGATIONS OF IRREGULARITY (*Financial Times*); DELOREAN DENIES CASH ACCUSATIONS MADE BY TYPIST (*Daily Telegraph*). The pressure was easing; the sandbar was holding back the tide.

But DeLorean had to make another decision that day, one that was a real setback. He postponed the flotation of the new holding company—it could not go ahead until all the publicity had died away and the investigation was finished. Marian had accomplished what she set out to do.

Now he needed a London laywer, someone who would stop the Fleet Street press from nailing him to the cross. It was Rupert Murdoch who arranged it for him—and it was no less a person than Lord Goodman himself, from the suite in the Savoy Hotel where he was living at the time, who agreed to act for him. That was a major coup —there wasn't a paper on Fleet Street that did not tread more carefully when it knew Goodman was about.

The next day DeLorean announced that he had asked his lawyers to start libel proceedings against "those involved in the vicious slandering of the project." But it was necessary to counter the idea that the company was being investigated. That was easily enough arranged, since Mrs. Thatcher, through the attorney general, had not ordered an investigation of DMC or any of the DeLorean companies. She had simply asked the police to look into the allegations. If they found there was something in them, then an investigation into the companies would begin.

On Tuesday, October 6, the British solicitor general, Ian Percival, denied that the company's affairs were being investigated. He said that he had authorized "the sort of steps which are taken over and over again, indeed must be taken when allegations of the type now being bandied about are made." The government was now anxious to avoid any accusation that it was acting in a way that would endanger the jobs of the DeLorean workers in Belfast.

"It hardly needs saying," added Percival, "that it would be highly irresponsible for anyone to leap to any conclusions, especially when, by so doing, it could put men's jobs at risk."

Winterton was now on the defensive, instantly worried by the threats of libel action, as DeLorean intended he should be. "Nobody said the company was being investigated," he told the *Daily Telegraph*. "At no time have I said there is a full-scale inquiry into the activities of Mr. DeLorean. I find it interesting that Mr. DeLorean is to take libel action. I presume against Miss Gibson. If she is not that important, the best thing would have been to let the matter drop as soon as possible."

Winterton that day was angrily denying DeLorean's suggestions that he went public with the allegations in order to seek personal publicity. He only made the affair public, he insisted, after hearing that Miss Gibson gave an interview to a free-lance journalist in America. He was also certain she held a position of responsibility in the company—she had told him, he said, that she was an administrative assistant dealing directly with John DeLorean (which, in a sense, was true, although an exaggeration of her last position).

Now DeLorean focused on the police inquiry. That had to be nipped in the bud or the whole thing would get out of hand. DeLorean had planted the political pressure in London, dropping hints of closure of the plant with the blame being put at the government's door. That would deter even this government from pressing its inquiries too far.

He had created major doubts about the credibility of Marian Gibson and had forced Winterton to duck for cover. But if the police decided there *was* something to investigate, then everything would be over. Even if he came out of that perfectly clean—and there were plenty of doubts about that (although DeLorean deluded himself to the end that he was untouchable)—a long drawn-out inquiry would kill him as sure as anything.

He need not have worried. The Scotland Yard inquiry proved to be a nonevent, almost a charade. The two detectives were not to blame for that—they did what they were told to do, which was not much. In all, they spent a week on the inquiry and they interviewed just six people—Gibson's lawyer, Haddad's lawyer, Winterton, Mike Knepper and the only two people with any real evidence—Marian Gibson and Bill Haddad.

When Chief Superintendent John George and Detective Inspector John Hefford were ordered by the attorney general's office to begin their inquiries, they knew nothing of the background of the whole affair. After talking to Winterton, they soon discovered that the MP knew little more than they did.

They were as puzzled as he was by Haddad's memo: how could he write a memo on December 26, Boxing Day, a holiday in England when no one went to work? And what exactly were gold facets from Harrod's? What was this about John DeLorean and Chapman and Swiss bank accounts? What sort of public relations man could possibly use phrases like "given the Fleet Street nature of the British media"? What sort of people were they dealing with?

Their interview with Winterton did not enlighten them or reassure them. They could not contact Gibson. However, they learned she was on her way and would be staying with a cousin in the Thames Valley, not far from Heathrow Airport.

It was Monday, October 5, before they saw her. She did not want to meet them at her cousin's modest house, so they agreed she would come to the nearest police station. Here George talked to her while Hefford took notes: full name, Marian Frances Gibson; age of witness, forty-two years, born November 30, 1938. Occupation: she gave them "assistant public relations officer" and Hefford dutifully noted it down.

George then took her through her full story, starting in September 1979, when she went to work for DeLorean. She listed for them her allegations against her former employer: DeLorean claimed he had invested $4 million in the project, but it was only $750,000 and that had been put up by his wife, Cristina. Could Marian prove that? Hefford carefully noted down, "Rumour had it that the original investment. . . ." Then she claimed that £7 or £7.5 million paid for gasoline-bomb damage in Northern Ireland was a complete ripoff because only the personnel department offices were destroyed. Hefford wrote that she said it was "extremely excessive." Gibson also told them her belief that DeLorean used the money to buy his Bedminster, New Jersey, estate, but had no proof either. Hefford noted, "rumour was caused by the fact that the timing coincided with John DeLorean's purchase of the Bedminster, New Jersey, estate." He continued to write "rumours" or "the impression was gained," or, referring to the dealings of the Northern Ireland company with Colin Chapman, "deduced that all was not right." But again she had no proof.

They went through the gold facets memo, which now became Exhibit MFG/1. It was from this, she admitted, that she "deduced" that all was not correct in the dealings with Lotus. She knew nothing more.

Her own four pages of typed notes laid out not only her thoughts on DeLorean, but also her own personal particulars—her previous employment with references, plus two sheets outlining her job description, became Exhibit MFG/2. She demanded them back, claiming they had been included inadvertently in the papers handed to Winterton and were her personal property.

There was also, as Hefford wrote in his notebook, "one black binder containing copies of interoffice memoranda and letters marked Exhibit MFG/3 and one black binder containing copies of interoffice memoranda and letters marked Exhibit MFG/4."

It was not much to go on. The two policemen were not even sure if the allegations—assuming they could be proven—added up to anything illegal. DeLorean might have been spending money wildly, as the Haddad memo alleged, but the Northern Irish officials must know all about that—they had two men on the board. There did not seem to be anything too terrible, unless Haddad was inferring there were payments to the IRA. They weren't sure if he was.

Gibson told George and Hefford they must see two people in particular: Bill Haddad and her lawyer, Clarence Jones. Obviously they had to, George decided, and a few other people as well. It meant going to New York.

The next day they flew out of Heathrow—an adventure for both of them, since it was very rare that London police officers traveled overseas on business. Neither had ever been to New York and they were excited by the prospect. They were somewhat nervous, too, as they read the newspapers still full of front-page stories on DeLorean. A large responsibility seemed to rest on their shoulders and they were very much in the dark. They were rapidly becoming more curious, but not much wiser.

Even as the two policemen arrived in New York, DeLorean was beginning to relax, the tension slowly unknotting. He knew the situation was still serious, but the word he was hearing from London was that all would be well; the police inquiry was nothing to worry about. Lord Goodman was able to discover what the allegations were, and John DeLorean knew they could be handled. The Haddad memo was the one really damaging document.

DeLorean decided he would now begin to put the pressure on Haddad. He phoned him, telling him calmly that he knew he had given private memos and letters to Gibson, who carried them to Winterton. He was even able to tell him what they were.

DeLorean outlined the questions the police would ask. "They want to know why you wrote me a memo the day after Christmas," he said. "Nobody in Britain works on that day. They'll never believe you wrote that one. And they think these gold facets of yours are in my own house, one of my houses in the United States, not Belfast. And they're interested in the IRA angle."

Ignoring Haddad for the moment, DeLorean moved on to the next stage of his counteroffensive. He would bring on the secret weapon: Cristina. His wife always wanted to be an actress more than a model, and here was an unsurpassed opportunity for her to perform before the entire world. She was superb. The BBC cameras were allowed into their spacious Manhattan apartment and focused on an emotional Cristina, eyes welling with tears, at times so overcome she could barely get the words out, choking over her feelings of frustration and worry.

"It's so unfair. There are one or two people in Parliament who are against this project. He's put ten years of his life and four million dollars of his own into this project. He goes into this strife-torn area and creates 2,000 jobs and I worry one day he'll be brought home in a box. He hasn't seen a penny of personal profit yet. But he will, he will. And why shouldn't he?"

She pictured John DeLorean as a softy, a pushover for the likes of Marian Gibson, who were out to damage him for their own spiteful ends. It was nonsense that Gibson now feared for her life. "He never locks anything. It would have been so easy to get into his files. He's been audited three times by Parliament and always came out clean. As for Miss Gibson being in danger, he wouldn't hurt a fly."

As for paying for the house in Bedminster, that was easily explained away, too. "John sold a ranch to pay for that. I work hard. I make a lot of money. I helped buy that house."

At the same time, DeLorean was talking to the British ministers, illustrating to them his new relaxed, laid-back manner. "I'm not criticizing what was done," he told Adam Butler. "You have behaved quite properly. I know you did the same as you'd have done if it were any other company."

But he also wanted Butler to understand very clearly the damage a lengthy police inquiry would do to the project in Belfast. How long before there was a statement? It must be soon, he urged. Butler thought there would be a statement "very soon." And Goodman was more and more cheerful, pulling his powerful strings behind the scenes, letting people who mattered know that he, Lord Goodman, had looked at the allegations and there was nothing in them.

In New York the two policemen could not make up their minds either way—they simply did not have enough information to go on. They seemed to be getting nowhere fast as they tried to contact the witnesses who might help them. Even Haddad was proving difficult.

The next day DeLorean, Haddad and Knepper flew to Florida. DeLorean was giving a speech that Haddad helped write. Haddad was just along for the ride and a chat with DeLorean about his compensation. It did not work out as either intended. Haddad had a five-year contract at $125,000 a year, which still had three years to run. He also had options to purchase 100,000 DMC shares at ten cents a share (the dealers paid $5 and even Johnny Carson paid $2), but his right to exercise the option on 40,000 of them had already lapsed. Haddad was hoping they could agree to a golden handshake. He and DeLorean sat beside each other on the way down and talked desultorily. Haddad raised GPD and Lotus.

"Bill, that was all approved by the Northern Ireland people, by the auditors and even by the Bank of England. It doesn't concern us. I think it was a scam for Colin Chapman, but that was the way he wanted to do it, not us. You've met Colin Chapman, he was a racing driver and he's got ice in his veins. I think it was just his offshore thing. We looked at the directives and we still don't know who owns it, but I believe it is Chapman, personally."

The atmosphere on the way down was cold but polite. On the way back it was hostile. During the day DeLorean had a call from Tom Kimmerly. That morning's *Daily Mirror* had yet another Lisners story. It had printed Haddad's memo, complete with "gold facets." Everybody else was following it up. There was no more talk about amicable settlements. DeLorean now determined to do to Haddad what he had done with Dewey, Strycker, Gibson and anyone else who he felt had betrayed him: in his own phrase he would "put some shit on his shoes."

Haddad needed a new lawyer, of that he was certain, and he would not see the Scotland Yard detective until he had one. Ira Lee Sorkin of Squadron Ellenoff Plesent & Lehrer agreed to act for him. But Thursday was Yom Kippur and much of New York was closed, including Sorkin's firm. They finally arranged to see the detectives on Friday, Sorkin reluctantly agreeing to break what he had intended to be a long Jewish holiday weekend.

In the meantime George and Hefford managed to set up their first interview, with Clarence Jones. His only knowledge of DeLorean was what he had gained secondhand from Gibson and Haddad. He took them no further, except that he was calmer and more coherent than his client. DeLorean decided to strike at the heart of the controversy and caught a Thursday-night plane out of JFK, arriving at Heathrow the next morning. Wearing dark glasses, a turtleneck, blazer, and flannel trousers, John DeLorean started his hatchet job on Haddad as soon as he alighted from the plane.

"The memo is a forgery," he told reporters. "We now think Marian Gibson's whole concept was to create a story to be sold for money. Without a doubt money was her motive. She asked for $200,000 for the story."

It was a total lie.

DeLorean seemed increasingly confident, as even Haddad, viewing the situation from a distance, could see. DeLorean had flown to London, he said casually, "to get everything sorted out. I am confident everything will be cleared up, because it is so silly. The attorney general has retreated and they say the government will soon make an announcement which will clear up the whole thing."

Haddad's interview with the detectives did not calm his nerves. As DeLorean predicted, they started in on the date of the memo.

"Odd day to write, isn't it?" asked Chief Superintendent George with that deceptively understated politeness of the best British policemen. Boxing Day? Not a day for thinking about that sort of thing. Had he really written it?

Yes, said Haddad, certainly he wrote it. Boxing Day was not observed in the United States. It was not unusual to work on that day although, yes, the DeLorean office was closed. But was it delivered? DeLorean was saying he had never set eyes on it before. Haddad insisted he had. How could he be sure? He knew the systems, he insisted, and could prove to them that the memo was seen by De-Lorean. There were witnesses who would confirm it.

Then George turned to the "gold facets" and the sentences "I recently learned, for example, that we may have hidden some of the capital expenses of the house in expenses for the project. In short, the books were altered. Silly, because the house can be justified."

What was that about—what house was it? Haddad corrected their impression that it was a private DeLorean house in the United States. It was a house on the edge of the factory site in Belfast, and it was really Chuck Bennington, the managing director there, who spent the money, not DeLorean.

They also brought up the question of the IRA: did Haddad suspect any DeLorean money had gone to that organization? "To the best of my knowledge," replied Haddad cautiously, "the DeLorean Motor Company did not pay tribute to the IRA." He had never heard of any and had not meant to imply there was any in the memo. That was not what he was saying at all.

But he needed more files and Sorkin thought he could do with more time to go through the papers and documents Haddad had brought in only that day. They had been at it for hours and the detectives were starting to despair. Haddad, under instructions from his lawyer, would not talk openly and told them little. However, they agreed they would hold another meeting, preferably over the weekend or on Monday. That was awkward for Haddad and his lawyer. Sorkin suggested Tuesday and the officers, under pressure from London for a speedy resolution, reluctantly agreed. In the meantime Sorkin would attempt to retrieve more files from Haddad's office at the DeLorean Motor Company and would review them over the weekend.

But first Sorkin had to perform another duty. Reporters were now demanding to hear from Haddad whether he really was the author of that memo. Sorkin emerged from the meeting with the detectives and told the *Daily Mail*'s reporter, "I am authorized to confirm that Mr. Haddad is indeed the author of the memo." Such was the focus of interest in the story by now that the *Mail* built most of its front page around this one sentence alone the next day, together with a picture of DeLorean carrying his bags off the airplane.

The detectives now planned their schedule for the following week. They had not learned much since arriving in New York. There might be something here—they wanted to take a look at GPD, which seemed to be a fruitful area of investigation, particularly in view of the elaborate secrecy that surrounded it. Walter Strycker might be worth talking to also, although they were having difficulty locating him.

George and Hefford were not impressed by the witnesses so far. Aware of the political pressures in the matter, they were unwilling to accept at face value the allegations made by Gibson and Haddad. They had seen some memos and other papers, but they were not even convinced that Haddad had sent that memo or if he had that DeLorean received it. They had made no approach to the DeLorean office so far; DeLorean himself was back in London and they were not even certain whom else to interview.

They finally selected Haddad's successor, Mike Knepper, whose name they had seen in the papers answering some press queries. But it was Friday night and he had gone for the weekend. How could they reach him? They worked their way through the Kneppers in the phone directory, finally contacted him, and arranged a meeting for the next day.

On Sunday, however, a phone call from London changed their plans. It was from the Director of Public Prosecutions office, the formal link in the command chain between the attorney general and the police. No, they had to admit, they had not discovered anything so far to prove or disprove the allegations, but what with Yom Kippur and not being able to contact people, they had barely begun. they might make better progress next week. "No," said the voice at the other end. "The enquiry is over. Cancel whatever appointments you've made and come home."

The police investigators discovered nothing. The politicians remained in charge, still supporting John DeLorean.

DeLorean himself was under siege in London over the weekend. But outside events were going better for him than he could have hoped. The detectives were ordered home. Now the attorney general, Sir Michael Havers, informed colleagues that DeLorean would be cleared. There was nothing in Marian Gibson's allegations. He would make a statement Monday, October 12, to that effect. That weekend the *Sunday Telegraph* broke the news—they had already learned what the result would be. So had DeLorean.

Sunday night he went for a walk in London on his way to dinner at one of the smarter clubs where he was a member. (He had joined Les Ambassadeurs, Harry's Bar, and Annabel's.) On his way, he passed a church. The pressure had been intense and suddenly he wanted to go inside. Later DeLorean was to claim in an interview: "I am sitting in the church praying, and I turn around and here is some guy behind me holding a tape recorder. And it's a guy from the *Daily Mail.* I said, 'I can't believe this! Is nothing sacred to you people?' "

The *Daily Mail* had a different version. According to its editor, the reporter approached DeLorean on the pavement outside the church and did not try to interrupt his prayers. But it was just another example of the pressure that DeLorean still faced.

On Monday morning, October 12, the attorney general met with Sir Thomas Hetherington, who made the statement that lifted the weight of the world off DeLorean's shoulders for a few months.

No evidence had emerged, said Hetherington, "to support any of the allegations of criminal conduct against Mr. John DeLorean or the company which bore his name."

The police inquiry had ended, although, said Sir Thomas, "should any evidence of a criminal offense subsequently come to the attention of the Director he would give it consideration." It was to be thirteen months before any more evidence would surface and new inquiries started.

But for the moment DeLorean was in the clear. In triumph, he caught a plane to Belfast, where he had a press conference to further refute the allegations against him and throw a little mud himself with an accusation that shook everyone present, including his own executives.

"I have a strong feeling that the widespread publicity given to the allegations is part of a wider conspiracy." He paused for effect. "It appears to be an organized attempt to destroy this company. Wiser heads than mine will have to seek out the motives of those who would destroy us. The allegations could have been made for political or economic reasons. A foreign country may have been involved in the plot to destroy Ulster's proudest achievement."

There were gasps. What foreign country? What was he talking about? "I dare not name the country I have in mind," DeLorean went on. "It is unlikely that a group of minor people of limited ability could have created the problem alone. Why did it all happen suddenly when we started looking like we were going to make the grade? It is a distinct possibility that a competitor within the car industry was responsible."

He ended with a threat: "I will be issuing writs against the people who were the most serious perpetrators of terrible crimes against this company. Miss Gibson and Mr. Winterton have formed a combination of people with limited ability who caused all this trouble."

What was the country? he was immediately asked. Were other people in the automotive industry responsible for the conspiracy against him? "I do not know. It is a distinct possibility. It may even be a country," he repeated. But *what* country? DeLorean was using one of his favorite techniques: plant his idea and let it grow in the other's mind. He would go no further, not even to his own executives, who had never heard any of this before, nor would they again.

All that remained for him to do now was to carry out his threat. He flew back to London that night and the next day Lord Goodman went into action on his behalf. Nicholas Winterton, at the Conservative Party conference in Blackpool, learned that he personally was being sued for sums he could not possibly hope to pay. DeLorean spread the libel net wide: Marian Gibson and Haddad, the *Daily*

Mirror, the free-lance journalist John Lisners, the BBC, and Independent Television News were all included with the MP. DeLorean had settled on a nice round figure: $250 million was about right.

As he boarded the Concorde to fly back to New York on Tuesday morning, he allowed himself some further elaboration. "We feel we have been damaged to the extent of $250 million and we are now at the stage of figuring out who is going to pay," he told reporters. "Some of the media have claimed I have taken too much money from the company. My hope is that when these writs are served and we've won the libel action, I won't be taking any more from the company because various members of the media will support me for the rest of my life."

With that, he passed through customs and flew home. He has handled the affair with considerable skill and nerve, only losing himself slightly in the curious conspiracy theory in Belfast and with the *Daily Mail* reporter outside the church on Sunday evening. He had held back the tide during that one long week, even raising a sandcastle on the sandbar. He was cheerful as he boarded the plane, the pressure easing after one of the toughest weeks of his life. There would not be many more good moments.

17

THE MONEY RUNS OUT

It was to be a brief triumph. Events that had conspired in DeLorean's favor now moved against him. When he arrived in Belfast knowing that within a few hours he would be officially cleared of Marian Gibson's allegations, the tide had reached the top of the sandbar and was about to spill over.

He was running out of money and it was going to be harder and harder to find more—even to persuade his existing lenders to continue funding the shipment of his cars. At the Dunmurry factory, the large courtyard was chock full of cars. The docks in Belfast could take no more. They were piling up in the warehouses in California and in the showrooms all over the United States. The production lines were now churning them out at a rate of eighty a day, but sales were running at just half that.

DeLorean had gambled heavily the previous summer when he took on 900 extra workers. It probably saved his skin in the last week—2,400 jobs, conveniently rounded up to 2,500 by DeLorean at every opportunity, sounded so much more impressive than 1,500.

It indicated to the naive government officials and the outside world that demand was so great he could sell every car he could produce—and more. Against these jobs, what did a few "gold facets" matter? Or even a few million dollars here and there that he might or might not have invested? Would any official endanger those jobs and a successful business operation on the word of a sacked secretary, a former public relations man, and a maverick Tory MP?

That hiring decision, made solely to impress potential investors, did more to destroy the DeLorean empire than anything else. Components, wages, and overhead were all two to three times higher than they should have been for the volume of sales.

In the autumn the United States auto market fell deeper into recession than anyone had anticipated. Sales ran at their lowest levels since the 1950s, and although luxury cars held up remarkably well—Jaguar, for instance, doubled its U.S. sales in 1981—sales of DMC-12s were running behind production. DeLorean advertised heavily, but the car itself had not lived up to its promise, and driver reaction was not what he had hoped. John DeLorean no longer sounded quite the "ethical" person he had presented himself, the car no longer seemed to be the great, revolutionary machine the American public was expecting.

In California Dick Brown still believed he could sell all the cars Belfast could produce—and his optimism buoyed the others.

DeLorean's bloated payroll was eating the slender cash reserves, and so were sky-high stocks of unsold cars and the cost of financing them. Overhead in Belfast and in New York was huge compared to the size of the company—DeLorean was paying General Motors-size salaries and even more in severance pay. He had built an exceedingly top-heavy organization, using the British government's money, and was able to keep juggling with all the balls in the air while the car remained only a prospect. But it was a reality now, and it was beginning to show badly in the marketplace.

DeLorean could no longer convince the British government that unless it put in that extra few million pounds, they wouldn't even have a car to show for their previous £84 million and all their money would be wasted.

What he could—and did—say was to the effect that "I said I'd build a factory and I've built it; I said I'd build a car and here it is. Everyone in the United States is enthusiastic about it—here are reports to prove it. Our very success is creating a cash flow problem. The need to finance higher stocks and a higher volume of production, plus higher inflation (which is your fault) and the impact of strong sterling, are all draining away my cash. Just a small bit of extra money and you'll have a great investment."

* * *

Mr. Cryer asked the Secretary of State for Northern Ireland whether any further application for financial assistance had been received from DeLorean Cars Ltd.; and if he will make a statement.

Mr. Adam Butler: No application for selective assistance additional to that already notified to the House has been made by DeLorean Motor Cars Limited. The company has lodged a number of grant claims under the Industrial Investment (General Assistance) (Northern Ireland) Act 1966 (as amended) under which standard grants are payable in respect of eligible capital expenditure. These are under consideration.

Hansard, Written Answers.
October 23, 1981

Cryer's questions were usually based on firm knowledge; this October day was no exception. Butler's reply to Cryer's inquiry on "further application for financial assistance" was technically correct: there had been no application for more money. But just one week after DeLorean boarded the Concorde to return in triumph to New York, the McKinsey Company delivered its latest status report. In stark terms it warned NIDA chief executive Tony Hopkins that "the relationship between DMC, DMCL and H. M. Government is once again entering a particularly sensitive phase. There is a strong likelihood that the Company will approach NIDA, and through it the Department of Commerce, for further assistance."

The political difficulties that would ensue, the report cautioned—as if Hopkins were not already aware—"are clearly considerable—as are the economic risks for the Province if a satisfactory outcome cannot be negotiated."

That report was dated October 21. Two days later Butler was fending off Cryer's question and once more refusing his request to file either the British government's agreement with DeLorean (although most of it had already been revealed in U.S. Securities and Exchange Commission documents related to the planned issue of DeLorean Motor Holdings) or DeLorean's contract with Lotus, in the House of Commons library.

John DeLorean was still desperately anxious to get his stock issue off the ground, and that week he insisted to the Northern Irish officials and ministers that he needed all their help. DeLorean asserted that the major point of it was to fund the DMC-24, the gull-wing-door sedan that could be launched in 1983–1984.

But he also talked openly about the "tremendous damage done" to his company by two weeks of "scurrilous allegations" that had led to the delay of that issue. He was still astonishingly optimistic about his prospects. He continued to exaggerate, tossing about the type of unrealistic figures that British government officials hated to hear from him, knowing what nonsense it all was. For example, he planned to raise production of the car in the following year by 50 percent, he said, which would mean 3,500 to 4,000 jobs at Dunmurry.

The last questions from the SEC on the prospectus would be replied to that week, DeLorean told the officials, and the issue could go ahead quickly. But it had to take place within ninety days before the need for money for the sedan became urgent.

Once again this was a typically misleading DeLorean statement. The sedan would cost at least $80 million to develop. Bache was already saying that because of the slump in the car market and the troubles DeLorean was having, they would not now get the $28 million they once hoped for. It would be less than $20 million. Of that, $3.1 million would go to the limited partners in DeLorean Research Limited Partnership and another $2.4 million to Oppenheimer in fees. Then there was Bache's fee—DeLorean never mentioned how much he thought that would be, but it wasn't going to be less than Oppenheimer's total. So even if he took in $20 million gross from the stock issue, the company itself would get only between $11 million and $12 million toward its already critical finances. There would be nothing for the sedan, but DeLorean's own shares in the company would still have a value of nearly $100 million.

A week after the DPP cleared DeLorean of Marian Gibson's allegations, he was still smarting.

"At the end of the day it's like being given a certificate to say you're sane. You're still the only one with that certificate," he said wryly.

Behind the scenes, however, there was little humor that week as the skirmishing began in earnest about another infusion of government money—or else a closed factory in Belfast.

DeLorean was negotiating intensely again, claiming the furor caused by Gibson's allegations and relayed by a member of the Conservative Party had damaged his position badly. He arrived in London the following Monday, only a week after he had left, and on Tuesday turned up at Earl's Court for the annual Motorfair. The DMC-12 was on display at the show for the first time, and with all the controversy of the past weeks, it was getting star attention. For a few hours he stayed on the stand alongside the sales team, then hurried off for talks about the pressing matter of new money.

British government guarantees on £17 million in bank loans from Barclays and Citibank would run out at the end of the year, and if DeLorean could not extend those guarantees, then his company would be bankrupt.

The left-wing Labour MP Bob Cryer was once again on the prowl, probing the Northern Irish minister of state, who must have suspected by now that Cryer had a "deep throat" either in NIDA or the Department of Commerce in Belfast.

Time and again Cryer asked the most penetrating and embarrassing of questions. He had asked the very first question ever in Parliament on DeLorean, and he kept up the barrage. He brought up GPD, the Oppenheimer partnership, the Lotus deal, DeLorean's outside interests, the role of the outside directors on the DeLorean board, and many other issues, all more or less simultaneously with the first suspicions that all was not entirely above board. The unfortunate Adam Butler usually answered Cryer evasively. Sometimes Butler was made to look foolish within days by ensuing events; sometimes his responses were dead wrong. Cryer's sources kept him far better informed than the minister's. Other MPs asked questions on DeLorean, but on the whole they were ordinary and predictable ones, based on their own uninformed views or particular prejudices.

Butler could have done without Cryer's insider questions that week. He could also have done without an incident, amusing in retrospect but infuriating at the time, at the Dunmurry plant: the tea break dispute.

It happened on the Thursday nightshift, when the workers in the body shop went off for their tea break. There was a major problem: no water. The supply to the factory had been interrupted, and without water, there could be no tea.

Disgustedly the nightshift workers eventually strolled back into the body shop to find that the foremen had refused to wait for them and had started up some of the machines. The foremen were anxious to catch up with their production targets—there were presently no fiberglass body shells in stock.

A shouting match followed as the men strongly objected to supervisors trying to take over their work. When the dayshift came on, the shop stewards announced they would mount a token work stoppage. Management reacted by suspending all 250 of the men.

It was one of the few strikes at Dunmurry; the plant had been remarkably calm by British automobile industry standards. The striking workers belonged to the Transport and General Workers, whose leader in Northern Ireland was John Freeman, an intelligent, responsible man who was also on the NIDA board. Freeman had a sense of humor: he described the incident as a "storm in a teacup." He was right: the workers were all back on the job on Monday, although over the weekend some 700 of them had become involved.

At 280 Park Avenue the storm was in something larger than a teacup. John DeLorean was about to lose another of his senior executives, this time his president and chief executive, Eugene Cafiero. In reality, Cafiero had been on the way out since the end of September just before Marian Gibson blew the whistle.

Cafiero negotiated himself a handsome contract when he joined John DeLorean. Now that he was leaving, he intended to get the full benefit of it. He began work in May 1979 with a five-year contract at $375,000 a year plus options of 500,000 shares (then loosely valued at $10 each). To replace the benefits at Chrysler that he abandoned, DeLorean made him an interest-free loan of $168,000, repayment to be made only if he received benefits from Chrysler. In total, Cafiero got $3,200 from Chrysler—and the remaining $164,800 was now "forgiven" by DeLorean and treated as compensation.

As the tea break strike was being settled in Northern Ireland, Cafiero's attorneys were drafting a letter for him and John to sign jointly. It started:

> Dear John,
> This will confirm my acceptance of the severance offer which you made to me, during the week of September 28th.

It then went on to list the particulars: Cafiero would receive his full $375,000 a year, payable monthly, plus cost of living allowances, until May 15, 1984. In turn he would be available as a consultant (in the unlikely event that DeLorean would want to consult with him), but would not be required to travel or attend meetings if he did not want to. If DeLorean wished, he could stay on as president until December 15, 1981. He would also have the use of a DeLorean automobile "to be delivered not later than November 15" and replaced each year on October 1, while he remained a director—through 1983.

It was remarkable that a company trembling on the brink of bankruptcy and begging the British government for more money would agree to pay its former president some $1.2 million (and more, including pensions and other benefits) in compensation.

Since he formed the company, DeLorean had lost his senior executives in a steady stream. Bill Haddad had been terminated on September 23. That same day, DeLorean's third chief financial officer, James G. Stark, after long discussion with Roy Nesseth, had gone on medical leave and had not been back since. Nesseth was not directly responsible, although Stark was certainly afraid of him.

Stark's contract ran through October 31, 1982, at $300,000 a year. Under Nesseth's urgings, the financial officer, his neck in a brace and glad to be out of an office he had come to loathe, agreed to advance the expiration date to February 15, 1982—but he would be paid at his full salary rate until that date.

Bob Dewey now resigned again, too, for the third time. He had refused to return to his old position of chief financial officer and had served as a consultant and an executive at Composite Technology. But when Strycker left, Dewey discovered that DeLorean had re-elected him chief financial officer. Dewey resigned from that post the instant he learned of it, insisting it was a role he would never again occupy under any circumstances.

"The chief financial officer in this company is like a mushroom," Dewey would remark. "He's kept in the dark and fed manure." Dewey negotiated severance pay of $100,000 but never received it. He ended up on the five-man committee of DMC creditors appointed in January 1983.

Bill Collins served DeLorean as loyally as he knew how, and was forced out by the deal with Lotus.

Walter Strycker forged the deal with Northern Ireland, but left a year after that; DeLorean did his best to destroy Strycker's reputation, too.

Dick Brown still remained, but only by virtue of the fact that he ran his own operation in California, away from the mainstream. Even he had been removed from the main board of directors. Without Brown the company would not have survived. It was he who had the relationships with the dealers and it was only his efforts at the Quality-Control Centers that made the early cars marketable.

Haddad had been fired for objecting too loudly to the formation of the new holding company.

Marian Gibson was forced out by the classic DeLorean method of demoting and demoralizing.

In Belfast Chuck Bennington was sent to Coventry (literally as well as metaphorically) and was no longer an executive officer of either the Belfast company or DMC. And there were many others, including Terry Werrell and the Collins team.

Who was left? Who formed DeLorean's board at this stage?

Many of its members had significant financial and professional interests in the company, including DeLorean's closest confidant, Tom Kimmerly. The general counsel and his Detroit law firm had a five-year contract for $180,000 a year. In the previous four years, the DeLorean Motor Company had paid his firm $1,077,087 in fees—and Kimmerly, Gans, and Shaler would be a creditor in the amount of $208,228.51 when the company went bankrupt.

Robert W. Benjamin was a thirty-six-year-old New York lawyer who was also chairman of the audit committee. He was senior partner of Van Ginkel & Benjamin, which in the previous four years had received $221,585 in legal fees and would also be a creditor for $36,631.

There was another lawyer on the board—thirty-nine-year-old Henry "Bombastic" Bushkin, the designee of Johnny Carson. Bushkin's firm had been paid $108,306 in fees since 1978 and he went onto the creditor list for another $4,626.

Between 1978 and November 1981, DeLorean Motor Company paid out $1.65 million in legal fees to firms in which its own directors were partners—including the New York law firm Javits & Javits, which had first introduced John DeLorean to Oppenheimer, and whose partner Eric Javits was a director until May 1981.

There was another director on the board whose firm benefited from its DeLorean connection. Robert S. Gay was the owner of the insurance agency Robert S. Gay Associates, founded in Detroit in 1950. In 1980 alone DeLorean Motor Company paid that firm $857,640 in insurance premiums plus another $58,757 to Swanson Insurance

Company, a company controlled by another DeLorean director, Richard Swanson.

Edmund King, forty-eight-year-old head of Wood Gundy, one of the early investors in DeLorean, was also on the board. King arranged the introduction to the Northern Ireland authorities, for which his firm earned a fee.

Alex Fetherston and James Sim were the two directors on the board who represented the British government. They were both Belfast businessmen of some seniority and respect in their communities. They were paid the modest amount of £5,000 a year for their DeLorean duties (plus $600 a day for every day they spent on audit work that December). The two men were to display their naive assessment of the situation that December by proposing and seconding a motion— approved by the board of DMC in New York and DMC Ltd. in Belfast —granting bonuses of $760,000 to the most highly paid men on the team as a reward for their "excellent" work over the past year. DeLorean, who already had been paid more than $400,000, would get another $101,000. Kimmerly would receive $76,000.

There was another member of the board from whom John DeLorean could also hope for support: Cristina Ferrare DeLorean. She was elected in the boardroom reshuffle the previous year.

The so-called "audit committee" that was supposed to monitor the company's spending and, in particular, the British government's money, consisted of Benjamin as chairman, John DeLorean, Fetherston and Sim, plus Gay and Swanson.

Among the executive directors who remained were Jim Season, a thirty-seven-year-old financial man who was overawed by both DeLorean and Kimmerly. There was Buck Penrose, who joined DeLorean from Booz Allen & Hamilton at the height of the Northern Ireland negotiations and who was accused by the others of spending most of his time on DeLorean's outside activities. And there was Edward L. Smith, fifty-six, who ran the plastics company (CTC) and who kept his head down.

That was the composition of the top-heavy, expensive board that John DeLorean had built around himself by October 1981 as he moved into the thick of his financial crisis. Despite pressure from NIDA, he still occupied his luxurious offices on Park Avenue.

He was still building his empire that autumn with his outside projects: the hot-air engine; the "boutique" of DeLorean sunglasses, suede jackets, cosmetics, etc.; the Transbus; the snow-grooming company, and a dozen other ventures, most of which came to nothing.

The DeLorean art collection was now piled up on the floor in the quarters on the 35th floor, unappreciated. NIDA had made desperate efforts to make him sell some of the pieces, and at one point DeLorean surrendered marginally to the pressure.

Now more dependent than ever on British government money, DeLorean was still running an office and lifestyle worthy of an organization the size of General Motors. He used the Concorde on his frequent trips to London, stayed at the Connaught—one of the most expensive hotels in the world—and used London's best clubs, charging expenses to the company. He paid huge salaries to men like Cafiero and Stark when they were barely coming into the office any longer. John DeLorean thought it was nothing less than he deserved, and he resented the continual carping of Tony Hopkins. The prospectus published by Bache showed that in 1980 salaries had doubled to more than $5 million. Travel, entertainment, and promotion had risen from $540,000 to $1.1 million. Legal fees that year were $776,000. (Legal fees connected with the Bache issue in 1981 were nearly $2 million.)

Many of the DeLorean people were to remark afterward that "we should have been in a loft on Eleventh Avenue—or stayed in Detroit." California would probably have been an even more suitable place—that was where the market was and where the cars were being shipped.

The Northern Ireland officials were getting improper figures and sometimes no figures at all for months on end. By the end of October their anxiety was considerable. It was becoming clear to all those who knew John DeLorean that he could not go on like this—that bankruptcy might be only weeks, and certainly no more than months, away. The steady run of departures, the leaks, the lack of proper accounting, the misleading statements he continually made, all pointed to a company running out of control.

Wednesday, October 28, 1981: The board of the Northern Ireland Development Agency assembled for its monthly meeting at its usual time of 10 A.M. in its Maryfield offices. Dennis Faulkner chaired the meeting. Tony Hopkins, his chief executive, was present to report on DeLorean. NIDA had met twice during the height of the Gibson affair, but this was its first full board meeting since it had all blown up.

NIDA had set up a special monitoring committee for its largest investment, but that did not seem to be helping the situation. Hopkins had the latest McKinsey Report as well as his own report on the proceedings of the past month. Both were equally disturbing, but particularly McKinsey's assessment that DeLorean was running into another major cash shortage and would be coming back to them for at least £10 million—probably more. With DeLorean it always seemed to be more.

But Hopkins brought up another point that morning. The De-Lorean company in the United States was no longer holding board meetings. None had been held for some time; therefore the two Northern Ireland directors did not know what was going on. The audit committee was "not functioning," he reported. The entire board of NIDA was aghast, knowing full well that every one of them would take the blame for the venture gone wrong.

Hopkins could no longer get information from DeLorean. He was being treated resentfully and cavalierly, since DeLorean wanted to deal only with the ministers.

But it was still a NIDA responsibility. After all, NIDA had the equity investment and was responsible for monitoring the government money. The meeting was a long one as the board discussed in some despair the possible lines of access to the U.S. company. Trade union leader John Freeman was particularly vocal, insisting that NIDA set out clearly to DeLorean its concern over the lack of board meetings, the audit committee, expenditures, and access to DMC and warn him yet again that unless the situation improved immediately, NIDA would pull the plug.

Nevertheless everyone realized how powerless they really were. In New York DeLorean openly boasted how he had the British government over a barrel. They had all heard the remark and knew it was true.

No more money would mean that DeLorean would be bankrupt—and £84 million already spent would go down the drain—with 2,500 thrown out of work at the factory. It was an appalling prospect.

At this point NIDA itself was undergoing yet another reorganization. It was to be merged and beefed up with a new board and executive as the Northern Ireland Industrial Development Board.

The feeling that things were going badly had now permeated the factory as well. The *Irish Times* sent a reporter to talk to the workers on the assembly line.

"No way would I buy one of these cars," said one worker. "I've seen what I put in, and no way would I pay for it."

They had complained about the components and been ignored, the men claimed.

"Everybody more or less thinks it's not going to last. Everybody's attitude is 'What's the point of complaining? We'll not be here in a few months.' If they had anywhere else to go they wouldn't be here."

They complained that their foremen had been appointed without training and "haven't got a clue." One of the stewards was more explicit.

"I didn't think things were all that good. I knew that something was amiss but I didn't think it was misappropriation of funds. I thought that the systems on the floor had no rhyme or reason. They just push the cars out the door and I thought the cost was astronomical. When you get the heads of departments coming out and physically working on the floor, there is something wrong."

Someone else said he felt sorry for the finance department. "There are people working here seven days a week and getting a twelve-pound check. It's human error, but when there were 300 or 400 human errors a week, there is something wrong."

Through November DeLorean and NIDA worked toward what everyone was aware would be a major confrontation by the end of the year. If the British government guarantees on the loans from Barclays and Citibank lapsed, then there was no more DeLorean Company. But there would be no jobs, either—and there would be plenty of egg on the faces of a large number of politicians and ministers who had supported the American car man.

The car itself was coming in for some adverse publicity. Mike Knepper later recalled in an article he wrote for *Motor Trend* in July 1982:

The electrical system soon took over the No. 1 spot on the list. It was, as Brown called it, a mess. At the heart of the problem was an alternator that was drastically understrength. Its maximum output was 75 amps, but with all the systems running, the car could easily draw 80 or 90 amps. Batteries were down and DeLoreans were lying dead all across the country.

Other recurring problems that seriously damaged the car's early reputation included power windows that fell out of their tracks; fuel gauges that would never register full (sending units and gauges were incompatible); leaking cooling systems; side bolsters that were scuffed and eventually ruined by the doors.

Not all early customers had lengthy tales of woe, but there were problems with almost every car sold. Some were so bad the company gave the customer a newer model, and actually bought the cars back from two, maybe three, irate owners.

Entertainer Johnny Carson, after taking delivery of his new De-Lorean, drove only a few miles before it broke down. A new distributor was rushed to the scene; that part broke down, too. Carson was not amused.

Then there was the man who climbed into a DMC-12 at a special display in a Cleveland museum and closed the gull-wing door. To his considerable surprise, he could not get out again and was forced to stay there for hours as officials and mechanics worked frantically to extricate him.

More importantly, the car was recalled for a second time. Some of the problems that so concerned the engineers at Belfast were surfacing. Early in the fall the front suspension on two cars collapsed onto the wheel assembly after a nut gave way. There were then 350 DMC-12s on the road; from Park Avenue, John DeLorean sent out eighteen people to get them back and remedy the problem. He managed it then without having the secret leak out.

But in mid-November, DeLorean had to make a public recall. The nuts holding together parts of the front suspension began to unscrew themselves after just a few thousand miles. There were 2,200 cars on the road; there was no way a recall could be done quietly.

The engineers hastily substituted a "castle" nut with a hole drilled through for a locking pin. Unfortunately, it was soon discovered that the drilling had caused hairline fractures in about 10 percent of the castle nuts that were sent from Belfast to the United States. The whole batch had to be sent back.

Some of the engineers who were concerned about the problems with the front suspension suggested that the DMC-12 go back to the drawing board and that the suspension be redesigned. There was no time for that, insisted DeLorean. But he did consult Porsche in the hope that they might come up with a solution. DeLorean engineers also discovered that some of the antiroll struts that should have held the suspension rigid were made with the wrong-size threads on the end, making them insecure. The potential was disastrous. If either a nut or an antiroll strut failed at high speed, the driver would find it difficult to retain control.

Meanwhile, Dick Brown was working night and day in the United States to sort out the quality-control problems. He created a smooth but expensive operation. The figure of $2,000 per car fell back a bit in the summer, but by late fall it rose again as the untrained work force churned out DMC-12s at a rate of eighty per day. At one point Brown was spending 140 hours fixing up each car. The time involvement did diminish to sixty-eight hours, but the $600 per unit was still a hefty expense on top of all the other costs the DMC-12 had to bear.

Brown in California and Lander in Belfast were ensuring that the cars were salable once they arrived in dealers' showrooms. But they could not easily cure the more fundamental engineering problems that arose as the cars were driven, and about which the engineers had warned again and again.

DeLorean suffered another blow, this time at the hands of Mother Nature. In November the rate of U.S. auto industry sales was an annual 8.3 million, a fairly good pace. But in December the weather turned cold, bringing the worst winter the U.S. had experienced in a century. It was not the time to sell cars, and certainly not sports cars. The annual rate dropped to a mere 6.0 million, the lowest in twenty-five years. Sales plummeted further to 5.8 million cars in January. The frigid weather coincided with the start of a $500,000 DeLorean print advertising campaign designed by the agency of Averett, Free and Fischer. It was the familiar "Live the Dream" theme.

"Your eyes skim the sleek, sensuous stainless steel body, and all your nerves tell you 'I've got to have it.' "

Two-page, four-color ads soon began appearing in the "high-demographic" periodicals: *Business Week*, *Newsweek*, *The New Yorker*, *Forbes*, *Fortune*, and *The Wall Street Journal*.

"The DeLorean, surely one of the most wanted automobiles in automotive history," the ads proclaimed.

Only it was no longer true. In Dunmurry the cars still came off the production lines at 400 a week, but they were beginning to pile up.

November 25: At NIDA's monthly meeting, everyone was worried about the Cafiero settlement. How could DeLorean possibly justify paying him nearly half a million dollars a year (including his various allowances) while he did virtually nothing in return? The costs of Brown's quality-control operations were also revealed for the first time. What was happening at Dunmurry that all the extra money had to be spent in the United States? Hopkins promised to make his own investigation of the Cafiero settlement and would take up the cost of quality control with Don Lander in Belfast.

McKinsey informed Hopkins in its latest status report that "Throughout 1981 DMC produced a succession of earnings, balance sheet and cash flow projections that have proved over-optimistic— perhaps inevitably, given the need to maintain management morale and commitment and to secure continued financial support from HMG." Certainly that was no news.

Hopkins presented one nugget of information, also overoptimistic. He understood that the public stock issue would go ahead in January, although at a much lower level. There would be only a tiny injection of funds into the company after fees and expenses, he said.

Bache still hoped to go ahead, but the brokerage house was now talking about raising only $12 million. It had not reduced the price per share—instead of 2.25 million shares, it was now proposing to issue a million shares at the old price of $12. Yet another massive document was dutifully filed at the SEC.

The ministers and officials in Northern Ireland finally decided to get tough with DeLorean. He would be coming to Belfast in mid-December and by then they had to approve the company's plans. NIDA had been trying to get tough for more than two years—its attempts to renegotiate a better deal ruined by Humphrey Atkins' generosity in August 1980 when he had handed DeLorean the extra £14 million, and by the less skeptical and more accommodating attitude of the Department of Commerce.

Wednesday, December 3: John Banham of McKinsey, the members of NIDA, and the Commerce officials met to prepare the way for the big showdown meeting with DeLorean scheduled for December 16. It would be only two weeks away from the deadline on the bank guarantees, so they would have DeLorean against the wall.

How to handle him? DeLorean was now asking urgently for an extra £5 million and his guarantees to be extended for another year. For once there was an agreement. They must all be "tough." No more money. But they would propose extending the guarantees.

The first week in December was a very good one at the factory in Dunmurry. The target of 400 cars was exceeded by three. In the United States, sales totaled 123 during the first ten days of the month. Production during November had run at roughly twice the level of retail sales. McKinsey was now reporting accurate sales and production figures, although a little late, but not nearly as tardy as the minister Adam Butler, who continued to present the best face for DeLorean.

The House of Commons, December 3, 3:15 P.M. The prime minister had just entered the Chamber for her biweekly session of Prime Minister's Question Time. The previous day, her chancellor of the exchequer, Sir Geoffrey Howe, presented a minibudget that projected price increases by some one to one-and-a-half percent, a disappointing blow for a prime minister pledged to conquer inflation.

Mrs. Thatcher was bracing herself now for a battle with the leader of the Opposition, Michael Foot, who was already on the benches across the Dispatch Box. As she slid into a seat on the Government front bench, her attention was caught by the word "DeLorean," a topic discussed briefly at a Cabinet meeting that morning at Number Ten Downing Street.

At the Dispatch Box was the tall, elegant figure of Adam Butler, his old Etonian accent contrasting with the rougher, earthier voice coming from the back-benches on the opposite side. Bob Cryer was at it again. Once again, he knew more than the unfortunate minister.

As Mrs. Thatcher took her seat, her colleagues shuffling aside to make way for her, Butler was just telling Cryer that the factory in Dunmurry was making eighty DMC-12s a day.

Cryer came back with a long and cleverly worded retort.

"Does the minister accept," he stated in the time-honored House of Commons fashion whereby statements at Question Time must end in a query, "that it is very much to be hoped that sales will catch up with output and lead to longer term, stable jobs in the Province?

"As regards public accountability," Cryer continued, "given that eighty million pounds of taxpayers' money is involved, will the minister explain why he had failed to tell the House that three members of the audit committee have financial interests in the company, according to the minister's own paper, the *Sunday Telegraph?*

"In addition, will he explain why eighteen million dollars of taxpayers' money has been spirited abroad to a Panamanian company to pay Lotus Cars, which is in Norwich?"

The *Sunday Telegraph* was not Adam Butler's paper, but the wily Cryer knew that Conservative ministers were always more vulnerable to criticism from newspapers they regarded as being on their side.

Butler's reply could scarcely have been worse. He rose again from beside the prime minister, who was busily shuffling her notes for her own session due to start in exactly thirty seconds, to say: "The honourable gentleman's information about sales and production is erroneous, because sales are running ahead of production. The same comment might well apply to the honourable gentleman's other allegations. I ask him and others who attempt to detract from this exercise not to do so, because they will damage employment prospects in Northern Ireland."

He sat down and Mrs. Thatcher rose as the Speaker called out the first questioner, the Conservative Tim Brinton, for Prime Minister's Question Time.

It is not suggested here that Adam Butler was trying to mislead the House. That would be a serious offense. Clearly, he believed what he said. The question is, then, how could he have been so uninformed?

McKinsey's figures had gone to NIDA and the Department of Commerce. The financial interests of three DeLorean directors—Benjamin, Swanson, and Gay—were listed in the information filed for the public at the SEC in Washington and New York. That is where the *Sunday Telegraph* had obtained its facts.

And Cryer's question on the Panamanian company, GPD, was again dismissed by the minister, who never seemed to wonder why a deal should be made through a Panama-registered, Swiss-based post office box, and why it was that British government money paid out of Belfast to Norwich should first have to travel through Geneva. Even here, an investigation into GPD might have resulted in a different outcome. It would have required a good accountant, with access to the books of the Northern Ireland DeLorean company and Lotus, less than a week to establish that there really was $18 million (and more) that had been "spirited abroad."

Butler was to retain his confidence to the very end. Only a few hours before DeLorean was arrested for drug smuggling, the minister was interviewed in his Belfast office. He still insisted that DeLorean was essentially not dishonest. DeLorean, in Butler's view, was essentially a marketing man; some of his more optimistic statements could be ascribed to that. In negotiations he was a bully and tough, but that was understandable.

In New York DeLorean was preparing for his big meeting with NIDA and with the Northern Ireland secretary of state, Jim Prior himself. On Monday, December 14, he would fly to London. But now he assembled his board and senior staff, including Brown from California, for a major meeting. He produced a document listing the demands he was going to make of the British: the guarantees had to be extended on that crucial £17 million. There would have to be further grant money, more loans to fill in the cash gap, some $30 million of export credit from the British Export Credit Guarantee Department, with which he had been negotiating for months. The export credit is "our right as the biggest exporter in Northern Ireland and thirtieth biggest in Britain," he said.

DeLorean was not feeling the least bit penitent or outwardly concerned by the situation. To the contrary, he displayed that curious penchant of his to blame the other guy. In this case he blamed the Northern Irish officials and Tony Hopkins in particular. John Zachary DeLorean was doing his honest best.

DeLorean could be extraordinarily foul-mouthed and vicious about people who got in his way. Those close to him say they heard him deride everybody he knew, from the men at General Motors to presidents, civil servants, his own directors, and everybody who was anybody.

"He stood up and went through a long dissertation," recalled Dick Brown, "and he called the Northern Irish and British all sorts of derogatory names—ugly, dirty, filthy names. Things you would hear on 42nd Street. Just really bad names. And his theme was that they were going to do it his way."

According to Brown, DeLorean told those at the meeting, "We are going to do this thing the way we want to do it. We are going to keep the New York office, and keep California and keep all our operations. And if they don't like it, we'll close the plant."

He was still going to ask the British for $60 million to build the sedan, DeLorean announced. Brown described him as almost childish that day, a quality he had noticed before about him.

"He has fits of anger just like a child. But the thing is that we had no parent disciplining him, so as long as he got away with it, he continued to test the water even more.

"John was a great trial-balloon guy. He would say these crazy things. But if nobody challenged him, he would go even further. As if he was a child. Who knows what a child would be like if he had no discipline whatever? It was destruct, destroy, call names, fight, scream, holler. If nobody ever stops him, what does he become?"

It was a disturbing prelude to what lay ahead. DeLorean took the Concorde to London the following Monday—overnight at the Connaught, then the morning shuttle and Dunmurry by 10:20. That day the mountain was coming to Mohammed. The new Northern Ireland secretary of state for the Thatcher government was coming to Dunmurry for his first visit to see the factory, the car, and the workers. His appearance might soften the blow since Jim Prior, even if he had wanted to, could give DeLorean no more new money. The Cabinet committee dealing with it had refused. The Conservative government, which had put in another £30 million on top of the £54 million from the Labour government, had balked at last.

But Prior was sensitive to the political repercussions—the expected charges that the Tory government was pulling out of Northern Ireland and withdrawing from the project simply because it was a Labour-inspired endeavor. DeLorean was already setting the scene for that.

That December day, the two men met for the first time. Prior's early prejudice gave way before a tour of the impressive factory. He had also seen the latest McKinsey report and was impressed by that too. DeLorean managed to get in a few highly optimistic comments of his own.

"In the first six months of sales," he told Prior, "more than 3,000 cars were sold to retail customers. It took Mercedes five years to reach this sales level in America, BMW eleven years, Porsche thirteen years and your own Jaguar seventeen years." He had some $70 million worth of cars on the ground, with dealers clamoring for them. He just had no liquidity. "Things look great—we are oversold. We have orders of 5,000 against a production capacity next quarter of only 3,800 units."

A few days later DeLorean was again on the agenda at a Cabinet Committee meeting in Whitehall. Prior related his first experience with DeLorean. In view of his optimism and the forecast sales and cash flow, Prior proposed that the government should renew the guarantee of £17 million of bank borrowing, which would run out at the end of the year, but DeLorean was actually only using £8.5 million of the guarantees. "I propose we renew for ten," said Prior. Reluctantly his colleagues agreed.

DeLorean had won in his first meeting with his third Northern Ireland secretary of state. Prior, unsympathetic before they met, had actually argued his case for him. But it was to be a costly victory for DeLorean. It was not many weeks before Prior discovered he had been misled, and that he in turn had unwittingly misled the Cabinet Committee. It was something he would not forgive DeLorean for. From that point on, the project was doomed.

18

RECEIVERSHIP

By pleading or threatening, or a combination of both, DeLorean had usually triumphed. He did not get any more new money from Jim Prior, but he had persuaded the minister to support him, and that was no mean achievement. But Prior had yet to be tested in real battle, and a full-scale Waterloo was now looming. Back in New York, De-Lorean began to stake out the high ground. He started with a state-ment that unless he got $26 million of export financing "to which we're entitled," he would take a "strong look at curtailing our opera-tions by cutting production and jobs dramatically." Once again he was presenting a setback as something else, something it was not.

"All the politicians are scared to deal with us now," he said.

By then he must have known what was happening to sales, had to know that he could not indefinitely go on churning out cars that no one would buy, would have to cut back production within days rather than months, even if he got all the money in the Bank of England.

There was a lull in the factory during Christmas week. But during the following week, DeLorean insisted that the Dunmurry factory go back to full blast. In the week ending January 4, it produced 315 cars. But then came crisis after crisis. The tide of events was rushing in on John DeLorean as he ran out of goodwill and then money.

Bache Halsey could not get the public stock issue off the ground, and on January 6 asked for a postponement. It was the end of the issue —and with it went John DeLorean's paper fortune of $120 million that he had been so certain was within his grasp. If the stock offering had been less ambitious and more salable DeLorean might have been able to hold on to something. Now he owned half of nothing. De-Lorean Motor Holdings, which had cost nearly $2 million in fees and countless hours of executive time—the SEC documents alone were more than twelve inches thick—died.

DeLorean began to look for a partner, some "good, solid organization that would provide us with some of the facilities that we as a company lack." The Northern Irish were horrified. His agreement stipulated he could not sell any of his shares.

Only now did it become apparent how important Marian Gibson's intervention had been. The Bache issue had missed the deadline.

"We had to do it last July or August," admitted DeLorean. That had been the original intention, but it was Tony Hopkins' stubbornness over DeLorean's right to be able to sell his shares that had caused the issue to miss the target date. September or October would still have been possible, and it would almost certainly have happened then but for Gibson and Winterton.

Would it have helped DeLorean if the issue had gone ahead? The net amount the automobile company would have received was probably no more than $10 million, and that was supposed to go toward the sedan version of the car. In mid-January DeLorean was short $50 to $60 million and it was getting worse day by day as inventories overflowed and cars were not sold.

Now came a series of hard blows. The most serious was dealt by the Bank of America, which through Dick Brown's good offices had provided a $33-million line of credit. In December DeLorean asked the bank to increase it and announced that the Bank of America had agreed to go up to $47 million, although what he wanted was $60 million. This was all export credit—the Bank of America was financing the cars themselves, lending money against the collateral of actual cars once they were shipped out of Belfast.

There was a safety clause that tied the amount of money it lent DeLorean to the sales volume generated by the dealers. For weeks, as the cars piled up in the showrooms, the bank had not exercised that clause. But in early January it took that option. Instead of its hoped-for $47 million of credit, the company suddenly had only $24 million. The cash crisis deepened dramatically.

It also meant that a shipment of cars already at sea and valued in Belfast at £9 million had not been paid for—although the master agreement signed in 1978 stipulated very clearly that no cars leave Belfast without being paid for, a safeguard designed to ensure that DMC bore the cost of unsold cars in America and that the Belfast company got its revenues on time.

Another shipment of £6 million worth of cars was ready to go. It was canceled. The flow of cars across the Atlantic had now stopped, but the production lines were still running and the stocks of autos began to build up in Belfast. There were cars everywhere.

DeLorean boasted of how 6,500 cars worth £85 million had been shipped from Belfast. Indeed, they had been, but 4,000 of them were in inventories and 1,655 were with dealers.

The weather might have contributed to the predicament, but was it really the fault of the weather? That December period was actually a good one for luxury cars: Porsche sales more than doubled over the same month in 1980; Jaguar sales were up 69 percent; the Datsun 280ZX increased by 9 percent. Ironically, even Lotus did better.

The weather was not the whole story by any means. The simple truth was that there were not enough customers for John DeLorean's dream car. The factory in Dunmurry was turning them out at an annual rate of 20,000. The annual sales rate since the DMC-12 had first hit the market was 8,000. John DeLorean's hugely expensive operation requried sales of 25,000 to 30,000 units a year to support it and repay loans, let alone finance his ambitious new ventures, notably the sedan on which Giugiaro in Turin and Mike Loasby in Belfast were still working.

The result was that the company was now running at an annual cash shortfall of some $50 million. Even at twice the rate of sales achieved during the months the car was on the market, there would still have been a loss. And sales, far from improving, were getting worse. DeLorean Motor Company and its Belfast subsidiary were rapidly heading for disaster.

Belfast, January 11, 1982. When they arrived at work in Dunmurry, the men got the news they had been dreading: the factory was going on short time. That week they would work only three days. DeLorean had found a convenient excuse to explain it to the outside world: there was a strike on the Sealink Ferry from mainland Britain that carried some vital components. But no one really believed it—certainly no one at the factory.

The panic that had set in with the first reports of Marian Gibson's revelations now began to spread. Across the United States the weather worsened. During the first week of January, 100 DMC-12s were sold. This was better than the twenty-five sold the previous week, but it was still hopelessly low. In Dunmurry, working on their part-time basis, the men made sixty cars.

But shipments had stopped. The factory now had no revenue. Unless DeLorean could arrange that export financing, not a single car could move from Belfast to its market in the United States.

The unions in Northern Ireland were getting impatient and were supporting the government's attempts to force a showdown and find out what was really going on in the DeLorean empire. It was an unusual alliance: trade unions alongside a Tory government. John DeLorean had now turned everyone in Britain and Northern Ireland against him.

He was still remarkably untouched by it all. DeLorean was tough: his body armor was impervious to the objections and criticisms of the officials at NIDA, whom he regarded with vague contempt. His remarkable capacity for self-delusion, and the ability to convince himself that he was always right, had been let down by others, or betrayed, or deflected by incompetence, remained with him to the end of the project. His shell was never even visibly dented.

John DeLorean believed that only he at General Motors had glimpsed the truth of the matter, only to him had Divine Providence shown where the American auto industry was going wrong. His attitude now, as he moved toward his worst crisis, had not changed since the farewell speech he gave to GM in 1973 that so bemused all who had worked with him.

There was no hope of raising money from any banks. Bank of America had pulled the plug, and no one would touch him now. There was no chance of a private issue, no hope of a big investor. It would take too long to develop, and the money would be too late. But he still worked on it, as he always had.

He believed his one real hope lay with the British Export Credit Guarantee Department (ECGD), and he had been bombarding ministers, officials, and everyone he thought could be useful with letters and Telexes about how much he deserved and needed the credit. It was a "completely secured loan so far as the British government is concerned—secured by the cars themselves," he claimed.

The British government was less convinced. Export credit money was still government money, and there would be no more of it for DeLorean. In the Treasury, ministers including Bruce-Gardyne were arguing that the time to cut a bad investment "is always now." Any more money lent, given, or guaranteed would be more money down the drain.

On Monday, January 18, Don Lander and Joe Daly traveled to London from Belfast to persuade the ECGD to lend the needed $70 million. Lander was an impressive representative, far more so than DeLorean himself under the circumstances. The Canadian was well known in London after his years running the British Chrysler operation—which had received far more money from the British taxpayer than DeLorean ever did.

Lander was out of the Strycker/Brown/Collins mold—a straight, successful, professional auto-man who was not particularly interested in building a vast private empire for himself. His reputation was strong enough to withstand his involvement with DeLorean.

Daly was the financial man, out of his depth and hating the limelight and publicity. He never quite knew what his responsibilities were. DeLorean kept promoting him to acting chief financial officer of the New York company, even though he was in Belfast, and then demoting him again when a new financial officer was hired.

DeLorean caught the Concorde on Tuesday and arrived in London that evening. Before he left, he received another unpleasant shock. It was just a pinprick at the time, but it was nevertheless annoying. Bill Haddad had lodged a $19-million suit against him, alleging slander, libel, fraud, and "malicious termination of employment for reasons contrary to public policy." If it came to court, there would be a lot of nasty revelations that would do DeLorean no good.

When he arrived in London, there was not much to cheer him up. February is the worst month in London as far as weather goes—wet, cold, windy. Even the luxury of the Connaught did little to keep out the chill. As he was arriving, the morning papers had picked up the "performance bonuses" voted to DeLorean, Kimmerly, and other senior executives in December. That did nothing for the atmosphere either.

DeLorean had ordered the factory back onto a five-day work week in hopes of reviving some of the flagging confidence. But on that Tuesday, in listing the £84 million the government had invested so far, Butler announced that the government was arranging "major reviews" of the overall relationship with DeLorean.

The situation was getting worse and worse. The government was furious about the bonuses, desperately embarrassed that they had actually been recommended by its own representatives on the DeLorean board. Even if the government had wanted to—and it did not—it was now virtually impossible politically to help DeLorean further.

The *Financial Times* published a strong editorial that concluded, "Further financial backing would be a disservice not only to the tax-payer but also to the company's employees; there is no security in jobs which depend on permanent government subsidy."

John DeLorean himself was in Belfast, harping on his familiar theme of how unfairly the government was treating him.

"We're a political football," he claimed. His main complaint was that inflation clause in the master agreement. He had been given £14 million under its terms, but it was a loan, not a grant. He figured he deserved it as grant money.

DeLorean talked to Tony Hopkins and his team at NIDA and to the Department of Commerce. He talked to the unions, indicating he was "not optimistic." On Wednesday he was back in London to meet Prior, Hopkins, and Ken Bloomfield, the new Permanent Secretary of the Department of Commerce.

Meanwhile Prior was at Number Ten Downing Street for a Cabinet meeting, where he brought up the entire issue of DeLorean with the Treasury ministers. Prior told the ministers that he had been wrong about DeLorean. There was no hint of weakening, all the discussion was about how to minimize the impact on Northern Ireland's economy. The ministers were prepared to consider proposals involving the writing off of their investment thus far, including the leasing of the factory to DeLorean in a restructured company, but only if John DeLorean could be bound hand and foot. No one could come up with a way to keep the company going without him. DMC had the sole distribution rights to the car, and the Oppenheimer partnership owned the rights to the car itself. The full implications of the original 1978 agreement were only now becoming clear.

Late that Wednesday evening, Prior and DeLorean met at the Northern Ireland office in London. Prior was grim, adamant. What about the optimistic reports he had received just before Christmas? What had changed so much in a month? DeLorean ignored Prior's recriminations and came back with some of his own. He had now finally asked Prior for more money—£47 million. In return he was still refusing to give an inch to NIDA's demands: no renegotiation of the master agreement, no reorganization of royalties, no concession. Prior ripped into that. DMC's existing lines of credit were extended to the limit. There was no possibility of raising private funds, and the Bank of America was cutting its short-term credit. "We're not prepared to lend you £47 million or any other further money at all," he bluntly told DeLorean. It was a long, angry and heated exchange, with DeLorean continually playing the only card he now had left—closure of the factory. "Closure does not change the situation," said Prior. There would be no money.

It was late in the meeting when Prior revealed the counterproposal he had been saving to see how DeLorean would react. Now he unveiled it.

"You say your wish is to ensure the project's success. Well, it's mine too. I propose therefore that the DeLorean company in Belfast should invite an eminent accountant and solvency expert, who would be assisted by his own large firm, to look at the business. We would give him say, two weeks, to report on whether in its present form or in any restructured form the company could continue with any hope of commercial success. I have in mind Sir Kenneth Cork, whom I have already approached, and he is standing by for your invitation."

DeLorean barely knew who Sir Kenneth Cork was. But it did not take him long to work out the implication. "That is tantamount to receivership," he told Prior. "It would completely destroy the business. How could we ever raise the money we need with a receiver in the factory?" After some more shouting, Prior had to go to the House for a vote, and DeLorean took the opportunity to talk to his colleagues. Lander filled him in on Cork, and what he heard only filled DeLorean with even greater dread. This was not going the way he planned it.

For many years, Cork was "Mr. Receiver" in London industrial and financial circles. His firm, Cork Gully, had moved from ordinary audit and accounting work to specialize in receivership and had blossomed in the early 1970s, when Britain suffered a banking and real estate plunge comparable to Wall Street's 1929 crash.

At sixty-seven, Cork was a tall, owl-like man whose lugubrious expression could change in a flash when a grin spread across his features. He had been Lord Mayor of London, a year-long position achieved only by the most established figures in the very Establishment City of London. Cork had been involved with the precursor of NIDA, the Northern Ireland Finance Corporation, and had a connection with the Province.

Quite a few companies had been salvaged through the process of receivership—one stage short of liquidation. Rolls-Royce had been through the process. The receivers themselves always complained that they were brought in too late—a few months before, they told all who would listen, and much more might have been done. (Perhaps that might not have been the case with DeLorean.)

Receivership is a curious British institution with no direct American equivalent. It is a limbo, halfway between viability and liquidation. A company in receivership is suspended, in a sense; the creditors are unable to foreclose and seize the assets while the receiver tries to realize as much as he can for them. The principle is that the components of a company are often worth more on a going-concern basis than on a forced liquidation.

Unlike a liquidator, a receiver has the power to carry on "business as usual." In fact, he has almost unlimited power in a company to which he is appointed. He is president, chairman, chief executive and financial officer—all rolled into one. No money goes out or comes in, except through him.

Shareholders—in this case John DeLorean—have no power whatsoever over the receiver. He must answer in the long run to the creditors, but in the short run, while the receiver sorts out plans and proposals, he is in full charge.

Prior returned from the House and he and DeLorean met again. DeLorean still protested that the minister had not given enough consideration to his requests and to the other points he had raised. But he would call a board meeting for both companies in New York on the following Monday to discuss Sir Kenneth Cork. It was late when they finally broke up.

That evening Sir Kenneth had a phone call from a Northern Ireland Office official. DeLorean, he was told, had to catch the Concorde flight back to New York early the following morning. Could Sir Kenneth see him for breakfast. Eight o'clock at the Connaught?

"Well," replied Sir Kenneth, "in these circumstances it's more usual for people to come and see me." But there was some protest from the other end. "Mr. DeLorean's a very busy and important person," protested the official.

Cork relented, although with poor grace. He lived in Great Missenden, and never ate breakfast anyway. It meant leaving home exceptionally early to get into town by eight in the London traffic. And Cork was doing the job more as a favor to Prior than for any other reason.

The next morning he was at the Connaught by the appointed time and ordered a cup of coffee. No sign of DeLorean. Eight-fifteen arrived and still no DeLorean. Cork fumed. Finally, at 8:20, DeLorean swept in with his entourage, including Tom Kimmerly and Don Lander. Brief introductions were made, and as he sat down, DeLorean looked across the table at Cork.

"Sir Kenneth, I want to ask your advice."

"Yes, Mr. DeLorean, what is it?"

"I want to sue your government for fifty million pounds for war damages and criminal damages and breach of contract and other things. And what I want to know is, do I do that before or after you write your report?"

Afterward, Cork wished he had thought of a brilliant reply; but considering his surprise, he did not do badly.

"Well, it depends, Mr. DeLorean, on how much money you've got."

"What's it got to do with how much money I've got?"

"Well, Mr. DeLorean, you're going to lose it. So if you sue after my report, you may keep it in your pocket a little longer."

There were no more facetious remarks after that. But Cork found John DeLorean unpleasantly arrogant. DeLorean rattled on about what a wonderful project he had, but how the British government owed him this money and wouldn't pay up, and he'd been brought to his knees because of it.

Cork pointed out that the claims for the damages he was talking about—bombings of his factory and disruption—were arbitrated in the courts. To get the money, one had to go through the entire legal process. Few genuine claims were rejected, he said. In fact, it was quite the opposite, since the British government fought to keep industry alive in Ulster.

It was not a good beginning. After half an hour, DeLorean had to leave for his flight. Don Lander, watching the performance, was appalled. He knew the weight Cork carried in government and City circles, even if DeLorean did not. As they walked out of the hotel, Lander followed Cork and apologized for DeLorean's rudeness. His quiet Canadian manner and genuine concern caused Cork to thaw considerably.

John DeLorean flew home with cries of "No!" from every government quarter ringing in his ears. No export credit, no more loans, no grants, no money of any kind! Get his operation onto a viable footing and then "maybe." Cut out that fabulous penthouse and huge office expense. Stop spending government money on twenty different outside operations unrelated to the car. Put in some money of his own or from his friends. Then perhaps the factory could be supported at a lower production level. Prior had given DeLorean seven days to accept the appointment of Cork or to find a backer.

DeLorean summoned his board for a final meeting before the great confrontation.

On Tuesday January 26, every single director of both companies, except for Henry Bushkin and Cristina (who never attended board meetings), gathered in a hired room at the Waldorf-Astoria, because there were too many for the boardroom in the Park Avenue offices. At ten o'clock DeLorean opened the meeting with what one director later described as a vicious attack on the British government and those who worked for it. However, despite some sweeping statements (according to the minutes kept by Tom Kimmerly) to the effect that it would be better to shut down than turn the business over to Sir Kenneth Cork, it was finally agreed that Cork should at least be provided with information, although nothing more. "Members of the board were as usual compliant," reported one director to Prior, "and didn't raise a voice against him." But he did report that "there were some signs that the board was becoming more realistic than it had been in the past."

In New York John DeLorean emerged from the meeting to say that "prospects are still bright." In Belfast Prior warned that the position was "extremely serious." By now everyone knew whom to believe— and it wasn't John DeLorean.

Late in the evening on the following day, DeLorean arrived at Whitehall after yet another Concorde flight. He went straight to see Prior. It was one o'clock in the morning when he emerged. It had been a tough experience for both men. Prior told him flatly there would be no money, but there was a proposal. Sir Kenneth Cork had agreed to prepare a report within fourteen days. If he concluded that the project could be restructured in a way that would make it still viable—almost certainly at a lower production level—then the government might support that. No promises, of course.

DeLorean would have to cooperate and make considerable concessions: Cut down his lifestyle that attracted so much adverse publicity. Move out of his ridiculously pretentious office. And above all, find some money from one of those mythical buyers he always had in the background. The alternative was for the government, as the largest creditor, to appoint a receiver. In the meantime, the factory would have to cut back sharply, preferably the following day.

DeLorean did not give in without a fight. He had bluffed Humphrey Atkins by threatening to take the government to court and got an extra £14 million. Now he tried it again, insisting he was owed £10 million for criminal damages to his factory. There was war damage and the adjustment for inflation, he argued, and credit guarantees that should have been automatic and that were always promised to him. He had had his lawyers prepare a case and would take the government to the European courts, he threatened. Prior was not impressed. DeLorean could sue if he liked, but in the meantime Sir Kenneth was going to prepare his report.

The next morning a bizarre incident occurred—a moment of high comedy in a sea of corporate tragedy. It was ten in the morning in London and Belfast, but only two o'clock in Los Angeles, where Dick Brown was sleeping when the phone rang. It was a call from Belfast. Brown, still anxious about the quality of the car, had sent over a seven-man team, headed by Doug Paterson, to oversee the production line. It was Paterson, in some distress, who was calling him now.

He had just ended an early-morning meeting with Don Lander and the other staff at Dunmurry, Paterson said, and there had been an uproar. DeLorean had called up to tell Lander to pull Brown's quality-control people off the line and let the cars go through "regardless of quality."

Paterson had been there just a month and was making a fight, but he wanted Brown's support. As he talked, Brown suddenly heard another conversation coming in on top of them. It sounded like a crossed line, and he recognized the voice—it was John DeLorean!

"Hold on a minute," he said to Paterson as he heard his own name mentioned. "Doug, just a minute—I'm overhearing another conversation. Hold on, I'll be back to you—don't hang up."

Brown listened in for half an hour with Paterson hanging on at the other end, unable to hear anything. Brown came back to him every so often to insist he stay there and not break the connection. What he was overhearing was an extraordinary conversation. Brown knew DeLorean was at the Connaught in London. He was speaking to Roy Nesseth in Huntington Beach, California, only ten miles from Brown's home.

All Brown's recent suspicions that his phone might have been tapped revived dramatically. His wife had been complaining for weeks that there was something strange about it.

The words that had caught his attention were John DeLorean's: "Don't tell Brown, don't tell Brown."

A shaken Dick Brown heard DeLorean order Nesseth to make arrangements to get ships over to Northern Ireland and clean out the plant, take parts, machinery, cars, everything, and ship it, "but don't tell Brown." It seemed that DeLorean had decided that once the receiver went in he would lose control over those assets, but if he could get them to the United States, he could still sell them and would leave the receiver nothing more than an empty factory.

Brown never discovered if his phone was tapped. But it seemed an incredibly strange coincidence that he should cross-connect with DeLorean and Nesseth. "I suspect my lines *were* tapped," said Brown later.

Over the next few weeks, Sir Kenneth Cork got to know Don Lander quite well, and they came to like each other. With Lander still around, Cork thought, there might still be a chance. While DeLorean went home, Cork went to Belfast, feeling jaundiced against the whole operation.

What he saw there, however, caused him to think again. The factory was first class. Lander and his team, despite everything, were hardworking and dedicated. Given half a chance, Cork began to feel, they might make a go of it if they could get the financial structure right.

In his years as a receiver, Cork had seen many similar situations— a perfectly good operation that could be viable with half the employees, a quarter of the overhead, and without the enormous burden of interest charges on borrowings.

Clearly there was not a market for 20,000 cars a year, but there might be for 8,000 or so. Keep the best men, make it a lean, tight operation, and maybe it could go on, although it would still need an injection of cash from outside. Prior had made it very clear to Cork from the beginning that any proposal he put forward must start with the premise that there was no more government money.

In Belfast that weekend 1,100 of the 2,400 employed had been laid off. In New York DeLorean gave a press conference in which he said he had a "serious offer" from an American company that would solve his problems.

"We do have a short-term liquidity problem," he admitted. "But rest assured, DeLorean is here to stay."

And then he endeared himself even less to those in Belfast who were desperately trying to save him.

"Looking back," he said nonchalantly, "I probably made a mistake in going to Belfast."

In February, as Cork worked on his report with a team of accountants who looked at every angle, the factory went onto a one-day work week.

For the moment, however, the newspaper headlines were focused elsewhere—a name even better known in Britain than DeLorean's went bust on February 5. Sir Freddie Laker, the pioneer of supercheap transatlantic airfares and Prime Minister Thatcher's favorite entrepreneurial businessman, fell from the sky. Laker and DeLorean were almost too much in one week, with the London Times also being threatened with closure by its new owner, Rupert Murdoch.

There was one DeLorean news item that caused howls of rage in all quarters, however. DeLorean had always been outrageous in his comments, but now he excelled himself. While talking about selling the company, DeLorean was simultaneously bad-mouthing it.

He suddenly made public his claim for £10 million in damage to the plant as a result of terrorist incidents. He had been "told to stay away from windows when at the facility" and that "bullets had landed in the area." He went on to say that there had been a total of 140 firebombings at the factory and that executives had been the targets of sniper attacks.

One hundred forty incidents? No one could believe it. DeLorean himself wouldn't even stay overnight in the place, insisting to his staff that the "Brits want me out of here by nightfall—I'm a target."

He never was a target. And there was only one serious incident— at the height of the Bobby Sands hunger strike. For the damage done then, DeLorean got £425,000.

An investigation showed there were several other incidents when gasoline bombs, no more than milk bottles half-full of gasoline, had been thrown in over the perimeter fence. There had been no sniper incidents—not a single one. It was pure make-believe!

Tuesday, February 9, Sir Kenneth finished his report. It was not unhelpful to John DeLorean—in fact, it was astonishingly supportive under the circumstances. But Cork showed the true financial picture. In 1981, instead of the profit about which DeLorean still boasted, losses amounted to £23.1 million and the share capital had been wiped out. There had been a huge outflow of money from Belfast to New York, with virtually all New York operations paid for by British money.

DeLorean had a report of his own prepared at the same time by the accounting firm of Peat Marwick Mitchell & Company, and was now busily passing that document around. It showed that if operations were cut back and an injection of £20 million made, the business would become profitable. This was the basis for John DeLorean's search for new money that week. He kept repeating to Cork—who went to see him in New York and was astonished by the grandeur of the offices—and to everyone else, that he had buyers lined up to help.

That evening, in an office under the shadow of St. Paul's Cathedral in the City of London, Sir Freddie Laker was in conference with the man whom he hoped would bail him out. Tiny Rowland was the chief executive of Lonrho, a British conglomerate with mines, ranching, and trading interests all over Africa. Lonrho also owned the Sunday newspaper *The Observer* and 30 percent of the retail group House of Fraser, which owned Harrod's.

Rowland was one of the most remarkable businessmen on the British—or the world—scene. He was the first person whom Daniel K. Ludwig, the "world's richest man," had trusted enough in fifty years to make a joint deal with. Rowland ended up buying the Princess Hotel chain from him.

Rowland had a penchant for companies on the rocks, and, by coincidence, had met DeLorean ten years before. One of the companies Rowland bought for his Lonrho Group was Wankel, the rotary engine group. At one point he had gone to Detroit to see Ed Cole, who brought DeLorean into the talks with him when General Motors was planning a major push on Wankels.

Unfortunately for Rowland, the oil crisis intervened and the Wankel was not particularly fuel efficient. But DeLorean told him afterward that if it were not for the huge increase in the price of oil, "Lonrho would be as big as GM." Now DeLorean turned again to Rowland.

Rowland was lecturing Sir Freddie on why things had gone wrong for him.

"Your problem is that you've been selling ten-dollar bills for nine dollars and sooner or later that catches up with you."

The phone rang. The voice was vaguely familiar.

"Hi," said John DeLorean. "This is Margaret Thatcher's biggest headache. I've got a deal for you—the biggest you've ever made."

Rowland laughed appreciatively. He knew all about DeLorean, and one sick company was enough in one week. He bailed out Freddie Laker and set him up in business again in a smaller way. He refused DeLorean.

By mid-February, DeLorean had exhausted every possible source he could think of. He sent out documents signed by eminent accountants such as Peat Marwick to hordes of people. Sir Kenneth Cork had done his best for him, too. DeLorean was able to suggest to potential investors that they call Cork, and the receivership expert would agree there was a viable proposition if the company were run correctly and enough new capital were available.

Cork's scheme was very generous to DeLorean. DeLorean Motor Company could lease all the production facilities and tooling in Belfast simply by assuming two long-term notes: a Department of Commerce loan (with no interest for two years) of £14 million, and £7.72 million of fourteen-year mortgage, also with a possible interest freeze. It came to roughly £22 million or $40 million. The finished and unfinished cars, worth $30 million, would be paid for as they were shipped.

It was an extraordinarily attractive deal, and all it required was for DeLorean to come up with that famous investor of his to put up working capital. For those weeks, he always had an investor, or so he told anyone who asked. Usually it was an Arab, the head of a state that could not be identified.

No one knew whether he really existed or not. DeLorean would not tell Jim Prior. He would not tell Cork. All he would say in those final days was, "He's from an oil-rich country." Of course the United States and Great Britain both fall into that category.

Prior studied Cork's report over the weekend of February 13 to 14 and then Telexed DeLorean to come in and see him as soon as possible. He wanted DeLorean in London on Monday. DeLorean stalled, insisting he needed more time. He could not be there until Wednesday, he replied, when he would have his buyer and the money.

Prior was furious, but he had other things on his hands that week. He was persuading his Cabinet colleagues to adopt a daring plan for Northern Ireland involving an elected assembly, a sort of rolling devolvement from direct rule by Westminster for the Province. He achieved it, and later was to regret it bitterly. Ironically, the elections would take place on the day John DeLorean was arrested in California.

On Tuesday DeLorean sent over Robert Benjamin, head of the audit committee. Benjamin took a DeLorean team consisting of the Belfast lawyer Robin Bailie and Don Lander along with him to see Cork. DeLorean himself arrived on Wednesday, too late for a scheduled meeting with Prior, which had to be canceled. This time he checked in at Claridge's; one of his "prospects," whom he hoped might come up with the money, was staying at the hotel.

Cork met with DeLorean that night. Prior was going to make his statement the next day, Cork said. He was going to appoint a receiver. DeLorean protested that he could come up with the money but he had to have more time.

Time had run out, Cork told him. The statement was already being prepared to go out to the press. Jim Prior would tell the House of Commons the news the following day.

The choice was a bald one: either DeLorean could now accept his offer of a voluntary receivership or the British government would appoint a receiver anyway, with all the resultant damage to his reputation, to sales of the car, and to everyone involved.

Cork explained the details of the scheme he had worked out in New York the previous week. It was an ingenious arrangement. A new company would be set up. It would either lease the factory and equipment or take over the outstanding debts; revenues from the sales of the completed cars would go to the old company. Perhaps most important of all, DMC in New York would pay for those cars that had left Northern Ireland without payment; they would be paid for as and when they were sold. But to make it work, Cork had decided that DMC in New York would need a cash injection, and it would not come from outside. John DeLorean must put at least $5 million of his personal money into DMC. Reluctantly, DeLorean agreed. But he continued to protest strongly against the appointment of a receiver. He had a backer, "the head of an Arab state" who would put up $30 million over the next few days, perhaps even the very next day.

By now Cork was getting used to DeLorean's wiles. In his long career, he had seen all sorts of people and could be forgiven a certain cynicism.

"What state?" Cork asked.

An Arab state, replied DeLorean. His man did not want to be identified.

There was also a potential backer on the West Coast whose representative he wanted Cork to meet the next morning. The money was there, he insisted; just hold off on the receivership.

For once, Cork was at somewhat of a loss. He was a man who dealt in crisis or—more often—the aftermath of crisis. Usually when he was appointed, it was already too late and it was his job to go into a company, look at the books, and tell the shocked management and staff that they now had no job. Too often in his career, Cork had had to close down entire companies and pick over the bones for the bits that could be resurrected in another life. He had lived with corporate death most of his career and was inured to the tragedy and human drama of it. His specialty was to identify those parts of a company that could survive after the death of the parent and, freed of the burdens of debt and overhead, might still stay in business. He had turned receivership into a fine art, employing his skills to save companies that would have disappeared under a different system. Cork was a master.

The scheme he discussed again with DeLorean that night was what he called his "Rolls-Royce" plan. When Rolls-Royce failed in 1971, its receiver created a new company, Rolls-Royce 1971. The assets of the airplane-engine side, whose contract to build the RB-211 engine for the Lockheed Tri-Star had proven too costly, had been transferred to the new company. The auto side was spun off with its own separate stock market quotation (it has since merged with Vickers). In that case, creditors got their money back and shareholders received a substantial repayment, too. The company is still running, although with government assistance.

Now Cork was proposing to create "DeLorean Motor Cars Limited 1982." To succeed, it would still need John DeLorean's active participation. He would have to sell the cars—he owned the distribution rights—although Cork was proposing to renegotiate that provision, too. The license to the car was owned by the DeLorean Research Limited Partnership, so the company could not make the cars without permission from that group. DMC was the only general partner.

That evening the two men conducted a tough bargaining session. Cork's main advance was an agreement from DeLorean that he would inject $5 million of his own personal money into DMC in New York.

Cork had been appalled by the drain of funds from Northern Ireland into that company. It was "absolutely crazy," he told Prior. For his part, DeLorean persuaded Cork to meet his "prospect" the next morning and do his best to get Prior to hold back for another few days.

At 9:30 the next morning, the men met again at Claridge's. DeLorean's prospect was not willing to deal; he wanted more time and his interest was only exploratory. It was to become a familiar pattern.

"You only had to walk into DeLorean's office," Cork would say later, "and say 'I'm interested in your car' and he'd say, 'Can you put up $50 million?' and the man would agree he could if he wanted to. And then if any interest was expressed, DeLorean would say, 'I've got a man who wants to invest $50 million.' It was as immediate as that."

But at the same time, Cork had met some of the prospects with whom DeLorean was negotiating and they were often highly reputable people. He had talked to General Motors and Chrysler, for instance, and Oppenheimer, too. Thus he could not easily dismiss the potential investors whom DeLorean always seemed about to produce.

By midmorning there was still an unnamed person on the West Coast, and there was the Arab head of state, whoever he might be. Cork was skeptical that he ever existed.

Noon, Thursday: Cork and DeLorean went together to the Northern Ireland office in Whitehall. Jim Prior was not in a receptive mood. His two predecessors, Roy Mason and Humphrey Atkins, had been damaged politically by DeLorean, and Prior had enough problems of his own—both in the Cabinet, where he now had been maneuvered away from one of the key economic posts into the turbulent waters of Northern Ireland, and in the Province itself. Prior wanted a solution *now* to DeLorean, and he had decided that meant receivership.

Perhaps Cork could salvage something from it, although privately Prior must have doubted it. But receivership would at least provide some breathing time, soften the blow. The government could not be accused of not trying to the very end.

But Prior was not prepared for the news that DeLorean gave him. He had an Arab head of state who was going to come to the rescue, he said. Prior glanced at Cork, incredulous. The press releases were ready. He was planning a statement within a few hours. All of a sudden, there was this. Surely DeLorean could have found the money before?

Cork indicated it might be worth waiting for. Abruptly Prior made his decision. He would postpone his statement, delay the press release. DeLorean had until midnight New York time to have the money transmitted.

After thirty minutes, Prior ended the meeting. DeLorean returned to Claridge's to spend the rest of the day on the telephone. He almost certainly believed he could persuade *someone* to come up with the money that day. There is no other obvious reason for his last desperate stall.

He seemed incapable of facing defeat—intent on hanging on until the final seconds, unwilling to surrender an inch of ground. That night, as hope ran out, he could not even tell Sir Kenneth Cork the news himself.

It was midnight when Cork's phone rang at his home in Great Missenden, north of London. Robin Bailie, DeLorean's Belfast attorney, was on the line. The Arab had not come through with the money. DeLorean needed more time. There was no other prospect who could come through in the time allotted. DeLorean would agree to the voluntary receivership. It was all over.

By six the next morning, the press release had gone out. Cork issued his own reassuring statement to the work force at 9:30. At 11:00 Jim Prior rose to address the House of Commons. He had appointed Sir Kenneth Cork and his partner, Paul Shewell, as joint receivers, he announced, although he warned this did not "guarantee a way ahead" for the company.

"It is clearly a matter of concern to the government that this position should have been reached."

It would be wrong, he emphasized, to be too optimistic about the company's survival—as if anyone were still optimistic. But "there is more goodwill to try to reach some successful position than one might have thought possible over the past few weeks."

Typically, DeLorean was already twisting the story to his own advantage. From Claridge's that morning, he issued a brief press statement. He was "delighted" with the outcome, he said, and emphasized that the receivership was voluntary rather than enforced by creditors. Then he went to Heathrow for his Concorde flight home. Curiously, he was not booked under his own name for that flight. He chose to travel, for whatever reasons, under the name of Nesseth, although his whereabouts were certainly no secret.

On the four-and-a-quarter-hour flight, DeLorean had enough time to prepare yet another counteroffensive. Cork's mention of Rolls-Royce had struck a chord. By the time he arrived at Kennedy Airport, DeLorean had a statement ready. It never once mentioned receivership. Instead, it announced he had just completed an "extremely advantageous reorganization plan" that was comparable to the "similar restructuring of Rolls-Royce in 1973" (it was 1971).

He was already translating an event that, for anyone else, would have been halfway to disaster, as something entirely different—as he had done time and time again.

"By this action, the government has removed $130 million of primarily government debt from the balance sheet. Using this turning point agreement as a springboard, the many DeLorean customers who have hesitated to conclude the purchase of their automobile may now do so with complete confidence."

John DeLorean ended his statement with thanks "to Her Majesty's Government for this powerful support."

That afternoon DeLorean defiantly faced the world. He chose to do it on the 35th floor of 280 Park Avenue, where it would be crowded, rather than the more plush 43rd floor, which would not fit so well with the new image.

He was beginning to show the strain, but he was still full of vigor. He had traveled to London on Wednesday, stayed up most of the two nights there, and then traveled back only that day. For weeks he had been under intense pressure on every side. If he had allowed himself to think about it, he would have given up weeks—perhaps even months—before. But John DeLorean could not accept defeat. By that point, another man would have been a physical and emotional wreck and would have tried to hide away—at least for a weekend—to lick his wounds. Instead, DeLorean held a press conference.

"Are you a con man?" asked an American reporter. "Is your conscience clear?"

"My conscience is very, very clear," replied DeLorean.

He had one final trick up his sleeve for that press conference. When Freddie Laker went down, his traveling public bombarded him with checks and cash to get him flying again. Two weeks later, that was still fresh in DeLorean's mind. Now DeLorean displayed some checks of his own: one for $10, the other for $20. It was not much, he admitted, but it was proof of the affection the public had for him.

He ended with a statement that would be far more prophetic than anyone at the time ever imagined.

"We won't go out of business. Whatever it takes in the world, we will do it to keep in business."

19

"YOU HAVE THE RIGHT TO REMAIN SILENT...."

Late in January 1982 an old acquaintance of John DeLorean's faced some bad news of his own. James Timothy Hoffman was as tired as he had ever been in his life, and as scared. Yet there was no relief in sight. He was in a safe house kept by the United States government's drug strike force near San Diego. Special Agent John Valestra was congratulating Hoffman on a job well done.

He had successfully infiltrated a cocaine-smuggling ring run by a United Airlines pilot and a Manhattan Beach, California, real estate developer. Hoffman worked his way into the ring, worked with the smugglers, and even went to Colombia to help with the buy. He gathered enough evidence to enable the agents to catch the ring red-handed with $14 million worth of coke. The two leaders drew ten-year jail sentences. It was one of the biggest cases won by the feds in California in years.

This was not Hoffman's first job undercover in the dangerous, murky world of international drug trafficking. Late in 1981 he had been less successful gathering evidence in a federal prosecution of a Lebanese arms dealer who the authorities were convinced also smuggled drugs into the United States. A grand jury in Baltimore let the man go, and agent Valestra had not been as happy as he was that night in San Diego.

But although his agent-controller was happy, Hoffman still had his own problems, for the strike force was about to hand him three more cases to work on. Hoffman protested but he knew he had no choice. He was what the feds call a "confidential informant," or a "cooperating individual," or simply a "CI," a drug smuggler who had been caught and rather than face imprisonment had agreed to take the agents where they themselves could not easily go—down into the underworld of dealers.

Valestra and the feds had Hoffman on a short leash and they all knew it. In February 1981 he had just turned forty and had been indicted by a grand jury on charges that he was part of a cocaine-smuggling ring from 1975 to 1977. Hoffman's special task was to arrange transport, to buy or rent the aircraft to bring the drugs into California from Ecuador. In working out the logistics of each trip, he often recruited unknowing friends and even family members, some of them children, to give his frequent visits to Latin America an aura of respectability.

The feds used the hold over Hoffman's family as effectively as their hold on him. So while he protested, he knew he had no choice but to work on the three new probes Valestra had for him; even the risk of death was better than the reality of prison. Besides, something might turn up; he might get free somehow.

He was not prepared when Valestra handed him the list of prime suspects to be investigated—one of the names was that of William Morgan Hetrick. The two were old acquaintances from John De-Lorean's days as a Pauma Valley swinger, and now all three men were on a fateful collision course.

Hetrick was a man who had spent much of his life around the rich at play, and he had a burning desire to be one of them. He loved money as much as he loved flying, and the Texas-born Hetrick had begun flying when he was fourteen.

After World War II, Hetrick acquired some war surplus B-25s and embarked on the raffish career of a free-lance cargo pilot, hauling exotic and occasionally illegal cargos from South America and Africa. In the process he gained a reputation as one of the best pilots in the business. In the late 1950s his flair won him a job as test pilot and personal pilot for William Lear, designer of the Learjet. The stint with Lear involved transporting his friends from show business, including such stars as Glen Campbell. And this led Hetrick to another job as pilot with another millionaire named Fletcher Jones.

By the middle 1960s Fletcher Jones was many times a millionaire. The Computer Sciences Corporation, which he helped found in 1959 with $100, was bringing in $50 million a year in sales. Preferring to take it easy, Jones created Westerly Stud Farms, a 3,600-acre ranch, in the Santa Ynez Valley near San Diego. He spent his time working on the 22,000-square-foot villa and the miles of flowerbeds, white fencing, and modern barns for his livestock. Jones also favored the company of beautiful women, and part of Hetrick's job was to fly them from Los Angeles to San Diego for long party weekends at Westerly. Cristina Ferrare soon became a favorite of Jones' and a friend of Morgan Hetrick and his wife; it was to them that she confided that Jones had asked her to marry him and that she was about to say yes.

But on a bright May morning in 1972, Jones was piloting his single-engine plane for a landing at the Santa Ynez airport when he crashed eight miles short of the runway and was killed on impact. Exactly one year later, Cristina Ferrare married one of Jones' friends, John DeLorean, whose Pauma Valley swinging days were soon forgotten. Westerly remains abandoned and unfinished more than a decade later.

After Jones' death Hetrick drifted north again into a series of unhappy partnerships with firms that maintained airplanes or customized private jets for the wealthy. It is generally agreed he was a good mechanic, as good as he was a pilot. One of the enterprises centered on an antiskid airplane braking device Hetrick invented. He hired Hoffman, a Pauma Valley neighbor and young playboy who spent more than he seemed capable of earning, as a salesman. In 1975 the business and the friendship unraveled in a complicated court battle between the partners. One of the highlights of the case was Hoffman's appearance as a witness to testify that Hetrick had taken a $100,000 kickback from him on the sale of an airplane. He also accused Hetrick of demanding a kickback of one-third on all commissions on braking systems sales.

So Hoffman and Hetrick had gone their separate ways. Both men apparently developed ties with the burgeoning drug trade in the region. Hoffman, according to federal agents familiar with his case, was not very successful as a smuggler. But since 1975 Hetrick had been doing very well indeed. According to federal authorities, he used his extensive contacts among the network of private pilots to build up his own drug-transporting business between Colombia and the United States via a refueling stop at a field outside Biloxi, Mississippi. By the end of 1981, U.S. authorities considered him one of the major drug importers in the region. They also knew he would be hard to catch.

Part of the problem in any drug prosecution is to provide adequate proof of the flow of currency needed to pay for the drugs, to prove that money was handed over at the sale, and to show what happened to that money after the sale. The agents believed that Hetrick was doing so well that the simple logistics of handling such huge sums of cash were beginning to cause problems. Hetrick's own aviation repair and maintenance business was not very successful, yet in early 1981 he established Morgan Aviation Company in a hangar at the end of the Mojave Airport at Mojave, California, ninety miles north of Los Angeles on the edge of the vast desert. Morgan Aviation quickly became the talk of the little community of pilots and mechanics based there. The hangar was air conditioned, and a computer-driven lathe was installed to handle sophisticated machining jobs. Hetrick moved into a nice home and began to drive a Cadillac. His fleet of airplanes, half a dozen at a time, was parked around the hangars along with an equal number of vans and cars owned by the firm.

The only thing missing was the customers. Hetrick was frequently absent, leaving a son in charge. Yet he appeared to prosper and was a genial free spender who always reached for the restaurant check. He also freely invited guests to fly with him to Fort Lauderdale for parties on his forty-six-foot Kita trawler, the *Highland Fling*. And although he was turning fifty, he was an active scuba diver and snorkeler. Often he would take off on his trawler or his Hattaras yacht, the *Ivory*, in the company of his pal and protégé, Stephen Arrington, a thirty-four-year-old former U.S. Navy frogman in Vietnam whom the unkinder souls at the air terminal called "Morgan's glorified gofer."

Apparently few people really wondered about Hetrick's strange success. Mojave Airport General Manager Dan Sabovich was proud of the new state-of-the-art addition to his community airport. "I used to take friends there just to show it off."

Visitors were especially impressed by the aviation machine shop and computer, which were better than the facilities at most larger airports. Everything about it was first class, and expensive. "I thought he must have an angel—a financial backer," said Sabovich. "The business he was doing didn't warrant the operation he had here."

But the government agents knew that Hetrick was his own angel by then, and that his planes were logging thousands of hours of flight time to Colombia and back to Mojave, where the hangar was put to more profitable uses. They even knew that Hetrick boasted about his bank account in the Cayman Islands and that he complained ironically about the problems of converting the volume of profits from his smuggling operation into legally usable bank deposits.

But knowing and suspecting is a long way from catching and proving. That is where Hoffman came in.

If the use of such a dubious character as informer and infiltrator on so many major felony cases appears odd, remember the time in which the early probes were launched. Ronald Reagan had campaigned the year before on a strongly worded pledge to launch a war on organized crime and in particular against the drug trade. The word moved out quickly through the myriad U.S. government law enforcement agencies that the president had declared an end to the long-running intertribal war between the various agencies. He appointed department heads who were determined to make his war on crime a success; agency careerists were well advised to put aside their disagreements and get in line, whether they were from the Justice Department and FBI or the Treasury and IRS. There was to be a new government strike force that pooled the resources and information of all the agencies in a cooperative venture. And it would work—or else. Prodded by the direct interest of the Chief Executive, the hunt was on in earnest.

Other powerful voices were being raised against the scandal of uncontrolled drug trafficking in California. The permissive political tide symbolized by Governor Jerry Brown had ebbed and turned. Even Hollywood studio chiefs, by tradition indifferent to the morality of their stars—unless caught—had begun to fret over the public scandal and the production problems caused by talented casualties of drug abuse.

But however welcome the new support was to the agents in the field, the campaign against drugs caught most law enforcement agencies short of manpower, equipment, and contacts within the growing community of Americans who had set themselves up as entrepreneurs and who operated within a tightly controlled network of people known only to themselves. The real problem was how to penetrate these self-contained units with the speed being demanded from Washington. However shopworn he might be, James Timothy Hoffman was a valuable link with this new underworld. At least he knew who they were. At least he knew Morgan Hetrick.

Back in New York City, the shock of the bankruptcy of the company had generated such a siege atmosphere at the Park Avenue offices that some of the employees referred to the place as "the Bunker"—out of DeLorean's earshot to be sure. As February became March, John DeLorean returned to New York from London after the

veek spent trying to stave off the receivers. He had some hard
ʒ to do. The dozen or more outside schemes and business
ventures he was working on were abruptly abandoned.

From this point on, DeLorean devoted himself to a single-minded
effort to revive his empire or, at the end, to preserve his diminishing
role and control over the remnants. To the traumatized staff waiting
for him, DeLorean radiated quiet confidence. He showed no sign of
being especially worried, but his grueling work schedule was now
focused on finding some sort of financial rescue plan for the company.

The ultimate objective was to get the entire operation back on its
feet, but failing that, to preserve DMC's control over the distribution
of the DMC-12s in North America and John DeLorean's personal
control over DMC. And there were immediate pressing problems to
deal with too. His cash flow was cut off—the $290,000-a-month fee
from the Belfast company would no longer arrive. No cars were allowed out of Belfast unless they were paid for in cash. The production
line at Dunmurry, still running, would have to be paid from DMC
funds in New York—in other words by John DeLorean personally.

True, there were plenty of unsold cars in the United States, but
DeLorean, Kimmerly, and Nesseth, meeting in DeLorean's office the
day after Secretary of State James Prior pulled the plug, were only too
aware that the Bank of America had a lien against most of them; in
effect, they were already mortgaged. Kimmerly pointed out that the
date of the latest installment payment to Bank of America was long
overdue; the bank could seize the cars and strangle the company at
once.

Economies were hastily introduced. First to go were the penthouse
offices. DeLorean fought for two years to keep the suite, against the
constant complaints of Tony Hopkins and NIDA. Now he had no
choice. It cost $1 million a year to keep the offices, so he, Kimmerly,
and the rest of the now-shrinking staff moved to the 35th floor to
smaller, less expensive quarters. In early March DeLorean cut the staff
to a minimum. Where once his empire had numbered 3,000 employees, fewer than forty were left.

DeLorean also restructured the DMC board of directors. Kimmerly
was taken off the board, which he had been reluctant to join in the
first place for fear of conflicts of interest. Over the ensuing months,
DeLorean also bought nearly $600,000 worth of DMC properties—
furniture, art work, cars (including Ken Dahlinger's 1955 gull-wing

Mercedes-Benz)—at discount prices as a gesture that he was putting his own money into the sagging corporation.

Yet the real job was to find major financing. A few hundred thousand dollars was not even relevant to saving DMC or keeping the Belfast plant running. And there were plenty of businessmen who were interested, however briefly, in coming to John DeLorean's aid. The old reputation was still holding, helped largely by credulous press reports stressing each fifty-car-per-month gain in sales (the DMC-12 was selling at less than 300 per month during this period) instead of the tremendous gap between the sales and the 1,700-car-per-month total that had to be met to save the venture. A spurious press release claiming profits for DMC during the last half of 1981 was widely reprinted at this time—unquestioned by most of the general news media.

The company version of its plight was easily credible if one did not look too hard. The DMC-12 had been successfully launched; those firm orders were still in place. Only the severe winter and the slump in the general automobile market in the United States had slowed things down. The British government had panicked (as governments will), but an injection of $30 million or so could tide DMC over until the widely predicted economic recovery revived the demand for new cars. The facts of course were quite different. Even the widely publicized car-sales slump was something of a red herring where the DMC-12 was concerned. While general car sales had sagged, sales of luxury cars had boomed.

It was this belief that luxury cars could be sold that attracted California financier Alan Blair, who pulled together a private group and offered DeLorean a rescue package of $30 million. The price would be little enough for what Blair wanted: control of DMC and John DeLorean's job. DeLorean might be kept on in a public relations capacity, but Blair wanted to run the revival attempt. Even as the talks began, Blair did what any sensible businessman did or should do. He ran a check on DeLorean and on the key men around him. He very quickly ran into Roy Nesseth's reputation.

"Based on what I learned, I would not be involved in anything that included a man like Nesseth." He withdrew his offer.

The unidentified Arab head of state never appeared. There is no evidence that he existed except in John DeLorean's imagination.

Early in March there was a new proposition, one that Sir Kenneth

Cork in London was cautious about, but at least it sounded hopeful. Budget-Rent-a-Car of Boston, the third-biggest car rental chain in the United States, approached Cork directly during the weekend after the bankruptcy. Budget was interested in 2,000 DMC-12s. There were some 3,750 cars in the pipeline from the factory through the Quality-Control Centers to the dealers. Cork knew he could not sell them to Budget without going through DMC—he tried and DeLorean flatly refused to surrender any of the rights enjoyed by DMC as sole distributor. He would not budge an inch. So a new scheme was quickly conceived: DeLorean would enter into negotiations with Budget to sell the rental company all the cars it wanted. Budget was interested in 1,000 cars immediately and another 1,000 over the next year. "A lot of people would probably love to drive one, even if not to own one," said a Budget representative. "If Mr. DeLorean had been able to sell his product at a lower price, he would have sold every car he made. If Sir Kenneth feels he can let the cars go at a little less, then we should have a deal." The idea then was that DMC would use the money to repay some of what it owed to the Belfast company— after it had paid off Bank of America.

DeLorean himself retained a sort of gallows humor during this period. The week of the bankruptcy, a line of men's toiletries had been launched bearing his name. He told the *New York Post:* "We're thinking of calling it 'A scent for losers,' or 'A smell for those on the way down.'" He also talked about moving the operation out of Belfast: "We have an alternative site—it's in a warm, sunny clime on the Mediterranean." This was nonsense: he no longer owned a thing in Belfast. It was all in the hands of the receivers, who would never release any of it. Moving to another site would mean starting all over again with a new car—and even rushing things, that would take another five years. The way the money was running out, DeLorean did not have five months, let alone five years.

During this new period of austerity, DeLorean took another action that would later cause considerable controversy among the lawyers and investigators picking over his estate. Henceforth, all checks in and all money paid out went through John DeLorean's personal account. His explanation was that he needed tighter financial controls. It also made him interested in economizing, perhaps for the first time since the Northern Irish had come up with money. For the rest of his corporate days, John DeLorean was tight-fisted about expenditures— he never used the Concorde again.

On Monday, March 1, DeLorean met Budget president Morri̇.
berg to discuss the delicate three-cornered deal. Cork could not au-
thorize DeLorean to negotiate about the sale of the cars already
financed by Bank of America. But title to some of the remaining cars
was far from clear. "There were numerous instances of double-dip-
ping," said J. Bruce McWilliams, DeLorean vice president in charge
of sales in the final days, in an article he wrote for *Car & Driver* in
October 1982:

> In effect, dealers had paid for cars but had not received them,
> and their money had been used to keep operations going. Not
> surprisingly, banks as well as dealers take a dim view of double-
> dipping. As cases of it became known, good gray institutions
> such as the Bank of America, Security Pacific, and GMAC sum-
> marily shut off floor-plan arrangements with DeLorean dealers, a
> devastating new blow to the company. Even if the Bank of
> America could be paid the $20 million owed to it and cars could
> be released from the depots for sale, the whole financial systems
> for selling to dealers would need rebuilding, and there were no
> immediate funds available to pay back those who had been dou-
> ble-dipped.

However, as DeLorean and Belzberg sat down to discuss the details
of a deal, there was optimism. "We think we can put together an
agreement," said Belzberg, "but if we are going to it has to be in a
week or two at the latest." No deal was possible without Bank of
America endorsement. It soon became clear that the money raised on
the Budget deal would first have to go to the bank, which was holding
out for its pound of flesh. Sir Kenneth Cork would have to get in line.

While DeLorean and Belzberg bargained, things were falling apart
rapidly in the rest of the organization. The number of DeLorean
dealers was quickly reduced. At one point it had been 345, but by the
end of February it was 285 and falling. In Belfast creditors were filing
suits or going broke. C. P. Trim, a Northern Irish company set up by
DeLorean and NIDA specifically to supply the car project, appointed
a receiver. At one stage it had provided 400 sets of interior and seating
trim each week. It had already halved its work force in January. Now
it closed with the loss of another 113 jobs. Most of the creditors,
however, were desperately trying to keep the factory going—their
only hope of getting any money back.

Then an event occurred that contributed heavily to wrecking the Budget deal and frightening off some of the other would-be investors. It started on Tuesday, March 2.

Earl Hansen was the general manager of American Auto Inc., a subsidiary of Pasha Industries Inc. of California, which specialized in security and shipments and which processed the DeLorean cars imported on the East Coast through Wilmington. He met the ships bringing the cars in, supervised their unloading, saw them safely through customs, and then transported them to Dick Brown's Quality-Assurance Center at Bridgewater, New Jersey. His duties did not stop there, however. Because of the arrangement with Bank of America whereby it lent DMC $33 million and in return had a written security interest in the stock of DMC-12 cars in the U.S. (except for the last 1,000, which had been shipped without financing), Hansen's operation also had a regulatory aspect. When a car was to be shipped to a dealer, DMC would send an order to Hansen, a letter of release from the Bank of America would follow immediately, and the car would go off to the dealer. That way the bank made sure it got its money at the same time the car was moved. It was a simple and effective operation —until the first week of March.

The day after DeLorean opened his talks with Budget, Hansen received orders from 280 Park Avenue to ship fourteen cars out of the Bridgewater facility, but no letter of release came from Bank of America. Hansen was well aware of the problems DeLorean was having and had no intention of breaking the strict terms of the agreement, which stated that Pasha and AAI "agree to recognize Bank of America's security interest in the vehicles." No letter of release, no vehicles, he decided. To be on the safe side, he checked with the head office in California. He phoned Glenn S. Yamaguchi, Pasha's general counsel, to check whether Bank of America had agreed to release the cars. Yamaguchi called back to tell him no. So Hansen ordered Fran Clark, his manager at the DeLorean Bridgewater facility, not to release them.

The next day, however, Bill Mahr, one of the few DeLorean executives remaining at the Park Avenue office, turned up at Bridgewater. The cars must be released, he told Clark. Clark was taken aback, but he knew his orders. He called California, seeking guidance from headquarters. George Pasha III gave it to him: don't release those cars. Pasha was now aware of the heightening tension at Bridgewater and was concerned about being caught in the middle of it all. Ostensibly his company was still working for DeLorean, but in Belfast DeLorean was in the hands of the receiver. If he defaulted on the Bank of America loan, which Pasha suspected might happen, the rest of the cars would be owned by the bank. It was the job of Pasha's company to guard those cars.

Clark passed on Pasha's decision to Bill Mahr, and the young De-Lorean executive finally went away grumpily. But at seven that evening he was back. This time he brought two armed private security men with him. The men, he told Clark, would stay on the premises to secure it. Clark's Pasha men were already doing that. Now there were two sets of guards, each eyeing the other warily. Clearly, the Pasha men decided, something was about to break.

The next day it did. Oskar Stutz of the Bank of America National Trust and Savings Association passed the news on to George Pasha: DMC was in default. It had missed its payment on an outstanding balance of $18 million, the commitment from its dealers had fallen below the level of the Bank of America's credit agreement, and all cars should now be held to the benefit of the Bank of America, as specified in Pasha's contract.

Hansen was at the Bridgewater facility all that day, ordered there by George Pasha personally. There was trouble in the air and he wanted his top man at the site. The Pasha counsel, Yamaguchi, passed on the news: all cars now belonged to Bank of America and in effect Pasha had changed sides; DeLorean was no longer a client. Pasha was now working for Bank of America, and no cars were to leave the site without Bank of America's approval.

It was a long, tense day, the DeLorean staff and the Pasha men walking around each other carefully, no cars coming or going, the long lanes of cars parked carefully in the enclosure gleaming dully in the pale sunshine. If the DeLorean people were going to make a move, it would have to be soon.

It was nine that evening when Bill Mahr turned up again, this time accompanied by four "unidentified associates," in the staid language of Hansen's later affidavit, or four "armed thugs" according to Dick Brown's secondhand description. No polite language this time, no attempt to bluff and insist that the cars had been formally released. This time it was open threat. Mahr demanded fifteen cars, one more than the original fourteen. Hansen again refused. "Mr. Mahr in-formed me that because of my refusal to release the fifteen automobiles to him," said Hansen in his sworn affidavit in support of Bank of America's later court action against DMC, "Pasha's employment by DMC was thereby terminated upon the direct orders of Mr. John DeLorean."

Hansen believed that DeLorean no longer had the power to fire him, but he had to let California know what was happening. He picked up the phone to call Pasha or Yamaguchi and began to dial. A hand slammed down on his, forcing the receiver back into its cradle. No calls, said the DeLorean men. Hansen could scarcely believe it. He decided this was a police matter. "Call the cops," he told one of his security guards. "No," insisted one of the DeLorean men. "Not from here. This is DeLorean property. You can't use the phones." The guard went around the corner and used a public phone. In the meantime Hansen decided he would prepare documentary proof of his position. Again he was stopped. "The DMC personnel, along with the two armed security personnel they had installed the day before, also prevented me from utilizing the office's telecopy equipment to receive copies of Pasha's lease agreement with DMC and of the notice of default," said Hansen in his affidavit.

The local police arrived soon afterward. Mahr told them that Hansen and all other Pasha personnel had been dismissed by DMC and had no right to be there. Hansen was stuck without a copy of Pasha's lease agreement or of the Bank of America's notice of default, so he had no documents proving his right to be there. The police, perplexed by what was clearly a complex situation, finally sided with DMC and asked the Pasha people to leave.

Hansen asked Fran Clark to hang around outside and watch what went on. If the DeLorean people were going to take some cars, he wanted to know where they went. It did not take long. By 10:30 P.M., the men inside started loading. They took fifteen cars, with Clark following at a safe distance. They didn't go far—just twelve miles. To John DeLorean's Bedminster estate.

Across the country, Dick Brown was suddenly hearing about it. Bill Morgan, his man running the Bridgewater facility, called him. "He told me five armed thugs were physically throwing out the guards and taking the inventory." In fact, the guards left without physical violence.

"I told Bill he had to stop it. He tried, and got fired," says Brown. A few minutes later, George Pasha called. He had learned that a similar raid was planned at the Santa Ana facility. "You've got to be kidding," gasped Brown. Pasha was not. "I'll handle it," said Brown. He called his people at Santa Ana and told them what was happening. "Call the police. I'll be there in thirty minutes."

By the time Brown arrived the police were there. Fifteen minutes later a car pulled up containing four armed men who tried to get in. But the police were there in force and this time they were stopped. Fifteen minutes later Brown was called to the phone. It was Roy Nesseth calling from Peacock Alley, a fashionable promenade in New York's Waldorf-Astoria. "Hey, Brown," he started, "if you want to continue living and if you want your wife and children to stay healthy, you'll cooperate."

"Is that a threat, Roy?"

"You call it anything you want. But you know I can back it up."

Brown handed the phone to a police officer, but he was shaken. A few minutes later he was called back to the phone. This time it was Tom Kimmerly, who was also at Peacock Alley.

"What are you doing there?" he demanded of Brown.

"I'm trying to straighten out this ruckus at the Quality-Assurance Center," said Brown reasonably.

"Well, you are not supposed to be there," said Kimmerly.

"Why not?"

"Because you were fired!"

"Nobody's advised me I was fired."

"You don't have to be advised," said Kimmerly.

"I don't know what you guys are up to," said Brown, "but I certainly don't want any part of it." He handed the phone to the police officer.

On Friday, the day after the Bridgewater incident, DeLorean and Brown talked on the telephone. Brown wanted confirmation of what Kimmerly had told him the night before, that he was fired. Yes, DeLorean told him, he was. DeLorean explained that the takeover of the cars was all a misunderstanding, but "he provided no coherent explanation of the incident," said Brown in his sworn affidavit for the Bank of America's action. "Based upon my observation of the operation of DMC and of the behavior of Nesseth and Kimmerly, I do not believe that [these] events . . . could have taken place without the knowledge and consent of . . . John Z. DeLorean."

Brown was now gone, and Bruce McWilliams, a mild, bespectacled, bald man who knew Dewey and Collins and who ignored their advice not to join DeLorean, suddenly found himself shoved into Brown's place. On Friday, according to McWilliams, "DeLorean asked me to pack my bags for California." The only thing that stuck in his memory about that meeting was DeLorean's statement "that Roy Nesseth would accompany me and that he would take care of any dirty work." DeLorean told him, "Roy is mean. There are people with mean streaks that may surface from time to time, but Roy is different —he enjoys being mean."

McWilliams found the office in chaos when he got to Irvine. "Events in previous weeks had traumatized the staff. There had been numerous firings, dire predictions of events to come by the management, even a staff party at which Big Roy was burned in effigy. One was reminded of the apprehensions of Berliners as the Russian tanks drew nearer."

While McWilliams started sorting out the immediate disaster areas —thousands of warranty claims had piled up, amounting to $1.5 million, all systems and services such as the computer operation were a shambles—Nesseth began dealing with the creditors. He used a combination of threats, evasion, and hard bargaining, much to the consternation of the staff. Now many of them drifted away or were fired. "There was no money, none at all," said McWilliams in his article for *Car & Driver*. "We were flat broke, even running out of necessities such as coffee, stamps, and envelopes. The cleaning service was a creditor and had packed up, and offices became grungy, restrooms smelly. We owed the city of Irvine $330 for water, but they didn't cut their supply because we would have become a health hazard. In order to participate in Los Angeles's Auto Expo, we had to borrow exhibit cars from dealers because we no longer owned any. Shrubbery was carried to our stand at the show from the executive offices."

About this time United States Department of Transportation safety researchers were wondering whether the DMC-12 should be allowed on the road at all. In the autumn of 1981 Brown had donated to the government two DMC-12s—machines that could not be brought up to sale quality—for its research program on the controversial airbag safety restraint device for the front compartment of passenger cars. The airbag study was a pet project of DeLorean's—the publicity and goodwill were valuable and the cost of the two cars could be deducted. In September they were sent to the Dynamic Sciences track in Phoenix to be outfitted with airbags and testing dummies and crashed at speeds above the 35 mph minimum for passenger cars in the United States.

Until that moment there had been absolutely no government inspection of the safety or emission control or fuel-efficiency numbers provided to DOT or other agencies by DMC. Contrary to what most citizens believe, government safety regulators cannot test every car model that comes into the dealer showrooms. As one DOT official explains it, "The Congress gives us just enough money for a minimum amount of testing; it costs as much as $10,000 in addition to the price of the car to crash-test a car, and I would rather be testing the basic models of the Chevys and Fords that millions of people drive than concentrating on limited editions such as the DeLorean."

Besides, the basic numbers had originated at Lotus, which had an unquestioned reputation for engineering integrity, and there was no rash of customer complaints about a specific part or design feature to alert the DOT.

One of the scientists present during the Phoenix crash-tests remembers, "We were extremely pleased about the design of the DMC-12 cockpit and the numbers we got out of the crashes. They were among the best data we got in the entire program. If it hadn't been for the fuel spills it would have been a perfect test."

One of the precautions the DOT testers take in crashing cars into fixed barriers is to use a fuel solvent with a highly visible red dye that makes it easy to spot gasoline spillage resulting from crash damage to the fuel system. To their surprise, they noticed considerable quantities of the fuel's telltale stain not only on the pavement around the car but in the passenger compartment as well.

"We tore the car apart to find the reason. The gasoline tank was still intact and had been well placed in the front Y-area of the chassis. But we found that the electric fuel pump hung down into the tank and was held in place by two heavy rubber flanges. The heat of the day must have weakened the rubber because the impact—and you can generate up to twice the impact by going 45 mph instead of 35 mph —sent the pump moving forward and up and that raised the lid of the fuel tank and allowed the spillage," one of the researchers said.

The government scientists were not about to keep quiet about the fuel spillage. A report was filed in Washington along with the other test data. By the time the appropriate office had received the report and realized its seriousness, DMC was bankrupt. A notification was sent, but what could they do then? "Who do you tell to recall the cars, even assuming we decided to recall them? The Belfast plant? John DeLorean personally? Dick Brown wasn't even in California by the time we realized what was going on," a DOT official said later.

John DeLorean was probably never personally aware of the spills. By this time he was trying to put together his deal with Budget. But the Bank of America was no longer interested in making things easy for him. It filed suit in federal court in New York seeking repayment of its loans and asking the court to order DMC to make 1,950 cars available to it. The bank was owed $18 million; the value of the cars at list price was nearly $50 million. But the cars were not selling, and those that were brought less than list price. The days of early premiums were long gone.

DeLorean remained aloof from it all, as he had from the building of the factory and the car. He was now holed up in a much more modest office on the 35th floor, without the panoramic views, the telescope, or the space he had enjoyed in the penthouse. The art collection so painstakingly gathered by Maur Dubin was now piled up in stacks, some of it already sold. DeLorean remained as calm and determined as ever—failure was not something he could countenance even now.

Sir Kenneth Cork had left him a chance, in fact a very good chance, of survival. Cork had sculpted an ingenious scheme, one which he was proud of and could still work if just one of DeLorean's many prospects came through with some money. It was essentially the same deal he had suggested to DeLorean before receivership, with minor refinements: a new company, DeLorean Motor Cars Limited (1982), would be formed; the factory, tooling, and other equipment would be leased to it for a nominal sum. The new company would be debt-free, but it would pay off the debts of the old company when it sold completed cars.

DeLorean leaped on the plan as enthusiastically as a drowning sailor grasping at a lifeline, except that typically he turned it around so that it came out advantageously for himself. "This means that as we see it," he wrote in the document he prepared for prospective investors, "all the tooling, plant and equipment and learning curve having been transferred without the capital payment to the new company, the new company will be responsible for providing sufficient finance, to provide the working capital starting from a position where there is no work in progress and no finished stock, or indeed, as an empty factory. Therefore, there is in fact no purchase price."

Cork had persuaded Prior that the government should go along with the plan. And Prior agreed, not without a battle with his Cabinet colleagues. If something could be saved from the ashes, however small, then Cork's scheme was worth trying. At Dunmurry there were still 1,300 people building cars from parts already bought, mostly on credit. The parts would have no value unless they could be converted into cars. During those final months DeLorean had ordered parts for a production rate of 30,000 cars a year.

DeLorean also prepared a six-year plan, showing some healthy projections. Most observers didn't give him six weeks, but DeLorean never wavered. "Shorn of the written-off debts," he wrote in the document with the plan, "the company is much stronger and healthier than ever before. DMC today is in a far better position to compete and fulfill its potential to become a smaller, extremely profitable, BMW. BMW, incidentally, went through a similar reorganization two decades ago. Today it is one of the finest automobile enterprises in the world." It never occurred to him that statements like that, made from the bunker of a visibly bankrupt and dying enterprise, must have raised ironic chuckles from readers. To John DeLorean, with his extraordinary tunnel vision and determination to shut out the reality of his situation, there was a real prospect of building not just a BMW but a Mercedes.

But he needed $30 million. The Budget deal would only get his major creditors off his back, pay off Bank of America and some of the others. It would not produce the cash he needed to provide working capital for Belfast. He needed a straight equity injection of some $30 million. He spent hours drawing up his proposals: "During the major public offering planned for July 1981 (which was aborted due to the government's procrastination) the company was valued at $12–$15 per share, approximately $300 million. Under today's proposals the company represents a much greater value, most debt has been written off and by elimination of the government's 7 million shares the dilution is reduced."

He played with sales figures. In 1982 he could still sell 6,300 cars, he forecast. In 1983 he would introduce a turbocharged version whose sales would steadily build up. By 1985 there would be a sedan as well, and by 1987, the end of his six-year plan, he would be selling 33,600 units for revenues of nearly $1 billion and profits of $161 million. The only year the new company could operate at a loss would be year one, when it would lose $1 million. By year two it would already be making a profit of $50 million, producing a very decent return for anyone clever enough to invest $30 million now.

Through March and on into April he sent this plan with his accompanying glowing statement and projections to potential investor after investor. He bombarded Sir Kenneth Cork with news that he had at last found his man, willing to put up $30 million. Cork made the journey to New York several times, but after a while he stopped going. He had to have every new investor checked out, and very often got a negative answer. They invariably had the money, but didn't want to invest it in DeLorean. DeLorean had convinced himself that every slight expression of interest amounted to a firm commitment.

At the beginning there were some good people: Alan Blair was a serious prospect. And there was a possible deal with General Motors itself, although DeLorean may have exaggerated that. Cork was astonished at the figures in the documents DeLorean was sending out. "They have no relevance to the facts at all," he bluntly told DeLorean. "These cash flow forecasts and profit forecasts—they're pie in the sky." DeLorean ignored his criticisms.

"Nobody ever follows up," Cork complained to one of his colleagues after some weeks. "Every time there is a new voice. Someone rings up and says, 'I'm so-and-so and you can check me out.' We do and he has the money and we are just getting used to him when he disappears. And someone new rings up."

Cork found something else to dislike in DeLorean's office: Roy Nesseth. At first he didn't know what to think of him, but he soon made up his mind. After Nesseth had interrupted a discussion between Cork and DeLorean with threats of libel writs against Cork and against the British government and had run on for some minutes about the stupidity of everyone in Belfast and London, Cork turned on DeLorean.

"You'd better get that man out. I'm not having him in here while I'm talking to you."

DeLorean was taken aback. "Well, he's my partner."

"I don't care if he's your brother," snapped Cork. "If you want to talk to me get him out of this room!"

Nesseth went.

Cork soon noticed one intriguing little pattern: every new investor was offering the same amount of money. "Why is it always $30 million?" he said half-jokingly to DeLorean on one occasion, his renowned grin flashing across his features. "Surely to God you could find the grace to vary the figure every now and again, if only for appearance sake."

DeLorean laughed.

Cork kept setting deadlines for the injection of new money; DeLorean kept missing them. The Budget deal ran into problems familiar to DeLorean watchers. Budget was enthusiastic about the cars, but it was having trouble negotiating with him. Belzberg had been a DeLorean fan, as caught up with his reputation as anyone. He saw DeLorean's present plight as a personal tragedy and was keen to help. He also thought the cars would be a major attraction at his airport outlets. At the start negotiations had gone well. The Bank of America battle had soured relations for a while but they recovered. By the end of March they had arrived at a deal, but then it collapsed again. Belzberg revived it in a different form, and by mid-April they again had a deal: 1,000 cars to be leased rather than sold to Budget for up to six months and then sold as used cars by DeLorean dealers. This was a solution to the problem of the title to the cars. Bank of America had now won its court order preventing DeLorean from selling any cars until it had been repaid. Cork claimed the other cars belonged to the Belfast company because they had never been paid for. DeLorean denied both. Budget could not deal without having title—unless it could lease.

Then, as the deal was about to move forward, another complication arose. While negotiating to sell or lease to Budget, DeLorean and Nesseth were also negotiating to sell or lease to another company: Consolidated International Corporation of Columbus, Ohio. This was the deal that DeLorean probably hated more than any other. Consolidated was a purchaser of liquidated stock. It had bought the remains of the Bricklin stock and still charged pretty high prices for Bricklin parts. A deal with Consolidated meant that there would be two suppliers of DeLorean cars—DMC, if it could manage to free some cars, and Consolidated. And Consolidated was offering a low, low price: just over $11,745 each for 1,193 units. It would infuriate the dealers, wreck all DeLorean's careful marketing plans, harm the image of the high-priced, low-volume car—but it would bring in money. By the middle of April DeLorean was unveiling his new $54-million package: $14 million would come from Consolidated, which would provide short-term operating cash. Then there would be another $40 million in long-term funding, DeLorean told *Auto News*: $35 million of it would come from a Southern California financial institution, the other $5 million from his own personal funds, as he had promised Cork. It would be enough, said DeLorean, to allow him to reacquire the Belfast facility and get going again.

In London Cork was wary to the point of skepticism. "Frankly I would like to see the money before going too deeply into things," he told the *Daily Telegraph*. "Mr. DeLorean has come up with proposals before, but they don't seem to have got very far."

Only a slight wave of hope went through the Belfast factory—there had been too many false dawns already. But DeLorean became more hopeful by the day: "We have the bankers' letters but we need to get some form of arrangement made," he said after sending the proposals off to Cork and his partner, Paul Shewell. On Friday, April 16, the 1,300 workers still in the Belfast factory emerged from their eighth week of receivership with no idea what their future would be. They were now building only thirty-five cars a week, surviving basically because of another form of government aid—temporary-employment subsidy. They were now three weeks past Cork's original deadline and they were resigned, fatalistic. The newspapers carried conflicting headlines day by day: RECEIVER MAY DASH LAST DELOREAN HOPES (*Guardian*, April 21), DELOREAN MAY BE SAVED (*Daily Telegraph*, April 23), FRESH HOPES OF BUYER FOR DELOREAN CAR PLANT (*Times*, April 23).

Then the Budget deal fell through, killed by the lawyers, who would not allow it to go ahead unless they could guarantee the title to the cars. DeLorean himself was holding back on the Consolidated deal, but it was finally going through against all his instincts. "He really hated like hell dealing with Consolidated—regarded them as Shylock, taking their pound of flesh," said a DeLorean executive. But he had no choice. Consolidated paid $14 million for 1,174 cars, most of it going straight to Bank of America. It did not relieve the cash squeeze, but it did mean the cars were for sale again.

Two days later, as Cork was about to close the factory, a savior finally arrived on the scene. With the legal wrangle between DMC and Bank of America finally out of the way, the cars were moving again. The combination of that fact and the potential rescuer persuaded Cork to allow a stay of execution. He extended again, giving DeLorean another five weeks.

The savior came from New York. He was thirty-eight-year-old real estate magnate and financier Peter Kalikow, whose family company, H. J. Kalikow, owns several Manhattan apartment buildings and some major office buildings. Cork quickly discovered that if Kalikow wanted to invest, he would have no trouble finding the money from his own resources—he had the money all right. But would he go through with it?

It was Kalikow who set himself a deadline: May 14. "It must be ready for signing then. Otherwise this thing could go on forever," he told DeLorean and Cork. Kalikow had gone above the repetitive $30 million figure. He was offering $35 million. He recalls:

> I had known John for some time and known of him for longer than that. I saw him from time to time at the Boardroom [A private club one floor below DeLorean's penthouse office.] and a friend of his had done some legal work for me. The friend asked if I would be interested in pursuing some type of investment. I said I would and that's how it came about.
>
> I was not a social friend at all and there was nothing that led me to believe that the company's problems were any different from what a lot of auto companies were running into at the time. I was impressed that they did so well in the period of time that they were involved in the project; that they managed to get the whole thing going with all the tooling and get a credible product on the market.
>
> The deal was put together in a short period of time but it was a comprehensive proposal as far as I was concerned. Basically it would have been an amalgamation of the companies here and it would have assured DMCL that every car sold to us would have been paid for. There would have been no problem for them once a car was made, it would have been paid for.

Not surprisingly, Kalikow demanded majority control of DMC and John DeLorean tentatively agreed. The next step was to win the approval of the receivers. Paul Shewell flew to New York and met with Kalikow.

"Shewell was very nice and polite and told me that he could not entertain my offer. We talked it over for three hours in my office. They wanted somebody to come there and bail out the place, replace their investment 100 cents on the dollar and there was just no way that I could do it that way. So I thanked him very much and that was the end of it."

The Kalikow offer would have done nothing for the receiver's position. Cork and Shewell wanted an equity investment, not just financing for the cars already made. Their interest was in trying to keep the factory going, thereby getting something back for the creditors as well as preserving jobs in Northern Ireland. Cars made would have been paid for, yes. But who paid for the cars to be made in the first place? Kalikow's offer did nothing for the Belfast company.

Kalikow, however, kept the deal open beyond his original deadline while DeLorean continued to wax optimistic. "The entire arrangement will be completed by the end of May," he announced on May 17. Two days later Kalikow pulled out.

With the Bank of America repaid $13 million of its money and now moving for its remaining $5.3 million, crisis was again looming. By now Prior and even Prime Minister Thatcher were pressuring Cork to come up with a solution or close the plant. Anything was better than this uncertainty. But with Kakilow out, DeLorean announced yet another new backer and again Cork had to go through the motions.

On Monday, May 25, Shewell flew to Belfast and Dunmurry. He assembled the 1,500 workers and gave them the news. Three months of fruitless searching for backers had failed. The production line would be shut down the following week. Some 200 or so men would be kept on for the time being to run the servicing operation for those cars already sold and to keep efforts going to sell more cars. The other 1,300 would be laid off at the end of the week. It was "another nail in the coffin of our dying economy," said a spokesman for the joint Protestant-Catholic Alliance. Shewell's statement aroused fury across the Province, expected though it was. The shop stewards talked about discrimination against Northern Ireland and accused the government of economic withdrawal from Ulster, insisting that London was preparing the way for a complete retreat from Northern Ireland, a move that would please no one except the IRA. Two days later they climbed a perimeter fence and started a sitin in the factory. "We will eat and sleep on the site for as long as is necessary," said Sean O'Neill, the senior shop steward.

All summer long it was the same pattern. Every time Cork was about to close the factory, there would be a new prospect. At one stage it was a consortium of British suppliers, led by Barrie Wills and Chuck Bennington, who came forward with a deal. It appealed to both Cork and Prior. They found a bank—Hill, Samuel, one of the leading merchant banks in the City of London—and the bank felt it could be made to work. Hill, Samuel's Tim Frankland went to Northern Ireland to talk to Cork about it. It was an ingenious plan: the factory would be reopened but would build two cars rather than one. British Leyland had recently eliminated its TR-7 sportscar line at Speke, near Liverpool. Why not buy the rights to that (it was government owned anyway) and build two sports cars in Dunmurry? Reduced work force, tight controls, proper management—it might work. Hill, Samuel thought it could probably raise the money from the City of London—possibly £10 million.

There was one snag. Hill, Samuel wanted its £80,000 fee up front before it would take the risk of preparing the prospectus and going ahead. And the consortium didn't have that sort of money. Would the government pay for the prospectus? Prior took the proposal all the way to Margaret Thatcher. She looked at it and said, "It seems to me if they can't raise the fees to pay the bankers they haven't got much of a chance of raising the rest." Prior and Cork agreed, much as they both approved of the scheme. And so another rescue bid died. Others would be raised in the spring and early summer. All came to nothing. The downhill slide picked up speed.

Chance continued to play a large role in DeLorean's fortunes. In early March another bizarre string of coincidences began to unfold, beginning in the small town of Ventura, California, halfway between Los Angeles and Morgan Hetrick's base of operations near Mojave.

Ventura Police Chief Paul Lydick began surveillance of a local resident suspected of transporting large sums of currency out of the state. A local informant had overheard the suspect brag about his currency-hauling exploits and of his contacts with a man named Morgan. The surveillance spread to include several other men and led the local police to Morgan Aviation.

"We thought it might be a money-laundering operation. Take a hypothetical case . . . if you know somebody who's broke and all of a sudden starts making flights to Miami and New York and driving new cars, you might ask yourself what's going on here." Lydick asked the help of the United States Customs Service and the Internal Revenue Service, whose agents quickly learned that Morgan Aviation and Morgan Hetrick were subjects of a drug probe. Thus, under the new ground rules from Washington, the money probers and drug busters pooled resources and mounted a far larger operation against Hetrick than might have been the case a few years earlier. Rather than wait for the wily pilot to make a mistake, the government decided to mount a sting, to shut down the operation for good.

According to the authorities, the original plan had FBI agent Benedict Tisa pose as "James T. Benedict" and claim to be an official of the Eureka Federal Savings and Loan Association of San Carlos, California, another small town about forty miles southeast of San Francisco. James Hoffman was given specific orders. He was to make contact with Hetrick and get back in his good graces. He was to convince Hetrick that the Savings and Loan official would help him with the growing problem of shifting his drug profits into legally usable cash. Hoffman was also to hint that not only was "James Benedict" willing to launder Hetrick's money, but he would also like a piece of a future drug deal as well.

Hoffman did as he was told. Hetrick was interested but still cautious. The net was getting tighter around him but he was far from caught.

On July 11 John DeLorean and James Hoffman, who was barely able to believe his good luck, met at the Marriott Hotel in Newport Beach, California. DeLorean complained to his old neighbor about his business frustrations. One of the key points of contention by prosecutors and DeLorean's defense lawyers is what happened next. Who moved first? Who first mentioned a drug deal? In the stilted language of law enforcement, the agents charged that DeLorean sought out Hoffman because he "had a sense" of the younger man's involvement with drug trafficking and that DeLorean initiated the idea that a drug deal might generate the kind of cash he needed to save DMCL before Sir Kenneth Cork abandoned any rescue attempt.

Whatever happened then, the next event is not disputed. Hoffman told his control, Valestra, that John DeLorean, the big-name automobile tycoon, might be coaxed into a drug deal. Better yet, De-

Lorean was acquainted with the prime target, Morgan Hetrick. One could be used to land the other. The federal agents quickly agreed, ever mindful of the publicity value of busting a major business executive.

The agents now say the plan was changed and Hoffman was to tell Hetrick that DeLorean could be used as a source of new capital for a major coke or heroin transaction, something large enough to let banker Benedict have a piece of the action too.

In the meantime, DeLorean kept Sir Kenneth Cork and the British government searching for ways to avoid abandoning the project. On August 3 Shewell reported that the British investors group was asking for more time to work out a deal. During this period a certain amount of tension was developing between the receivers and the British government in the person of James Prior. The Northern Ireland Secretary was becoming increasingly skeptical about whether DMCL and the Dunmurry factory could ever be hoisted back into operation again.

But this time Cork prevailed, partly because the plan involved the ouster of John DeLorean. On August 9 he flew to New York and presented the plan to DeLorean: the investors wanted to produce a British Leyland Triumph or TR-7-type car as well as the DMC-12. Donald Lander would become chief executive of both the Belfast and U.S. operations. The investors insisted that DeLorean be ruled out of the decision-making process before they would come in. DeLorean remained impassive. Under the agreement the receivers group had until the end of August to put their deal together. DeLorean correctly judged that they would not make it; they didn't, and a thirty-day extension was asked. After September 30 it would be DeLorean's turn again to come up with a rescue plan; he had to have the money by then.

On September 4 DeLorean met Hoffman at the L'Enfant Plaza Hotel, a luxury complex in Washington, D.C., just south of the museums of the Smithsonian Institution and the great tree-shaded mall that stretches out from the Capitol. At this meeting DeLorean was introduced to "Mr. Vicenza": in reality Valestra pretending to be a heavyweight dope distributor tied to organized crime.

While the conversation was being monitored and recorded by nearby FBI agents, DeLorean and the two men discussed, in the language of the government affidavits, "the importation and distribution of heroin from Thailand and cocaine from South America as a means of generating large amounts of capital for the DeLorean Motor Company." According to the transcriptions of the tapes, DeLorean agreed to supply $1.8 million to bankroll the drug buy. Vicenza-Valestra then volunteered to put up about $3 million so that the group could purchase a 220-pound load of coke. As the discussion rolled onto the government tapes, the three men agreed that Mr. Vicenza was to handle the distribution of the drugs and that DeLorean was to get most of the profits from the deal. They agreed to meet again and set the final terms.

There was no reminiscing about the Pauma Valley days when Hoffman, Hetrick, and DeLorean finally met September 20 in a room at the Bel Air Sands Hotel in Los Angeles. The eager bank official Benedict (agent Tisa) was on hand, but most of the meeting was dominated by Hetrick, who bragged about his skill as a smuggler. It was agreed Hetrick would bring in 100 kilos (220 pounds) at $50,000 a kilo, of top-quality cocaine from his supply source in Colombia. Benedict was to handle the distribution of profits to DeLorean. A final meeting was set for a week later.

At about this time a most disturbing warning began to filter through the very highest levels of the Thatcher government. Highly placed United States diplomatic sources passed the word to drop any contact or future dealings with John DeLorean. Something was up. He was involved, or soon would be involved, in a major government prosecution. There were no more details than that, no mention of drugs, no hint of an arrest date. Just a word to the wise. Not even Sir Kenneth Cork and the receivers could be told. Whatever happened, the DeLorean affair must be wound up as painlessly as possible; the receivers must be persuaded to give up any future rescue attempts and to close Belfast down for good.

But Sir Kenneth was far from willing to let the DeLorean project fold. Indeed, in that final week of September it appeared that his long search for a legitimate investor was on the verge of success. Best of all, it was a British firm that was trying to wire the deal together, a deal that could inject as much as $100 million into the enterprise. Such a major investment would not only help put the Belfast production lines back in operation and cover the cost of the cars already languishing in lots on both sides of the Atlantic, but it might also buy out the entire British government's stake—something even Prior dared not hope for.

The firm negotiating with Sir Kenneth was Minet Financial Management, a branch of the Minet Group, which in turn was a major
member of the Lloyd's of London insurance network. Minet Financial
specialized in placing money from various British tax-haven banks in
the Cayman Islands and British Virgin Islands in high-risk, high-yield
investments outside the reach of the U.K. Inland Revenue.

The framework of the proposed deal was simplicity itself. Minet's
clients would lend the money directly to DeLorean Motor Company
Inc., the Delaware shell which was to have held John DeLorean's
assets if the Bache public stock offering had gone through successfully.
DMC Inc. had lain dormant since that time.

The $100 million would have been more than enough to rescue
DeLorean. The investment could have settled the Belfast company's
$30 million in creditors' debts, bought the assets of the Dunmurry
plant (perhaps another $25 million), taken over the inventory of cars,
and put the sales network back together again. This time DeLorean
could have it all without the interference from NIDA and London
officials, whom he now blamed for the venture's collapse.

The deal was also attractive to the Minet investment managers.
They thought of DeLorean as a genius executive who had hit a patch
of bad luck. The American car market had to turn around one of
these days, and placing their clients inside the revival of the DMC-
12 would be a neat trick indeed.

But neither the Minet managers nor Sir Kenneth were fools. Both
were aware of the weathervane changes that could occur in negotiations with DeLorean. And Sir Kenneth would still have to persuade
the Thatcher government and ultimately Parliament to ratify the
deal.

So, in the flurry of telephone calls and Telexes that crisscrossed the
Atlantic, Sir Kenneth and the investors imposed one condition that
could not be negotiated away. If John DeLorean wanted to be part of
this deal and to control the resurrection of his company, he would
have to come up with a capital investment of his own by a fixed
deadline. The sum required was $20 million, and it would be nonre-
fundable if the deal failed. The deadline date was October 20.

DeLorean complained to Sir Kenneth that while he had $10 mil-
lion on hand, he feared he could not raise the rest. The Minet managers came to his rescue. The British firm had done business for some
time with a small American investment bank in the Washington,
D.C., suburb of McLean, Virginia.

F.S.I. Financial Services Inc. is a small firm that places about $100 to $200 million a year in loans to individual clients. Its other distinction is that it is one of three such investment firms headed by a woman.

Jeanne Farnan is a shrewd and circumspect expert on the almost invisible threads that make up the international syndicated-loan network. She was in London on another deal in the first week of October when she was asked if she could come up with a short-term loan for John DeLorean. After a day trip to inspect the Dunmurry plant, Farnan said she would return to Washington and try.

In the meantime, DeLorean returned to New York and immediately called Farnan in Virginia to see how her loan was coming. Farnan recalls:

> It seemed to me that DeLorean almost had the pieces together when I got involved in this. He called me at home one night and we talked. I explained that it would have to be a standby loan for $10 million for a term of ninety days. The interest rate at that time was 12 percent and the closing fee was about 2 or 3 percent.
>
> The only problems we really had were with the receivers, who objected to the bank where we first proposed to put the money. Finally we changed banks and then backed the loan funds with another investor's certificate of deposit. So it was a doubly colla-teralized loan. The money was to go to DMC Inc.

DeLorean did not haggle over the terms, nor did he ask for help on the other $10 million. "He said he had that $10 million but he needed the rest to show the British government that he was operating in good faith," Farnan says. "He also did not tell me the money would be nonrefundable. No one told me that until after the affair was long over. You can imagine how I felt."

The last meeting involving the drug-ring planners took place September 28 at the Bonaventure Hotel in Los Angeles—again in a room that was monitored and recorded by the agents. Discussing the deal were Hoffman, DeLorean, and Vicenza, who told the automaker that sales from the coke buy could gross more than $50 million. As payment for fronting the $3 million in seed money, Vicenza said he wanted a 50 percent interest in DeLorean Motor Company. De-Lorean's voice is heard agreeing; he later transferred to Vicenza 50 percent of DMC Inc. Talk of a heroin deal was finally dropped because, as Vicenza explained, it might take five weeks after delivery before profits could be realized. DeLorean didn't have that kind of time. In early October Hetrick left the Mojave Airport and the scheme was in motion.

In New York at the DMC offices, John DeLorean kept up his daily routine without a hint that something special was in the wind. He continued to make public statements predicting that a final investors-group plan would be put together by the end of October. There were reports that a Hong Kong organization was holding discussions, but DeLorean laughed when journalists pressed him for confirmation. Something's going to happen soon, he assured them. They would be the first to know.

The tension at the DMC headquarters in New York was more than matched among the federal agents waiting to spring the trap on Hetrick and DeLorean. Hetrick had telephoned the Eureka bank and told Benedict-Tisa that he planned to arrive in Los Angeles on Monday, October 18, on Pam Am flight 442 from Miami.

Always cautious, Hetrick jarred Benedict somewhat by announcing he would bring only 25 of the 100 kilos promised. If that went well and he could get $1.8 million from the DeLorean-Vicenza partnership, the remaining 75 kilos would follow very soon. There was no thought of waiting; the agents moved to close the trap for good.

According to plan the agents secured room 501 at the Sheraton Plaza hotel near the L.A. Airport. The room was a minisuite, its rooms divided by a glass wall. On the other side cameras and recorders were set and manned.

At 3:55 P.M. on the afternoon of October 18, Hetrick met Benedict at the airport and picked his luggage off the conveyor belt. By 4:20 they were in room 501 and Hetrick announced that he was ready to go. The agents were not. It was not until 7:45 P.M. that DEA agent Gerald Scotti and Vicenza-Valestra arrived and began their act as underworld drug wholesalers come to make the buy. The suitcase containing $1.8 million in cash was placed on a plexiglass coffee table in full view of the cameras. Hetrick looked at it but did not bother to count the money; the suitcase was closed and set aside.

Now it was Hetrick's turn. As the cameras turned he told the agents that the cocaine was hidden in a car that would be driven to the hotel by his aide, Arrington. He called the younger man and told him to bring the car to the front entrance of the hotel lobby; the group would meet him there.

But Arrington misunderstood the message and arrived in Hetrick's own Cadillac. The cocaine was in another car. The men agreed on an impromptu plan of action—Arrington would take agent Scotti and Hoffman to the cocaine car and turn it over to them. Hetrick and Benedict-Tisa would go to dinner and make the transfer of funds later from Vicenza. Convoys of agents trailed after both groups.

On the way, Arrington chatted freely with Scotti and Hoffman. He explained how the coke car—a Chevrolet Caprice—had been rigged with a lever under the dashboard to unlatch the back seat and expose the hidden cargo section. He boasted about similar jobs he had done for Hetrick and complained about the low pay he got for such danger-ous work. By agreement, Arrington left the two agents with the Cadillac and went by himself to get the delivery car, which was parked elsewhere in a public parking lot. Within a few minutes he arrived and as he stopped the Caprice, Scotti could see Arrington lean forward and pull the seat lever. The rear seatback popped forward.

"Go ahead, take a look," Arrington told Scotti, who clambered in the back and pulled the seat forward to expose a compartment full of "multiple kilo-size packages, mostly wrapped in brown wrapping paper with masking tape," as his affidavit would later recount.

The official Scotti narrative continues in the officialese used by policemen the world over:

> I removed one of the packages, which I noted was marked "RCX" in blue felt-tip pen. I pierced the outer wrapper of the package with a key and took out a pinch of white crystalline powder in my fingers. By its distinctive smell and appearance, I believed this substance to be cocaine from my experience as a narcotics investigator. I exited the vehicle and gave a prear-ranged "bust" signal, at which time the agents and officers on surveillance effected the arrest of Stephen Arrington. I advised Arrington of his Constitutional Rights under *Miranda,* but he declined to make any statement at that time.

The time was 9 P.M. At 11:15 P.M. Morgan Hetrick and Benedict-Tisa had finished their meal at the posh La Cage aux Folles restaurant on La Cienega Boulevard and were leaving when other agents closed in and made the arrest. Hetrick, too, kept silent after being read his rights.

He and Arrington were taken to the Terminal Island federal correctional facility nearby for fingerprinting and processing. Suddenly the agents had a brief scare. No one had foreseen what Hetrick might do when he was allowed his mandatory telephone call after processing. Would he call DeLorean and warn him off? The fears were unfounded as Hetrick placed an understandably urgent call to his lawyer.

It was well into the morning of October 19 back on the East Coast by now. In McLean, Virginia, Jeanne Farnan and an aide had worked all weekend to complete the loan documents and get them off to New York by courier. Farnan had to turn around then and pack for yet another trip to London. This time she would be part of the negotiations between Sir Kenneth and the Minet managers about what to do next.

John DeLorean arrived at his Park Avenue offices at the usual time and immersed himself in the daily routine. By midmorning the F.S.I. loan documents were delivered and lay on his secretary's desk unopened. When Farnan called to see if they had been signed, the secretary said she would see that DeLorean got them right away. Farnan said she would call back.

Just before noon she called again. Yes, Mr. DeLorean had received the loan forms personally. They were on his desk, still unsigned. The secretary promised she would remind him to act soon because he was about to leave for Los Angeles and she did not know when he would be back. This alarmed Farnan.

She told the secretary that DeLorean must sign those forms before he left—there could be no delay. She was leaving soon for London for talks about the company's future; there would be no future if he failed to sign those documents today. He must understand that.

An hour later John DeLorean left his office for the flight to Los Angeles. Three FBI agents followed him to the airport and sat behind him on the planeride out.

Once he arrived at the Los Angeles airport, DeLorean paused and made a quick telephone call back to his office. He had not signed the F.S.I. document and his secretary asked when he would be returning so she would have something to tell the now-frantic Jeanne Farnan. He brushed the question aside and took the other messages without commenting or betraying any of the excitement he must have felt. Then he went briskly to the nearby Sheraton Plaza Hotel, to room 501. It was nearly 3 P.M. Within fifteen minutes he was under arrest. The dream of John Z. DeLorean was ended. The nightmare was about to begin.

EPILOGUE

"I don't care what you say about John DeLorean, you have to give him credit for what he accomplished or nearly accomplished. He was a maverick. He took a swampy field in Northern Ireland and in two years turned it into a state-of-the-art factory that produced a damn good car. Whatever else he did, you have to give him that."

In one form or another, this soulless definition of success has been used to justify a surprisingly persistent sympathy for DeLorean's public image since his arrest. Of course one should not pass judgment on the criminal charges against him until his day in court is over. But there is good reason to measure DeLorean's life up to the point of his arrest by something other than this supposedly pragmatic standard of morality.

Implicit in the "only results count" view of DeLorean's automobile career is the totally false premise that the entrepreneurial spirit in the world is so threatened that any person brave enough to set off on his own is justified in using any means to succeed. This does not jibe with the facts of life in the United States over the past twenty years, or for that matter in the United Kingdom. This period has seen a blossoming of individual business founders, men and women who have invested sweat and vision to create new economic growth. Indeed, the revolution in high-technology industry is almost exclusively the result of just the kind of small-shop mavericks who possess the courage supposedly monopolized by John DeLorean.

Undeniably, DeLorean began his career equipped with engineering skills that bordered on genius, plus an inexhaustible supply of energy and ambition. One can only guess with sadness at what an enormous contribution he might have made to all our lives had those talents been used for good.

Ironically, it is when one applies that engineer's definition of success—the "does it succeed" standard—that the barrenness of DeLorean's subsequent career stands out in stark relief from what it might have been. However high-flown the rhetoric about his ethical car was at the beginning, John DeLorean's dream car must be judged as being not even close to a success.

Through his indifference, greed and cynicism he debased his own dream. Over the years the car was reduced to being a plaything for those whose only standard of judgment is the price tag. The DMC-12 at its best is a low-performance counterfeit of better cars and will never be the museum piece of quality its sellers claim today. At its worst, individual models are seriously flawed and in some cases may be dangerous. Nevertheless, car dealers around the country are getting a premium price of $25,000 to $30,000 for it.

And consider the cost of DeLorean's dream. Hundreds of millions of dollars were thrown away on the project on both sides of the Atlantic. It will take many years before any British government can muster the political mandate to undertake a job-creation program of comparable size in Northern Ireland.

Here is the core of the tragic result of DeLorean's dream. More than 2,500 men lost their jobs when the Dunmurry plant was closed, and it is not an exaggeration to say that the entire terror-ravaged region has lost the best hope for peace it may have for years to come.

There were other human casualties too. The lives of the men and women who invested their money, careers and talents in the DMC-12 project were squandered, and all endured the emotional trauma of betrayal at the hands of a man whom they believed could make their dreams come true. Some have regained their footing. C. R. Brown is currently an executive for Avanti Inc., the small, luxury-car maker whose twenty-year history of success and high quality of product is the epitome of everything that the DeLorean project lacked.

Bob Dewey and Bill Collins are partners in a joint venture to produce a lightweight, fuel-efficient family motor home, due out next year. Walter Strycker has returned to San Francisco and resumed his independent venture-capital business. William Haddad was a major campaign aide to New York's new governor, Mario Cuomo, and is writing his own book about his experience.

Others have not been so lucky. Marian Gibson has resumed her business career but still bears the financial and emotional costs of the continuing lawsuits DeLorean's lawyers are waging in London. Most of the Dunmurry plant executives have been left stranded by the collapse. At Norwich, Mike Kimberley and Fred Bushell struggle Swiss francs to its Amsterdam affiliate banking house Pierson, to revive Lotus Group after the twin blows of Colin Chapman's death in December 1982 and the undeserved taint of the firm's DeLorean ties.

The final chapter on the DeLorean car saga and on the life of John Z. DeLorean will be many more years in the writing. (See the chart illustrating the flow of funds on the DMC-12 project.) Just how much money was siphoned from the various fund-raisings may never be fully known, but a fair accounting will probably unfold very soon indeed.

This much is known. Late in the summer of 1979, Rothschild Bank AG of Zurich transferred 13,761,650 Swiss francs to its Amsterdam affiliate banking house Pierson, Heldring, Pierson, for conversion into $8.9 million. That money was transferred via Citibank in New York to the John DeLorean loan account at Continental Illinois Bank in Chicago. On October 2, 1979, DeLorean's Cristina Corp. used $7.5 million of that money to buy a new issue of preferred stock in De-Lorean Manufacturing Company of Detroit. Since John DeLorean already owned 100% of both Cristina and Manufacturing, the stock purchase was merely a transfer of capital. In turn, Manufacturing reduced its outstanding loans from Continental Illinois and, in subsequent negotiations, shifted its line of credit and debts to Logan Manufacturing Company of Utah, which Manufacturing had purchased control of earlier in the summer.

An irony in John DeLorean's life is that he may have less to fear from the criminal charges lodged against him in Los Angeles than he does from those in the bankruptcy court sitting in judgment in Detroit on the affairs of the DeLorean Motor Company. In the criminal proceedings, DeLorean could win and go free immediately. If he is convicted and sentenced, at least it will be a fixed term that eventually will be over with.

But the bankruptcy proceedings could last for years. Under the 1980 bankruptcy law revisions, the power of creditors of firms such as DMC was vastly expanded. The courts can subpoena records and reach beyond the barrier of a corporation's identity to recover assets and resources wrongly taken by the firm's principals. The reach of the creditors and the judge now extends across the Atlantic, where FBI agents cannot go, to delve into Swiss bank accounts and Cayman

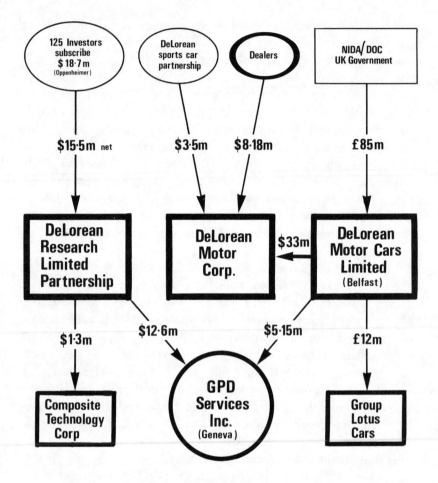

Islands deposit boxes. Immunity from future criminal prosecutions can be given to those who cooperate, and that alone could set information flowing that would have been inaccessible just three years ago.

But as fascinating and important as the final chapter on DeLorean may be, it is doubtful that future events will substantially alter the tenor of his recent career. Other people used him to get what they wanted; that is undeniable. Those who worked for him frankly admit that his enormously positive public image was an asset they could use to achieve their own dreams and goals. Governments, too, bowed before that public image. Agencies charged with safeguarding the public welfare took shortcuts to accommodate him. Financiers ignored their duties to their clients in the race to get a piece of the DeLorean action. Politicians rushed to give him money, in order to solve their own problems. The public press—especially the American business press—bears a special guilt for its lazy gullibility in swallowing and ballooning the image of the iconoclastic, socially compassionate corporate maverick.

All of this is true, but it does not fully explain the enormous devastation that resulted from DeLorean's career of corporate banditry. After all, some individuals did resist his predations. There were government officials who disengaged themselves from his schemes and others who protected their constituents with determination. From the start, there were journalists who sounded a warning for all to hear that the car was a failure, a project doomed by DeLorean's avarice.

The missing ingredient, then, is John DeLorean's character. We will never know why he became the way he is. Other men have emerged from more impoverished backgrounds without his visible self-destructiveness. Others have overcome the frustrations of corporate life with individualism that did not become predatory. It is still possible to have a vision and realize it fully and with honor, and it is still possible to get what one wants without destroying the dreams and lives of others in begetting it.

John DeLorean struck a chord in all of us twenty years ago when he railed against a philosophy of greed, insensitivity and self-enrichment —in the products offered by corporations and in the lives of individuals. In the end he became what he hated most—a parody of the General Motors he so despised.